Lecture Notes in Computer Science 1806
Edited by G. Goos, J. Hartmanis and J. van Leeuwen

Springer
Berlin
Heidelberg
New York
Barcelona
Hong Kong
London
Milan
Paris
Singapore
Tokyo

Wil van der Aalst   Jörg Desel
Andreas Oberweis (Eds.)

Business Process Management

Models, Techniques, and Empirical Studies

Springer

Series Editors

Gerhard Goos, Karlsruhe University, Germany
Juris Hartmanis, Cornell University, NY, USA
Jan van Leeuwen, Utrecht University, The Netherlands

Volume Editors

Wil van der Aalst
Eindhoven University of Technology
Faculty of Technology and Management, Department of Information and Technology
P.O. Box 513, 5600 MB Eindhoven, The Netherlands
E-mail: w.m.p.v.d.aalst@tm.tue.nl

Jörg Desel
Katholische Universität Eichstätt
Mathematisch-Geographische Fakultät, Lehrstuhl für Angewandte Informatik
Ostenstraße 28, 85072 Eichstätt, Germany
E-mail: joerg.desel@ku-eichstaett.de

Andreas Oberweis
J.W. Goethe-Universität Frankfurt am Main
Institut für Wirtschaftsinformatik, Lehrstuhl für Wirtschaftsinformatik II
Postfach 111932, 60054 Frankfurt am Main, Germany
E-mail: oberweis@wiwi.uni-frankfurt.de

Cataloging-in-Publication Data applied for

Die Deutsche Bibliothek - CIP-Einheitsaufnahme

Business process management : models, techniques, and empirical
studies / Wil van der Aalst ... (ed.). - Berlin ; Heidelberg ; New
York ; Barcelona ; Hong Kong ; London ; Milan ; Paris ; Singapore ;
Tokyo : Springer, 2000
    (Lecture notes in computer science ; 1806)
    ISBN 3-540-67454-3

CR Subject Classification (1998): D.2, H.2, H.4, J.1

ISSN 0302-9743
ISBN 3-540-67454-3 Springer-Verlag Berlin Heidelberg New York

Springer-Verlag is a company in the BertelsmannSpringer publishing group.
© Springer-Verlag Berlin Heidelberg 2000

Typesetting: Camera-ready by author, data conversion by Steingraeber Satztechnik GmbH, Heidelberg
Printed on acid-free paper   SPIN: 10720204   06/3142   5 4 3 2 1 0

Preface

Business processes are among today's hottest topics in the science and practice of information systems. Their management comprises design and engineering efforts but also activities later in the life-cycle (e.g., business process reengineering, continuous process improvement, exception handling, and change management). Recent publications on business process management consider the entire spectrum from theoretical aspects, conceptual models and application scenarios, down to implementation issues.

The editors of this book have organized a number of scientific events in recent years, partly together with other colleagues, where business process management played a central role. Amazed at the variety, novelty, and quality of contributions we decided to share this knowledge with a wider audience. In addition, we invited other well-known scientists from the field to contribute their respective view to the state-of-the-art in business process management. We are very happy and proud that our efforts have resulted in the compilation of articles in your hand.

We are convinced that the material in this book is of great interest and value for researchers in many different areas and also for practitioners, as the authors come from different fields inside computer science or economics and industry. Since the topic is interdisciplinary in nature, it can only be captured by taking many different views into account. The structure of this book does not reflect the respective authors' backgrounds but concentrates on the three core issues in Business Process Management: design, analysis, and application:

I   Design of Business Processes

The papers of this part review modeling techniques and give concrete guidelines for modeling business processes and their organizational context.

II   Formalisms and Analysis

This part of the book discusses formal approaches to business process management, analysis techniques for validation, verification, and performance consideration, and the problems associated to dynamic change.

III   Systems and Applications

The final part of the book focuses on IT aspects and the application of techniques for business process management in practice. It describes practical experiences, tool evaluations, and the application of new technologies in various application domains.

We should like to express our gratitude to all authors. Only their perfect cooperation in providing their papers in time and in the required form allowed us to have this book in print in a relatively short time. Also, we cordially acknowledge the excellent cooperation with Springer-Verlag, namely with Alfred Hofmann and his colleagues in the preparation of this book.

February 2000

Wil van der Aalst
Jörg Desel
Andreas Oberweis

For most contributions to this book, prior versions or abstracts appeared in one of the following proceeding volumes:

van der Aalst, W.M.P., G. De Michelis and C.A. Ellis (eds.): *Workflow Management: Net-based Concepts, Models, Techniques, and Tools (WFM '98)*. Workshop at the 19th International Conference on Application and Theory of Petri Nets (Lisbon, 22.6.1998)

Desel, J., A. Oberweis, W. Reisig and G. Rozenberg (eds.): *Petri Nets and Business Process Management* (Seminar at Schloss Dagstuhl 5.7.1998 - 10.7.1998). Dagstuhl-Seminar-Report No. 217

Paul, H. and I. Maucher (eds.): *Integration von Mensch, Organisation und Technik: eine partielle Bilanz*. EMISA-Fachgruppentreffen 1998 (Gelsenkirchen, 7.10.1998 - 9.10.1998). Graue Reihe des Instituts Arbeit und Technik No. 1998-04

van der Aalst, W.M.P., J. Desel and R. Kaschek (eds.): *Software Architectures for Business Process Management*. Workshop at the 11th International Conference on Advanced Information Systems Engineering (CAiSE '99) (Heidelberg, 14.6.1999 - 15.6.1999). Institut für Angewandte Informatik und Formale Beschreibungs-verfahren, Universität Karlsruhe, Forschungsbericht No. 390

Table of Contents

Part III: Systems and Applications

Techniques for Modelling Workflows and their Support of Reuse

Gerrit K. Janssens, Jan Verelst, Bart Weyn

University of Antwerp - RUCA
Information Systems & Operations and Logistics Management
Middelheimlaan 1, B-2020 Antwerp, Belgium
E-mail: {gerritj, verelst, bweyn}@ruca.ua.ac.be

Abstract. Several authors propose their own technique based on Petri Nets to model workflow processes. Most of them recognise the adaptability problem inherent to workflows, viz. the frequently and/or radically changing character due to changing business process rules, but suggest totally different solutions. Because the proposed techniques are fundamentally different, eleven of these techniques are briefly discussed and compared. Next, we survey approaches to reuse in the workflow field and we classify them in a framework derived from the information systems literature.

1 Introduction

Recently, both the domain of workflow modelling by using Petri Nets and the area of reuse in software engineering have gained much attention. We share the opinion that it could be opportune to take a closer look at the application of the reuse concept to workflow modelling. It is our intention to make an informal introduction to the subject and an attempt to make a broad outline of desirable future developments and some topics that need further research. First we summarise the different topics concerning this field that have already been covered and treated by several authors.

2 Definition of Basic Workflow Concepts

Despite the increased interest in the domain of workflow management, the field still lacks precise definitions for some of the concepts. Little agreement exists upon what workflow exactly stands for and which specific features a workflow management system must provide. For an overview of existing definitions and interpretations of workflow and workflow management systems we refer to Georgakopoulos et al. [21]. In the following we will use the formal definition of workflow presented by the WfMC [25].

W. van der Aalst et al.(Eds.): Business Process Management, LNCS 1806, pp. 1-15, 2000.
© Springer-Verlag Berlin Heidelberg 2000

3   Workflow Concepts Translated into Petri Nets

Since Zisman [53] used Petri Nets to model workflow processes for the first time in 1977, several authors have made attempts to model workflows in terms of Petri Nets, amongst which De Cindio et al. [10,12], Ellis and Nutt [13,14], Nutt [40], van der Aalst [3], Ferscha [16], Wikarski [50], Li et al. [33], Adam et al.[7], Oberweis et al. [41], Badouel and Oliver [9], Merz et al. [35,36], and Schömig and Rau [45].

3.1   Why Petri Nets to Model Workflow?

Van der Aalst [2] identifies mainly three reasons for using Petri Nets for workflow modelling. The first reason is the fact that Petri Nets possess formal semantics despite their graphical nature. The second reason is that instead of being purely event-based, Petri Nets can explicitly model states. In this way, a clear distinction can be made between the enabling and execution of a task. The final reason lies in the abundance of available and theoretically proven analysis techniques.

Oberweis et al. [41] identify five different reasons to opt for using Petri Nets when modelling workflows. They are:
- Integration of data and behaviour aspects,
- Support for concurrent, cooperative processes,
- Different degrees of formality,
- Availability of analysis techniques,
- Flexibility.

Merz et al. [35] finally state that the combination of a mathematical foundation, a comprehensive graphical representation, and the possibility to carry out simulations and verifications is the main strength of Petri Nets when modelling workflows.

Han [23], however, warns and states that despite the popularity of Petri Nets to model workflows, he does not believe that Petri Nets are directly applicable for modelling workflows, mainly due to their fixed structures. The author criticises the lack of flexibility of most of the proposed net models and indicates the mechanisms to support abstraction and compositionality as the main reason.

3.2   High Level Versus Low Level Petri Nets

In this section we give a brief overview of the Petri Net classes proposed by various authors. Because of the problematic nature of modelling business processes, Petri Nets in their conventional form are not well suited as a modelling language. Common problems encountered when modelling workflows include high complexity when dealing with other than just toy models and lack of flexibility, especially where structural changes are necessary.

As already mentioned, the structure of workflows is extremely volatile as a consequence of changing business process rules. Business environment and conditions change very quickly. System evolution is unavoidable because business processes evolve continuously caused by internal organisational reforms, external environmental changes, etc.

Hence, business models are subject to mainly two types of changes: on the one hand changes in the data of the workflow systems and on the other hand changes in the rules of the workflow systems.

In order to deal with these issues, various authors propose their own Petri Net class. We synthesise the different approaches of various authors and compare them in Table 1.

Author	Petri Net class	Brief description
Van der Aalst W.M.P [1]	Workflow-nets (WF-nets)	Abstraction into P/T-nets of High Level Petri Nets with two special places *i* and *o*, indicating beginning and end of the modelled business procedure.
Ellis C.A., Nutt G.J. [13]	Information Control Nets (ICN)	High Level Petri Net variant intended to represent control flow and data flow.
Oberweis A., et al. [41]	INCOME/WF	High Level Petri Nets are used to describe the so-called core workflows on a relatively abstract level. Integration of a relation-like data model, considering tokens as database tuples.
Adam N. R., et al. [7]	Temporal Constraint Petri Net (TCPN)	Ordinary Petri Net extended with an interval function and a timestamp function to model absolute as well as relative time.
Agostini A., et al. [8]	Subclass of Elementary Net Systems	A WFMS consists of two basic components: namely a WF model and a WF Execution model. Simplicity of the WF model is stressed because it enhances the flexibility and adaptability of the WF Execution Module.

Wikarski D. [50]	Modular Process Nets	Low Level Petri Nets provided with a hierarchic module concept and with constructions designed to realise communication between net instances and their environment and constructions to create and destroy the net instances.
Schömig A.K., Rau H. [45]	Coloured Generalised Stochastic Petri Nets (CGSPN)	CGSPN are used as a tool to measure performance and to model dynamic behaviour.
Merz M., et al. [35]	Coloured Petri Nets (CPN)	CPN are used to introduce dynamic workflow modelling in the distributed systems architecture COSM
Ferscha A. [16]	Generalised Stochastic Petri Nets (GSPN)	GSPN are used to model and quantify WF (performance and structural analysis).
Badouel E., Oliver J. [9]	Reconfigurable Nets	Extension of the WF-nets of van der Aalst [1], intended to support dynamic changes in Workflow systems.
Wikarski D., Han Y., Löwe M. [51,23]	Higher Order Object Nets (HOON)	In contrast to Modular Process Nets [50], which are used to model workflow processes, this approach is intended to model additionally the structure of the organisation and the organisational resources.

Table 1. Overview of the proposed Petri Net classes

3.3   High Level Petri Nets

Ellis and Nutt [13] and van der Aalst [6] make a resolute choice in favour of High Level Petri Nets. They both state that High Level Petri Nets are an indispensable necessity when modelling real world applications because Low Level Petri Net models tend to become extremely complex and very large. Moreover, Ellis and Nutt [13] state that, when modelling large sets of office procedures, Low Level Petri Nets lead to "an exponential explosion" of the model.

The Workflow nets (WF-nets) proposed by van der Aalst [1] are an abstraction into P/T-nets of High Level Petri Nets with two special places *i* and *o*, indicating the beginning and the end of the modelled business procedure. These WF-nets are suitable not only for the representation and validation but also for the verification of workflow procedures.

The question: "Given a marked Petri Net graph, what structural changes can or cannot be applied while maintaining consistency and correctness", is an important and pressing problem which has also been recognised by Ellis and Nutt [13]. However, van der Aalst [4] provides a partial answer to this question for Workflow nets in the shape of transformation rules. These rules should not be confused with the more common reduction rules. Eight basic transformation rules allow the designer to modify sound WF-nets while preserving their soundness.

Badouel and Oliver [9] extend the WF-net formalism of van der Aalst [1] and propose the Reconfigurable Nets. These Reconfigurable Nets intend to support dynamic changes in Workflow systems. A Reconfigurable Net consists in fact of several Petri Nets which constitute the different possible configurations of the system. Each configuration gives a description of the system for some mode of operation. The authors denote that Reconfigurable Nets are self-modifying nets, meaning generalisations of P/T-nets where the flow relation between a place and a transition depends on the marking. The authors conclude that it might be interesting to extend a Reconfigurable net with a control part to regulate the flow in the system.

Ellis and Nutt [13,14] and Nutt [40] propose Information Control Nets (ICN), derived from High Level Petri Nets to represent office workflows. By adding a complementary data flow model, generalising control flow primitives and simplifying semantics, ICN are in fact a generalisation of Coloured Petri Nets. ICN represent control flow as well as data flow. The authors provide an exception handling mechanism. They note, however, that the mechanism allows users to escape the model, rather than helping them to analyse and cope with the exceptions.

Finally, Merz et al. [35,36] use Coloured Petri Nets in order to enhance the distributed systems architecture Common Open Service Market (COSM), with concurrent workflow modelling. The authors introduce the Coloured Petri Nets which were developed by Jensen [27], as a modelling and simulation technique for concurrent activity management and control.

3.4   Stochastic Petri Nets

Ferscha [16] proposes Generalised Stochastic Petri Nets (GSPN) to model workflows. The author exploits the natural correspondence between the GSPN enabling and firing rules and the dynamic behaviour of workflow systems. With respect to quantitative analysis, the Markovian framework is used within the GSPN formalism to derive the performance metrics. For qualitative analysis the author refers to the available broad body of Petri Net structural analysis techniques.

Schömig and Rau [45] propose a variant of the above GSPN, i.e. the Coloured Generalised Stochastic Petri Nets (CGSPN). CGSPN are based upon Coloured Petri Nets as pure Petri Net formalism instead of Place/Transition Petri Nets. Compared to the classical approach which is based on P/T Petri Nets, this approach requires more sophisticated analysis techniques.

3.5   Low Level Petri Nets

Wikarski [50] states that complex Petri Net classes with various kinds of tokens, arc or place inscriptions, were developed to increase the expressiveness of the net models. He further states that the introduction of High Level Petri Nets has created a number of problems amongst which is the reduction of the intuitive aspect when modelling and the impossibility to describe dynamic or changing behaviour. To counter these problems, Wikarski proposes Modular Process Nets, which can be described as Elementary Net Systems with minimal syntactic extensions. Elementary Net Systems (EN-systems) have originally been introduced by Rozenberg and Thiagarajan [44].

Like Wikarski [50], Agostini et al. [8] plead for simplicity of workflow modelling and also opt for Elementary Net Systems. Their final objective is to create a workflow model that allows its users to design workflows having little or no experience with computer science, programming or formal languages. For this purpose, they define a subclass of these Elementary Net Systems. The authors stress that EN-systems possess adequate mathematical properties which allow the modeller to generate a large class of behaviours. They state that a WFMS consists of two basic components: a WF model and a WF Execution model. Simplicity of the WF model is stressed because it enhances the flexibility and adaptability of the WF Execution Module.

Adam et al. [7] state that an ordinary Petri Net fulfils the basic needs to model the control flow and value dependencies of a workflow system. In order to model the temporal dependencies between two tasks in a workflow, however, the authors propose a Temporal Constraint Petri Net (TCPN). According to the authors, existing Timed Petri Nets are not capable of modelling both relative and absolute time. Their functionality is limited to modelling relative time. The definition of a TCPN states that each place and each transition is associated with a time interval and a token with a time stamp.

3.6   Petri Nets Extended with Object-Oriented Concepts

Modular Process Nets proposed by Wikarski [50], have sensor transitions which can detect triggering signals from the external environment. These signals, however, only contain control information in a predefined context. In contrast to Modular Process Nets, resource management is explicitly embodied in Higher-Order Object Nets

(HOON), the other formalism proposed by Wikarski et al. [51]. The central idea of HOON is to arrange net models and their surrounding environments in a client/server manner and to model the client/server interfaces explicitly [23].

Moldt and Valk [38] propose the use of Object-oriented Petri nets in the context of workflows. Their work is an integration of earlier work by Moldt and Wienberg [39] and the concept of Elementary Object Nets by Valk [49].

4   The Reuse Concept for Workflow Modelling

4.1   Real World Workflow Modelling

In contrast to the field of software engineering where the concept of reuse is widely explored, few authors have developed a theoretical framework to reuse in workflow modelling by Petri Nets. Nevertheless, the concept of reuse is definitely encountered or applied in practice by many modellers of real world workflows. This is due to the fact that specifying and modelling real world workflows is highly complicated and complex and that they are usually not developed in a single step.

As Oberweis [42] stated, there are mainly two potential strategies for the development of large, real world workflow models. A first strategy is incremental construction by iteratively refining, evaluating and formalising net fragments. This strategy can be based upon composing certain elementary net building blocks from an existing Petri Net library. Another strategy is adapting application-specific reference process models and reference object models to the requirements of a specific case. These application-specific reference models are sometimes denoted as generic models because they have always captured a certain generic process knowledge.

In both cases, the importance of a well-documented library in which the reference models or the Petri Net fragments are stored cannot be underestimated in any way. Since the whole concept of both approaches is based upon the library, the quality of the library is a discriminating factor between failure or success of both systems.

Van der Aalst [1] also states that when dealing with the high complexity of real world workflows, designers can refer to reuse on the basis of hierarchical decomposition, especially in communicating with end-users.

4.2   Approaches to Reuse of Petri Nets for Workflow Modelling

In this section, the existing approaches to reuse of Petri Nets for workflow modelling are discussed and classified into a framework used in the information systems (IS) literature (see Table 2).

The classification used in this paper is a summarised version of the classification framework by Krueger [28], which was later adopted and refined by Mili et al. [37]. We choose this framework because, as Mili explicitly states, it focuses on the « paradigmatic differences between the various reuse methods ». A classification according to fundamental differences allows us to explore to what extent current approaches to Petri Net-reuse cover the whole reuse-spectrum.

Krueger's [28] framework distinguishes between two main types of reuse: the building blocks approach (compositional approach) and the generative approach. The building blocks approach is further subdivided into the reuse of software patterns and into software architectures.

4.2.1   Patterns
A (software) pattern is a proven solution to a certain standard type of problem. It is described by four essential elements:
- a pattern name
- a problem description, which clarifies in which situations the pattern can be used
- the solution to the problem
- the consequences and trade-offs involved in applying the pattern.

A limited amount of design patterns [19] and analysis patterns [18,24] has been published. An example of an analysis pattern is an Object-Oriented (OO)-conceptual model for the concept of a 'customer' or a 'bookkeeping account'. Although these patterns tend to be domain-specific, many of them can be used outside of their original domains [18]. For example, a pattern of a bill of material can also form the basis for modelling an organisation's hierarchy. Design patterns are situated at a lower level of abstraction. An example is the observer-pattern [19]. An observer is an object which monitors the state of a certain 'subject'. When the subject changes state, the observer notifies all interested objects of this change. A typical application of the observer pattern is found in spreadsheets. When a graph is produced based on data in a spreadsheet, it is important that the graph is notified of any changes in the underlying data. The observer-pattern describes how an observer can be built to achieve this goal.

Many of the existing approaches to reuse of Petri Nets for workflow modelling can be interpreted as reuse of a pattern. Especially approaches discussing compositionality of Petri Nets fall into this category: these authors implicitly assume that some existing elements (workflows) are composed. We interpret these existing elements as patterns.

However, before we enumerate which authors fall into this category, we add a level in the classification: black-box vs. white-box reuse of patterns.

Black-box reuse is defined as the reuse of existing software components without any modification. White-box reuse does allow adaptation of the components, usually using the mechanism of inheritance.

In the IS-literature, a preference for black-box reuse has developed over the years. For instance, Fayad [15] claims that black-box reuse leads to systems that are easier to use and extend. Zweben [54] provides experimental evidence: his experiments show that black-box reuse is superior to white-box reuse in terms of required effort and correctness of the resulting system. The main disadvantage of white-box reuse is that the inheritance mechanism violates the encapsulation-principle. The aim of this principle is to minimise interdependencies between modules by defining strict interfaces. A subclass, however, has access to some of the data and code of its superclass. The subclass is allowed to change the values of these data items, to call functions of the superclass etc. As a consequence, several dependencies between the super- and subclass are introduced. These dependencies compromise reusability, as changes in a superclass frequently induce changes in the subclass. [19, 47].

In the context of Petri-Nets, white-box reuse is discussed by Lakos [30,31], who defines the notion of inheritance for Object Petri Nets. Black-box reuse, through the notion of compositionality of Petri Nets, is discussed by Christensen [11], Han [23], Holvoet [26], Kruke [29], Wikarski [50] and van der Aalst [1,3].

For example, van der Aalst [1] briefly draws attention to reuse of WF-nets on the basis of 'task refinement' which is the refinement of a task by a subflow. In this way it becomes possible to decompose a complex workflow into subflows which, in their turn, can be built up from other subflows. In other words, one achieves a hierarchical decomposition.

Compositionality is an important property for hierarchical construction of WF-nets and more in particular for the reuse of subflows. The author [1] proves seven characteristics about compositionality with regard to verifying the correctness of subflows in the same way as verifying the entire workflow on a more abstract level.

4.2.2   Software Architectures
A Software Architecture is a high-level design of a software system, i.e. the subsystems and their interactions [46]. Examples of architectures are compiler architectures (consisting of analysers, parsers and code generators), database architectures and rule-based architectures for expert systems. Software architectures are similar to very large-scale patterns. However, patterns tend to focus on a small part of a system whereas an architecture contains the overall structure of the system.

In the context of reuse of Petri Nets for workflows, both Han [23] and van der Aalst [3] define software architectures for workflow management systems.

4.2.3   Application Generators and Very High-Level Languages
Application generators and very high-level languages constitute the class of generative reuse. Forms of generative reuse are based on reusing the process of previous software development, rather than reusing existing products (such as patterns or software architectures) [37].

Application generators and very high-level languages allow the user to specify the requirements at a very high level of abstraction. From these requirements, code is automatically generated. This approach to reuse is considered, in the long term, to have the highest potential payoff. However, at the current moment, it remains very difficult to build generators that scale up to industrial production [43].

In the context of Petri Nets for workflow modelling, only van der Aalst [3] describes a number of Petri Net tools that belong to this category.

4.2.4   Evaluation

By far the most common approach to reuse of Petri Nets for workflow modelling is black-box reuse of patterns. Most authors discuss this kind of reuse implicitly through the notion of compositionality.

However, very few authors, if any, discuss the notion of reusability explicitly and/or in great detail. In other words, questions such as which advantages exactly can be achieved or which type of reuse leads to these advantages, remain unanswered.

Reuse Type		Authors
Software Patterns	Black-box reuse	Christensen [11], Han [23], Holvoet [26], Kruke [29], Wikarski [50], van der Aalst [3]
	White-box reuse	Lakos [30]
Software Architectures		Han [23], van der Aalst [3]
Application Generators and very high level languages		van der Aalst [3]

Table 2. A classification of techniques for reuse of Petri Nets for workflow modelling

4.2.5   A Critical Remark Concerning Reuse in the IS-Literature

The idea of building software by assembling reusable components dates back to 1968 when Doug McIlroy proposed the idea of libraries of shared components at the NATO Conference of Software Engineering [34].

Since then, most programmers have continued to informally reuse their own code, but in an ad hoc way. Up to now, it has remained extremely difficult to realise a systematic approach to reuse [43,32,17]. Also, Prieto-Diaz [43] observes that the state-of-the-practice is still source code reuse, in spite of numerous claims that reuse at the design- or even analysis-level would have higher payoffs. Finally, Szyperski [48], for example, observes that at this moment, relatively few catalogues of reusable objects actually exist.

The literature contains a wide variety of potential reasons for the lack of systematic reuse: some technical, but many are managerial (relating to management commitment, organisational issues etc.) [52]. We now focus on one of the fundamental technical problems that underlie reuse.

4.2.6   Hidden Assumptions

A fundamental problem of software reuse is the problem of the hidden assumptions. This problem refers to the fact that software components make assumptions about their intended environment which are implicit and either don't match the actual environment or conflict with those of other parts of the system. Such conflicting assumptions make reuse extremely difficult or even impossible [20].

For example, Garlan [20] describes an example in which several software packages were combined in order to build a software engineering tool. However, the assumptions that the different packages made about which program held the main thread of control, were incompatible, which drastically complicated building the new system. As these assumptions tend not to be documented, they are extremely difficult to detect when deciding which software components could be reused.

Glass [22] provides an example in which a sort program was reused. However, the program performed extremely slowly when sorting strings. The undocumented assumption was that the structure of the sort program was far more appropriate for sorting numbers than strings.

Garlan [20] suggests possible solutions for the hidden assumptions-problem: amongst others, make architectural assumptions explicit, provide techniques for bridging mismatches between assumptions and develop sources of architectural design guidance. Although we agree with these suggestions, it is clear that these solutions are more workarounds to the problem than an elimination of it.

4.2.7   Final Remarks

We have briefly shown in this paragraph that, in the IS-field, systematic reuse has been pursued for up to 30 years, but that the practical state-of-the-art is still rather disappointing. Realising a systematic form of reuse has proven to be a very ambitious goal with a wide variety of problems (technical and managerial) along the way. Good modelling constructs alone (such as objects) have been insufficient to reach this goal.

It is our impression that the field of workflow modelling with Petri Nets is currently making quick progress towards deciding which modelling constructs are most appropriate. In order to determine whether this will be sufficient to realise systematic reuse in the workflow field, empirical and experimental studies are required. We have yet to find these in the literature.

5   Conclusion

In this paper we have tried to identify the existing Petri Net formalisms proposed by various authors used for modelling workflow. We found that, at the moment, there is not yet unanimity about which class of Petri Nets suits best the specific needs of workflow modelling. Especially the different approaches between Low Level Petri Nets and High Level Petri Nets can in this view be mentioned as exemplary.

An interesting remark, however, is that even a very good Petri Net formalism for modelling workflows is not worth much if there are no Workflow Management Systems or other computer tools based on it. This has also been stated by van der Aalst [5] concerning the usability of High Level Petri Nets. The author [5] notes that the availability of adequate computer tools is a critical factor in the practical use of High Level Petri Nets and related analysis methods.

Compared to database models, workflow models are far from being mature. There is definitely a need for standards in workflow modelling (like in the field of conceptual modelling with Entity Relationship Modelling). This has also been recognised by van der Aalst [1]. In our opinion, when speculating about the best formalisms to serve as a possible standard, it is likely that the Petri Net formalism which is best supported by computer tools, turns out to become the standard.

With respect to reuse, much progress is being made towards developing an adequate modelling construct for modelling workflows using Petri Nets. However, we have the impression that adequate modelling constructs alone were not sufficient to achieve systematic reuse in the IS-field. Whether the same applies to the workflow field should be further investigated.

6   References

1. W. M. P. van der Aalst, *Structural Characterizations of Sound Workflow Nets*, Eindhoven University of Technology, Computing Science Reports 96/23, 1996.
2. W. M. P. van der Aalst, *Three Good Reasons for using a Petri Net based Workflow Management System*, in Proceedings of the International Working Conference on Information and Process Integration in Enterprises (IPIC '96), T. Wakayama, S. Kannapan, C. M. Khoong, S. Navathe and J. Yates, Eds., Cambridge, Massachusetts, pp.179-201, 1996.
3. W. M. P. van der Aalst, *The Application of Petri Nets to Workflow Management*, The Journal of Circuits, Systems and Computers, pp. 1-53, 1998.
4. W. M. P. van der Aalst, *Verification of Workflow Nets*, in Proceedings of 18th International Conference, ICATPN'97; Toulouse, France; 23-27 Jun 1997, P. Azema and G. Balbo, Eds., Lecture notes in Computer Science, Application and theory of Petri nets 1997, vol. 1248, Springer-Verlag, pp. 407-426, 1997.
5. W. M. P. van der Aalst, and K. van Hee, *Framework for Business Process Redesign* in Proceedings of the Fourth Workshop on Enabling Technologies: Infrastructure for Collaborative Enterprises (WETICE 95), J. R. Callahan, Ed., IEEE Computer Society Press, Berkeley Springs, pp. 36-45, 1995.
6. W. M. P. van der Aalst and K. van Hee, *Business Process Redesign: A Petri-net-based approach*, Computers in Industry, vol. 29, no. 1-2, pp. 15-26, 1996.
7. N. R. Adam, V. Atluri, and W. K. Huang, *Modeling and Analysis of Workflows Using Petri Nets* Journal of Intelligent Information Systems: Special Issue on Workflow and Process Management, M. Rusinkiewicz and S. H. Abdelsalam, Eds., vol. 10, no. 2, pp. 1-29, 1998.

8. A. Agostini, G. De Michelis and K. Petruni, *Keeping Workflow Models as Simple as Possible*, in Proceedings of the Workshop on Computer-Supported Cooperative Work, Petri Nets and Related Formalisms within the 15th International Conference on Application and Theory of Petri Nets, Zaragoza, Spain, June 21st, pp. 11-29, 1994.
9. E. Badouel and J. Oliver, *Reconfigurable Nets, a Class of High Level Petri Nets Supporting Dynamic Changes within Workflow Systems*, Publication Interne IRISA PI 1163, 1998.
10. L. Bernardinello and F. De Cindio, *A survey of Basic Net Models and Modular Net Classes*, G. Rozenberg, Ed., Lecture Notes in Computer Science, Advances in Petri Nets 1992, vol. 609, Springer-Verlag, pp.304-351, 1992.
11. S. Christensen and L. Petrucci, *Towards a Modular Analysis of Coloured Petri Nets*, in Proceedings of the 13th International Conference Sheffield, UK, June 1992, K. Jensen, Ed., Lecture notes in Computer Science, Application and Theory of Petri Nets 1992, vol. 616, Springer-Verlag, pp. 113-133, 1992.
12. F. De Cindio, C. Simone, R. Vassallo and A Zanaboni, *CHAOS: a Knowledge-based System for Conversing within Offices*, Office Knowledge Representation, Management and Utilization, W. Lamersdorf, Ed., Elsevier Science Publishers B.V., North-Holland, pp. 257-275, 1988.
13. C. A. Ellis and G. J. Nutt, *Modeling and Enactment of Workflow Systems*, in Proceedings of the 14th International Conference Chicago, Illinois, USA, June 1993, M. A. Marsan, Ed., Lecture notes in Computer Science, Application and Theory of Petri Nets 1993, vol. 691, Springer-Verlag, pp. 1-16, 1993.
14. C.A. Ellis and G. J. Nutt, *Workflow: The Process Spectrum*, in Proceedings of the NSF Workshop on Workflow and Process Automation in Information Systems: State-of-the-Art and Future Directions, Athens, Georgia, pp. 140-145, 1996.
15. M. A. Fayad and D. C. Schmidt, *Object-oriented Application Frameworks*, Computers in Industry, vol. 40, no. 10, pp. 32-38, 1997.
16. A. Ferscha, *Qualitative and Quantitative Analysis of Business Workflows using Generalized Stochastic Petri Nets*, in Proceedings of CON '94: Workflow management - Challenges, Paradigms and Products, Linz, Austria, October 19-21, 1994, G. Chroust, A. Benczur (Eds.), pp. 222 - 234, Oldenbourg Verlag, 1994.
17. R. Fichman, C. Kemerer, *Object Technology and Reuse : lessons from early adopters*, IEEE Computer, pp. 47-59, October 1997.
18. M. Fowler, *Analysis Patterns: Reusable Object Models*, Addison-Wesley, 1997.
19. E. Gamma and R. Helm, *Design Patterns: Elements of Reusable Object-Oriented Software*, Addison-Wesley, 1995.
20. D. Garlan, *Architectural mismatch: why reuse is so hard*, IEEE Software, pp 17-26, November 1995.
21. D. Georgakopoulos, M. Hornick and A. Sheth, *An Overview of Workflow Management: From Process Modeling to Workflow Automation Infrastructure*, Distributed and Parallel Databases, vol. 3 (2), pp. 119-153, 1995.
22. R. Glass, *A word of warning about reuse*, ACM SIGMIS Database, vol. 28 no. 2, pp. 19-21, Spring 1997.
23. Y. Han, *HOON - A Formalism Supporting Adaptive Workflows*, Technical Report #UGA-CS-TR-97-005, Department of Computer Science, University of Georgia, November 1997.
24. D. Hay, *Data model patterns: conventions of thought*, Dorset House Publishers, pp. 268, 1996.
25. D. Hollingsworth, *Workflow Management Coalition: The Workflow Reference Model*, 4-29-1994, The Workflow Management Coalition, Brussels, Belgium.
26. T. Holvoet and P. Verbaeten, *Petri Charts, An Alternative Technique for Hierarchical Net Construction* in Proceedings of the 1995 IEEE Conference on Systems, Man and Cybernetics (IEEE-SMC'95), pp. 1-19, 1995.
27. K. Jensen, *Coloured Petri Nets*: Vol. 1, Springer-Verlag, 1992.

28. C. W. Krueger, *Software Reuse*, ACM Computing Surveys, vol. 24, no. 2, pp. 131-183, 1992.
29. V. Kruke, *Reuse in Workflow Modelling*, Diploma Thesis, Information System Group, Department of Computer Systems, Norwegian University of Science and Technology, 1996.
30. C. Lakos, *From Coloured Petri Nets to Object Petri Nets*, 16th International Conference on the Application and Theory of Petri nets, Torino, Italy, pp.278-297, 1995.
31. C. Lakos, *The Consistent Use of Names and Polymorphism in the Definition of Object Petri Nets*, in Proceedings of the 17th International Conference on Application and Theory of Petri Nets, Osaka, Japan, June 1996, J. Billington and W. Reisig, Eds., Lecture Notes in Computer Science, vol. 1091, Springer-Verlag, pp. 380-399, 1996.
32. N-Y, Lee, C.R. Litecky, *An empirical study of software reuse with special attention to ada*, IEEE Transactions on Software Engineering, vol. 23 no. 9, pp 537-549, September 1997.
33. J. Li, J.S.K. Ang, X. Tong and M. Tueni, *AMS: A Declarative Formalism for Hierarchical Representation of Procedural Knowledge*, IEEE Transactions on Knowledge and Data Engineering, vol. 6, no. 4, pp. 639-643, 1994.
34. M. McIlroy, *Mass-Produced Software Components*, 1968 NATO Conference on Software Engineering, pp. 138-155, 1968.
35. M. Merz, D. Moldt, K. Müller and W. Lamersdorf, *Workflow Modeling and Execution with Coloured Petri Nets in COSM*, In Proceedings of the Workshop on Applications of Petri Nets to Protocols within the 16th International Conference on Application and Theory of Petri Nets, pp. 1-12, 1995.
36. M. Merz, K. Müller-Jones and W. Lamersdorf, *Petrinetz-basierte Modellierung und Steuerung unternehmensübergreifender Geschäftsprozesse*, in Proceedings of the GI/SI Jahrestagung 1995, Tagungsband der GISI 95 Herausforderungen eines globalen Informationsverbundes für die Informatik, F. Huber-Wäschle, H. Schauer and P. Widmayer, Eds., Springer-Verlag, Zürich, pp. 1-8, 18-20 Sept. 1995.
37. H. Mili, F. Mili, and A. Mili, *Reusing software: issues and research directions*, IEEE Transactions on Software Engineering, vol. 21 no. 6, pp. 528-561, 1995.
38. D. Moldt and R. Valk: Object Oriented Petri Nets in Business Process Modelling. Part II, Chapter 9 in this volume.
39. D. Moldt and F. Wienberg, *Multi-Agent-Systems based on Coloured Petri Nets*, in Proceedings of 18th International Conference, ICATPN'97; Toulouse, France; 23-27 Jun 1997, P. Azema and G. Balbo, Eds., Lecture notes in Computer Science, Application and theory of Petri nets 1997, vol. 1248, Springer-Verlag, pp. 82-101, 1997.
40. G. J. Nutt, *The Evolution towards Flexible Workflow Systems*, Distributed Systems Engineering, vol. 3-4, pp. 276-294, 1996.
41. A. Oberweis, R. Schätzle, W. Stucky, W. Weitz and G. Zimmermann, *INCOME/WF- A Petri-net Based Approach to Workflow Management*, H. Krallmann, Ed. Wirtschaftsinformatik '97, Springer-Verlag, pp. 557-580, 1997.
42. A. Oberweis, *An Integrated Approach for the Specification of Processes and Related Complex Structured Objects in Business Applications*, Decision Support Systems, vol. 17, pp. 31-53 ,1996.
43. R. Prieto-Diaz, *Status Report: Software Reusability*, IEEE Software, pp. 61-66, May 1993.
44. G. Rozenberg, P.S. Thiagarajan, *Petri Nets: Basic Notions, Structure, Behaviour*, in: J.W. de Bakker, W.-P. de Roever, G. Rozenberg, Eds., Current Trends in Concurrency, Lecture Notes in Computer Science, vol. 224, Springer-Verlag, pp. 585-668, 1986.
45. A.K. Schömig and H. Rau, *A Petri Net Approach for the Performance Analysis of Business Processes*, University of Würzburg, Report n° 116 Seminar at IBFI, Schloss Dagstuhl, May 22-26, 1995.
46. M. Shaw and D. Garlan, *Software Architecture: Perspectives on an Emerging Discipline*, Addison-Wesley, 1996.

47. A. Snyder, *Encapsulation and Inheritance in Object-Oriented Programming Languages*, in Proceedings of the International Conference on Object Oriented Programming, Systems, Languages and Applications (OOPSLA), 1986.

48. C. Szyperski, *Component software : beyond object-oriented programming*, Addison-Wesley, 1997.

49. R. Valk, *Petri Nets as Token Objects – An introduction to Elementary Object Nets*, in Proceedings of 19th International Conference, ICATPN'98; Lisbon,Portugal; June 1998, J. Desel and M. Silva, Eds., Lecture notes in Computer Science, Application and theory of Petri nets 1998, vol. 1420, Springer-Verlag, pp. 1-25, 1998.

50. D. Wikarski, *An Introduction to Modular Process Nets*, International Computer Science Institute (ICSI) Berkeley, Technical Report TR-96-019, CA, USA, 1996.

51. D. Wikarski, Y. Han and M. Löwe, *Higher-Order Object Nets and Their Application to Workflow modeling*, Technische Universität Berlin, Forschungsberichte der FB Informatik 95-34, 1995.

52. M. Zand, M. Samadzadeh, *Software reuse: current status and trends*, Journal of Systems and Software, vol. 30, pp. 167-170, 1995.

53. M. D. Zisman, *Representation, Specification and Automation of Office Procedures*, University of Pennsylvania Wharton School of Business, PhD Thesis, 1977.

54. S. H. Zweben, and S. H. Edwards, *The effects of layering and encapsulation on software development cost and quality*, IEEE Transactions on Software Engineering, vol. 21, no. 3, pp. 200-208, 1995.

Modeling Processes and Workflows
by Business Rules

Gerhard Knolmayer[1], Rainer Endl[1,2], Marcel Pfahrer[1,3]

[1] Institute of Information Systems, University of Bern,
Engehaldenstrasse 8, CH 3012 Bern, Switzerland
{knolmayer, endl, pfahrer}@ie.iwi.unibe.ch
[2] igim ag, Felsenstrasse 88, CH 9001 St. Gallen, Switzerland
[3] Urs Sauter + Marcel Pfahrer AG, Mettlenweg 7,
CH 2504 Biel, Switzerland

Abstract. This contribution describes a rule-based method for modeling business processes and workflows. Business rules are defined as statements about guidelines and restrictions with respect to states and processes in an organization. After introducing an extended Event-Condition-Action (ECA) notation, an approach for the refinement of business rules is developed in order to achieve a consistent decomposition of the business processes. Thus, ECA rules serve as an integration layer between different process modeling and (workflow) specification languages. Finally, we propose an architecture of a rule-oriented repository supporting the modeling and refinement process.

1 Introduction

Several methods and tools have been developed to describe business processes and workflows. These methods and tools differ in their constructs, notation, ease of use, and other aspects. Often different methods are employed at different stages of the development process.

In this contribution we propose a rule-based methodology to provide a uniform modeling approach at different abstraction levels. This approach suggests to transform a rule-based description of a business process in one or several refinement steps into a rule-based workflow specification. The (business) rules that underlie the business process are first described in natural language. In subsequent steps these rules are refined in a structured manner. This results in a set of structured rules representing the business process at different abstraction levels. Comparisons and case studies [KEPS97] show that this rule-based methodology has advantages compared to established approaches like Petri-Nets [cf. Ober96] and Event-Driven Process Chains [cf. Sche92]. Recently, business rules are often considered as a very important component of modern information systems [cf., e.g., MWBG98; dPLL98]. Several software and consulting companies focus their activities on business rules.

There are two kinds of relationships between business rules: First, there is a relationship at the same abstraction level, establishing the control flow between the components that are defined at this level. Second, we propose a hierarchical relationship representing the derivation of business rules that are relevant at a lower

W. van der Aalst et al. (Eds.): Business Process Management, LNCS 1806, pp 16-29, 2000

abstraction level from higher-level rules. During the overall modeling process the same basic constructs are used; these may be extended by additional constructs according to the level of abstraction. The proposed approach should lead to a more consistent modeling procedure than applying various methods at different abstraction levels.

In a decentralized organization, a virtual enterprise, or in coordinating processes in a supply chain often different methods and tools are employed for representing processes and workflows. To support the development of coordinated process or workflow models across enterprise boundaries or locations, a layer into which the different (sub-)process models can be transformed and another layer from which the specifications for different workflow tools may be derived, are highly desirable. We suggest to use business rule layers for these descriptions (cf. Fig. 1) [cf. Knol98].

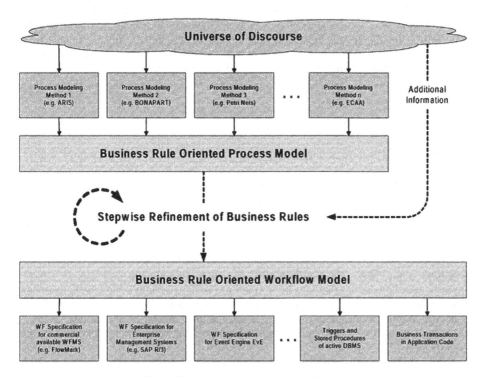

Fig. 1. Business rules as integration layers.

The business rule approach can serve as an integration platform for different process modeling techniques and different target systems that implement the workflow or parts of them. For the representation of business rules we use the ECAA-notation which is based on events, conditions, actions, and the selection construct; the resulting constructs are enhanced with different constructs for representing static components of business processes, i.e., organizational units, roles, actors, and entity-relationship-models.

In order to maintain the dependencies between process and workflow models at different modeling levels, it is helpful to store the business rules in a rule repository.

This repository serves as the core of a development environment which may provide the following functionality:

- Process modeling tool
- Import functions for different process modeling tools
- Refinement tool
- Data modeling tool
- Organization modeling tool
- Generators for different workflow management systems.

In this contribution we describe the constructs and fundamental concepts of a rule-based methodology for modeling business processes and the specification of work-flows. In section 2 we discuss the meaning, notation and origin of business rules and their suitability for modeling business processes. The third section shows how different types of control flows can be described by business rules. The fourth section deals with some extensions to the business rule approach, particularly with constructs for representing a data model and an organizational model. The refinement process is described in section 5. The results are summarized in section 6.

2   Business Rules

2.1   Definition

A lot of knowledge and many rules exist in an organization to prescribe and/or restrict the way in which the organizational goals are achieved. Some of these rules exist in a formalized way, e.g., in an organizational handbook; others are not documented and exist only informally. Some rules are so precisely defined that they can be automated, others allow for discretion of a human actor.

Originally, business rules were defined in connection with integrity constraints, resulting, e.g., from the cardinalities of entity-relationship models or more sophisticated constraints that can be defined in NIAM [NiHa89]. However, business rules do not only cover data integrity but usually also define or restrict organizational behavior. We define business rules as „... statements about how the business is done, i.e., about guidelines and restrictions with respect to states and processes in an organization." [BBG+90].

2.2   The EC^mA^n Paradigm

In active database management systems, rules are often perceived to consist of the three components *event*, *condition*, and *actions* and, thus, are called ECA rules [Daya88]. These rule components can be defined as follows:

- The event component specifies when a rule has to be executed. It indicates the transition from one process relevant status to another. Events are not time consuming and do not include any activity to be performed by an actor.

- The condition component indicates a condition to be checked before any action is triggered. It is a special case of a time consuming action resulting in a boolean value (true / false).
- The action component states what has to be done depending on the result of the evaluation of the condition component. In analogy to the condition component, the action is time consuming too, but its termination is characterized by raising one or more process relevant events.

Business rules are regarded as the main result of the system analysis phase [KiRo94; dPPL98]. ECA rules may not only be used to specify dynamic behavior in database management systems, but also for formalizing business rules at the conceptual level. The notation has been extended to ECAA rules that allow to specify an alternative action to be executed when the evaluation of the condition component returns false (Fig. 2) [HeKn96; Herb97].

With respect to decision tables and CASE-constructs of some programming languages, rules could also be seen as allowing m branches, and, therefore, as EC^mA^n constructs. Special appearances of this construct are ECAA-, ECA- and (condition-less) EA-rules. Since actions may raise one or more subsequent events, EC^mA^n rules are well suited for representing business processes and workflows. In order to reduce the complexity and readability of the models, the proposed notation is restricted to EA, ECA, and ECAA rules. It is obvious that EC^mA^n-rules can be transformed into a sequence of ECAA rules still providing the possibility to specify binary XOR selections within one rule. Furthermore, we do not suggest to use the ECA notation because this would lead to logically redundant and incomprehensible models.

ON	Event
IF	Condition
Then DO	Action
Else DO	Alternative Action

Fig. 2. ECAA-notation.

3   Process and Workflow Modeling in the ECAA-Notation

3.1   Necessary Constructs

With respect to modeling the control flow, the following situations have to be covered [Jabl95; EnMe99]:

- Sequence of actions,
- parallel actions,
- alternate actions, and
- iterations of actions.

All of these necessary constructs may be represented by EA rules or combinations of EA and ECAA rules, as described in the subsequent sections.

3.2   Modeling Sequential Actions

To model a sequence of actions within a business process, we simply link the associated business rules. This may be achieved by raising an event when the preceding action terminates. An event can be raised either explicitly, e.g., with a special modeling construct "RAISE EVENT", or implicitly, e.g., by an update command in a database. The sequential link between the actions is based on the fact that the event resulting from the previous action appears as triggering event in the subsequent rule (cf. e_2 and e_3 in Fig. 3).

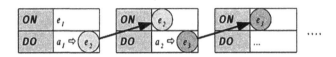

Fig. 3. Modeling a sequence of actions

3.3   Modeling Parallel Actions

Splitting the control flow into parallel paths (AND split) can be modeled in different ways: One way is to raise by one action several events that trigger the subsequent actions in parallel (cf. e_{2a} and e_{2b} in Fig. 4). The other way is to reference the same event in different EA rules (cf. e_2 in Fig. 5).

The synchronization of the two or more parallel sub-processes may be done by specifying a rule with a *conjunction event* [cf. Gatz95; HeKn95] (cf. e_{ia} and e_{ib} in Fig. 5).

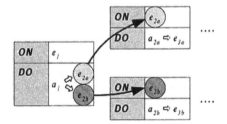

Fig. 4. AND split using two events

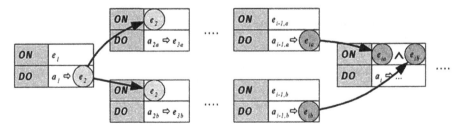

Fig. 5. Modeling parallel actions (AND split using one event).

3.4   Modeling Alternate Actions

Alternate actions may be either exclusive (XOR-split) or non-exclusive (OR-split). Exclusive alternatives can be modeled by different action parts of an ECAA rule that raise different events (cf. e_{2a} and e_{2b} in Fig. 6). The resulting paths may be joined by a rule in which event components are combined by a disjunction operator [cf. Gatz95, HeKn95] (cf. e_{ia} and e_{ib} in Fig. 6).

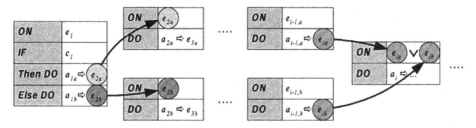

Fig. 6. Modeling exclusive alternate actions.

A way to specify non-exclusive alternate actions is using several ECA rules triggered by the same event but formulating different conditions (cf. c_{2a} and c_{2b} in Fig. 7). Either e_{3a}, e_{3b}, both events, or none of these events may occur. The ELSE-branches do not trigger actions but simulate the occurrence of the final events e_{ia} and e_{ib} to ensure joining the parallel branches and allow the execution of subsequent subprocesses.

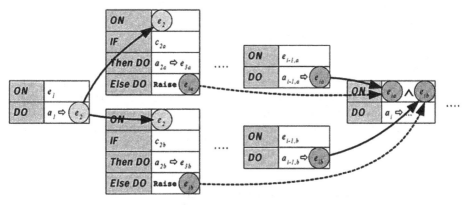

Fig. 7. Modeling non-exclusive actions.

3.5   Modeling Iterations of Actions

Modeling iterations may be done by repeatedly raising an identical event, either implicitly or explicitly (e.g., event e_2 in Fig. 8). Loop control has to be modeled by an ECAA rule: If the condition component (c_i) is evaluated as true, the action component leads to an event outside the loop (e_{i+1}); otherwise the action component raises the event inside the loop (e_2).

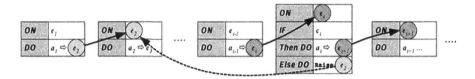

Fig. 8. Modeling iterations.

3.6   Additional Modeling Options

Additional modeling options are offered by appropriate complex event constructs [HeKn95]:

- Event selection: m events out of $\{e_1, e_2, ..., e_n\}$, $m < n$,
- Event sequences: Events $(e_1, e_2, ..., e_n)$ in a well-defined sequence,
- Periodical event: every n-th event e,
- Interval: e within an interval $[e_1, e_2]$.

The use of these complex events allows to model additional control flow structures, e.g., modeling a combination of parallel and alternative branches of a process [cf. KEPS97].

Even more important for business process modeling is the specification of valid times or derived valid times of events:

- Absolute time: t
- Relative time: Δt after an event e
- Repeated time: every Δt within an interval (t_{start}, t_{end}).

These types of event expressions allow the modeling of time schedules, periodically performed activities, or limitations on processing time, waiting time, transfer time, and throughput time. Furthermore, temporal event expressions allow to react on "non-events", defined in such a way that no "real" event happened during a certain time interval.

4   Supplementing Actors and Data Models

4.1   Modeling of Actors

An important element of workflow models is the specification of persons and/or application systems being responsible for checking the conditions and executing the actions. Consequently, the ECAA-notation must be extended with constructs dealing with these static components of a business process or workflow. Fig. 9 shows an ECAA rule in which the condition and action blocks are extended with an *actor* component, modeling human and/or automated system components responsible for the execution.

ON	E vent		
IF	C ondition	Actor	Human and/or automated system components
Then DO	A ction	Actor	Human and/or automated system components
Else DO	A lternative Action	Actor	Human and/or automated system components

Fig. 9. Extension of the ECAA construct with actor components.

4.2   Data Modeling

Another static component are entity/relationship-types that are relevant for checking conditions and executing actions. The condition and action blocks of an ECA rule are extended with the appropriate components (Fig. 10).

ON	E vent		
IF	C ondition	Actor	Human and/or automated system components
Then DO	A ction	Actor	Human and/or automated system components
Else DO	A lternative Action	Actor	Human and/or automated system components

Fig. 10. Extension of the ECA construct with data models.

5   Stepwise Refinement of Business Rules

Most methods for developing information systems employ stepwise refinement. The basic ideas of this concept go back to [Wirt71]: "During the process of stepwise refinement, a notation which is natural to the problem in hand should be used as long as possible." Some methods and tools have been proposed for a stepwise refinement of program specifications to code using the refinement calculus [MoGR93]. The refinement of Petri Nets is discussed in [Padb96]. In practical application development, the refinement usually also provides additional, more detailed information about the universe of discourse.

5.1   The Refinement Process

Methods for workflow specification should provide similar functionality, leading from a semi-formal description of a business process to a formal workflow specification. The refinement process should be accomplished with identical modeling concepts and structures.

At the beginning of the modeling process, the components of the rule may be described informally (Fig. 11). Each non-elementary rule has to be refined separately, describing it by a set of more precise rules. The starting and terminating events of the refined representation are often identical to the events of the refined rule (cf. e_2 and e_{i-1} in Fig. 12). In other cases the refinement process may also lead to a more precise description of events.

ON	Order entry
DO	record the order in the order processing system

Fig. 11. EA rule with informally described components.

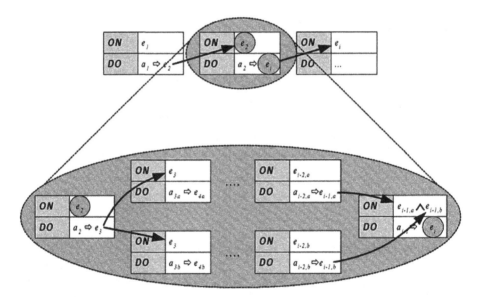

Fig. 12. Refinement of a business rule.

The refinement process may consist of several steps. At the lowest level, the components of the rules must be so elementary and precise that a workflow specification can be derived (Fig. 13).

ON	Order entry		
IF	Exists (SELECT Customer-Nb FROM Customer WHERE Customer-Name = :Name)		
Then DO	Raise Event (customer data found)	Actor	Event engine
Else DO	"record customer data" Raises (customer data recorded)	Actor	Sales employee; "SAP R/3" (Transaction=TA4711)

Fig. 13. ECAA rule with elementary components.

5.2   The Refinement of a Business Rule

As stated above, a rule consists of event, condition and action components. However, the activities for checking a condition can be interpreted as actions, resulting either in a true or false status (cf. Fig. 13). This result can be regarded as an (internal) event. Therefore, conditions and actions are called *active parts* of a rule. During the refinement process, the modeler has to focus on these active parts because events are implicitly modified when refining conditions and actions.

To illustrate the refinement of the active parts we consider the rule shown in Fig. 14 which represents the process of a special health insurance claim (SHIC) at the context level.

E1	ON	customer wants to effect a SHIC insurance contract
C1	IF	existing customer
A1	Then DO	update customers insurance contract portfolio (⇒ insurance portfolio updated)
A2	Else DO	create customers insurance contract portfolio (⇒ insurance portfolio created)

Fig. 14. Business rule at context level.

For illustration purposes we refine the starting event E1 into two exclusive events E11 and E12, depending on the previous customer relationship. This results in a set of four rules at the next abstraction level (cf. Fig. 15). After applying this set of rules, either a true- or a false-event is raised, triggering the actions A1 or A2 defined in Fig. 14.

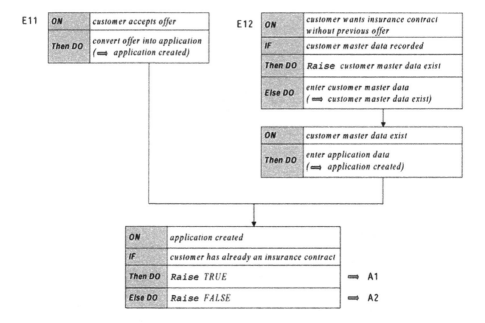

Fig. 15. Refinement of the condition part of the context rule.

The refinement of the action parts of a rule is performed analogously to the refinement of the condition part.

5.3   Architecture of the Rule Repository

To assist the modeler in obtaining consist representations over all abstraction levels, the modeling process should be supported by appropriate tools. A main concept for developing and maintaining workflow specifications is the availability of a rule-repository [HeMy97]; a rule-repository is a special case of a knowledge repository [ZaAz97]. A prototype based on the commercially available repository-tool Rochade is described in [Herb97]. A more extended architecture for process and workflow modeling is suggested in [KEPS97] (Fig. 16). Process model repositories are also discussed in [GrSc98].

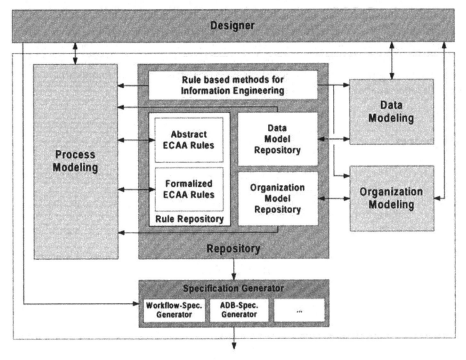

Fig. 16. Architecture of a rule-oriented process and workflow modeling environment.

6   Conclusion and Outlook

The business rule approach seems to be suitable for modeling business processes and workflows. This approach can serve as an integration platform for different process modeling techniques resp. tools and different target systems that implement the workflow or parts of them [KEPS97]. To achieve this, the ECAA-notation is used, enhanced with different constructs representing static components of business processes, i.e., actors and entity/relationship types. There is a need for a methodology for stepwise refinement which supports the transition from the semi-formal process model to a formal workflow specification. This methodology has to state constraints to be fulfilled by semantically correct process and workflow models. Related work has been published in [BeRS95; AaHe97].

In order to allow the administration of the dependencies between process and workflow models at different degrees of accuracy, the business rules have to be represented in a rule repository. This repository is the core of a development environment providing appropriate tools for process, workflow, data, and organization modeling, process refinement, as well as import and export capabilities to and from different process modeling and workflow management systems.

A rule repository system also provides the opportunity to implement capabilities for analysis and simulation. The system may detect incomplete models (missing components) and inconsistencies (dangling events, infinite loops, etc.), and it may be used to improve processes and their implementation in WfMS. A repository facilitates also the maintenance of changes in process models over their whole lifecycle. One approach, allowing the representation of rule evolutions based on a bi-temporally extended relational database, is proposed in [HoPf99].

References

[AaHe97] van der Aalst, W.; van Hee, K.M.: Workflow Management: Modellen, Methoden en Systemen, Schoonhoven: Academic Service 1997.

[BBG+90] Bell, J.; Brooks, D.; Goldbloom, E.; Sarro, R.; Wood, J.: Re-Engineering Case Study - Analysis of Business Rules and Recommendations for Treatment of Rules in a Relational Database Environment, Bellevue Golden: US West Information Technologies Group 1990.

[BeRS95] Becker, J.; Rosemann, M.; Schütte, R.: Grundsätze ordnungsmäßiger Modellierung, in: Wirtschaftsinformatik 37 (1995) 5, pp. 435 - 445.

[Daya88] Dayal, U.: Active Database Management Systems, in: C. Beeri, J.W. Schmidt, U. Dayal (Eds.), Proceedings of the 3rd International Conference on Data and Knowledge Bases, San Matheo: Morgan Kaufmann 1988, pp. 150 - 169.

[dPLL98] do Prado Leite, J.C.S.; Leonardi, M.C.: Business rules as organizational policies, in: Proceedings of the Ninth International Workshop on Software Specification and Design, Los Alamitos: IEEE Comput. Soc. 1998, pp. 68 - 76.

[EnMe99] Endl, R.; Meyer, M.: Potential of Business Process Modeling with regard to available Workflow Management Systems, in: B. Scholz-Reiter; H.-D. Stahlmann; A. Nethe (Eds.): Process Modelling, Berlin: Springer 1999.

[Gatz95] Gatziu, S.: Events in an Active, Object-Oriented Database System, Hamburg: Dr. Kovac 1995.

[GrSc98] Gruhn, V., Schneider, M.: Workflow Management based on Process Model Repositories, in: IEEE Computer Society (Ed.), 1998 International Conference on Software Engineering, Los Alamitos 1998, pp. 379 - 388.

[Herb97] Herbst, H.: Business Rule-Oriented Conceptual Modeling, Heidelberg: Physica 1997.

[HeKn95] Herbst, H.; Knolmayer, G.: Ansätze zur Klassifikation von Geschäftsregeln, in: Wirtschaftsinformatik 37 (1995) 2, pp. 149 - 159.

[HeKn96] Herbst, H.; Knolmayer, G.: Petri nets as derived process representations in the BROCOM approach, in: Wirtschaftsinformatik 38 (1996) 4, pp. 391 - 398.

[HeMy97] Herbst, H.; Myrach, T.: A Repository System for Business Rules, in: R. Meersman, L. Mark (Eds.), Database Application Semantics, London: Chapman & Hall 1997, pp. 119 - 138.

[HoPf99] Hoheisel, H.; Pfahrer, M.: Ein temporales Regel-Repository zur Unterstützung evolutionärer Workflow-Modellierung, in: A.-W. Scheer; M. Nüttgens (Eds.): Electronic Business Engineering, Heidelberg: Physica 1999, pp. 565 - 583.

[Jabl95] Jablonski, S.: Anforderungen an die Modellierung von Workflows, in: H. Österle; P. Vogler (Eds.): Praxis des Workflow-Managements - Grundlagen, Vorgehen, Beispiele, Wiesbaden: Vieweg 1995.

[KiRo94] Kilov, H.; Ross, J.: Information Modeling, An Object-Oriented Approach, Englewood Cliffs: Prentice Hall 1994.

[KEPS97] Knolmayer, G.; Endl, R.; Pfahrer, M.; Schlesinger, M.: Geschäftsregeln als Instrument zur Modellierung von Geschäftsprozessen und Workflows, SWORDIES Report 97-8, Bern 1997.

[Knol98] Knolmayer, G.F.: Business Rules Layers Between Process and Workflow Modeling: An Object-Oriented Perspective, in: S. Demeyer; J. Bosch (Eds.), Object-Oriented Technology, Berlin: Springer 1998, pp. 205 - 207.

[MoGR93] Morgan, C.C.; Gardiner, H.B.; Robinson, K.A.: On the Refinement Calculus, Berlin: Springer 1993.

[MWBG98] Mens, K.; Wuyts, R.; Bontridder, D.; Grijseels, A.: Workshop Report - ECOOP'98 Workshop 7: Tools and Environments for Business Rules, in: S. Demeyer; J. Bosch (Eds.): Object-Oriented Technology, Berlin: Springer 1998, pp. 189 - 196.

[NiHa89] Nijssen, G.M.; Halpin, T.A.: Conceptual Schema and Relational Database Design: A fact oriented approach, New York et al.: Prentice Hall 1989.

[Ober96] Oberweis, A.: Modellierung und Ausführung von Workflows mit Petri-Netzen, Stuttgart, Leipzig: Teubner 1996.

[Padb96] Padberg, J.: Abstract Petri Nets: Uniform Approach and Rule-Based Refinement, Ph.D. Thesis TU Berlin 1996,
http://www.cs.tu-berlin.de/~padberg/Publications/Year96/AbstrPetriNetze.ps.gz.

[Sche92] Scheer, A.-W.: Business Process Engineering - Reference Models for Industrial Companies, 2nd Edition, Berlin et al.: Springer Verlag 1994.

[Wirt71] Wirth, N.: Program Development by Stepwise Refinement, in: Communications of the ACM 14 (1971) 4, pp. 221 - 227.

[ZaAz97] Zarri, G.P.; Azzam, S.: Building up and making use of corporate knowledge repositories, in: E. Plaza, R. Benjamins (Eds.), Knowledge Acquisition, Modeling and Management, 10th European Workshop, EKAW '97, Berlin: Springer 1997, pp. 301 - 316.

Guidelines of Business Process Modeling

Jörg Becker[1], Michael Rosemann[2], Christoph von Uthmann[1]

[1] Westfälische Wilhelms-Universität Münster
Department of Information Systems
Steinfurter Str. 109, 48149 Münster, Germany
Phone: +49 (0)251/83-38100, Fax: +49 (0)251/83-38109
{isjobe|ischut}@wi.uni-muenster.de
[2] Queensland University of Technology
School of Information Systems
2 George Street, Brisbane QLD 4001, Australia
Phone: +61 (0)7 3864 1117, Fax: +61 (0)7 3864 1969
m.rosemann@qut.edu.au

Abstract. Process modeling becomes more and more an important task not only for the purpose of software engineering, but also for many other purposes besides the development of software. Therefore it is necessary to evaluate the quality of process models from different viewpoints. This is even more important as the increasing number of different end users, different purposes and the availability of different modeling techniques and modeling tools leads to a higher complexity of information models. In this paper the Guidelines of Modeling (GoM)[1], a framework to structure factors for the evaluation of process models, is presented. Exemplary, Guidelines of Modeling for workflow management and simulation are presented. Moreover, six general techniques for adjusting models to the perspectives of different types of user and purposes will be explained.

1 Complexity and Quality of Business Process Models

The popularity of different process management approaches like Lean Management [58], Activity-based Costing [52], Total Quality Management [21, 35], Business Process Reengineering [16, 17], Process Innovation [7, 8], Workflow Management [14], and Supply Chain Management [39] has two main effects concerning the requirements on process models. First, the number and variety of model designers and users has spread enormously. Especially, representatives from various business and technical departments, who are not necessarily modeling experts are increasingly involved in the design of process models. As a consequence, the understandability of process models is of growing importance. Secondly, the number and variety of

---

[1] This paper presents results from the research project Guidelines of Modeling (GoM), which was funded by the German Ministry of Education, Science, Research, and Technology, project no.: 01 IS 604 A.

W. van der Aalst et al. (Eds.): Business Process Management, LNCS 1806, pp 30-49, 2000
© Springer-Verlag Berlin Heidelberg 2000

purposes process models are used for is growing. Besides the "traditional" use of process models within software engineering these models are more and more used for pure organizational purposes like process reorganization, certification, Activity-based Costing or human resource planing (see as well [37]).

Process modeling is supposed to be an instrument for coping with the complexity of process planning and control. Existing models show as well considerable complexity themselves, though. Hence, the *design* of process models often turns out to be very problematic. It has direct influence on the economic efficiency of the underlying process-related project. In the first place the model design requires personnel resources and (if necessary) the purchase of software tools. Moreover, the risk exists that the process models, referring to their purpose, are not sufficient. For example, semantic mistakes or the disregarding of relevant aspects can lead to possibly expensive misjudgments. Consequently, the design of models always is an economical risk and not only a modeling exercise.

Especially in enterprise-wide process management projects the design of integrated process models can become a comprehensive challenge. The number of process models can easily be higher 500 with five or more different levels. The related risk will be increased if the model design is seen as a domain of "modeling specialists" who are supposed to be the only ones who understand "their" models. In contrast to this, a business process model should serve as a communication base for *all* persons involved. Consequently, the quality of process models can beyond the fulfillment of syntactic rules defined as its "fitness for use".

Within this context a framework called *Guidelines of Modeling (GoM)* has been developed to assure the quality of information models beyond the accordance to syntactic rules. The GoM-framework includes six guidelines, which aim to improve the quality of information models (product quality) as well as the quality of information modeling (process quality). The *design of business process models* is one core field within the project.

This paper describes first the general intention and the framework of the Guidelines of Modeling (section 2). Exemplary, Guidelines of Modeling for workflow management and simulation, two main purposes of process modeling, are discussed in the third section. Section 4 presents six different techniques for the adaptation of models to perspectives of different users and purposes. The paper ends with a brief conclusion.

2   The Guidelines of Modeling (GoM)

Various frameworks for quality assurance of information models were already presented. Usually, they are either focussing only one kind of information models, in particular data models (like the approaches from [1] or [31, 32]), they focus only special requirements [2, 59], or they contain such high-level-statements, that it is difficult to derive useful recommendations for modeling projects [24, 27].

The aim of the Guidelines of Modeling (GoM) is the development of specific design recommendations in order to increase the quality of models beyond the fulfillment of syntactic rules [3, 41, 42]. The term GoM has been chosen as an analogy to the Generally Accepted Accounting Principles (GAAP) [9, 29, 38]. On the one hand, the GoM result from the selection of the relevant aspects for information modeling from the GAAP.

On the other hand, the GoM adapt elements of the existing approaches for the evaluation of information models. The Guidelines of Modeling, which are presented here (see for an alternative suggestion [49]), contain six guidelines to ameliorate the quality of information models. These are the principles of correctness, relevance, economic efficiency, clarity, comparability, and systematic design (figure 1, see also [31]). While the observance of the principles of correctness, relevance and economic efficiency are a necessary precondition for the quality of models, the principles of clarity, comparability and systematic design have a mere optional character.

The GoM-framework includes besides the six *general guidelines* (level 1) recommendations for different *views* (level 2, e.g. process models) and for different *modeling techniques* (level 3, e.g. Event-driven Process Chains (EPC) or Petri Nets).

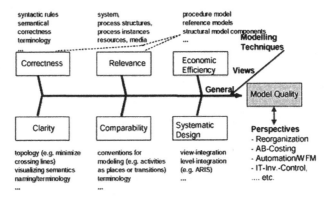

Fig. 1. The Framework of the Guidelines of Modeling (GoM)

2.1   The Basic Guidelines

The basic guidelines consist of the guideline of correctness, the guideline of relevance, and the guideline of economic efficiency.

The *guideline of correctness* has got two facets [1]: the syntactic and the semantic correctness. A model is syntactic correct, if it is consistent and complete against the meta model (see for definitions of meta model ([33], p. 38, [44], pp. 104-105) the model is based on. For the evaluation of the syntactic correctness of a model it is indispensable to have an explicit (documented) meta model. Semantic correctness postulates that the structure and the behaviour of the model is consistent with the real world. Finally, the consistency between different models is viewed as a part of the correctness of the model [59].

While many frameworks use completeness as a quality factor of information models [1, 31], the GoM express this criteria in more relative terms.

The *guideline of relevance* postulates

- to select a relevant object system (universe of discourse),
- to take a relevant modeling technique or to configure an existing meta model adequately, and
- to develop a relevant (minimal) model system.

A model includes elements without relevance, if they can be eliminated without loss of meaning for the model user.

The *guideline of economic efficiency* is a constraint to all other guidelines. In the GAAP-context it is called the cost/benefit constraint ([9], p. 51). It is comparable to the criteria "feasibility" of LINDLAND ET AL. [27] and restricts e.g. the correctness or the clarity of a model. Approaches to support the economic efficiency are reference models, appropriate modeling tools or the re-use of models.

2.2   The Optional Guidelines

The pragmatic aspect of the semiotic theory [27] is integrated in the GoM by the *guideline of clarity*. Without a readable, understandable, useful model all other efforts become obsolete. This guideline is extremely subjective and postulates exactly, that the model is understood by the model user. It is not sufficient, if a model designer regard the model as understandable (see also understandability in the GAAP ([9], p. 52). "Construct overload", the situation in the framework of WAND and WEBER in which one object type of an information modeling technique map to at least two ontological constructs is an example for missing clarity as additional knowledge outside the modeling technique is required ([56], p. 211). Mainly layout conventions put this guideline in concrete terms.

The *guideline of comparability* demands the consistent use of all guidelines within a modeling project. It is one of the guidelines which corresponds directly with one GAAP principle, the comparability principle ([19], pp. 551-552). Like the GAAP which aims to increase the comparability between businesses and periods (e.g. avoid different inventory methods like LIFO and FIFO), this guideline includes e. g. the conform application of layout or naming conventions. Otherwise, two models would follow certain, but different rules. The necessity to compare information models is obvious if as-is-models and to-be-models or enterprise-specific and reference models have to be compared.

The *guideline of systematic design* postulates well-defined relationships between information models, which belongs to different views, e.g. the integration of process models with data models. Every input and output data within a process model has to be specified in a corresponding data model. Further interdependencies exist, following for example the ARIS-approach [45, 46, 47], concerning the functions (function view), the organizational units (organizational view), the results of a process (output view) and the involved applications and databases (resource view). One demand is to use a meta model which integrates all relevant views.

2.3   The GoM Meta Model

Within the research project Guidelines of Modeling a meta model was designed in order to structure and integrate the different project topics (figure 2, [42]). This model shows that a *perspective* is defined as a person-purpose-model-relationship. The purpose represents the intention of the modeling project. Besides the purposes the perspective is determined by the involved persons. Here are two facets of relevance: the existing methodological knowledge (expert, novice) which influences the selection and configuration of the modeling technique, and the role (model designer or user, active or reactive role), which influences the content of the model. Other, more elaborated definitions of the terms perspective and also viewpoints can be found in [6, 36].

Obviously, the guidelines vary in their perceived importance for different perspectives. For example, information models used within the phase of requirements engineering for the purpose of developing individual software and ideally automatically processed by CASE-tools call for syntactical correct models (primacy of the guideline of syntactical correctness in comparison with the guideline of clarity). In contrast to this, process models which are used to explain the business to end-users may include syntactical mistakes, if this supports compact and clear models and if the economic efficiency and the clarity is more important. Consequently, it is necessary to define also *perspective-specific guidelines*.

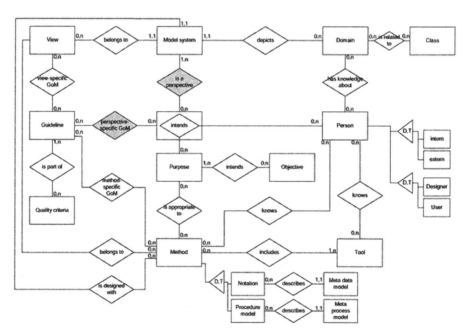

Fig. 2. The GoM meta model

In the following workflow management and simulation will be taken as two examples for popular modeling purposes. Various recommendations for these two purposes will be presented.

3   Guidelines for Selected Purposes of Business Process Modeling

3.1   Workflow Management

The economic efficient development of workflow-based applications [26] does not only require a well considered planning and implementation of systems, but demands the efficient design of workflow models (see also [22]). Workflow models serve in all stages of system planning and development as a communication platform for those who work on the project. However, the recent discussion of workflow modeling is often focussing on syntactic questions. It neglects criteria that go beyond the notation rules and include the specific semantic context of the individual modeling process.

In order to establish standards for the design of information models it is advantageous to have a modeling technique that can be regarded as a quasi-standard (like the ER-approach [4] for data models). Currently, this is not the fact with workflow models. Every workflow management system uses rather its proprietary modeling technique. Therefore, after a workflow management system has been chosen, a revised workflow modeling according to the system-specific modeling technique is in the most cases indispensable.

Experience has shown that the general number of business process models to be transformed into workflow models is rather small. It is not unusual that a company has 100 or more business process models, but only two or three workflow models. Furthermore, concerning breadth and length, only a part of a business process model can usually be controlled workflow-based. Thus, the manual revision of workflow models often is more economic efficient than the use of interfaces (see WfMC interface no. 1). These interfaces might provide some syntactical translation but can not bridge the semantic gap between business process models and workflow models. In the following, specific recommendations for workflow modeling will be given, which focus on comparing these models with business process models. Moreover, it will be distinguished between a first workflow model that is used for selecting a workflow management system or discussing workflow alternatives, and the final executable workflow model.

Function View
Concerning the functions (or activities) within a workflow model, usually a n:m-relationship between business process models and workflow models exist.

Compared to organizational process models, in workflow models *manual functions* should be largely *avoided*, in particular if one follows after the other immediately. On the other hand the amount of functions rises, if the application systems or organization units involved allow further splitting of a function. In general one can state that the granularity of the functions in workflow models are determined by a (possible) change of the organizational unit and/or the application system. Figure 3 shows how with every change of the involved organizational unit and/or the application system a new function has to be introduced. One has to consider the fact that most workflow management systems do not allow a reuse of functions. In this case, a redundant function specification is necessary.

For every function the start and end conditions should be precisely determined. In particular, it has to be indicated if the function shall be started manually or automated. As an option, for every function a deadline can be declared. When this deadline is exceeded, a higher authority can be informed, ideally the person in charge for the process (the process owner). It should be taken into account that not all workflow management systems support a hierarchical modeling.

Thus, business process models can be used as a starting point for the development of workflow models. In order to derive the workflow model, functions have to be deleted and new functions have to be modelled. For the design of an executable model, also further attributes (start and end conditions) have to be specified.

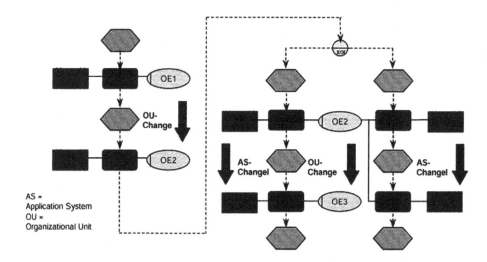

Fig. 3. Granularity of functions within workflow models

Data View

Unlike a business process model, a workflow model requires for every function the description of the necessary *input and output data*. On the level of entity types, attributes, etc. the workflow model has to depict these input and output information. Due to the considerable modeling effort being necessary for the data view of a workflow model, only data that is critical because of the underlying interfaces has to be specified within the first workflow model. After a workflow management system is selected and an executable workflow model is required, the data view has to be completed with information like the data type or the exact data location (database server, table, etc.).

Besides the input and output data, the *data flow* is to be described. The data flow determines the flow from the function that produces data to the function that consumes data. The data flow is restricted by the control flow as the data flow can not precede the control flow. Consequently, the control flow has to be completed before the data flow can be specified. A workflow model should include the data flow as this enables an analysis of further interfaces beyond the use of the control flow information. However, existing workflow management systems often do not allow the visualization of the data flow and show only the (local) input and output data.

Organizational View

Every function within a workflow model must include a link to an organizational construct, if it is not completely automated and shall be executed autonomously. Relevant organizational constructs in the context of workflow management are role (in the sense of a qualification or a competence), organizational unit (permanent or temporary like a project team), position, position type and person as a static information. Figure 4 describes using an extended ER-approach the relationships between these organizational constructs. Moreover, a workflow owner should be specified for the entire workflow.

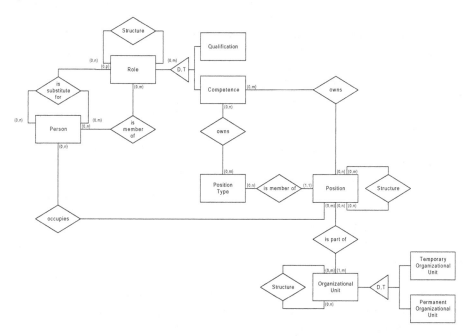

Fig. 4. A reference model for the organizational constructs within workflow models [44]

The organizational constructs in workflow management systems differentiate to a considerable extent. Concerning the assignment of organizational constructs to workflow functions, always the minimum set of organizational constructs which is required for the workflow execution has to be chosen. The organizational constructs, which are used for workflow modeling should refer to the "usual" organizational constructs of the enterprise specified in an organizational chart. If information about the workflow runtime history is of importance, (i.e. function no. 6 should be executed by the same employee who was responsible for function no. 3), a detailed note has to be placed in the workflow model (e.g., "RTH" (Run Time History)).

It has to be taken into consideration that in a workflow model the link between a function and an organizational construct means "*executes*". During the run-time the workflow management system interprets this link and the identified organizational population receives the corresponding work item. In contrast, in business process models this link often means "is responsible for".

If *several organizational constructs are connected with only one function*, there is always an XOR-relationship between them. This means that the number of at run-time addressed members of the organization is extended (e.g. procurement department, all members of a special project and Mr. Smith receive the work item). If a certain rule exists, according to which the relevant organizational constructs can be selected, but the function itself as well as the involved application systems and data are identical, a workflow-split (control flow) has to be defined. If there shall be an AND-relationship between the organizational constructs, it has to be explicitly declared at the borderline between function and organizational construct ("AND"). This could for example mean that both, task executive *and* project executive, must sign a document. Again, it should be stressed that these comprehensive modeling conventions can only apply for the general workflow model. As soon as a special workflow management system is selected, its constraints usually do not allow this elaborated specification between the workflow functions and the involved organizational constructs.

In addition to the organizational constructs, further involved resources have to be depicted. Again, it should be differentiated between a general specification of resources in a first workflow model, which serves as a basis for discussions and the executable workflow model. Only the final workflow model has to include the complete and exact specification of all involved resources. All referred IT-applications have to include specifications of the server, program parameters, etc.

Control View

The control flow describes the logic relationships between the workflow functions. Whereas a linear sequence does not require special considerations (but see the requirement to specify the start and end conditions), split and join constructs are far more demanding. This is an important difference to business process models, which can easily include various splitting and joining connections without that the modeler has to be concerned about the process execution.

Possible (inclusive or exclusive) OR -splits have to be specified exactly in order to become executable by the workflow management engine. If it is not a simple transition condition (e.g., order value > 10.000 $), a reference has to be set that leads to an explanatory document (i.e. rules of signatures, organizational handbook). It is advantageous expressing the respective transition conditions by using dedicated nodes in the models (e.g., predicates, places or arc-inscriptions in Petri Nets or events in Event Driven Process Chains (EPC)).

As an optional construct, many workflow modeling tools allow an ELSE-exit (also: default-connector). This connector is rated as "true", if the conditions of the other corresponding connectors do not fit. This semantic relationship can be stressed by explicit indication of the relevant connector with "ELSE".

OR-Joins require special consideration as many workflow management systems execute them wrongly as an XOR-Join. While this is not critical within business process models, inclusive OR-joins demand further information about the connections, which are evaluated with true at run-time. One approach is the dead path elimination [25]. In this case, the corresponding OR-split forwards an information to the OR-join about all workflow paths, which will not be executed. With this input the OR-join has all required information for the determination of the continuation of the workflow.

Many workflow management systems demand one explicit start and final state node respectively. This is usually not required in business process models. Therefore, these nodes have to be added.

3.2   Simulation

Business Process Simulation (BPS) [12] has been mentioned, albeit only briefly, by many researchers as a technique that could be helpful in the context of business process change. HANSEN (1994) also advocates the appropriateness of simulation for Business Process Reengineering, arguing that "an engineering approach to process reengineering that incorporates modeling and simulation is necessary". Similarly, KETTINGER ET AL. (1997) argue that there is a need for more user-friendly and 'media-rich' capture of business processes and simulation can accommodate these requirements by providing easy visualization and allowing team participation in process redesign. V. UTHMANN and BECKER [53, 54] discuss some detailed aspects of the use of simulation within the business process management life-cycle (figure 5).

The design of simulation models, although it is a problematic task, is mostly treated as a black box. There are only some unsatisfactory isolated hints like "use refinements" or "formalize successively". For the reduction of complexity and the efficient management of designing models three principles have been established in systems engineering: the structuring of similar objectives in phases, the reuse of solution components and the application of conventions to restrict the degree of freedom. The central idea behind this is the identification of analogies in the problems and the reuse of analogous solutions. The identification and utilization of such analogies within the context of simulation models lead to phases, components and conventions.

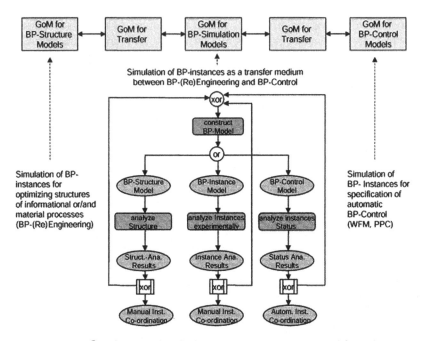

Fig. 5. Simulation within the business process management life-cycle

Model design recommendations should be applicable to a variety of simulation tools. While the phases are independent of tools the components and conventions have to be put in concrete form in terms of certain simulation modeling techniques using their specific construction elements and terminology. As a reference method higher Petri Nets [40] were chosen. Besides some other good reasons the Petri Net specific design recommendation can, thanks to their general process understanding, be transformed to other process modeling techniques pretty easily [53, 55].

A *phase model* of seven phases has been developed (figure 6, a more detailed description of the guidelines is given in [54]). The *separated* view of process object flows is directed to the purposes of processes and simplifies the process identification. This meets the BPR objective of analyzing processes without taking care about departments (= resources). In view of the widely used structure- and function-oriented process descriptions (see [18]) it can be assumed that such a view of processes is intuitively easier to understand than simulation models, especially by modeling novices, and therefore, better accepted. Processing from phase 1 to 2 leads towards a systematic successive transition from static structure models to dynamic models. A further advantage of a separated view of process object flows is that corresponding process models can easier be hierarchically refined without the assignment of resources over different levels. Traditionally, from a *function view* a process is understood as a succession of object-using, modifying and/or deleting functions (activities), and from *data view* as a succession of states corresponding to the existence of process-related objects. This differentiation is reflected in the phase model: First in phase 1 (process object flows) it is recommended to start with a function oriented process mapping (s. above). In phase 3 the object types are specified within the static data view before the functions are procedurally (in contrast to descriptively) described in phase 4. In the phases 1 to 4 there are considered process structures, coordination mechanisms, operation and state times. Input, disturbances/changes and initial states are designed in phase 5 to 7.

The phases offer a framework to decompose the design of process simulation models in less complex subtasks. Within the phases certain objectives are to be modeled applying to specific components and conventions.

The aim of using *model components*, which can be individually composed, is a more efficient and correct model construction. There are reference simulation models in the form of context-related model components [45]. Complementary to these ones the guidelines comprise components, which are not related to concrete organizational or engineering problems, but structure context independent analogies. These *structure components* describe coordination mechanisms on different complexity levels where components can consist of less complex components (down to the elements of the meta model of the simulation language). Their higher abstraction level allows the use of these components for a simplified individual construction of simulation models from the scratch as it usually is necessary within process simulation. Moreover, the structure components help model designers to be more sensitive towards possibly relevant coordination mechanisms. The structure components are related to single objectives, and therefore, are assigned to certain construction phases.

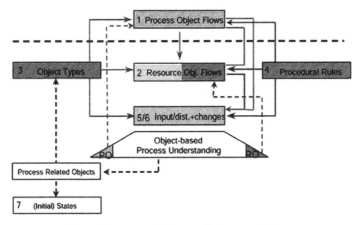

Fig. 6. Phase model for simulation model design

Finally, some *design conventions* should be presented. Methods of process modeling contain generally just a set of syntactic rules, which give model designers a wide degree of freedom. Therefore, one objective can be depicted in (different) models which are correct but do not have sufficient quality, e. g. they are misleading or badly arranged. This has to be taken into account especially because of the (in simulation models) usually high number and variety of involved model designers and users of model. Conventions are supposed to restrict this freedom and lead to a higher quality. One important intention of this is to ensure a uniform, clear (GoM-principle of clarity) and unequivocal understanding of models of all involved users. A further important aspect of model conventions is the support of coping with the requirements perspectives. Important conventions for simulation models refer especially to the use of terminology, topology, start and end markings of processes, the visualization of process and resource object types (including the media type) within their organizational context, documentary aspects and the explication of different views (e.g. data, function and organizational view). For the definition and consolidation of terms the use of a business term model is proposed. Besides the discussed semantic aspects the performance of simulation models has to be taken into account.

4   Techniques for Adjusting Models to Perspectives

Perspectives on process models can be distinguished by the involved persons and by the modeling purpose. While a process model which specifies a workflow has to depict among others the control flow, the data flow and program parameters (see section 3.1), a model which is used within an organizational handbook or for certification purposes includes mainly organizational facts (process owner, roles, etc.). A rough impression of the great variety of perspectives on information models which exists especially concerning process models can be found in figure 7.

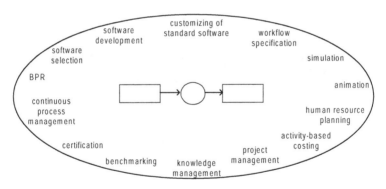

Fig. 7. Potential perspectives on process models [42]

Within the research project Guidelines of Modeling we identify, characterize and compare these perspectives using empirical studies. In the following, this paper is not concentrating on these content-specific questions, but it will be discussed how perspectives can methodically be distinguished. Six ways of customizing different perspectives will be explained. They have an adjunctive relationship to each other, which means that they can be used in combination. As an application of the guideline of relevance they suppose to reduce the model complexity for every individual perspective.

4.1   Different Layout Conventions

Different layout conventions exist, if the models of two perspectives concerning the number and the naming of the information objects are identical, but different in their representation (aesthetics). This kind of model differentiation is more determined by the way of using the model than by the model content. It can be realized with "reasonable effort", if the placement is identical and only form, color, size, etc. of the objects are different. The transformation of "typical" information models with cycles and squares into more colorful, more or less self-explanable models is important to gain the acceptance in the business departments. Figure 8 portrays, taking ARIS Easy Design as an example [20], how a process model designed for end users from business departments can look like (see also [30] for a similar approach).

Different layout conventions become much more difficult to handle, if also the placement of the information objects can vary. One example in (large) data models is that different entity types are of different importance for different users. As a consequence, in every model different entity types should be right in the middle of the model, the area of most attention. For that, sophisticated algorithms are necessary, which optimize models concerning metrics like the minimal (average, maximum) length of edges, the minimal number of crossings, or the minimal drawing area [2, 34, 51]. Potential constraints are that only two directions are allowed (vertical, horizontal) or symmetries have to be stressed (e.g. sons in hierarchies).

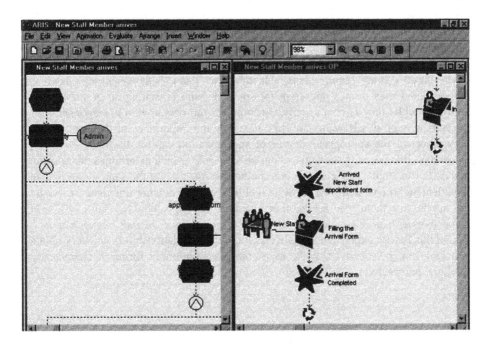

Fig. 8. A process model in ARIS Easy Design [20]

4.2   Different Naming Conventions

A different naming in models related to different perspectives is of high importance in distributed, especially international modeling projects and requires the possibility to administer synonyms for the relevant model constructs. It is recommended to use a *business term catalogue*, which defines and relates the main terms within a company ([23], pp. 127-133). Furthermore, one cluster of the business term catalogue should as a part of the meta model define the constructs, which are relevant for information modeling (e.g. entity type, cardinality) [50]. Between the single business terms exist typical semantic relationships like "is related to", "classifies", "is part of", "is a" or "is synonym of". A business term catalogue should substitute existing (textual) glossaries and be as far as possible completed before the process modeling activities start. The attributes of the business terms contain links to the different purposes and characterize a term e.g. as a software-specific term (e.g. "Company Code" within SAP R/3) or to specific qualifications (e.g. the German term "Unternehmen" for model users familiar with German). The user or the user group has corresponding attributes, so that for every user (group) the adequate terms can be selected automatically.

4.3   Different Information Objects

In comparison with different layout or naming conventions the perspectives are much more individual, when different information objects are relevant for them. For example, a workflow developer would not be interested in a detailed description of the manual functions within a process, while someone who is responsible for the implementation of activity-based costing may be especially interested in these time-consuming functions (see also [43] for a comparison of workflow management and activity-based costing requirements). On the other hand, batch-tasks depicted in a process model may be not important for someone who is writing an organizational handbook, while they have a specific meaning for the person who is responsible for the customization of ERP software. In a next step the importance of the attributes of every object or the appropriate degree of specialization can be discussed for every perspective. It is not only the purpose but also the role, which determines the relevant objects. For example, a doctor has got another perspective on the same process than the patient and the person who allows traveling expenses another one than the person who applies for them (see for another example ([28], pp. 60-61)). Thus, different perspectives can be characterized as *different projections on one common model*. Though this is very expensive to realize as it requires a relationship from every object to the relevant perspectives, it is one of the most important forms to characterize individual perspectives.

4.4   Different Information Object Types

In some cases the requirements of different perspectives can be generalized in a way, that between the perspective and the information object types (e.g. entity type, organizational unit type, etc.) of the common meta model a relevance relationship can be identified. That means, different perspectives can be characterized as *different projections on a common meta model*. For example, it is indispensable to depict the object type role in a workflow model, while in ERP-specific reference models like the ones from SAP [5] or BAAN [13] system organizational units (e. g. company code, plant or sales organization in SAP R/3) are relevant.

This requirement is already realized in some modeling tools. For example, ARIS-Toolset is offering method filters which reduce the meta model in a way that the user is not confronted with the over-complexity resulting out of a non-appropriate modeling technique [20].

4.5   Different Use of a Process Modeling Technique

The high number of different modeling techniques with a common root (e. g. Entity Relationship model or Petri Nets) leads to the fact, that in many cases perspectives can be distinguished because they are slightly different in their meta model. As an explanation, the event-driven process chains (EPC) are taken as an example [45, 46]. EPC consist mainly of functions, events and control flow connectors. One notation rule, which was stressed about the EPC, is that an OR-split never succeeds directly an event. Nonetheless, in the most important book which is using the event-driven process chains, "Business Process Engineering" [45] the included reference models do not consider this rule (to get a higher clarity, because of shorter processes).

This kind of perspective differentiation requires individual rules to transform one model into the other. It is one objective of the Guidelines of Modeling to identify for widespread modeling techniques like the ERM or event-driven process chains typical differences in using the meta model and as far as possible to prioritize one alternative (see [41] for examples for the event-driven process chains).

4.6   Different Meta Models

As the first five approaches assume that one modeling technique serves for all the different perspectives, the requirements for such a language are quite high [36]. Single perspectives have got the highest degree of individualization if they are designed with different modeling techniques. Therefore, they already can be distinguished by the underlying meta models. Such a differentiation may be necessary, if a BPR-project requires easy to understand models designed for example with event-driven process chains, while the introduction of workflow management requires precise Petri Nets and the increase of the customer orientation of the processes needs customer-supplier-protocols [48]. If this form of perspective differentiation is tolerated within a modeling project, it is recommended to design relationship meta models: meta models which relate the elements and relationships of the involved modeling techniques to each other [33]. They can be used for the horizontal model transformation (within analysis) and for the vertical model transformation (from analysis to design).

5   Summary and Outlook

A continuously growing number of different purposes for process modeling, of involved model designers and model users, and available comprehensive modeling tools increases the complexity of process modeling. Thus, the management of the quality of process models is becoming challenging.

This paper presented a framework called Guidelines of Modeling (GoM), which structures different quality criteria and levels of abstraction in two dimensions. We discussed the six guidelines of correctness, relevance, economic efficiency, clarity, comparibility and systematic design (section 2). Workflow management and simulation were taking as examples in order to put the modeling recommendations in concrete terms for two selected purposes (section 3). More general, six different techniques for the differentiation of process models for alternative purposes were presented (section 4). The introduced concepts offer less experienced model designers some hints for a systematic and adequate design of process models. The overall GoM architecture and the detailed recommendations make more sensitive for critical quality factors beyond the consistent use of a modeling technique.

The aim of the further work is the design of a "comprehensive" set of guidelines for process models with Petri Nets as the uniform reference modeling technique within the entire process life-cycle [10, 11]. Modeling Guidelines should force to construct the common elements adequately for the core purposes of process modeling, namely Business Process (Re)Engineering, workflow management and simulation [53]. Furthermore, we are currently analyzing the potential for the integration of an IS-related ontology into the GoM-framework. First results taking the Bunge-Wand-Weber models [57] can be found in [17].

References

[1]   Batini, C., Ceri, S., Navathe, S. B.: Conceptual Database Design. An Entity-Relationship - Approach. Benjamin Cummings, Redwood City, California (1992)

[2]   Batini, C., Furlani, L., Nardelli, E.: What is a good diagram? A pragmatic approach. In: Chen, P. P.-S. (ed.): Proceedings of the 4th International Conference on the Entity-Relationship Approach: The Use of ER Concept in Knowledge Representation. Elsevier, North-Holland, 312-319

[3]   Becker, J., Rosemann, M., Schütte, R.: Guidelines of Modelling (GoM). Wirtschafts-informatik 37 (1995) 5, 435-445 (in German)

[4] Chen, P. P.-S.: The Entity-Relationship Model: Toward a Unified View of Data. ACM Transactions on Database Systems 1 (1997) 1, 9-36

[5] Curran, Th., Keller G.: SAP R/3. Business Blueprint: Understanding the Business Process Reference Model. Prentice Hall, Upper Saddle River (1998)

[6] Darke, P., Shanks, G.: Stakeholder Viewpoints in Requirements Definition: A Framework for Understanding Viewpoint Development Approaches. Requirements Engineering 1 (1996), 85-105

[7] Davenport, T.H.: Process Innovation: Reengineering Work Through Information Technology. Boston, Massachusetts (1992)

[8] Davenport, T.H., Short, J.E.: The New Industrial Engineering: Information Technology and Business Process Redesing. Sloan Management Review 31 (1990) 4, 11-27

[9] Davis, M., Paterson, R., Wilson, A.: UK GAAP: Generally Accepted Accounting Principles in the United Kingdom. 5th ed., Clays Ltd, Bungay, Suffolk (1997)

[10] Deiters, W.: Information Gathering and Process Modeling in a Petri Net Based Approach: Part III, Chapter 1 of this volume

[11] Deiters, W.; Gruhn, V.: The Funsoft Net Approach to Software Process Management. International Journal of Software Engineering and Knowledge Engineering 4 (1994) 2, 229-256

[12] Desel, J., Erwin, T.: Simulation of Business Processes: Part II, Chapter 2 in this volume

[13] van Es, R. M.; Post, H. A.: Dynamic Enterprise Modeling. A Paradigm Shift in Software Implementation. Kluwer, Deventer (1996)

[14] Georgakopoulos, D.; Hornick, M., Sheth, A.: An Overview of Workflow Management: From Process Modeling to Workflow Automation Infrastructure. Distributed and Parallel Databases 3 (1995) 2, 119-153

[15] Green, P., Rosemann, M.: An Ontological Analysis of Integrated Process Modelling. In: Jarke, M., Oberweis, A. (eds.): Advanced Information Systems Engineering. Proceedings of the 11th International Conference - CAiSE '99. Lecture Notes in Computer Science, Vol. 1626. Springer-Verlag, Berlin et al. (1999), 225-240

[16] Hammer, M.: Reengineering Work: Don't Automate, Obliterate. Harvard Business Review 68 (1990) 4, 104-112

[17] Hammer, M., Champy, J.: Reengineering the Corporation: a Manifesto for Business Revolution. London (1993)

[18] Hess, T., Brecht, L.: State of the Art des Business Process Redesign: Darstellung und Vergleich bestehender Methoden. 2nd ed., Gabler-Verlag, Wiesbaden (1996) (in German)

[19] Horngren, Ch. T.; Harrison, W. T.: Accounting, 2nd ed. Prentice Hall, Englewood Cliffs, New Jersey (1992)

[20] IDS Scheer AG: ARIS Methods. Version 4.1. Saarbrücken (1999)

[21] Ishikawa, K.: What is Total Quality Control? The Japanese Way, Prentice Hall, Englewood Cliffs (1985)

[22] Jannsens, G. K., Verelst, J., Weyn, B.: Techniques for Modelling Workflows and their Support of Reuse: Part I, Chapter 1 in this volume

[23] Kirchmer, M.: Business Process Oriented Implementation of Standard Software. Springer-Verlag, Berlin et al. (1998)

[24] Krogstie, J., Lindland, O. I., Sindre, G.: Towards a Deeper Understanding of Quality in Requirements Engineering. In: Iivari, J., Lyytinen, K., Rossi, M. (eds.): Proceedings of the 7th International Conference on Advanced Information Systems Engineering – CAiSE '95. Springer-Verlag, Berlin et al. (1995), 82-95

[25] Leymann, F., Altenhuber, W.: Managing business processes as information resources. IBM Systems Journal 33 (1994) 2, 326-348

[26] Leymann, F., Roller, D.: Workflow-based applications. IBM Systems Journal 36 (1997) 1, 102-123

[27] Lindland, O. I., Sindre, G., Sølvberg, A.: Understanding Quality in Conceptual Modeling. IEEE Software 11 (1994) 2, 42-49

[28] Macaulay, L. A.: Requirements Engineering, Springer-Verlag, Berlin, Heidelberg, New York (1996)

[29] Miller, M. M.: Comprehensive GAAP Guide. Harcourt Brace Jovanovich, Publishers, San Diego et al. (1988)

[30] Moody, D. L.: Graphical Entity Relationship Models: Towards a More User Understandable Representation of Data. In: Thalheim, B. (ed.): Proceedings of the 15th International Conference on Conceptual Modeling: Conceptual Modeling – ER '96. Springer-Verlag, Berlin et al. (1996), 227-244

[31] Moody, D. L.; Shanks, G. G.: What makes a Good Data Model? A Framework for Evaluating and Improving the Quality of Entity Relationship Models. The Australian Computer Journal, 30 (1998) 3, 97-110

[32] Moddy, D. L.: Shanks, G.: Improving the Quality of Entity Relationship Models: An Action Research Programme. In: Edmundson, B., Wilson, D. (eds.): Proceedings of the 9th Australiasian Conference on Information Systems. Vol. II, Sydney (1998), 433-448

[33] Nissen, H. W., Jeusfeld, M. A., Jarke, M., Zemanek, G. V., Huber, H.: Managing Multiple Requirements Perspectives with Metamodels. IEEE Software 13 (1996) 3, 37-48

[34] Nummenmaa, J.; Tuomi, J.: Constructing layouts for ER-diagrams from visibility-representations. In: Kangassalo, H. (ed.): Proceedings of the 9th International Conference on the Entity-Relationship Approach - ER `90: Entity-Relationship Approach. Elsevier, North-Holland (1991), 303-317

[35] Oakland, J.S.: Total Quality Management: The Route to Improving Performance. 2nd ed., Nichols Publishing, New Jersey, NJ, (1993)

[36] Opdahl, A. L.: Towards a faceted modelling language. In: Galliers, R. et al.: Proceedings of the 5th European Conference on Information Systems - ECIS '97. Cork 1997, 353-366

[37] Pagnoni, A: Management-oriented Models of Business Processes: Part I, Chapter 7 in this volume

[38] Pareira, V., Paterson, R., Wilson, A.: UK/US GAAP Comparison. 3rd ed., Briddles Ltd, Guildford and King's Lynn (1994)

[39] Poirier, C. A.: Advanced Supply Chain Management: How to Build a Sustained Competition. Publishers' Group West (1999)

[40] Reisig, W.: Petri Nets - An Introduction. Berlin (1985)

[41] Rosemann, M.: Complexity Management in Process Models. Gabler-Verlag, Wiesbaden (1996) (in German)

[42] Rosemann, M.: Managing the Complexity of Multiperspective Information Models using the Guidelines of Modeling. In: Fowler, D., Dawson, L. (eds.): Proceedings of the 3rd Australian Conference on Requirements Engineering. Geelong (1998), 101-118

[43] Rosemann, M, Green, P.: Enhancing the Process of Ontological Analysis - The "Who cares?" Dimension. In: Dampney, K. (ed.): Proceedings of the IS Foundations-Workshop. Sydney, 29. September (1999)

[44] Rosemann, M., zur Mühlen, M.: Evaluation of Workflow Management Systems - a Meta Model Approach. Australian Journal of Information Systems 6 (1998) 1, 103-116

[45] Scheer, A.-W.: Business Process Engineering. 3rd ed., Springer-Verlag, Berlin et al. (1998)

[46] Scheer A.-W.: ARIS - Business Process Modeling. 2nd ed. Berlin et al. (1999)

[47] Scheer, A.-W., Nüttgens, M: ARIS Architecture and Reference Models for Business Process Management, Part III, Chapter 8 in this volume

[48] Scherr, A. L.: A new approach to business processes. IBM Systems Journal 32 (1993) 1, 80-98

[49] Schütte, R., Rotthowe, Th.: The Guidelines of Modelling as an approach to enhance the quality of information models. In: Ling, T. W., Ram, S., Lee, M. L. (eds.): Conceptual Modeling - ER '98. 17th International ER-Conference, Singapore, November 16-19, 1998. Springer-Verlag, Berlin et al. (1998) 240-254

[50] Spencer, R., Teorey, T.; Hevia, E.: ER Standards Proposal. In: Kangassalo, H. (ed.): Proceedings of the 9th International Conference on the Entity-Relationship Approach – ER `90: Entity-Relationship Approach. Elsevier, North-Holland (1991), 425-432

[51] Tamassia, R., Di Battista, C., Batini, C.: Automatic graph drawing and readability of diagrams. IEEE Transactions on Systems, Man, and Cybernetics 18 (1988) 1, 61-78

[52] Tunney, P.B., Reeve, J.M.: The Impact of Continuous Improvement on the Design of Activity Based Cost Systems. Journal of Cost Management (1992) 43-50

[53] von Uthmann, C., Becker, J.: Petri Nets for Modeling Business Processes - Potentials, Deficits and Recommendations. In: Proceedings of the Colloquium on Petri Net Technologies for Modelling Communication Based Systems. Berlin 1999 (to appear)

[54] von Uthmann, C., Becker, J.: Guidelines of Modeling (GoM) for Business Process Simulation. In: Scholz-Reiter, B., Stahlmann, H.-D., Nethe, A. (eds.): Process Modeling. Berlin, Heidelberg (1999)

[55] van der Aalst, W.M.P., van Heh, K.M.: Business Process Redesign: A Petri-net-based approach. Computers in Industry 29 (1996) 1-2, 15-26

[56] Wand, Y.; Weber, R.: On the deep structure of information systems. Information Systems Journal 5 (1995) 3, 203-223

[57] Weber, R.: Ontological Foundations of Information Systems. Coopers & Lybrand Accounting Research Methodology Monograph No. 4, Melbourne (1997)

[58] Womack, J. P., Jones, D. T., Roos, D.: The Machine That Changed the World: The Story of Lean Production. Harpercollins (1991)

[59] Zamperoni, A., Löhr-Richter, P.: Enhancing the Quality of Conceptual Database Specifications through Validation. In: Elmasri, R. A., Kouramajian, V., Thalheim, B. (eds.): Proceedings of the 12th International Conference on the Entity-Relationship Approach – ER `93. Springer-Verlag, Berlin et al. (1993), 85-98

A Knowledge-Based Approach for Designing Robust Business Processes

Chrysanthos Dellarocas and Mark Klein

Center for Coordination Science
Sloan School of Management
Massachusetts Institute of Technology
Room E53-315, Cambridge, MA 02139, USA
{dell, m_klein}@mit.edu

Abstract. This chapter describes a novel knowledge-based methodology and computer toolset for helping business process designers and participants better manage exceptions (unexpected deviations from a normal sequence of events caused by design errors, resource failures, requirement changes etc.) that can occur during the enactment of a process. This approach is based on an on-line repository exploiting a generic and reusable body of knowledge, which describes what kinds of exceptions can occur in collaborative work processes, how these exceptions can be detected, and how they can be resolved. This work builds upon previous efforts from the MIT Process Handbook project and from research on conflict management in collaborative design.

1 Introduction

Business process models typically describe the "normal" flow of events in an ideal world. For example, the model of a product development process typically includes a "design product" activity, followed by a "build product" activity, which, in turn, is followed by a "deliver product" activity. Reality, however, tends to be more complicated. During the enactment of a business process a lot of *exceptions,* that is, deviations from the normal sequence of events, might occur. For example, product design might prove to be inconsistent with the capabilities of the manufacturing plant. Manufacturing stations might break down in the middle of jobs. Delivery trucks might go on strike. To assure that a process is still able to fulfill its organizational goals, process participants must be able to detect, diagnose and successfully resolve such exceptional conditions as they occur.

Traditionally, managers have relied on their experience and understanding of a process in order to handle deviations from the expected flow of events. However, the increasing complexity of modern business processes and the accelerating pace with which these processes change has made the reliance on individual managers' experience and intuition an increasingly less satisfactory way to deal with exceptions. There is an increasing need for *systematic* business process *operational risk*

W. van der Aalst et al. (Eds.): Business Process Management, LNCS 1806, pp 50-65, 2000

management methodologies. Such methodologies will assist business process designers to anticipate potential exceptions and instrument their processes so that exceptions can either be avoided or be detected in a timely way. Furthermore, when exception manifestations occur during process enactment, these methodologies assist in selecting the best way of resolving them.

Current process modeling methodologies and tools [6, 11, 12] do not make any provision for describing exception handling procedures separately from "main-line" processing. This approach, however, is problematic for a number of reasons. First, it results in cluttered, overly complex, models, which hinder instead of enhancing understanding and communication. Second, the anticipation of possible failure modes once again relies on the experience and intuition of the model designers. Third, the approach cannot help with exceptions that have not been explicitly hard-coded into the model.

This chapter describes a knowledge-based approach for designing robust business processes. Rather than requiring process designers to anticipate all possible exceptions up front and incorporate them into their models, this approach is based on a set of novel computerized process analysis tools, which assist designers in analyzing "normal" process models, *systematically* anticipating possible exceptions and suggesting ways in which the "normal" process can be instrumented in order to detect or even to avoid them. When exception manifestations occur, these tools can help diagnose their underlying causes, and suggest specific interventions for resolving them. The approach is based on an extensible knowledge base of generic strategies for avoiding, detecting, diagnosing and resolving exceptions.

The remainder of this chapter is structured as follows: Section 2 provides an overview of the proposed approach. Section 3 describes how the approach has been successfully applied to analyze operational risks of the Barings Bank trading processes. Section 4 discusses related work. Finally, Section 5 presents some directions for future work.

2 A Knowledge-Based Approach to Exception Handling

2.1 What is an Exception?

We define an exception as any deviation from a "normal" collaborative process that uses the available resources to achieve the task requirements on an optimal way. An exception can thus include errors in enacting a task or distributing results between tasks, inadequate responses to changes in tasks or resources, missed opportunities and so on. To make this more concrete, consider the possible exceptions for the generic coordination process known as "subcontracting". Subcontracting can be used whenever one wants to share agents who do a service among requestors of that service. The requestor for a service sends out a request for bids (RFB) asking for agents to perform a given task. Interested subcontractors respond with bids. The requestor awards the task to the subcontractor with the best bid (based for example on anticipated cost, quality or timeliness), at which point the subcontractor performs the task and returns the results to the requestor. This mechanism makes many implicit assumptions; violations of any one of them can lead to exceptions (Figure 1):

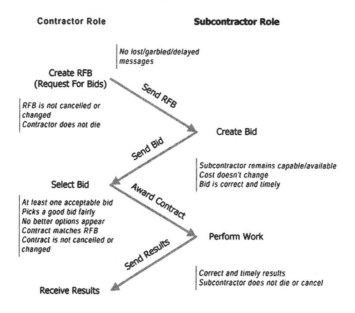

Fig. 1. Implicit Assumptions for Subcontracting.

Plain text items on the left and right represent tasks done by the Contractor (on the left) on the Subcontractor (on the right). Labeled arcs represent interactions between the Contractor and Subcontractor. Items in italics represent implicit assumptions made by this mechanism (for example that the task required by the Contractor does not change after it has sent out the RFB, that the Subcontractor does not cancel the task it was assigned, become incapable of doing it, make a mistake etc.). Any event that results in the violation of any of these assumptions represents a possible exception for the subcontracting process. In addition to that, some exceptions take the form of dysfunctional systemic behavior that may result even when the mechanism is followed perfectly. Deadlock (where several agents are each waiting for another one to do something) and resource poaching (wherein high-priority tasks are unable to access needed resources because these resources they have already been reserved by lower priority tasks) are all examples of this.

We have developed, as a result of analyses like that shown above, a growing taxonomy of exception types, a subset of which is show below (Figure 2):

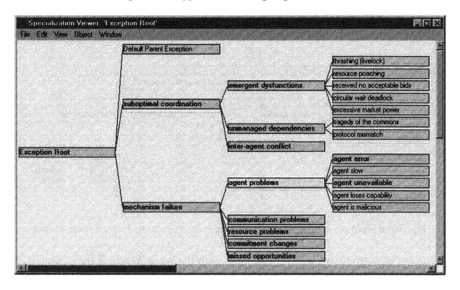

Fig. 2. A Subset of the Exception Type Taxonomy.

As we shall see, the essence of our work is developing a knowledge base that captures such exceptions and relates them to (1) the processes that they can occur in, and (2) the processes that can be used to manage (anticipate, detect, avoid and resolve) them.

2.2 Preparing for Exceptions

The first step in our approach helps process designers to anticipate, for a given "normal" process model, the ways that the process may fail and then instrument the process so that these failures can be detected or avoided. The principal idea here is to compare the process model against a taxonomy of elementary process elements annotated with possible failure modes.

A process element taxonomy can be defined as a hierarchy of process element templates, with very generic elements at the top and increasingly *specialized* elements below. For example, Figure 3 depicts a small activity taxonomy. Each activity can have attributes, e.g. that define the challenges for which it is well-suited. Note that activity *specialization* is different from *decomposition*, which involves breaking an activity down into subactivities. While a subactivity represents a part of a process; a specialization represents a "subtype" or "way of" doing the process [20, 21]. Resource, goal and assumption taxonomies can be defined in a similar manner.

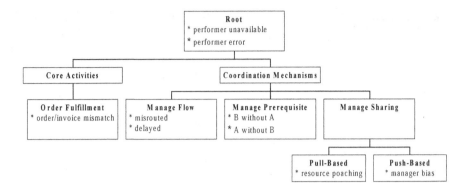

Fig. 3. An Example of a Generic Activity Taxonomy Annotated with Failure Modes.

Process element templates are annotated with the ways in which they can fail, i.e. with their characteristic *exception types*. Failure modes for a given process template can be uncovered using failure mode analysis [24]. Each process element in a taxonomy inherits all characteristic failure modes of its parent (generalization) and may contain additional failure modes which are specific to it.

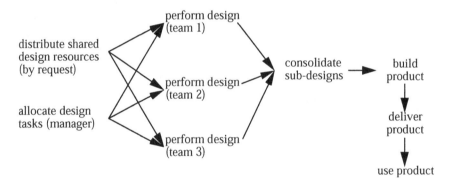

Fig. 4. An Example "Normal" Process Model.

Given a "normal" process model, to identify failure modes we need only identify the generic process element templates that match each component of the model. The potentially applicable exception types will then consist of the union of all failure modes inherited from the matching templates. We can see, for example, that the "distribute shared design resources" activity in Figure 4 is a subtype of the generic "pull-based sharing" process template in Figure 3, since the resources are "pulled" by their consumers rather than "pushed" (i.e. allocated) by their producers. This template includes among its characteristic failure modes the exception called "poaching", wherein resources go disproportionately to lower priority tasks because agents with lower priority tasks happen to reserve them first. The "deliver product" activity is a specialization of the "manage flow" template, with characteristic exceptions such as "item delayed", "item misrouted" and so on. All activities also inherit the characteristic failure modes from the generalizations of these matching templates, such as "responsible agent is unavailable", and so on.

The process designer can select, from this list of possible exception types, the ones that seem most important in his/her particular context. He/she might know, for example, that the "deliver product" process is already highly robust and that there is no need to augment it with additional exception handling capabilities.

For each exception type of interest, the process designer can then decide how to instrument the process in order to detect these exceptions. While processes can fail in many different ways, such failures have a relatively limited number of different manifestations, including missed deadlines, violations of artifact constraints, exceeding resource limits, and so on. Every exception type includes pointers to *exception detection* process templates in the process taxonomy that specify how to detect the symptoms manifested by that exception type. These templates, once interleaved into the "normal" process model by the workflow designer, play the role of "sentinels" that check for signs of actual or impending failure. The template for detecting the "resource poaching" exception, for example, operates by comparing the average priority of tasks that quickly receive shared resources against the average priority of all tasks. The "item delayed", "agent unavailable", and "item misrouted" exceptions can all be detected using time-out mechanisms. Similar pointers exist to *exception avoidance* processes, whose purpose is to try to prevent the exceptional condition from occurring at all.

2.3 Diagnosing Exceptions

When exceptions actually occur during the enactment of a process, our tools can assist process participants in figuring out how to react. Just as in medical domains, selecting an appropriate intervention requires understanding the underlying cause of the problem, i.e. its *diagnosis*. A key challenge here, however, is that the symptoms revealed by the exception detection processes can suggest a wide variety of possible underlying causes. Many different exceptions (e.g. "agent not available", "item misrouted" etc.) typically manifest themselves, for example, as missed deadlines.

Our approach for diagnosing exception causes is based on heuristic classification [5]. It works by traversing a diagnosis taxonomy. Exception types can be arranged into a taxonomy ranging from highly general failure modes at the top to more specific ones at the bottom (Figure 2). Every exception type includes a set of defining characteristics that need to be true in order to make that diagnosis potentially applicable to the current situation

When an exception is detected, the responsible process participant traverses the exception type taxonomy top-down like a decision tree, starting from the diagnoses implied by the manifest symptoms and iteratively refining the specificity of the diagnoses by eliminating exception types whose defining characteristics are not satisfied. Distinguishing among candidate diagnoses will often require that the user get additional information about the current exception and its context, just as medical diagnosis often involves performing additional tests.

Imagine, for example, that we have detected a time-out exception in the "deliver product" step (see Figure 4). The diagnoses that can manifest this way include "agent unavailable", "item misrouted", and "item delayed". The defining characteristics of these exceptions are:

- **agent unavailable:** agent responsible for task is unavailable (i.e. sick, on vacation, retired, etc.)
- **item misrouted:** current location and/or destination of item not match original target destination
- **item delayed:** item has correct target destination but is behind original schedule

The user then has a specific set of questions that he/she can ask in order to narrow down the exception diagnosis. If the appropriate information is available on-line, then answering such questions and thereby eliminating some diagnoses can potentially be at least partially automated.

2.4 Resolving Exceptions

Once an exception has been detected and at least tentatively diagnosed, one is ready to define a *prescription* that resolves the exception and returns the process to a viable state. This can be achieved, in our approach, by selecting and instantiating one of the generic exception resolution strategies that are associated with the hypothesized diagnosis. These strategies are processes like any other, are captured in a portion of the process taxonomy, and are annotated with attributes defining the *preconditions* that must be satisfied for that strategy to be applicable. We have accumulated roughly 200 such strategies to date, including for example:
- IF a process fails, THEN try a different process for achieving the same goal
- IF a highly serial process is operating too slowly to meet an impending deadline, THEN pipeline (i.e. release partial results to allow later tasks to start earlier) or parallelize to increase concurrency
- IF an agent may be late in producing a time-critical output, THEN see whether the consumer agent will accept a less accurate output in exchange for a quicker response
- IF multiple agents are causing wasteful overhead by frequently trading the use of a scarce shared resource, THEN change the resource sharing policy such that each agent gets to use the resource for a longer time
- IF a new high-performance resource applicable to a time-critical task becomes available, THEN reallocate the task from its current agent to the new agent

Since an exception can have several possible resolutions, each suitable for different situations, we use a procedure identical to that used in diagnosis to find the right one. Imagine, for example, that we want a resolution for the diagnosis "agent unavailable".

We start at the root of the process resolution taxonomy branch associated with that diagnosis. Three specific strategies are available, with the following preconditions and actions:

- **wait till agent available:** IF the original agent will be available in time to complete the task on the current schedule THEN wait for original agent to start task
- **find new agent with same skills:** IF another agent with the same skills is available, THEN assign task to that agent
- **change task to meet available skills:** IF the task can be performed a different way using agents we have currently available THEN modify and re-assign.

The system user can prune suggested strategies based on which preconditions are satisfied, and enact or customize a strategy selected from the remainder. Note that the substantial input may be needed from the user in some cases in order to refine a generic strategy into specific actions.

2.5 Summary

Figure 5 summarizes the knowledge structure which serves as the basis of the approach described in the previous sections. It consists of two cross-referenced taxonomies: a specialization taxonomy of process templates and a taxonomy of exception types.

During process design time, process models are compared against the process taxonomy in order to identify possible failure modes. Once failure modes are identified, the exception type taxonomy provides links to appropriate detection and avoidance processes. During process enactment time, exception manifestations are compared against the exception type taxonomy in order to identify possible diagnoses. Once plausible diagnoses have been identified, the exception taxonomy provides links to resolution processes.

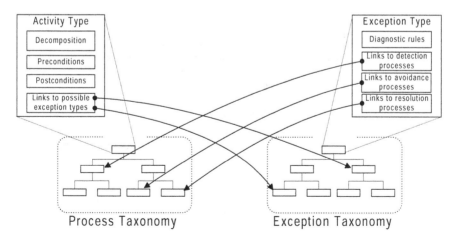

Fig. 5. Overview of Exception Handling Knowledge Structures.

3 Case Study: Barings Bank

The approach described in the previous section can be applied in order to help design robust new processes. It can also be a helpful tool when testing the robustness of existing business processes. This section illustrates how the method has been used in order to systematically expose potential dangers (and suggest possible fixes) in a well-known case of a failed business process.

In February 1995, 233-year old Barings Bank, one of the oldest and most respected investment houses in the United Kingdom, went bankrupt. The entire bank collapsed because of losses of $1.4 billion incurred in a matter of days by a single young trader, Nicholas Leeson. Nicholas Leeson was a futures trader in the Singapore branch of the bank. For a number of reasons, which are still not entirely clear, Leeson began to engage in unauthorized futures trading in the Singapore exchange. Due to inadequate internal controls and other process failures, Leeson was able to maintain his unauthorized and highly risky activity undetected by the bank headquarters in London until the very end.

The collapse of the Barings Bank is one of the most dramatic and talked about recent disasters in financial markets. There exist several detailed accounts and analyses of why and how it happened (for example, [10, 27]). From our perspective, the Barings disaster is interesting because it was the result of a series of undetected exceptions in one of the bank's secondary business processes: the futures trading process in Singapore.

In this section, we will demonstrate how the approach described in this paper can be used to systematically point out the gaps in the Barings trading process controls, as well as to suggest ways for closing those gaps.

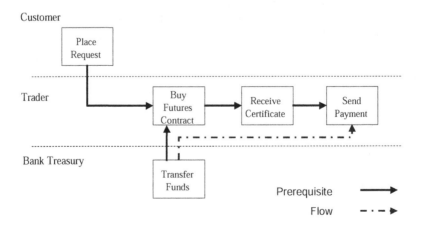

Fig. 6. The Barings Futures Trading Process

As described in the previous section, the approach begins with a "normal" model of the process. Figure 6 depicts a simplified but accurate model of the futures trading process, based on the descriptions contained in [10] and [27]. The model consists of boxes, which describe process activities, and lines, which describe various dependency relationships, that is, constraints that must hold true in order for the process to succeed. The following is a brief description of the process: When a customer requests a futures trade, the trader asks the bank headquarters for advances of funds in order to cover the customer's margin account[1]. Once the funds have arrived, the trader performs the trade, waits to receive the corresponding security certificate and finally pays the exchange. In an "ideal" world, a trader only performs trades when authorized to do so by customers, correct certificates are always received, and payment for trades exactly match the funds forwarded to the trader by the bank headquarters. These conditions are implied by the "prerequisite" and "flow" relationships, which are part of the "normal" process model.

The first step in our exception handling methodology consists of identifying the possible exceptions that are associated with each element of the "normal" process model. For simplicity we will only consider here exceptions associated with dependency relationships in the model.

According to the failure mode taxonomy shown in Figure 3, one possible exception of any prerequisite relationship is a prerequisite violation ("B without A"), that is, the possibility of activity B happening without a prior occurrence of activity A. In the context of the Barings trade process such violations would translate into unauthorized trading, unwanted security receipts and unnecessary payment (Figure 7).

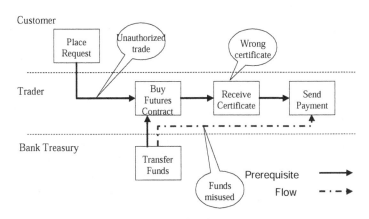

Fig. 7. The Barings Futures Trading Process with Associated Exceptions

---

[1] To find out more about derivatives trading and the meaning of margin accounts, the interested reader is referred to Zvi Bodie, Alex Kane, Alan J. Marcus, *Investments* (4th Edition), Irwin, 1998 (Part IV).

Likewise, one possible exception of a "flow" process is mismatch between the amount produced and the amount consumed. In the context of the Barings process this would translate into a misuse of headquarter funds.

After possible exceptions have been identified, the next step is to use the information stored in the exception type taxonomy (Figure 2) in order to find ways for avoiding or detecting the exceptions. It turns out that, because the trading process at Barings involves several independent entities (customer, bank, exchange) and requires some initiative from the part of the trader, there are no practical mechanisms for avoiding the exceptions. There were, however, several mechanisms for detecting them.

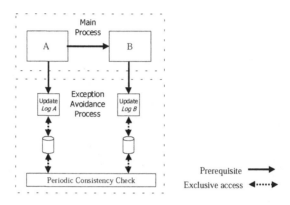

Fig. 8. Logging is a Generic Process for Detecting Prerequisite Violations

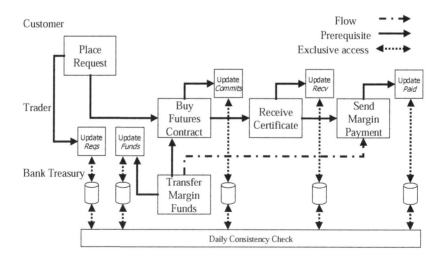

Fig. 9. Barings Process Properly Instrumented with Logging Processes.

For example, *logging* is one (out of several) generic mechanism for detecting prerequisite relationship violations (Figure 8). Logging involves recording all occurrences of activities A and B in some reliable storage medium and periodically conducting checks for prerequisite violations. In order for logging to be successful it is, in turn, required that (a) all occurrences of A and B are reliably logged and (b) the log can only be modified by the processes that do the logging.

If we insert a logging process for all dependencies listed in Figure 8 we get a model of a properly instrumented trading process (Figure 9).

At this point, we can compare the process derived using our approach with the actual Barings described in [10, 27]. It can immediately be seen that, although Barings did log some information about trades, it had two crucial gaps relative to the properly instrumented process of Figure 9 (see Figure 10):

First, it failed to log and compare the amount of funds forwarded by headquarters to the trader to the amounts actually paid by the trader for customer trades (in other words, the log labeled "Funds" in Figures 9-10 was missing from the Barings process). Second, Nick Leeson, in addition to being a trader, was also in charge of the back room operations in the Singapore branch. This gave him the authorization to modify the trades logs (and thus violated requirement (b) above of the logging process).

Nick Leeson was able to use these two gaps to his advantage as follows: Whenever he received a trade request from a customer, he requested an amount of funds far greater than what was required for the customer trade. He then performed the customer trade, as well as some additional unauthorized trades on his behalf. All of these trades were automatically logged into logs "Commits", "Received" and "Paid" (see Figures 9-10). Leeson then erased the records of his unauthorized trades from logs "Commits", "Received" and "Paid". Therefore, at the end of each day, the log of "Requests" matched perfectly the other three logs. By not checking for discrepancies between the funds forwarded to Leeson and the total funds recorded at the "Paid" log, headquarters remained unaware of Leeson's activities until it was too late.

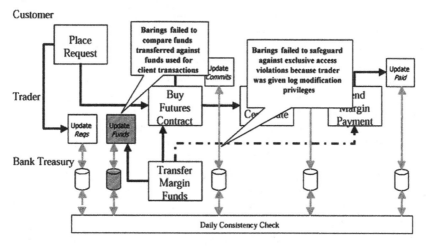

Fig. 10. Comparison between Ideal and Actual Barings Process

It is probably too simplistic to claim that the Barings disaster would have been avoided if the management of Barings had at their disposal knowledge-based exception handling methodologies, such as the ones described in this paper. Nevertheless, this exercise demonstrates that these methodologies and tools can be used in real-life cases to alert management of potential weaknesses and suggest ways for making vital business processes more robust.

4 Related Work

The approach described here integrates and extends two long-standing lines of research: one addressing coordination science principles about how to represent and utilize process knowledge, another addressing how artificial intelligence techniques can be applied to detecting and resolving conflicts in collaborative design settings:

One component is a body of work pursued over the past six years by the Process Handbook project at the MIT Center for Coordination Science [8, 20, 21]. The goal of this project is to produce a repository of process knowledge and associated tools that help people to better redesign organizational processes, learn about organizations, and automatically generate software. The Handbook database continues to grow and currently includes over 4500 models covering a broad range of business processes. A mature Windows-based tool for editing the Handbook database contents, as well as a Web-based tool for read-only access have been developed. A key insight from this work is that a repository of business process templates, structured as a specialization taxonomy, can assist people to design innovative business processes more quickly by allowing them to retrieve, contrast and customize interesting examples, make "distant analogies", and utilize "recombinant" (mix-and-match) design techniques.

The other key component of this work is nearly a decade of development and evaluation of systems for handling multi-agent conflicts in collaborative design [15, 16] and collaborative requirements capture [17]. This work resulted in principles and technology for automatically detecting, diagnosing and resolving design conflicts between both human and computational agents, building upon a knowledge base of roughly 300 conflict types and resolution strategies. This technology has been applied successfully in several domains including architectural, local area network and fluid sensor design. A key insight from this work is that design conflicts can be detected and resolved using a knowledge base of generic and highly reusable conflict management strategies, structured using diagnostic principles originally applied to medical expert systems. Our experience to date suggests that this knowledge is relatively easy to acquire and can be applied unchanged to multiple domains.

The work described in this paper integrates and extends these two lines of research in an innovative and, we believe, powerful way. The central insights underlying this integration are that (1) business process exceptions can be handled by generalizing the diagnostic algorithms and knowledge base underlying design conflict and (2) the exception handling knowledge base can be captured as a set of *process templates* that can be retrieved, compared and customized using the principles embodied in the Process Handbook.

This work also constitutes, we believe, a substantive and novel contribution to previous efforts on exception handling, which have been pursued in the context of workflow [1, 9, 13, 18, 22, 25, 28-30] manufacturing control [14, 23, 26], model-based fault diagnosis [3, 7, 19], planning [3, 4], and failure mode analysis research [24]. Most workflow research has focused on languages for expressing correctness-preserving transforms on workflow models, providing no guidance however concerning *which* transforms to use for a given situation. There has been some manufacturing and workflow research on providing guidance for how to handle exceptions, but this has been applied to few domains (mainly software engineering and flexible manufacturing cell control) and/or has addressed a small handful of exception types. The planning work, by contrast, has developed a range of computational models but they are only applicable if the planning technology was used to develop the original work process. This is typically not the case for workflow settings where processes are defined by people rather than planning tools. Model-based fault diagnosis approaches use a single generic algorithm to uncover the causes of faults in a system without the need for a knowledge base of failure modes and resolution heuristics. This approach is predicated, however, on the availability of a complete and correct model of the system's behavior. This is possible for some domains (e.g. the analysis of electrical circuits) but not for many others including, we would argue, most collaborative work settings that include human beings and/or complex computer systems as participants. Model-based fault diagnosis also typically assumes that resolution, once a fault has been diagnosed, is trivial (e.g. just replace the faulty component) and thus does not provide context-specific suggestions for how to resolve the problem. Current work on failure mode analysis describes a systematic process. However, the actual work must be done by people based on their experience and intuitions. This is potentially quite expensive, to the extent that this analysis is rarely done, and can miss important failure modes due to limitations in the experience of the analyst [24].

5 Future Work

This chapter has emphasized the use of our exception handling knowledge base as a decision support tool for humans. Our ongoing work is also focused on connecting our technology with automated process enactment systems, such as workflow controllers and software agent systems. It is widely recognized that state-of-the art workflow technology provides only rudimentary support for exception handling [2, 9]. The result of our work will be a prototype implementation of a domain-independent *exception handling engine*, which oversees the enactment of a workflow script, monitors for exceptions and decides (automatically for the most part) how to intervene in order to resolve them. Given a "normal" workflow script, the engine first uses the exception handling knowledge base in order to anticipate potential exceptions and augment the system with additional actions that play the role of *software sentinels*. During enactment time, these sentinels automatically trigger the diagnostic services of the engine when they detect symptoms of exceptional conditions. The diagnostic services traverse the taxonomy of exception types, select (possibly with human assistance) a diagnosis and then select and instantiate a resolution plan. The resolution plan is eventually translated into a set of workflow modification operations (e.g. add tool, remove tool, modify connection, etc.), which are dynamically applied to the executing workflow.

For further information about our work, please see the Adaptive Systems and Evolutionary Software web site at http://ccs.mit.edu/ases/. For further information on the Process Handbook, see http://ccs.mit.edu/

Acknowledgment

The authors gratefully acknowledge the support of the DARPA CoABS Program (contract F30602-98-2-0099) while preparing this paper.

References

1. E. Auramaki and M. Leppanen. Exceptions and office information systems. In B. Pernici and A.A. Verrijn-Stuart, editors: *Office Information Systems: The Design Process*, pp.167-182, North Holland Publishing Co., 1989.
2. P. Barthelmess and J. Wainer. Workflow Systems: a few Definitions and a few Suggestions. *Proceeding of the Conf. On Organizational Computing Systems (COOCS'95)*, pp. 138-147, 1995.
3. L. Birnbaum, G. Collins, M. Freed and B. Krulwich. Model-Based Diagnosis of Planning Failures. *Proceedings of the 8th National Conf. on Artificial Intelligence (AAAI-90)*, pp.318-23, 1990.
4. C.A. Broverman and W.B. Croft. Reasoning About Exceptions During Plan Execution Monitoring. *Proceedings of the 6th National Conf. on Artificial Intelligence (AAAI-87)*, pp. 190-195, 1987.
5. W. J. Clancey. Heuristic Classification. *Artificial Intelligence* 27(3), pp. 289-350, 1985.
6. T. Davenport. *Process Innovation: Reengineering Work through Information Technology*. Harvard Business School Press, 1993.
7. J. deKleer and B. Williams. Reasoning About Multiple Faults. *Proceedings of the 5th National Conference on Artificial Intelligence (AAAI-86)*, pp. 132-9, 1986.
8. C. Dellarocas, J. Lee, T.W. Malone, K. Crowston and B. Pentland. Using a Process Handbook to Design Organizational Processes. *Proceedings of the AAAI 1994 Spring Symposium on Computational Organization Design*, pp. 50-56, 1994.
9. C.A. Ellis, K. Keddara and G. Rozenberg. Dynamic Change Within Workflow Systems. *Proceedings of the Conf. On Organizational Computing Systems, (COOCS'95)*, pp. 10-21, 1995.
10. S. Fay. *The collapse of Barings*. W.W. Norton, New York, 1997.
11. V. Grover and W. J. Kettinger, editors. *Business Process Change: Concepts, Methodologies and Technologies*. Idea Group Publishing, 1995.
12. M. Hammer and J. Champy. *Reengineering the Corporation: A Manifesto for Business Revolution*. Harper Business, 1994.

13. B.H. Karbe and N. G. Ramsberger. Influence of Exception Handling on the Support of Cooperative Office Work. In S. Gibbs and A. A. Verrijin-Stuart, editors: *Multi-User Interfaces and Applications*, Elsevier Science Publishers, pp. 355-370, 1990.
14. D. Katz and S. Manivannan. Exception management on a shop floor using online simulation. *Proceedings of the 1993 Winter Simulation Conference*, pp.888-96. 1993.
15. M. Klein. Conflict resolution in cooperative design. University of Illinois at Urbana-Champaign Technical Report UIUCDCS-R-89-1557.
16. M. Klein. Supporting Conflict Resolution in Cooperative Design Systems. *IEEE Transactions on Systems, Man and Cybernetics*, 21(6), pp. 1379-1390, 1991.
17. M. Klein. An Exception Handling Approach to Enhancing Consistency, Completeness and Correctness in Collaborative Requirements Capture. *Concurrent Engineering: Research and Applications*, 5 (1), pp. 37-46, 1997.
18. T. Kreifelts and G. Woetzel. Distribution and Error Handling in an Office Procedure System. *Proceedings of IFIP WF 8.4 Working Conference on Methods and Tools for Office Systems*, Pisa, Italy, 1987.
19. M. Krishnamurthi and D.T. Phillips. An expert system framework for machine fault diagnosis. *Computers & Industrial Engineering* 22 (1), Jan. 1992, pp.67-84.
20. T.W. Malone, K. Crowston, J. Lee and B. Pentland, Tools for Inventing Organizations: Toward a Handbook of Organizational Processes, Proceedings of 2nd IEEE Workshop on Enabling Tech. Infrastructure for Collaborative Enterprises (1993) 72-82.
21. T.W. Malone, K. Crowston, J. Lee, B. Pentland, C. Dellarocas, G. Wyner, J. Quimby, C. Osborne, and A. Bernstein. Tools for inventing organizations: Toward a handbook of organizational processes. *Management Science*, in print.
22. P. Mi and W. Scacchi. Articulation: An Integrated Approach to the Diagnosis, Replanning and Rescheduling of Software Process Failures. *Proceedings of the Eighth Knowledge-Based Software Engineering Conference*, IEEE Comput. Soc. Press. 1993, pp.77-84.
23. S. Parthasarathy. Generalised process exceptions-a knowledge representation paradigm for expert control. *Proceedings of the Fourth International Conference on the Applications of Artificial Intelligence in Engineering*, 1989, pp.241-56.
24. D. Raheja. Software system failure mode and effects analysis (SSFMEA)-a tool for reliability growth. *Proceedings of the Int'l Symp. on Reliability and Maintainability (ISRM'90)*, Tokyo, Japan, pp. 271-77, 1990.
25. D.M. Strong. Decision support for exception handling and quality control in office operations. *Decision Support Systems* 8(3), June 1992, pp. 217-27.
26. A. Visser. An exception-handling framework. *International Journal of Computer Integrated Manufacturing* 8(3), May-June 1995, pp.197-203.
27. G. Zhang. *Barings bankruptcy and financial derivatives*. World Scientific Publishing Co, Singapore, 1995.
28. M. Klein, C. Dellarocas and A. Bernstein, editors. Special Issue on Adaptive Workflow Systems, *Computer-Supported Collaborative Work*, January 2000.
29. S. Ellis and K. Keddara. A workflow change is a workflow. Part II, Chapter 6 in this volume.
30. A. Agostini and G. de Michelis. Improving Flexibility of Workflow Management Systems. Part II, Chapter 7 in this volume.

The "Organized Activity" Foundation
for Business Processes and Their Management

Anatol W. Holt

Via Panzini 12
20145 Milano, Italy
anatolholt@iol.it

Abstract. This paper introduces a new notional and notational tool – "organized activity" (OA) and its theory (TOA) – to the BP/BPM community. Most of this "introduction" is accomplished via an example – the "Pulsar" – which is: (a) an "organized activity" claimed to be useful to business, but also other activities; (b) new; (c) easy to understand; (d) suitable to computer support; (e) richly illustrative of OA ideas, in its "computerized" and non-computerized versions.

A significant terminal part of the paper is devoted to a comparison of OA/TOA to Petri nets – for two reasons: (a) OA/TOA grew out of Petri nets; (b) many readers of this paper are familiar with Petri nets, and rely on them professionally.

1   Introduction

In the last decade (or two) a new "theory" has been born: the "theory" of (human) *organized activity* – TOA for short. In effect this was the birth of two new things:
- a new subject matter – OA for short;
- a new type of "theory". The subject matter is treated in a *technical* manner – using the methods of the exact sciences; yet the approach differs from the rest of science appreciably – not discussed extensively in this paper, though touched on in Subsection 4.3.

OA/TOA is relevant to the present volume for an intellectual and a practical reason; intellectual, because business processes – whatever else they are – are certainly an example of human organized activity; practical, because many of the "problems" that naturally arise in the area of business process support, are problems that naturally arise for *any* organized activity – problems that can be analyzed and approached by means of the new field.

Associated with TOA there has also developed a graphical planning language – called DIPLAN. In previous work (and published results) DIPLAN has had two roles to play: (a) as a means to illustrate, and make visible TOA; (b) as a means to specify

W. van der Aalst et al. (Eds.): Business Process Management, LNCS 1806, pp 66-82, 2000

and communicate *plans*. DIPLAN (and TOA) are both descendents of Petri nets and related theory.

Briefly, let me explain the concept *organized activity*, and its relationship to BP/BPM. "Organized activity" is a human-social universal; at least as much as human language – for there are certainly organized activities which do not require verbal communication, but verbal communication requires organized activity. OAs have the following general characteristics:

- always linking many roles; sometimes linking many flesh-and-blood people - there may be millions - or only one flesh-and-blood person involved;
- always associated with a guiding plan, but exceptional circumstances can always arise requiring unplanned responses;
- always involving coordinated actions (*all* examples of coordinated action imply organized activity);
- usually repeatable (*all* examples of repetition imply organized activity);
- always motivated – by business, religion, politics, fun, etc.;
- always involving material (bodies) and (human) effort (actions) – and therefore "space" and "time" as ordinarily understood.

Likely Examples of OAs are games, political parties, BPs and bucketbrigades. TOA provides analytic and communicative techniques that apply to OAs.

Are *all* human activities OAs? This could be discussed at length, but one thing is certain: they should only be so regarded if the application of TOA "pays". (Analogously: a physicist may look at a person's body and see physics; but if that person has an ache, a doctor is better.)

And now BP/BPM. This is a domain that has established itself for pragmatic reasons. Businesses frequently have "problems" that can be solved by means of new information technological "systems", especially computer-based. What is more, businesses are likely to pay for such solutions. Unlike OA, BP/BPM was not isolated as an area for intellectual/philosophic/scientific reasons. Therefore it is entirely possible that a significant part of the technological effort involved in helping a business may also help a non-business (and/or vice versa – workflow only being one of many examples). In other words: basing one's technical solutions on OA will, in general, lead to better architectures than basing them on BP/BPM (for, whatever else is true, the skeleton of a BP/BPM "problem" will normally be based on the fact that a business process *is* an organized activity; furthermore: TOA may improve the community's ability to define "business problems" that are capable of solution – using technological "systems", or other means).

This paper exemplifies a computer-supportable OA which (a) differs from the more common type of BP/BPM system; (b) can obviously be useful to BP/BPM but also to non-business OAs; (c) is unlikely to have been defined without OA/TOA; (d) suggests new software (and possibly hardware) architecture which might be useful to BP. Moreover, it compares TOA/DIPLAN to Petri nets – introducing just barely enough of TOA/DIPLAN to accomplish the comparisons.

As can be understood from the foregoing: the point of this paper is *not* an explicit introduction to TOA/DIPLAN; rather, its point is to: (a) provide the reader with practical benefits which seem to derive from thinking in terms of OAs; (b) implicitly introduce OA/TOA; (c) build up the reader's motivation to study OA/TOA with the help of available publications.

2   An Example: the "Pulsar"

The reader should be warned in advance: the example may seem over-abstract and over-simple, yet: (a) in its "abstractness" lies its power; (b) it is more seemingly simple than really simple; and finally (c) at most useful scales this pattern of *organized activity* can *only* be realized with the help of a computer network, even though it seems so primitive and easy to understand.

The reader should also be warned: the example does not address the typical preoccupations of BP/BPM. In that fact too, lies its power. Obviously it is not "workflow"; obviously it leaves out many issues that arise in every business; but they are not issues that the example cannot accommodate! And: even though it does not offer a service that has been conceived – by businesses and/or their advisers – it may nevertheless be eminently useful to businesses.

And lastly, the reader should be warned: much of this paper is like the Pulsar – seemingly more simple than really simple. To profit from its content, it is useful to keep this point in mind.

2.1   Informal Description of the Pulsar

There are $N+1$ participants: 1 manager, m and N contributors, c_j.

The plan of operation is cyclic – in principle unlimited, forwards or backwards. We can name a cycle Z, arbitrarily by assigning it an integer i. Thus the cycle designation becomes Z_i. Of course, in practice, there will always be a first cycle, and we will find it convenient to call it Z_0. The cyclic scheme is expressed in Figure 1.

Each Z_i is grossly built as follows: (a) the manager m prepares and broadcasts a stimulus S_i to all contributors; (b) each of the contributors (c_j) prepares a response R_{ij} to the stimulus and returns it to m. The manager m uses all of these responses as background for the preparation of the next stimulus S_{i+1}.

In more detail: each Z_i consists of a "stimulus phase" SP_i, and a "response phase" RP_i. In course of SP_i m prepares and broadcasts S_i; in course of RP_i all contributors c_j prepare and return their responses R_{ij}.

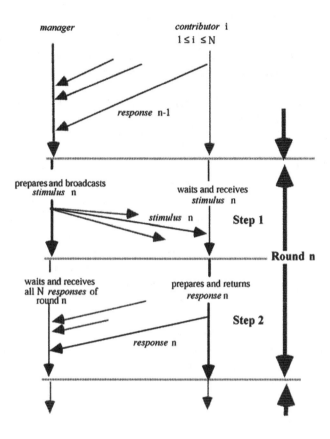

Figure 1

The beginnings and endings of cycle phases are relative to clock and calendar: the manager m determines the clock and calendar beginning and end of SP_i and RP_i. He may do this once and for all, for every cycle of the Pulsar or cycle by cycle. For example: for Z_8 the manager may decide: SP_8 is to begin at 0900 April 10, 1999 and end at 1200 of the same day; RP_8 is to begin at 1200 and end at 0900 April 11. On the other hand, the manager could determine once and for all at the beginning that all cycles are to be divided analogously during the 5 workdays of each week.

The details of a cycle Z_i: by the time SP_i begins, the manager m has a right to expect that all responses from the previous cycle have reached him (including "null responses"); thus, *after* its beginning, the manager can prepare the S_i. He must broadcast it enough before the end of SP_i (and therefore the beginning of RP_i) that, *after* this point, each contributor c_j can assume that S_i is in his possession.

Thus, after the end of SP_i (and the beginning of RP_i) each c_j can prepare R_{ij}. He must return it to the manager *before* the end of RP_i (and therefore the beginning of SP_{i+1}).

Additional communication: any participant at any time can send a message M to any other participant. Since all participants can be expected to have some idea of "what time it is" in terms of cycles, and of communication speeds, these messages M can be weakly synchronized with the cycles. M messages can be used by the manager to manage the Pulsar on an ongoing basis.

Desirable physical organization: all participants in a Pulsar would do well to keep all Pulsar-related files together – segregated from everything else. This includes a record of S's, R's and M's.

Additional (optional) features:

- Common area, CA: the content is controlled by m, and it can be read by all c's. All c's can assume that CA changes state at each end of SP (beginning of RP). CA can be seen as a method for reducing the amount of information that must be included in the stimuli.

- Null responses: it is desirable that the manager m be able to distinguish, on a given cycle, between a contributor who for some reason was unable to respond, and a contribute or who, though perfectly able, chose not to. This might be handled by introducing an explicit "null response" which a contributor makes if he has nothing to say, but is not prevented from responding.

- Categories of contributors: in the case of some Pulsar controlled processes it is desirable to distinguish between several types of contributor – such as "observers", "specialists", "editors", "correctors", etc. In producing his stimuli, the manager may be given aid in specializing these to contributor category; in any case, the manager should be able to specialize a stimulus to a particular contributor.

2.2   Some Comments (on the Pulsar)

Pulsar use: the Pulsar is a simple device for accomplishing any joint project under a central authority (the manager). However: this central authority may contribute nothing but *order* (as in the case of a traffic policeman, or meeting chairman), or may exercise arbitrary degrees of directive power over the project as a whole. Examples (by type) of such "joint projects":

- operating a department under a manager (a "business process");
- processing an item under someone's direction (another "business process").

None of the next-following examples are usually treated as "business processes":

- a meeting under a chairman;
- producing a document (under someone's direction);
- trying something out (under someone's control and observation).

Rights and responsibilities: flesh-and-blood persons can decide – probably freely – whether to participate in a Pulsar or not; but once having decided, they have Pulsar-related rights and responsibilities which the Pulsar imposes. For example: a contributor has a "right" to gain access to the next stimulus and/or the Common Area (if it exists); he has a "duty" to produce a response *within the given time interval* (for no duty to *do* something can be meaningful without a time limit).

We said above "probably freely" because: in accepting a job, the flesh-and-blood person may have pre-agreed to participate in Pulsars, or at the least, in joint efforts that may be pursued by means of a Pulsar.

The inclusions of (some) exceptions in the plan: TOA is "true to life" in the following respect: it asserts: *organized activities* always follow a *plan,* but are always subject to *exceptions.*

It is often possible to "enlarge" a plan by taking some classes of exceptions into systematic account. The Pulsar contains an example of this, in making provision for M messages which are only weakly synchronized with the dominant Pulsar cycle. (Aside from being useful to the control and management of a Pulsar-implemented joint project) M messages make it possible to raise "afterthoughts", requests for clarification, suggestions for the improvement of substance or procedure, etc.

There are 3 ways in which the inclusion of M messages in the Pulsar does more than ordinary e-mail: (a) because the M messages are understood as belonging to the Pulsar framework they can make use of Pulsar-relative identifiers without explanation; (b) the M messages accumulate in the Pulsar area; (c) their processing is governed by a priority which, in part, derives from the priority of the Pulsar-relative project as a whole.

The Pulsar and networks of computers: we assert that networks of computers become ever-more indispensable to Pulsar implementation as: (a) the participants are dispersed over wider geographic regions; (b) the desirable cycle time shrinks. In particular, a Pulsar with a cycle time of 20 minutes – possibly useful to the conduct of a meeting – *cannot* be implemented by anything other than computer means, even if the participants are all in the same building.

3   OA/TOA, the Pulsar, and Computer Support

It was claimed above in Section 1 that the Pulsar is an example of a "computer supportable OA". Now that the Pulsar has been described, I want to: (a) justify this statement; (b) expand on the idea OA above-and-beyond Section 1; (c) show that practically useful suggestions follow from this.

The "practical suggestions" concern computer support for any-and-all OAs – not just Pulsars. The link between TOA, the Pulsar example, and these suggestions, is the following: the Pulsar provides concrete illustrations for features common to *all* OAs, including more traditional BPs. Identification of these features suggests new-and-better computer services; since the services in question pertain to all OAs, and since a significant part of what computers do today is to support OAs, these suggestions imply structural features of computer systems to render them better adapted to deliver these services *in a uniform manner.*

3.1   Features of OAs illustrated by the Pulsar

The Participants: The participants in a Pulsar are identified by roles ("manager", "contributor") and not by personal name. Of course not: the roles are Pulsar-characteristic; the personal names are not. Yet, in every realization of the Pulsar specific persons must play these various roles (possibly even more than one role per person; and possibly also more than one person per role); however: the persons will certainly change from Pulsar to Pulsar; they may even change while a particular copy of the Pulsar is running.

These relationships between organizationally defined roles and flesh-and-blood persons are characteristic of *all* OAs (including BPs; including workflow). Further-more: (a) because performances of OAs can *always* involve deviations from the plan, OAs must always be managed, and (b) managers of an OA must always be prepared to change the assignment of persons to roles; therefore computer support for an OA should *always* provide for these reassignment operations.

The Actions: Actions (performed by the participants) are characteristic of all OAs. (as mentioned in Section 1). Assuming that the reasoning above is right, everything that has to do with participant actions should also be part of the system architecture. A participant's relationship to the actions he/she performs is an important part of TOA, and a much more significant aspect of computer system architecture than you might suspect.

Calendar and Clock: The relations of the actions of participants to the calendar and clock are also not a Pulsar specialty, but rather part of every OA (not deducible from Section 1).

Additional Communication: This too is a facility that is appropriate to *all* OAs. It is a generally applicable way to "foresee" the "unforeseen" – a capability that can be significantly based on (a modified version of) e-mail. More discussion of this follows at the end of this subsection.

N-Person Applications: Who is "the user" of a Pulsar (and therefore of its computer support)? Obviously a group of persons who – for one reason or another – want to accomplish something together. In other words: the "user" is a group! The same is true of most OAs.

Some years ago, I invented the distinction between a "solitary tool" and a "contact tool"; a solitary tool is taken in hand by a single person to accomplish one of *his/her* purposes; a "contact tool" is used by a group to ease (or even enable) their cooperation. The difference is profound; a contact tool certainly does not consist of N solitary tools. Each of the latter is used at a single person's pleasure; the contact tool is used by individuals when the pattern of cooperation that is supported decrees that it is appropriate.

The Pulsar is obviously a contact tool. Since every participant is supposed to do his part, the Pulsar as a piece of software should be distributed, with a different piece on each participant's computer. When for some reason the list of participants changes a piece of one person's computer memory must be moved to another site. Keep in mind: this (and earlier) technical problems derive ultimately from TOA – even from the little of TOA presented in Section 1.

Miscellaneous: Here I want to comment on a few other aspects of computer support for OAs. To begin with there is the question of organizing one's files and directories in a manner adapted to participating in OAs. This issue becomes particularly serious if person A who participates may later on be replaced by person B; if B is to continue where A leaves off, B must inherit the appropriate files and directories from A and must appropriately integrate these in his own work environment.

It is easy to see that these considerations interact with e-mail used as above. Clearly: if B is to replace A, B must also get copies of the relevant "additional communications". It follows: in building support for OAs, e-mail is no less important (structurally) than the file/directory system; indeed both of these need to be considered together.

3.2   Computers and OA/TOA

Although OA/TOA was historically born to help understand the use of computers, it still seems strange that a subject matter so "social-scientific" should have emerged; the word "computer" does not suggest this; what is more, nothing social-scientific – other than "Human Factors" – is today considered a necessary part of a young computer scientist's training!

Although it no longer seems particularly outlandish to think that computers extensively support organized activities, the computer pioneers (such as Babbage, Turing, Eckert and Mauchly, von Neumann, Perlis, Zuse, and many others) would have been surprised. The motivations which brought computers into existence really didn't seem related to OAs; they were created as solitary tools for people with computational problems. Even the fact that computational results were usually wanted by some people to satisfy the needs of other people was too remote from "computing" to influence computer design. This – I think – is a reason why hardware and software to the present day is mostly designed for "the user", a real or imagined person, and not for groups. Note that even in the design of "big" machines that serve many individuals, the group is an afterthought. This is also key to why the advanced computers of today, though so often used in support of OAs, are not architecturally "friendly" to OAs, and in particular not "friendly" to the Pulsar (as we see from 3.1

above). Finally, this also explains why inventing OA/TOA was so late, so difficult, and so little appreciated by the "computer community".

4   TOA/DIPLAN vs. Petri Nets in Some Detail

OA etc. owe their existence to Petri nets. This is particularly evident in DIPLAN – a graphical planning language which yields bipartite graphs with a Petri-net-like interpretation of little circles and little squares (two symbols that are used in both). But there are also major differences: (a) DIPLAN is more complex (and therefore less well adapted to the development of mathematics); (b) DIPLAN has no tokens (and therefore no "firing rule"); (c) DIPLAN is more scrupulous (pedantic) in its distinction between repetition (itself repeatable) and historical uniqueness; (d) DIPLAN leans on TOA, which stands on its own feet; Petri nets do not lean on a system theory which stands on its own feet.

In what follows, I will concentrate on a few outstanding DIPLAN/Petri-net differences which seem particularly important to me – to wit:

- the interpretations of (little) square, circle, and their interconnection;
- the role of persons;
- the definition and role of "state";
- the treatment of "information" and decision (so critical to computing).

4.1   Square and Circle; Actions and Bodies; Space and Time

TOA asserts: OAs can be efficiently described in terms of human actions performed on bodies; accordingly DIPLAN specifies a class of bipartite graphs; one vertex type, represented by small square symbols, standing for actions; another vertex type, represented by small circular symbols, standing for bodies; the bodies are said to be "involved in" the actions – represented in a DIPLAN diagram by an undirected link, verbally expressed as "an action involves a body" or equally "a body is involved in an action". According to TOA/DIPLAN every example of an action is a "lump" of human effort; every example of a body is a "lump" of material.

What is a lump of human effort? It isn't easy to say, considering that the effort may be any combination of mental and physical. But three things are certain: all efforts are performed by an effort maker; all efforts "take time"; all efforts involve lumps of material – even if only the flesh-and-blood body of the effort maker.

With equal certainty we can say: all bodies (lumps of material) will "take space"; with less certainty we can assert: all bodies must be involved in actions (that is, in lumps of human effort). We do in fact make this "less certain" assertion, at least for OAs. (It follows that bodies stored for future but uncertain use must be subject to ongoing human effort, namely maintenance effort!)

The DIPLAN model of an OA involves the following stronger assumptions: (a) actions take time *but not space*; bodies take space *but not time*; (b) a body persists only because it is involved in actions; an action takes space only because it involves bodies. Since every OA take both space and time, we have a particularly attractive interpreted justification for the Petri net axiom that forbids "isolated elements".

The foregoing makes clear: TOA/DIPLAN is concerned with the space and time of ordinary practice – and not with the space and time (or space/time) of modern physics. Nevertheless TOA/DIPLAN shares with modern physics: the idea that space and time are strictly interdependent; that neither of these can exist without "substance" (actions and bodies in the case of TOA/DIPLAN).

Petri nets seem to adopt a neutral attitude towards time and space taking. But these are matters of such overwhelming practical importance (even more than cost) that neutrality simply doesn't work. Most practitioners have therefore taken their time-spatial cue from the token game; the transitions (boxes) are assumed to be more-or-less instantaneous; the places (circles) account for all space, duration, and substance, of the "system". Not that other attitudes haven't prevailed – particularly in the realm of "timed" Petri nets. But the fact alone that "timed Petri nets" are thinkable, differentiates them from TOA/DIPLAN. Here, the categories of "time taking", "space taking" (and cost) are as built in as in they are in the consciousness of everyone concerned with practical arrangements.

4.2   Persons

Since Petri nets are about "systems" one cannot expect the formalism to take persons into special account. Since TOA/DIPLAN deals with the actions of people within OAs, they must take the action performers into special account. What does TOA/DIPLAN posit about these performers?

- *Persons* (and only persons) perform actions and own bodies.
- OA actions will only be performed if suitably powered – the "power" coming from the performers and taking the form of *interest. Interests* reside in bodies (which makes body ownership important).
- The performer of an action is always a flesh-and-blood person performing some OA-determined function that inheres in an organizational entity. *No other artifact – robot or computer, etc. – can perform actions*; for action performance *always* entails responsibility, and responsibility can never be carried by a non-human artifact. (Thus, even computer actions, which take place at nano-second speeds, are ultimately attributable to persons – a matter of no importance when computers were exclusively solitary tools, but now of utmost importance, while continuing to be technologically ignored.)
- DIPLAN contains graphic techniques for expressing these relationships. This fact alone makes DIPLAN more complex than Petri nets.

4.3   State

Petri nets, in theory or in practice, do not contain a clear concept of *state*. Many Petri net practitioners therefore equate a Petri net marking with a "system state" – an idea implicit in the famous "reachability problem". This idea may be frowned upon, or even objected to on reasonable grounds, but how can one frown or object in the absence of a clear concept of *state*? Do Petri nets represent "systems"? If so, do "systems" have "states"? I have had plenty of Petri net experience, but I cannot say with certainty. Contrastively TOA/DIPLAN deals with such questions (and many others that have to do with "state") in a way that leaves no room for mental clouds. Briefly, the TOA idea is this:

- Bodies and only bodies B can have states S.

But also (according to TOA):

- A body-in-a-state (for example B-in-state-S) is also a body – (actually a *case of* B).

TOA says: organized activity consists in (suitably interrelated) actions which involve bodies. There are various effects which actions can have on the bodies they involve – among others *state change*. So let us consider an action X which changes the state of B from S to S':

- X involves B; X also involves B-in-state-S; and also B-in-state-S'; X must consume B-in-S, and produce B-in-S'. Thus: a *change of state* requires an action which involves (at least) *three* bodies and *three* different effects: (a change-of-state, and a consequent consumption and production). Therefore from TOA's point of view: if an OA called V were to have states, it would have to be represented as a body subject to state change within some other OA called W. There is no simpler sense in which V has states. (As far as I can see, this is a reasonable conclusion.)

The concepts *state* and *state change* are not minor matters – in the description of OAs or "systems". Among other things, they are critically involved in the treatment of "information" and "decision" – obviously of great importance to computer support. It is this matter to which we now turn our attention.

4.4   Decision, Conflict, and "Information"

In the world of Petri nets, two transitions (or events) are "in conflict" if (a) both are enabled; (b) the taking place of either destroys the enabling of the other. This is considered to be the basis for "decisions" – and of course for "information". Let us illustrate by means of a "low-level" net.

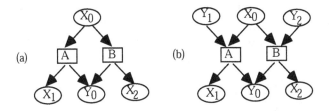

Figure 2

Assume an "initial marking" in Figure 2 (a) is a token on X_0. In this marking transitions A and B are in conflict; if A "fires", we produce X_1 and Y_0; if B "fires" we produce X_2 and Y_0. Note that, in the "elementary net" the meanings conveyed by the form of the place labels is not part of the net.

At any rate, it is (meta) clear that a "decision" between A and B must be made; this decision could be represented explicitly by augmenting Figure 2 (a) to become Figure 2 (b). Assume that the initial marking of (a) cited above is included in an initial marking of (b), namely: X_0 combined with Y_1 or Y_2, exclusively. Under this circumstance we see that A and B are no longer in conflict. Thus we might say: Y – in the form Y_1 or Y_2 – carries "information" into the situation depicted, information which "resolves the conflict" and (what comes to the same) allows the rendering of a (binary) decision.

This is a version of "making a decision" rejected by TOA; it insists: "making a decision" is an *action* – that is to say, a lump of effort – that must be expended by a participant in an OA. Regardless of all other interpretive differences, Figure 2 (b) makes the opposite seem true.

(This reminds me of a matter which I found puzzling as a young programmer.) In the graphical form of a flowchart one could write:

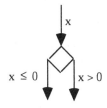

Figure 3

The diamond represented a decision with two outcomes: one outcome in case x is greater than 0; another outcome in case x is less-than-or-equal-to 0. I wondered: is this binary decision "work"? Is it in this respect like any other operation – addition say? The apparent mystery deepened in thinking about the "x" which "flows" into the decision; isn't this "x" *already* greater than, or less-than-or-equal-to, 0 before it "arrives" at the decision point? Isn't this a confirmation of the fact that the decision should require no work (and therefore take no time)? The Petri net solution comes down on the "no work" side of the issue; the TOA solution on the other side. (This conclusion is not entirely obvious, but it is worth thinking through.)

Let us consider the situation depicted in Figure 3 from the TOA point of view – using DIPLAN.

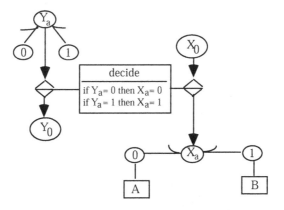

Figure 4

This is the first DIPLAN diagram which appears in this paper, and deserves some discussion in the light of the previous section.

Grossform of Figure 4: there is one central action labeled "decide" which changes the state of X and Y (as per 4.3). Figure 4 leaves several things out: (a) there is no explicit representation of X and Y (only of X and Y in their respective pre- and post-states.); (b) there is no explicit indication of *who* performs the deciding action – X or Y, or perhaps a Z that has been left out altogether. Given the nature of decision, it is simplest to assume that X decides, based on the input state of Y; after deciding, X will perform action A or action B, depending.

The "change-of-state" effect: in DIPLAN the change-of-state effect is symbolized by a diamond; thus we see that the "decide" action changes two states: that of X (on the right) and that of Y.

Case of: the DIPLAN symbol signifying this relationship is ⟍ , the element at left end of this connector being the *case of* the element on the right. From a more careful explanation of "state" it is clear that X_a and X_0 are both *cases of* X – and the same with Y_a and Y_0 with respect to Y. These examples of *case of* are understood and therefore not signaled explicitly. On the other hand, both X_a and Y_a have cases in turn. (Thus we see that TOA/DIPLAN allows for a state of a state (or case of a case) as is true-to-life.)

The evaluation function: Decisions and other informational operations require the specification of an "evaluation"; in DIPLAN, this evaluation is specified under the bar which can divide an action symbol. In effect, this evaluation is the computational burden imposed by the decision. Enough has been explained above to make the symbolism used in specifying the evaluation in Figure 4 evident.

The greater complexity of Figure 4 when compared to Figure 3(b): No doubt Figure 4 is more complex, and every increase in complexity should be justified. So: in what way is Figure 4 superior? (a) in its verisimilitude; (b) in its explicit represent-ation of the "work" of deciding; (c) in its applicability to *every* case of deciding, no matter at what "level", no matter where the "information" comes from, etc.; (d) in the scope it leaves for: representing things explicitly or implicitly; for coping with "mistaken decisions"; for representing decisions whose outcomes wholly, partially, or not-at-all, depend on input information; etc.

5   Review and Conclusion

The principal purpose of this paper has been to "advertise" the existence of a new theoretical framework – focused on *organized activity* OA, and its theory TOA, plus a related graphical method of representation (called DIPLAN) This framework is not only claimed to be applicable to BP/BPM; it is even claimed to bring advantages that a more specialized approach cannot match. This paper is an "advertisement plus", since it is also means to impart some substance that may be useful to BP/BPM experts.

Rather than attempting the impossible (namely, within the compass of a paper, introducing the reader to OA/TOA/DIPLAN explicitly), this paper is based on an illustrative example, the "Pulsar". The Pulsar constitutes an unusual form of organization which (a) is particularly easy to understand, (b) is particularly useful when implemented by means of a network of computers; (c) is obviously relevant to business processes – but also relevant to other types of *organized activity*. Detailed discussion of the Pulsar is used to "flesh out" OA/etc.

It is shown that the aspects of the Pulsar which fit in with the OA/etc point of view apply to *all* OAs, and therefore have software (and possibly hardware) architectural implications. Even workflow – a much more traditional approach than the Pulsar – could be improved by taking these aspects into serious consideration.

A secondary theme animating this paper is a comparison of DIPLAN and Petri nets – because (a) it is obvious that DIPLAN (though more complex) is a descendant of Petri nets, (b) many readers of this paper have previous familiarity with Petri nets, (c) it is a method for revealing more of the theory which underlies DIPLAN, and (d) it is a way to reveal some "big issues" underlying the focus on *organized activity* as opposed to *systems* – a focus that applies to Petri nets, but also to other methods.

As this paper asserts: DIPLAN has advantages and disadvantages when compared to more traditional methods, including Petri nets; (a) the theory underlying DIPLAN is (we think) better adapted to "business processes" (and more generally *organized activity*) than previous ones – as the Pulsar helps to demonstrate; (b) TOA/DIPLAN have the disadvantage of inherent complexity; it remains an open question whether this complexity "pays its way", especially considering that notational and conceptual complexity militate against useful, applied mathematics; (c) even though TOA/DIPLAN have been long in the making, they remain immature products; they are little known and little applied. (Even the Pulsar with its evident utility has not yet been incorporated in commercial software.)

However, TOA/DIPLAN and its practical consequences in the development of computer support have been described in a number of publications, including a book [7] in print and much more briefly in this paper. Its future remains open.

6   A Guide to Related Efforts

The contents of this paper was developed in course of ca. 5 decades of work, not much related to "the literature". (Indeed, the beginnings of this work predate "the literature"!) Nevertheless, the existing literature *is* relevant. Here, we provide a brief guide to related work with some bibliographic references where it seemed warranted to me. In this way I hope to connect the above to the massive international effort that has been mounted in related directions.

6.1   Organized Behavior and Planning Languages

The reader may be surprised at the title just above: the technical community that has been concerned with planning languages (graphical or otherwise) has not been concerned with theories of organized behavior (nor have those concerned with organized behavior been especially interested in planning languages). However: as the above makes clear, in the context of this paper, it is appropriate to consider them together.

In spite of Section 4 above, it seems appropriate to begin with a brief discussion of Petri nets and Petri net theory – even at the cost of some repetition.

Although Petri nets are in fact associated with "theory", no one would be inclined to regard this a theory of "organized behavior"; indeed, most people have regarded Petri nets as applicable to the description and analysis of *systems* (whether human-organizational or not) – no doubt with the thought that the rules governing organized human activity can *also* be treated as a *system*. Surely this thought was connected to C. A. Petri's interest in "communication disciplines" [9],[10], an idea that (somewhat) approaches "organized activity". (It is easy to suppose that all such activities require "communication", but I have assumed instead: all communication (especially symbolic) requires OA, but OA certainly does not require symbolic communication – or perhaps communication at all, depending on definitions.)

At all events, Petri nets are (a) quite mature, and (b) are widely known in the community which is likely to read this paper. On Petri nets there is a literature (books and papers) too extensive to be included. I content myself by referring the reader to Petri's own most recent published views [11]. Here are a few other immediately relevant references: Skip Ellis's "Information control nets" [5] (also developed from

Petri nets, [11]); Eric Yu's "goal oriented processing model framework" [13]. (At all events: to the best of my knowledge, DIPLAN is the only example of a planning language directly related to a theory of organized behavior such as TOA.)

As regards planning languages, the field broadens out enormously; there are graphical planning languages that have been extensively used in Operations Research (such as PERT, GERT, CPM, etc.), Workflow languages, and finally graphical flowchart languages used to represent digital computer program – a step farther away from human organized activity, but only a step (as further explained in [7]).

6.2   New Software-Architectural Proposals

In the course of the last 25 years there have been numerous proposals for a basic change in software architecture, with diverse motivations, some of which are cousins of the motivations that lie behind the proposals above.

First, there have come into being a whole series of new operating system proposals, none of which (a) have caught on, and (b) are as radical in outlook as Igo (the proposal in [6]). Second: other new proposals have been conceived as aids to the construction of information systems – more specifically Simon Kaplan [1], and Giorgio De Michelis [3].

6.3   Over-all

Several authors and researchers have recognized that there are over-all issues involved in the use of computers. Among those personally known to me are C.A. Petri, Terry Winograd, J. S. Brown, and G. De Michelis. All of them have expressed their views in writing – note particularly: Cook and Brown [2], Winograd and Flores [12], and De Michelis [4].

Particularly important to mention is the (relatively recent) output of Special Interest Group 8.1 of IFIP in the form of a report "A Framework of Information System Concepts" (FRISCO for short) [6]. This report was painstakingly built by 10 persons with Prof. Eckhard D. Falkenberg in the lead. (Details may be learned at ifip@ifip.or.at).

FRISCO is, in some sense, competitive with OA/TOA: without doubt it is philosophically/scientifically motivated; it has been produced in recognition of the same generalized lack that has brought OA/TOA into existence; it thinks its topic is "information systems" (rather than "organized activity"), but it places considerable emphasis on the idea that "organizations" are the context in which information systems (along with technological hardware/software systems) are found. Without a doubt FRISCO regards BP/BPM a sub-department. To members of the BP/BPM community I strongly recommend: (a) a thorough acquaintance with OA/OAT; (b) a thorough acquaintance with FRISCO.

Finally, a fuller treatment of OA/TOA can be found in [7] and [8] (among others).

References

[1]   Bogia, D., W. Tolone, C. Bignoli and S. Kaplan: Issues in the design of Collaborative systems: Lessons from Conversation Builder, in: Proc. Schaerding International Workshop on Task Analysis, Schaerding, Austria, 1993.

[2]   Cook S. D. N. and J.S. Brown: Bridging epistemologies: the generative dance between organizational knowledge and organizational knowing. Organizational Science, (to appear).

[3]   De Michelis, G., E. Dubois, M. Jarke, F. Matthes, J. Mylopoulos, J. Schmidt, C. Woo and E. Yu: A Three-Faceted View of Information Systems: The Challenge of Change, Communications of the ACM, 41.12, 1998, pp.64-70.

[4]   De Michelis, G.: Cooperation and Knowledge Creation, in: Knowledge Emergence: Social, Technical and Evolutionary Dimensions of Knowledge Creation, I. Nonaka and T. Nishiguchi (eds.), Oxford University Press, New York: (to appear).

[5]   Ellis, C.: Information control nets: a mathematical model of office information, in Proc. of the 1979 ACM Conf. on simulation, measurement and modeling of computer systems, ACM Press, New York, 1979.

[6]   Falkenberg, E. et al.: A Framework of Information System Concepts, IFIP (ifip@ifip.or.at), 1998.

[7]   Holt, A.W.: Organized Activity and its Support by Computer, Kluwer Academic Publishers, Dordrecht, Holland, 1997.

[8]   Holt, A.W.: ripensare il mondo - il computer e i vincoli sociali, Masson-Dunod Zanichelli, Bologna, Italy, 1998.

[9]   Petri, C.A.: Communication Disciplines, In: Computing System Design. Proc. of the Joint IBM University of Newcastle upon Tyne Seminar, B. Shaw (Ed.), University of Newcastle upon Tyne, September 1976, pp. 171-183.

[10]   Petri, C.A.: Modelling as a Communication Discipline, in: Measuring, Modelling and Evaluating Computer Systems, H. Beilner, E.Gelenbe (Eds.), North Holland, Amsterdam, 1977, pp. 435-449.

[11]   Petri, C.A.: Nets, Time and Space, Theoretical Computer Science,153, 1996, pp. 3-41.

[12]   Winograd, T, and F. Flores: Understanding Computers and Cognition, Ablex, Norwood, N.J., 1986.

[13]   Woo, C. and E.C. Yu: A Three-Faceted View of Information Systems: The Challenge of Change, Communications of the ACM, 41.12, (1998) pp. 64-70.

Evaluation of Generic Process Design Patterns: An Experimental Study

Michael Zapf and Armin Heinzl

Department of Information Systems (BWL VII), University of Bayreuth
michael.zapf@uni-bayreuth.de, armin.heinzl@uni-bayreuth.de

Abstract. In this chapter we present a framework for evaluating generic process design patterns. This framework is developed and tested for call center organizations as one specific application domain at first but will be modified for other domains in the future. As starting point we briefly examine available contributions from organizational theory and operations research which are applicable for evaluating generic process design patterns. Based on this we will identify the most relevant process patterns in our application domain and work out relevant performance criteria. In the second part of the chapter the evaluation framework will be tested within an experimental study. Thereby we compare different process partitioning strategies as typical design patterns in call centers. Our analysis will provide insight to the question under which circumstances a specific design pattern is preferable towards another.

1 Introduction

During the last years extensive work has been done to establish new or adapt existing techniques for business process management. For example have Petri-nets proven to be a powerful and accurate instrument for modeling and analyzing business processes [1]. But as organizational theory provides little rationale how to design processes from a normative perspective, the application of any process management instrument might be limited to descriptive purposes only.

In order to derive more general knowledge about how to design business processes we develop a framework for evaluating generic process design patterns. This framework is constructed for call center organizations as one specific application domain at first but will be modified for other domains in the future. With the evaluation of process patterns in specific domains we want to bridge the gap between general domain-independent design suggestions and specific in-depth domain knowledge.

As starting point we briefly examine available contributions from organizational theory and operations research which are applicable for evaluating generic process design patterns. In Section 3 the field of call center management is introduced and the specific characteristics of this domain are shown. After that we identify the most relevant process patterns in call centers and work out relevant performance criteria and suitable measures. The evaluation framework will be tested in Section 4 within an experimental study. Thereby we compare different process partitioning strategies as typical design patterns in call centers. Our analysis will provide insight to the question

W. van der Aalst et al. (Eds.): Business Process Management, LNCS 1806, pp 83-98, 2000

under which circumstances a specific design pattern is preferable towards another. In the last section the chapter is summarized and future research directions are pointed out.

2 Related Contributions

In this section we identify relevant contributions from the literature which focus on recurring normative process design problems, especially on the evaluation of process design patterns. Although this short review is not comprehensive, it provides an impression of past and presents research in the intersection of business process management and operations research.

In the early nineties, Hammer and Champy published their "radical" view on (re-) designing business processes [5]. From their perspective as consultants they derive some general process patterns which are stated to be superior to other ones. They suggest, for example, that companies should maintain process versions to manage different business cases by multiple specialists instead of generalists. Unfortunately, they neither provide any evidence for the superiority of the suggested design patterns nor they do indicate under which conditions their guidelines hold true.

In 1996, Buzacott examined these guidelines with a series of queuing models [2]. He uses throughput time as a measure of process performance and demonstrates that the reengineering principles from Hammer and Champy are not valid for all circumstances. Buzacott concludes that the guidelines are relevant when task times are subject to high variability which is typical for office and service processes. However, the focus on throughput time as a performance measure is not pervasive and ignores other important dimensions like efficiency or flexibility.

In 1997 and 1998, the research of Seidmann and Sundararajan goes beyond, analyzing single reengineering concepts like the consolidation of tasks more intensive [11, 12]. They also use throughput time as a performance measure but unlike Buzacott, they do not isolate queuing effects. Instead, they examine the influence of technological and organizational factors on the superiority of certain design patterns while still neglecting design objectives other than throughput time. Therefore, their recommendations cannot entirely support normative design decisions for real business processes.

The introduced evaluation approaches have in common, that (a) throughput time is used as only performance measure and (b) the patterns are build on a very high level of abstraction which makes it difficult to use them for normative design purposes. In our approach we try to overcome this drawbacks by using multiple performance criteria for evaluation and building process patterns for one specific application domain which allows a detailed analysis.

3 Call Center Management

3.1 Overview

Today's organizations encounter an increasing demand for high-quality services. Customers expect courteous and rapid deliveries of value-added services which may be strategic differentiator in traditional markets. In order to fulfill these expectations, many organizations deploy call centers for communicating directly to their client base. Due to the fact that call centers represent another marketing, sales, and service channel, they are mostly managed as an independent organizational entity. It's objective is to establish efficient and satisfactory interactions with actual and potential clients through the use of information and communication technology[1].

Call centers follow both, qualitative and quantitative objectives. Whereas qualitative goals like "customer orientation" or "customer satisfaction" indicate a more general view, quantitative goals like "service cost reductions" or "market share increases" may even more important to measure the outcome delivered by this type of organization.

The direction of communication within call centers can be inbound or outbound. Inbound-oriented call centers try to cope with a huge stream of incoming calls preferably avoiding busy telephone lines and long waiting periods for the customer. They are mainly used for providing product information, offering technical support services, handling incoming orders, managing customer requests and complaints, or capturing client data.

Outbound-oriented call centers focus on planned telephone campaigns and bundle all outgoing calls initiated by the service organization. Their application domains are address authentication, telephone sales, including cross-selling of products and services, sales support, collection and encashment services, and market research. Outbound-oriented call centers contact (prospective) clients in a proactive way. In case of short capacity, the client will not realize the bottleneck since he will be simply contacted hours or days later.

In contrast, the direction of communication in an inbound center is reverse and provides less degrees of freedom with regard to operations. Since customers are initiating the communication process, they expect the services to be offered (and delivered) in a prompt and timely manner. Insufficient resources will inevitably lead to longer waiting times as well as customer frustration resulting in more terminated calls. For this reason, it is more challenging to focus on inbound call centers which are also more common in the field.

3.2 Characteristics of Inbound Call Centers

According to Cleveland, the overall goal of call center management is to handle the workload of incoming customer requests with the desired service level on a high-quality standard [3]. It is clear, that sufficient qualified employees (agents) and a suitable organizational structure are the prerequisites to reach this goal. But there is

---

[1] This following section is based on the contribution of [9] on call center management.

little general knowledge available how to design a "good" call center organization and how to answer the main questions which raise in this context:

- What qualification level of agents is suitable to reach high-quality standard?
- Does the call center require specialists, generalists or a mixture of both?
- What kind of process structure enables the agents to handle the workload with the service level desired by the clients?

For a homogeneous environment with deterministic parameters for workloads, call-duration, etc., it will be likely to find appropriate answers to these questions. But (un)fortunately real world is not as simplistic as described but rather extremely dynamic. Thus, we need to discuss some of the dynamic characteristics of inbound-oriented call centers in order to be able to utilize planning procedures to this non-trivial problem domain.

- *Random distribution of incoming calls*
  Exogeneous factors that are unlikely to be influenced by the service organization, determine the calling behavior of the clients, their mode of inquiry, the time needed for finding appropriate answers, as well as the number or incoming calls. Even if call distributions could be estimated from the past, it is almost impossible to forecast all future call occurrences and call intensities exactly. This problem increases if less data about the history of the calls is available.
- *Random call-duration*
  Communication behavior and customer requirements are divergent to a large extent. Thus, the duration of each single call will vary significantly. Moreover, it is difficult to estimate the length of a particular call in advance.
- *Different types of customer requests*
  Customers have varying questions on divergent problems. But they expect that their phone calls are handled without major delays by a competent and qualified service representative.
- *Different media of incoming requests*
  Nowadays, different media such as telephone, fax or e-mail may be used simultaneously for communication with the client basis. The processes within a call center must have the ability to utilize as well as integrate any of these media in order to meet customer needs. Coping with media diversity is in fact one of the greatest challenges for inbound call centers.

3.3 Generic Process Design Patterns in Inbound Call Centers

In the following we focus on processes which are directly embedded in the call center organization. Further processes which are initiated by this interaction and take part in other organizational units will not be subject of our analysis. As starting point for deriving generic process patterns we follow the guidelines of Hammer/Champy [5]. In this context, especially the following two design patterns seem to be relevant in the call center domain:

A. *Combining sequential tasks* into one task which is executed by one employee and
B. *Providing multiple process versions* for different jobs or customers.

Pattern A allows the organization in an easy way to present one contact person to the customer. Misunderstandings, multiple data acquisition and hand-off delays can be avoided, resulting in positive effects on customer satisfaction and service quality. As a thumb rule, customers do not accept more than one or two forwarding actions during one call without getting annoyed. So it is clear that as much combining of tasks as possible should be done in the direct interaction with the customer.

Applying pattern B has the consequence to partition the overall call volume according to certain criteria and provide separate process versions and resources for each partition. There can be different reasons for partitioning:

- *Market reasons*
  In order to provide customized services it can be necessary to partition the process according to certain customer preferences. In this case different process versions are offered to different customer types. In conjunction with a differentiated prices policy this can be an adequate way of income generation.
- *Specialization reasons*
  Sometimes partitioning can be necessary because of the service or product complexity which is continuously increasing. As humans have a large but limited qualification potential it is not possible for employees to offer a high-quality service for a broad and complex product range. Even if the service complexity is not high, it can be useful to partition the processes in order to realize specialization gains which lead to faster and better handling of requests. But it should be noted that overspecialization may have an negative impact on the employee resulting in strain or absenteeism and should therefore be avoided.
- *Managerial reasons*
  Partitioning can be applied in order to better cope with span of control issues. It is easier to manage small agent groups than large groups.
- *Technical reasons*
  Technical reasons like geographical or cultural circumstances can require partitioning. For example it may be necessary for international call center to partition according different languages or time zones.

In order to use partitioning pattern B successfully, some further aspects have to be taken into consideration. First, the partitioning scope has to be defined. It can be on the process, subprocess or activity level. It has also to be decided how many versions should be offered and whether a homogenous or non-homogenous partitioning should take place.

3.4 Performance Criteria for Inbound Call Centers

The planning of an inbound call center is a complex task that requires a careful performance evaluation approach. A comparison of emergent design alternatives should be based on the behavior and outcome on the performance evaluation models involved. The alternative that complies best to pre-specified design objectives will be likely to be the preferable process design. Thus, suitable design objectives have to be formulated as well as operable measures in order to quantify their degree of fulfillment.

As stated earlier, a call center should meet the service requirements of it's actual and future client base in a qualitative and efficient manner. Accordingly, "service quality" and "efficiency" are major design objectives which will be outlined and operationalized in the next.

3.4.1 Design Objective "Quality"

The literature offers a variety of important qualitative measures for determining the service quality of a call center. Often quoted examples are "conversation quality" or "consultation quality" [6]. These measures can be assessed through customer interviews or coaching sessions undertaken by staff consultants. Gathering data about qualitative measures is useful for monitoring and improving ongoing activities. Thus, it requires a call center which has already started operations. Since no corresponding data is available at the planning stage, qualitative measures cannot be applied directly for process design purposes.

Quantitative measures seem to be more applicable for design problems as described in this paper. They are mainly used for examining whether customers are able to get in contact with call center employees within an acceptable period of time or not. They do not measure whether customers get the expected quality of service, but they ensure a basis on which the service can be provided in an effective manner. The following measures are suitable for this purpose:

- *Service level*
  The service level indicate the percentage of calls which can be accepted in a certain period of time, e.g. 80/20 indicates that 80 percent of all calls can be answered within 20 seconds.
- *Speed of answer*
  The average speed of answer is the average time, one call can be accepted, e.g. 12 seconds indicates that one call can be accepted at an average time of 12 seconds. This measure has to be used carefully, because it does not provide any information about one specific call of a certain customer. So it is possible that the actual speed of an answer is higher or lower than the average speed of an answer in numerous cases.
- *Lost calls*
  The number of lost calls summarizes all communication activity related to customers who hang up during a certain period of time.
- *Throughput time*
  The average throughput time is the overall time a customer has to hold on for the desired service. It is composed of the average duration of a call and the average delay.
- *Waiting time*
  The average waiting time benchmarks the average time a customer has to wait under the present conditions. In this context the longest waiting time may be of special interest, because it indicates the maximum delay a customer has to accept under the current conditions.

3.4.2 Design Objective "Efficiency"

Before we are able to determine which process patterns are more efficient than others, we will briefly discuss which different types of costs are relevant for call center management and how these costs may be allocated to specific process patterns. Starting with the cost types, we consider the following types as relevant:

- *Labor*
  Labor costs may account for up to 60 percent of a call center's total operating costs [4]. Since not all labor costs can be physically traced to the services created by a call center representative in a "hands on" sense, a distinction between direct labor costs and indirect labor costs is necessary. For example, the labor cost of a call center agent who is providing technical support service for a specific product could be attributed as direct labor costs. On the contrary, costs incurred by the supervision and administration of a call center cannot be allocated directly to specific processes and will therefore be referred as indirect labor costs or overhead costs.
- *Technology*
  The costs of information and communication technology are comprised by hardware and software costs. Since establishing an inbound call center requires an estimated initial capital investment of $ 5.000 to $ 7.000 per workstation [4], the incurred costs will be mainly accounted as depreciation on equipment and maintenance fees within the overhead costs figure.
- *Communication*
  Communication costs include all fees imposed from telecom service providers for the use of (toll-free) phone numbers, e.g. installment, basic fees, rates per minute, etc. which will be caused by the service organization. Since the time-based rates can be directly allocated to calling service representative, this largest portion of communication costs may be handled as direct costs. Basic fees and installments are often treated as overhead costs.
- *Office facilities*
  Facilities costs make up another significant portion of a call center's overhead costs. Examples are rent and lease, depreciation on buildings and furniture, power, building security as well as office supplies.
- *Outsourcing*
  Outsourcing costs incur from subcontracting external service providers that offer specific functions, like conducting campaigns or buffering peak loads. Moreover, these costs may also include the costs of consulting and research.
- *Training*
  Training costs include all costs for extending the knowledge of the workforce in a call center. Whereas it is always considered critical, it is an often overlooked component of the call center's success.

The first three types of costs listed – labor, technology and communication – represent the largest portion of cost, which may represent up to 90% of the total costs [10]. Since their controllability depends mainly on the contractual arrangements surrounding the cost objects, not all costs can be treated as variable. Especially outsourcing, lease, rent, or even some telecommunication contracts may involve pre-specified payments over a certain periods of time which do not permit the cancellation of the contractual relationship at any time. Thus, the incurred costs are mainly fixed from a short term perspective.

For comparing the efficiency of design alternatives it is especially important to take the differing costs per process pattern into account. As the examined process alternatives have similar overhead costs (e.g. technology costs, facilities costs) we will concentrate on direct costs, especially the direct labor and telecommunication costs.

Costs are one way to measure the efficiency of a process design. They point out, how much you have to pay for the employed resources. But they don't show whether the resources are overloaded or whether they have much idle time. For measuring this kind of efficiency we use the resource utilization, which gives the percentage of time a resource is busy in respect to the total time of its availability.

4   Evaluation of Common Process Design Patterns in Inbound Call Centers

In this section we present some typical process partitioning strategies in inbound call centers. We do not refer to a specific process design in a real enterprise but deal with generic process patterns which can be found in several application domain areas. As the most challenging processes are those with an high share of conversation and consultation we will focus in our analysis on the technical product support process. The scenarios will be evaluated during a simulation study.

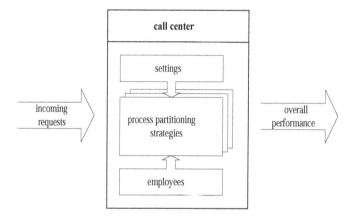

Fig. 1. Evaluation framework

4.1 Evaluation Framework

The examined *process partitioning strategies* constitute the core of our evaluation framework (see Figure 1). These strategies use different mixing ratios of *employees* to handle the *incoming requests*. As employees are the most important resources for a call center, the configuration of employees is likely to have a major influence on the *overall performance*. This performance is derived from multiple measures according to the criteria derived in the previous section.

4.1.1 Incoming Requests

The incoming customer requests are divided into two main categories, *standard* and *special requests*. Standard requests refer to simple or well-known problems an can be handled with basic knowledge of the application domain and the help of a solution database. Special requests refer to difficult or unknown problems and require in-depth knowledge on the side of the agent.

We consider incoming requests entering the call center with a certain "arrival rate". 80% of these calls are standard requests, 20% are special requests. The time period one agent needs to handle a request will be called "processing time" and the maximum time one customer accepts to wait for a free agent will be called "wait time until abandonment". These parameters are not deterministic but under stochastic influence. Table 1 shows the examined parameters, values and distributions.

Table 1. Parameters for incoming requests

parameter	value(s)
arrival rate	1000-1400 calls per hour
percentage of special requests	20%
processing time	
standard request	triangular(4, 8, 12)
special request	triangular(10, 16, 22)
wait time until abandonment	triangular(0.5, 1, 1.5)

4.1.2 Employees

In order to handle the incoming requests on a high-quality standard, enough qualified employees are needed. We include two qualification profiles in our analysis:

- *Generalists* with general knowledge are able to handle standard requests and
- *Specialists* with specific knowledge are able to handle special and standard requests.

The call center consists of 210 agents with possibly different payroll costs. We assume that generalists cost $12.50 per hour ($2,000 per month) and specialists $15.63 per hour ($2,500 per month).

4.1.3 Process Partitioning Strategies

The partitioning strategies can be first divided into *one-level* and *two-level designs*. In a one-level design all agents can accept calls directly from the customer and are organized in one common level. Whereas in a two-level design only a portion of the agents on the first level receives calls directly from the customer. The other part of the agents builds the second level, who receive calls by forwarding from their colleagues of the first level.

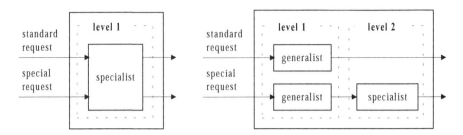

Fig. 2. Basic one-level and two-level designs

The *basic one-level design* without partitioning assumes that every agent can handle every incoming request and no forwarding is necessary (see Figure 2). The *basic two-level design* implies a partitioning between standard and special calls. Standard calls can be completely handled on the first level whereas special calls have to be forwarded to the second level.

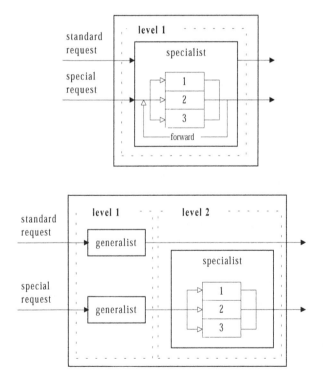

Fig. 3. One-level and two-level design with further process partitioning

These basic designs can be modified by *further process partitioning* for special requests. This partitioning implies also a partitioning of the specialist group into different teams. One team is responsible for the requests of one specialist field and is not able to handle requests for other fields. Examples for the one-level and two-level designs with partitioning into three specialist teams are shown in Figure 3. In our experiments we will assume a homogenous partitioning, which means an equal distribution of requests between the teams. Please note that in the one-level design, forwarding calls between different teams becomes invevitable. We assume that forwarding calls to the right agent takes two minutes per call, no matter whether the forwarding is done from one level to another or inside one level.

4.1.4 Performance Measurement

The overall performance of the process designs is analyzed according to the criteria and measures which have been discussed in detail in Section 3.4. The results are presented in two ways:

For a summary comparison of two or more design alternatives the performance measures are displayed in a single polar diagram (see Figure 4). The values for every measure are derived from the experiments with different workloads by calculating the arithmetic mean. This representation gives a first impression of the main differences between the analyzed designs. But it has to be treated very carefully because of the high degree of consolidation of the data.

Detailed comparisons are made by analyzing the changes of single performance measures with respect to different workloads.

4.1.5 Settings and Evaluation Technique

The evaluation of the overall performance of different process partitioning strategies will be conducted through a stochastic discrete event simulation study. We will use Call$im [13], a call center specific extension of the simulation tool ARENA [7], which suppports model design in a comfortable way. Some of the performance measures required were directly adopted from Call$im, while others have been implemented through individual routines..

The experiments have been undertaken in the form of multiple terminating simulation runs in order to reflect the nature of a typical call center. We assumed that the call center will be in service from 8 AM until 6 PM. In order to obtain expressive results, we lounched 100 runs for every experiment, every run representing one day of operation. The service is offered to the customer by toll-free phone numbers which cost 0,15$ per minute.

4.2 Results and Discussion

4.2.1 One-level versus Two-Level Design

In our first experiment, we compare the basic one-level and two-level designs (see Figure 2). As the one-level design includes solely specialists, which are able to handle any request, no process partitioning takes place. The two-level design provides two process versions for standard and special requests: Standard requests are handled on the first level, special requests pass through both levels.

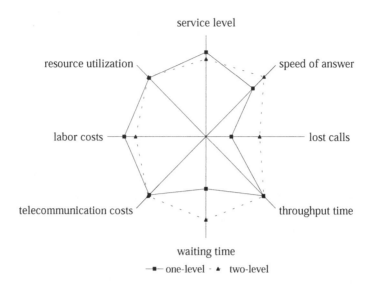

Fig. 4. One-level versus two-level design

Figure 4 presents the main performance differences between both designs. The quality measures service level, speed of answer, lost calls and waiting time show the disadvantage of the two-level design. This can be explained by the fact that (a) additional time has to be spend for call forwarding and (b) stronger queuing effects arise according to smaller agent groups. These effects are stronger for special requests than for standard requests and increase with the workload which is exemplary shown in Figure 5 for the waiting times. As we assume a limited "wait time until abandonment" accepted by the customer, the waiting times are relatively small and have little influence on the overall throughput times.

According to the higher call duration, the two-level design raises higher telecommunication costs. All advantages of the one-level design have to be paid with high labor costs, which are 15% higher than in the two-level design. The resource utilization does not differ significantly between the designs.

In summary it may be said, that the one-level design provides a higher quality level than the two-level design but causes higher labor costs.

4.2.2 One-Level versus Two-Level Design with further Process Partitioning

The second row of experiments deals also with the comparison between one-level and two-level designs but takes a partitioning of special requests into three specialist fields into account (see Figure 3).

Figure 6 shows that the performance differences between both designs are not as strong as in the case of no further partitioning. Since in the one-level design, two third of all special requests have to be forwarded on average, this observation can be easily explained. Please note, that the partitioning leads to stronger queuing effects which increase the percentage of lost calls significantly (compare Figures 4 and 6).

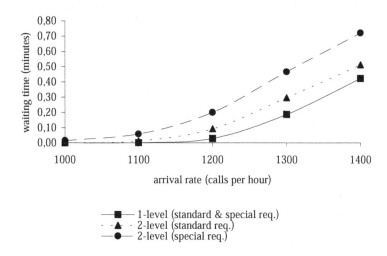

Fig. 5. Waiting time for one-level and two-level design

The cost comparison of both designs provides the same results as in the previous experiment: The agent costs in the one-level design are higher than in the two-level design. While comparing the resource utilization it should be noted that the one-level design guarantees a regular load sharing between the agents, whereas in the two-level design the high loads are not proportional shared between generalists and specialists.

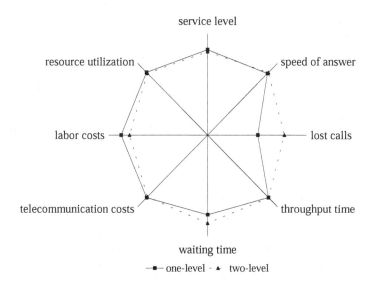

Fig. 6. One-level versus two-level design with further partitioning

With partitioning of special requests, the one-level design offers a higher quality-level than the two-level design but the differences are not as strong as in the case of no further partitioning. For this quality increase a higher price for employees has to be paid.

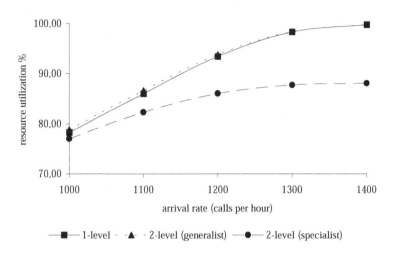

Fig. 7. Resource utilization for one-level and two-level design with further partitioning

4.2.3 Two-Level Design with Different Partitioning Strategies
The last set of experiments was carried out in order to examine the effects of different partitioning strategies in the two-level design. No partitioning was compared with partitioning into three and five specialist fields.

Further partitioning has mainly effected the percentage of lost calls, the other measures did not fundamentally differ from each other (see Figure 8). Figure 9 shows that the percentage of lost calls increases exponentially under high loads which complies with well-known results form queueing theory [8]. From there it is also to expect that the situation gets even worse for non-homogenous partitioning.

Thus, further partitioning leads to lower quality measures, which is especially relevant in high load situations.

5 Summary and Future Research Directions

In this chapter a framework for evaluating generic process design patterns was presented and applied in the domain of inbound call centers. In the first part we gathered special characteristics of inbound call centers, identified process patterns relevant for this domain and derived suitable performance measures for evaluating purposes. In the second part we evaluated multiple versions of one representative process pattern within a simulation study.

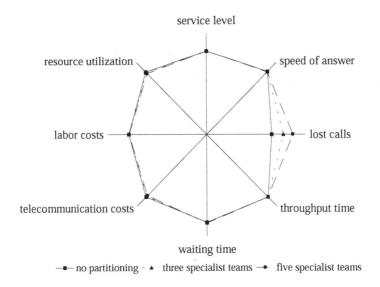

Fig. 8. Two-level design with different partitioning strategies

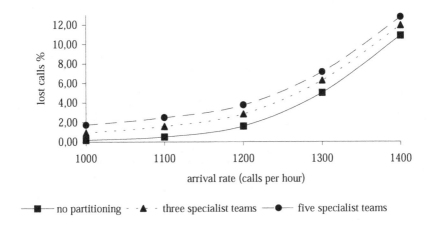

Fig. 9. Lost calls for different partitioning strategies

The results of the experiments showed that a one-level call center design reaches better quality measures than a two-level design from a quantitative point of view. It also leads to a more regular load sharing between the employees. But these advantages induce higher labor costs. Besides the fact that increasing process partitioning leads to worse quality measures, it should be only applied when other positive effects can be expected or no other alternatives are possible.

Our approach may be considered as a first step towards a comprehensive analysis of process patterns. Much work remains to been done on this way: (a) The presented patterns have to be analyzed for more parameter constellations to allow the extension of our results, (b) the dimension of multiple communication media has to be included into the design patterns to give more support for realistic design decisions, (c) the evaluation framework has to be extended with the design objective flexibility and (d) the evaluation framework should be applied for other application domains.

References

[1] van der Aalst, W.M.P.: The Application of Petri Nets to Workflow Management. In: The Journal of Circuits, Systems and Computers 8 (1998) 1, pp. 21-66.
[2] Buzacott, J.A.: Commonalities in Reengineered Business Processes: Models and Issues. In: Management Science 42 (1996) 5, pp. 768-782.
[3] Cleveland, B.; Mayben, J.: Call Center Management On Fast Forward. Call Center Press, Annapolis, Maryland 1997.
[4] Gilpatrick, K.: Costing out call centers. In: Credit Union Management, August 1998, pp. 19-22.
[5] Hammer, M.; Champy, J.: Reengineering the Corporation. New York 1993.
[6] Henn, H.; Seiwert, G.: Controlling im Call Center. In: Henn; Kruse; Strawe (eds.): Handbuch Call Center Management. Hannover 1998, pp. 251-268.
[7] Kelton, D.W.; Sadowski, R.P.; Sadowski, D.A.: Simulation with ARENA. McGraw-Hill, Boston et al. 1998.
[8] Kleinrock, L.: Queueing Systems. Volume II: Computer Applications. New York et al. 1975.
[9] Kruse, J.P.: Die strategische Bedeutung der Innovation Call Center. In: Henn; Kruse; Strawe (eds.): Handbuch Call Center Management. Hannover 1998, pp. 11-34.
[10] Mura, H.: Standortauswahl für deutschsprachige Call Center. In: Henn; Kruse; Strawe (eds.): Handbuch Call Center Management. Hannover 1998, pp. 95-112.
[11] Seidmann, A.; Sundararajan, A.: The effects of task and information asymmetry on business process redesign. In: International Journal Of Production Economics, 50 (1997) 2/3, pp. 117-128.
[12] Sundararajan, A.: Modeling and Designing Business Processes. Dissertation, William E. Simon Graduate School of Business Administration. Rochester, New York 1998.
[13] Systems Modeling Corp.: Call$im Template Users's Guide. Sewickley 1996.

Management-Oriented Models of Business Processes

Anastasia Pagnoni Holt

University of Milano, Department of Computer Science
Via Comelico, 39/41 - 20135 Milano, Italy
pagnoni@dsi.unimi.it

Abstract. This contribution addresses the relevance of Petri nets to the management of business processes in a general way. It is organized in three steps: (a) sorting out business processes are suitable to being represented by means of Petri nets; (b) setting up a comprehensive list of the typical questions a management-oriented model should help answer; (c) suggesting ways to answer questions in (b) for business processes sorted out in (a) by means of Petri net-based methods. In particular, we discuss how to obtain such answers by grafting algorithms of applied mathematics onto Petri net models. As a demonstration, a specific business problem—decision-making over alternative plan executions characterized by fuzzy properties—is worked out.

1 Introduction

Business processes are of very different types, as different as planning, production, marketing, bookkeeping, financial procedures, and negotiations of various kinds. Every business involves a number of intertwined processes, all of them marked by the involvement of interacting, interdependent actors, who may compete, cooperate, or conflict, and whose actions are usually difficult to untangle.

Designing effective computer support systems for processes of this level of complexity is a difficult task that requires an adequate formal model of reality. Setting up such a model amounts to deciding what information will be taken into account and what omitted, which questions will be answered and by which algorithms, and how key issues—costs, times, uncertainty, failure—will be dealt with. Any representation language that is going to be used will result in a further modeling constraint.

Researchers working in the areas of applied mathematics, economics, and computer science have suggested a number of formal models of reality. Every such model draws from a particular paradigm—that is, from a particular exemplary situation, and some problems it poses. So we have the paradigm of the decision maker trying to pick an action that minimizes his regret—or maximizes his utility;—the paradigm of the player driven by his want to beat some opponent, and that of the project manager seeking to complete his project within a certain time, or budget.

Petri nets are reality models of a different nature. They do not originate from the mathematization of some paradigmatic problem, but aim at representing the causal structure of discrete-event, concurrent systems of any kind, together with their operation. Petri nets do not come with a problem attached, but are meant to be a general representation tool. As a matter of fact, Petri nets have been used successfully for engineering quite different systems: production plants, computer networks, software systems, etc., though the representation and analysis capabilities provided by Petri

W. van der Aalst et al. (Eds.): Business Process Management, LNCS 1806, pp 99-109, 2000

nets—invariance analysis, liveness questions, etc.—have not yet been exploited by business analysts. Decision theory, game theory, operation research, statistics, bayesian networks, and other branches of applied mathematics provide a variety of methods for dealing with specific business-related problems, but all of these methods are based on some kind of oversimplification of reality. But for statistics, neither these methods nor the computer support systems based on them, are actually used in day-to-day business practice. Business people need their questions to be set, and answered, in a context that is true to the actual state of things. We believe that Petri nets can supply such a context in a number of cases.

In the next two sections we consider the specifics of Petri nets as a modeling tool, focusing on the features that make a business process apt for Petri net representation (Section 2), and delineating what decision problems can best be solved with the help of such a net model (Section 3). This done, in Section 4, we show how to exploit the flexibility of predicate-transition nets—a particular "brand" of Petri net—so as to render the algorithms of applied mathematics viable in the context of Petri net models. Finally, Section 5 illustrates the discussion above by working out a small application—the integration of priority orders characterized by imprecise attributes into the daily production schedule of a steel-manufacturing factory, via Petri net based fuzzy decision making.

In the sequel we shall assume that readers are already familiar with Petri nets, and the basics of fuzzy set theory.

2   Petri Nets and Business Process Representation

Petri nets allow us to draw clean-cut plans of general systems characterized be a high degree of concurrency. In a business framework, such plans will be global or partial outlines of a specific way of carrying out some kind of complex, mostly distributed, activity; they will be aimed at specifics, such as the scheduling of resources of various kind, or the controlling of failures, costs, workloads. Since every business may be regarded as a system involving a number of complex, concurrent operations—production, marketing, bookkeeping, financial procedures, negotiations, etc.—which, in their turn, consist of other complex, concurrent activities, using Petri nets for planning or analyzing business processes seems a rather natural idea.

However, every business also involves processes that are difficult, or even impossible, to represent by means of Petri nets: processes based on the ongoing interaction of actors who relate to each other in ways too difficult to untangle. Think, for instance, of the activities that take place at an emergency room, or of processes whose working depends on unpredictable factors, like consumer behavior or competitors' moves.

The building blocks of Petri nets are elementary state and transition components interconnected by a causality relation. But, while we may assume that the causal structure of any system of organized activities consists of interconnected state and transition components, some systems can not be represented as Petri nets at meaningful levels of detail. Complex activities with a very rich causal structure may be just impossible to break down in a useful way. For instance, drawing a Petri net plan of a soccer game—even if it were the occurrence graph of an already played match—is impossible. To draw such an occurrence graph, we would have to record every relevant event of that match: all actions that did and did not occur, together with the order in which they actually happened—or, did not happen. Every single action—or non-action—that actually influenced the outcome of the game would need to be modeled. And, even if it were possible to set forth such an occurrence graph, how many pairs of soccer pundits could then agree on it? On the other side, a meaningful a-priori Petri net model of a specific soccer game—say the final match of the last World Cup—is just unthinkable, because such is the combination of relevant actions.

For the same set of reasons, business processes involving several actors cooperating or competing in a relevant number of unpredictable ways are ill-suited for Petri net representation.

Another problem is that, being primarily a graphical representation language, Petri nets need to suite the capabilities of the human eye. The number of net elements—circles, squares, arcs—must be constrained accordingly. It is easy to see that few top-down unfoldings of several net elements are enough to make us loose track of the general picture. The same holds true for the "horizontal" aggregation of a substantial number of different net modules. Nor would it be more practical to rely on the incidence matrix of a "large" net. Only adjusting the granularity of our representation to human capabilities will make Petri nets a handy tool.

There is one more question to consider. Ordinary Petri nets have some element of indeterminacy about them, as enabled transitions are not bound to ever fire, and time is not taken into account explicitly. Timed and stochastic Petri nets allow us to associate times and/or probabilities with either state or transition elements, and then calculate asymptotic properties of net behavior: steady state features, home states, transient states, etc. But in general, asymptotic properties are of little interest to business managers.

So, what features make a business process suitable for representation and analysis by means of ordinary Petri nets? We suggest the following to be basic requirements.

Elementary state components of the business process model must represent well-defined pieces of reality. Resources must be easily identified, counted, or evaluated; conditions must be readily verifiable. Potential customers, expected orders, etc., are hard to count; employee motivation, or customer satisfaction are difficult to verify.

Complex activities must consist of a reasonable number of—alternative or concurrent—patterns of behavior. Such patterns must break-down to a few well-defined, repeatable actions. (This is the requirement which both the soccer game and the emergency room example fail to satisfy.)

The number of relevant state and transition components has to be fairly small. As a rule of thumb, we suggest that a net's incidence matrix never exceed 100 elements, with more zero entries as its size grows. (Too many arcs turn any net into a dish of spaghetti.) If high-level nets are used, the number of colors, the order of predicates, etc., also needs to be kept manageable.

Top-down unfoldings of net elements—state and transition elements alike—should not go too deep: after a number of top-down unfoldings, everyone looses track of the overall picture of the net.

Though some priority issues and synchronization problems are well modeled by means of Petri nets—like "if transition a fires first, then transition b will never be able to fire", or "transition a has to fire three times before b can",—time questions should not be the foremost concern of our planning effort. Petri nets are not recommended for solving timing problems. Other graphical methods—PERT or GERT networks,

GANT diagrams, etc.—work better, and can be combined with a Petri net plan of the project considered.

3 Management-Oriented Questions and Petri Net Plans

Decision theory provides us with a number of methods for choosing from among several actions, all of which rely on some mathematical formulation of the decision problem considered. However, such methods are not well-suited to answering questions about strategy—about choosing from among several possible *courses* of action,—because their formalisms do not allow for a dynamic representation of reality. This kind of question requires the formal representation of alternative sets of possibly concurrent actions, and is quite naturally expressed in the framework of Petri nets, because the notions of conflict and concurrency lie at the very heart of this formalism.

What is needed is a Petri net representation—a Petri net plan—of our decision problem, developed so that different *courses of action* do not interact (by this, we mean that the only places shared by alternative net executions are the sink and source). With this proviso, alternative net executions can be easily input to decision making techniques [1]. Of course, the decision-relevant attributes of the activities considered will have to be defined formally in some way.

Here is a list of business-relevant questions suitable to Petri net-based decision making.

- What action, or strategy, is best suited to achieve a given goal?

- How will prices, labor costs, market situation, a certain political issue, weather, etc., affect the outcome of a certain choice?

- What will the payoff, or the utility, of a certain course of action be?

- How are we to distribute this resource best?

- How are we to deal with conflicting goals?

- How are we going to steer this project?

- Can we detect, and possibly correct, unwanted situations as they appear?

In the next section we will show how to answer questions of this kind by grafting algorithms of applied mathematics onto Petri nets.

4 Tapping into Applied Mathematics

We found that the best way to apply algorithms of applied mathematics to Petri nets is to exploit the flexibility of predicate-transition nets [2], [3]. In this kind of net, the elementary state components are predicates of order n, that is, relations among n entries, possibly of quite different type (numbers, labels, functions, etc.), as their variety mirrors the variety allowed for predicate arguments.

At any given state, a predicate is satisfied by a (possibly empty) multiset of constant n-tuples. This multiset represents the predicate's extension, that is, the multiset of tuples for which the predicate actually holds true. Extensions of predicates make up net markings, and represent system states. As markings are changed by transition firings, in the lingo of Petri nets, we say that n-tuples "flow" through predicate-transition nets.

Because of the freedom allowed, such n-tuples are an ideal tool for representing objects together with their attributes, numeric or other. If the net is developed so that alternative net executions do not interfere—so that the only places they have in common are the source and sink—many algorithms of applied mathematics can readily be applied to alternative net executions via numeric entries in tuples.

In the next section, we will demonstrate this approach by showing how to apply fuzzy decision making in the context of predicate-transition nets. The method—fully described in [1],—also works with other algorithms.

5   Working Out a Small Example

The problem addressed is a typical decision making problem: the integration of priority orders—like small orders of best customers, or urgent orders of regular customers—into the production scheduling system of a factory making steel bars by order. Notice that this decision is about how to manage a certain business process, and not about the engineering of a production plant.

For the sake of simplicity, here we will present only a very small predicate-transition net representing the whole plant operation—net N, represented in Fig.1. Our approach requires predicate-transition nets with one source and one, or more, sink. All predicates but the source must be empty at the initial marking, and alternative net executions must not interfere. (A net execution is a set of sequential or concurrent transition firings that brings all tuples from the source to the sink. Transitions may either already be enabled at the initial marking, or become so as the net "proceeds".)

Transitions 1, 2, 3, and 4 of net N represent four draw machines. The markings of A represents metal chunks waiting to be drawn; the marking of B, bars already drawn. We assume that four kind of bars are produced by the factory: type-a, type-b, type-c, and type-d bars.

As we thought of using fuzzy sets in order to formalize the imprecise notions of best customers and urgent order, we had factory managers help us define the fuzzy attribute "best customer" and "urgent order".

Orders were represented by 3-tuples the first entry being the bar type ordered; the second and third entries being the membership degrees of the two fuzzy attributes above. For example, 3-tuple <a, 0.9, 0.3> would represent an order of a production unit of a-type bars, "urgent" with degree 0.3, and placed by a customer assessed to be a "best customer" with degree 0.9.

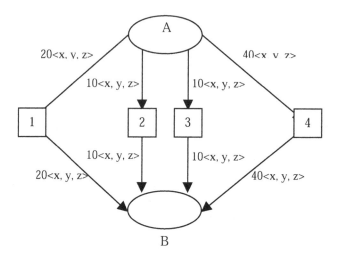

Fig. 1. Net N

Markings of predicate-transition net N are multisets of triplets, which we denote as

$$\sum_i m_i < t_i, \mu_c(k), \mu_u(q) >$$

where:

(i)   triplet $<t_i, \mu_c(k), \mu_u(q)>$ represents order q placed by customer k, for one production unit of t_i-type bars; $t_i \in \{a, b, c, d\}$;

(ii) $\mu_c(k)$ is the membership degree of customer k in fuzzy set $A_c = \{K, \mu_c(k)\}$ representing the fuzzy attribute "good customer"; K is the set of customers;

(iii) $\mu_u(q)$ is the membership degree of order q in fuzzy set $A_u = \{Q, \mu_u(q)\}$ representing the fuzzy attribute "urgent order"; Q is the set of orders;

(iv) m_i represents a number of triplets with same entries, that is, the number of similar production units ordered.

Let the initial marking of N be:

$$M(A) = 20<a, 0.9, 0.5> + 600<b, 0.4, 0.9> + 40<c, 0.3, 0.1> + 200<c, 0.3, 0.7>$$
$$M(B) = \varnothing .$$

Multiset $M(A)$ represents a set of orders waiting to be processed. Among others, we have 240 orders for c-type bars placed by mediocre customers ("good" with degree 0.3 only), 200 of which are rather urgent ("urgent" with degree 0.7), while 40 are not urgent at all ("urgent" with degree 0.1).

We call a *net execution* any multiset of enabled transition firings—sequential or concurrent— that brings all triplets in A from A to B. It will prove useful to characterize net executions as vectors of non-negative integers

$$e = [n_{11}, n_{12}, \ldots , n_{1s}, n_{21}, n_{22}, \ldots , n_{2s}, \ldots\ldots\ldots\ldots , n_{r1}, n_{r2}, \ldots , n_{rs}]$$

where r is the number of net transitions, s is the number of bar types, and n_{mt} the number of times transition m fires for bar type t. In our example, r = s = 4.

Table 1 shows six executions of net N with initial marking M.

Table 1. Six executions of net N

machine:	1	1	1	1	2	2	2	2	3	3	3	3	4	4	4	4
bar type:	a	b	c	d	a	b	c	d	a	b	c	d	a	b	c	d
e_1	1	0	0	0	0	60	0	0	0	0	20	0	0	0	1	0
e_2	0	0	2	0	2	0	0	0	0	60	0	0	0	0	5	0
e_3	0	0	10	0	0	0	4	0	2	0	0	0	0	15	0	0
e_4	0	10	0	0	2	0	0	0	0	0	4	0	15	0	0	0
e_5	0	10	0	0	0	0	60	0	2	0	0	0	0	0	1	0
e_6	0	30	0	0	2	0	0	0	0	0	4	0	0	0	5	0

For markings representing practical situations, there are usually very many alternative executions, which can be determined by computer. In this application, we had the additional constraint that orders for the same type of bar should not be split between different machines because of the long setup time required to shift from one bar type to another.

Let d(m) indicate the *run time of machine* m, with: d(1)=1, d(2)=d(3)=2, d(4)=3, and let the *run time for execution* $\mathbf{e} = [n_{11}, n_{12}, \ldots, n_{rs}]$ be defined as

$$d(\mathbf{e}) = \sum_{m,t} n_{mt} d(m) .$$

From these times, fuzzy attribute A_d—"short run time", defined over the set of executions E—can be derived:

$$A_d = (\mathbf{e}, \ \mu_d(\mathbf{e})) \quad \text{where} \quad \mu_d(\mathbf{e}) = \frac{\max_e d(\mathbf{e}) - d(\mathbf{e})}{\max_e d(\mathbf{e}) - \min_e d(\mathbf{e})}$$

($\max_e d(\mathbf{e}) \neq \min_e d(\mathbf{e})$, because if all executions had the same duration, we wouldn't even consider the attribute "duration".)

For the six executions of Table 1 we get:

$$\mu_d(\mathbf{e}_1) = 0.08, \quad \mu_d(\mathbf{e}_2) = 1.00, \quad \mu_d(\mathbf{e}_3) = 0.63,$$

$$\mu_d(\mathbf{e}_4) = 0.66, \quad \mu_d(\mathbf{e}_5) = 0.00, \quad \mu_d(\mathbf{e}_6) = 0.75.$$

Attributes A_c and A_u were defined over the set of customers and the set of orders, respectively. Since executions are multisets of transition firings, each of them occurring for a specific triplet, we can extend attributes A_c and A_u to net executions by considering the membership values carried by the firing triplets in the following manner.

Fuzzy attributes A'_c and A'_u—again called "good customer" and "urgent order"—over the set E of executions, will be defined as:

$$A'_c = (\mathbf{e} \in E, \ \mu'_c(\mathbf{e})) \quad \text{with} \quad \mu'_c(\mathbf{e}) = \sum_{i,j} n_{ij} \mu_c(j) ,$$

$$A'_u = (e \in E, \ \mu'_u(e)) \quad \text{with} \quad \mu'_u(e) = \sum_{i,j} n_{ij} \mu_u(j) \ .$$

For the six executions of Table 1, we get:

$$\mu'_c(e_1) = 0.67 \ , \quad \mu'_c(e_2) = 0.75 \ , \quad \mu'_c(e_3) = 0.58 \ ,$$

$$\mu'_c(e_4) = 0.61 \ , \quad \mu'_c(e_5) = 0.74 \ , \quad \mu'_c(e_6) = 0.70 \ ;$$

$$\mu'_u(e_1) = 0.84 \ , \quad \mu'_u(e_2) = 0.85 \ , \quad \mu'_u(e_3) = 0.71 \ ,$$

$$\mu'_u(e_4) = 0.71 \ , \quad \mu'_u(e_5) = 0.85 \ , \quad \mu'_u(e_6) = 0.78 \ .$$

Attributes A'_c, A'_u, and A_d are defined over E; all of them express desirable execution features. Saaty [4] suggested a method to assign a weight, between 0 and 1, to each such attribute in a way that expresses their relative importance to a decision maker. For this example, we will assume the weighting to be:

$$w_1 = (A'_c) = 0.55, \quad w_2 = w(A'_u) = 0.27, \quad w_3 = w(A_d) = 0.18 \ .$$

Weighted membership functions are obtained by raising membership functions to the relative weight. Here we get:

$$[\mu'_c(e_1)]^{0.55} = 0.81 \ , \ [\mu'_c(e_2)]^{0.55} = 0.86 \ , \ [\mu'_c(e_3)]^{0.55} = 0.74 \ ,$$

$$[\mu'_c(e_4)]^{0.55} = 0.77 \ , \ [\mu'_c(e_5)]^{0.55} = 0.85 \ , \ [\mu'_c(e_6)]^{0.55} = 0.82 \ ;$$

$$[\mu'_u(e_1)]^{0.27} = 0.95 \ , \ [\mu'_u(e_2)]^{0.27} = 0.96 \ , \ [\mu'_u(e_3)]^{0.27} = 0.91 \ ,$$

$$[\mu'_u(e_4)]^{0.27} = 0.91 \ , \ [\mu'_u(e_5)]^{0.27} = 0.96 \ , \ [\mu'_u(e_6)]^{0.27} = 0.93 \ ;$$

$$[\mu'_d(e_1)]^{0.18} = 0.63 \ , \ [\mu'_d(e_2)]^{0.18} = 1.00 \ , \ [\mu'_d(e_3)]^{0.18} = 0.92 \ ,$$

$$[\mu'_d(e_4)]^{0.18} = 0.93 \ , \ [\mu'_d(e_5)]^{0.18} = 0.00 \ , \ [\mu'_d(e_6)]^{0.18} = 0.95 \ .$$

The degree to which an execution e is characterized by a set of fuzzy attributes $\{A_i\}$—all attributes being defined over the same support E—is expressed by their intersection Δ (recall that, by definition, Δ is also a fuzzy set over support E):

$$\Delta = \underset{i}{I} \ A_i = (e, \mu_\Delta(e)) \quad \text{with} \quad \mu_\Delta(e) = \min_i \mu_i(e) \ .$$

Fuzzy set Δ can be interpreted as fuzzy attribute "desirable". We get

$$\mu_\Delta(e_1) = 0.63 \ , \quad \mu_\Delta(e_2) = 0.86 \ , \quad \mu_\Delta(e_3) = 0.74 \ ,$$

$$\mu_\Delta(e_4) = 0.77 \ , \quad \mu_\Delta(e_5) = 0.00 \ , \quad \mu_\Delta(e_6) = 0.82 \ .$$

Fuzzy attribute Δ can be used to chose a net execution. Of course, several executions may turn out to be optimal, though in our example only e_2 is.

Whenever a decision maker needs preference categories other than strict preference and indifference, we can resort to fuzzy outranking—a technique introduced by B. Roy [5]. Here is how it works.

For each fuzzy attribute $A_i = (e \in E, \ \mu_i(e))$ the decision maker has to provide three threshold values

$$I_i, P_i, V_i \in (0, 1) \quad \text{with} \quad I_i < P_i < V_i \ .$$

These values are interpreted as indifference, preference, and veto threshold, respectively, in the following way:

$$\mathbf{e}_h \text{ is as good as } \mathbf{e}_k \qquad\qquad \text{if} \qquad \mu_i(\mathbf{e}_h) \geq \mu_i(\mathbf{e}_k) + I_i \,,$$

$$\mathbf{e}_h \text{ is preferred to } \mathbf{e}_k \qquad\qquad \text{if} \qquad \mu_i(\mathbf{e}_h) \geq \mu_i(\mathbf{e}_k) + P_i \,,$$

$$\mathbf{e}_h \text{ is considerably better than } \mathbf{e}_k \quad \text{if} \qquad \mu_i(\mathbf{e}_h) \geq \mu_i(\mathbf{e}_k) + V_i \,.$$

Using these threshold values we can define for each attribute A_i its concordance matrix $C^i = [c^i_{ih}]$ and its discordance matrix $D^i = [d^i_{ih}]$:

$$c^i_{hk} = \begin{cases} 1 & \text{if} & \mu_i(e_k) \leq \mu_i(e_h) + I_i \\[2mm] \dfrac{P_i + \mu_i(e_h) - \mu_i(e_k)}{P_i - I_i} & \text{if} & \mu_i(e_h) + I_i < \mu_i(e_k) \leq \mu_i(e_h) + P_i \\[2mm] 0 & \text{if} & \mu_i(e_k) > \mu_i(e_h) + P_i \end{cases}$$

$$d^i_{hk} = \begin{cases} 0 & \text{if} & \mu_i(e_k) \leq \mu_i(e_h) + P_i \\[2mm] \dfrac{\mu_i(e_k) - \mu_i(e_h) - P_i}{V_i - P_i} & \text{if} & \mu_i(e_h) + P_i < \mu_i(e_k) \leq \mu_i(e_h) + V_i \\[2mm] 1 & \text{if} & \mu_i(e_k) > \mu_i(e_h) + V_i \end{cases}$$

The total concordance matrix C is defined as the weighted sum of the concordance matrices of all attributes: $C = [c_{hk}] = \sum_i w_i C^i$.

Concordance matrix C is aggregated with the matrices $D^i = [d^i_{ih}]$ to form the discordance matrix $D = [d_{hk}]$ with $d_{hk} = \dfrac{1}{n} \sum_i \alpha_{ihk}$, where n is the number of fuzzy attributes considered, and

$$\alpha_{ihk} = 1 \text{ if } d^i_{hk} \leq c_{hk} \,, \qquad \alpha_{ihk} = \frac{1 - d^i_{hk}}{1 - c_{hk}} \text{ if } d^i_{hk} > c_{hk}$$

$(d^i_{hk} > c_{hk} \text{ implies } 1 - c_{hk} \neq 0)$.

The outranking degree of execution e_h over execution e_k is finally defined as

$$r_{hk} = c_{hk} d_{hk} \,,$$

and yields the fuzzy outranking relation over E:

$$R = \{ ((e_h, e_k), \mu_R(e_h, e_k)) \mid (e_h, e_k) \in E \times E \wedge \mu_R(e_h, e_k) = r_{hk} \}.$$

In our case, after some algebra, we get:

$$C = \begin{array}{c|c|c|c|c|c|c|} & \mathbf{e}_1 & \mathbf{e}_2 & \mathbf{e}_3 & \mathbf{e}_4 & \mathbf{e}_5 & \mathbf{e}_6 \end{array}$$

	$\mathbf{e}_1$	$\mathbf{e}_2$	$\mathbf{e}_3$	$\mathbf{e}_4$	$\mathbf{e}_5$	$\mathbf{e}_6$
$\mathbf{e}$	1.00	0.11	0.73	0.73	0.36	0.43
$\mathbf{e}_2$	1.00	1.00	1.00	1.00	1.00	1.00
$\mathbf{e}_3$	0.22	0.00	1.00	0.76	0.18	0.08
$\mathbf{e}_4$	0.40	0.00	1.00	1.00	0.18	0.19
$\mathbf{e}_5$	0.85	0.76	0.82	0.82	1.00	0.82
$\mathbf{e}_6$	0.84	0.31	1.00	1.00	0.55	1.00

C =

	$\mathbf{e}_1$	$\mathbf{e}_2$	$\mathbf{e}_3$	$\mathbf{e}_4$	$\mathbf{e}_5$	$\mathbf{e}_6$
$\mathbf{e}_1$	1.00	0.67	0.67	0.67	1.00	0.67
$\mathbf{e}_2$	1.00	1.00	1.00	1.00	1.00	1.00
$\mathbf{e}_3$	0.97	0.28	1.00	1.00	0.72	0.91
$\mathbf{e}_4$	1.00	0.39	1.00	1.00	0.85	1.00
$\mathbf{e}_5$	1.00	0.67	0.67	0.67	1.00	0.67
$\mathbf{e}_6$	1.00	0.67	1.00	1.00	1.00	1.00

D =

	$\mathbf{e}_1$	$\mathbf{e}_2$	$\mathbf{e}_3$	$\mathbf{e}_4$	$\mathbf{e}_5$	$\mathbf{e}_6$
$\mathbf{e}_1$	1.00	0.08	0.48	0.48	0.36	0.28
$\mathbf{e}_2$	1.00	1.00	1.00	1.00	1.00	1.00
$\mathbf{e}_3$	0.22	0.00	1.00	0.76	0.13	0.07
$\mathbf{e}_4$	0.40	0.00	1.00	1.00	0.16	0.19
$\mathbf{e}_5$	0.85	0.51	0.55	0.55	1.00	0.55
$\mathbf{e}_6$	0.84	0.21	1.00	1.00	0.55	1.00

R =

The entries of the i-th row of R represent the degree to which execution $\mathbf{e}_i$ outranks the other executions. The minimum value of the i-th row—let us denote it by z_i—is the outranking degree of execution $\mathbf{e}_i$, that is, the degree to which $\mathbf{e}_i$ outranks all other executions. Here we have:

$$z_1 = 0.08 \ , \ z_2 = 1 \ , \ z_3 = 0 \ , \ z_4 = 0 \ , \ z_5 = 0.51 \ , \ z_6 = 0.21 \ .$$

These values can be used for clustering net executions into several preference classes. To this end, the decision maker will have to (a) determine the number n of preference classes he intends to consider, and (b) set n preference thresholds λ_j, with

$$0 < \lambda_1 < \lambda_2 < \ldots < \lambda_n < 1.$$

Best executions will be executions $\mathbf{e}_i$ for which $\lambda_n < z_i \leq 1$, second best executions will be executions $\mathbf{e}_i$ for which $\lambda_{n-1} < z_i \leq \lambda_n$, and so on.

In our example, by using two preference thresholds only, $\lambda_1 = 0.5$ and $\lambda_2 = 0.7$, we get one best execution $\mathbf{e}_2$—already found before—and one second-best execution, $\mathbf{e}_5$. Other threshold settings would make for empty preference classes.

That we only got one execution per desirability class is not surprising, given that we considered only six net executions out of the twenty four enabled at the initial marking of net N under the additional constraint that same-type orders should not be split between machines.

Actual applications usually encompass a substantially larger number of enabled executions, and preference classes with several members. Our algorithm may therefore take some computing time. If necessary, this can be shortened by reducing the search space by means of some heuristics, and by storing classification results in a data base for future reference.

6 Conclusions

We are convinced that a Petri net model of the causal structure of a business operation can provide a firm logical foundation and a realistic context for the application of algorithms of applied mathematics, decision theory, game theory, operation research, statistics, etc.—to business management questions. However, there certainly are important types of business operations not suitable to Petri net representation; specific requirements—discussed in Section 2—must be fulfilled. We argue that if they are, the key to the successful grafting of those algorithms onto Petri nets is provided by the modeling flexibility of predicate-transition nets. This will equip Petri net models with a very efficient computational toolkit.

References

1. Pagnoni A.: Project Engineering: Computer-Oriented Planning and Operational Decision Making, Springer-Verlag, Berlin Heidelberg New York (1992)
2. Genrich H.J.: Predicate/Transition Nets. In: Brauer, Reisig, and Rozenberg (eds.): Petri Nets: Central Models and Their Properties, Part I. Springer-Verlag, Berlin Heidelberg New York (1987) 207—247
3. Genrich H.J., Lautenbach K.: System Modelling with High-Level Petri Nets. Theoretical Computer Science, 13 (1981) 98—111
4. Saaty T.L.: The Analytic Hierarchy process: Planning, Priority Setting, and Resource Allocation. MacGraw Hill, New York (1980)
5. Roy B.: Partial Preference Analysis and Decision-Aid: Fuzzy Outranking Relation Concept. SEMA, Paris (1976)

Validation of Process Models
by Construction of Process Nets[*]

Jörg Desel

Lehrstuhl für Angewandte Informatik
Katholische Universität Eichstätt, Germany
joerg.desel@ku-eichstaett.de

Abstract. The major aim of this chapter is to describe an approach towards the development of techniques and tools to support the construction, validation and the verification of Petri net models of information
systems and business processes. To this end, the behavior of the models
is defined by partially ordered causal runs, represented by process nets.
We discuss how these runs are constructed and visualized for validation
purposes, and how they are analyzed. Moreover, we demonstrate how different dynamic properties can be formulated and checked by searching
respective patterns in process nets.

1 Introduction

Petri nets are frequently used for modeling both information systems and business processes. Whereas an information system model captures all its business
processes and their interplay, a business process model can be viewed as a part
of an information system model, leading from some input or trigger to some output or termination. We will not distinguish models of information systems and
models of their business processes in the first sections of this chapter because
most introduced concepts apply to both. We rather use the term "system" for
information systems and for business processes.

Each system has a dynamic behavior, given by its set of *runs*. In a run,
actions of the system can occur. We will distinguish actions from *action occurrences* and call the latter *events*. In general, an action can occur more than once
in a single run. Therefore, several events of a run might refer to the same action.

There are basically two different techniques to describe the behavior of a Petri
net model: A run of the model can either be represented by a sequence of action
names (a sequence of sets of action names, respectively) representing subsequent
events (sets of events, respectively) or by a causally ordered set of events. The
first technique is formally described by *occurrence sequences* (*step sequences*,
respectively). It constitutes the *sequential semantics* of a Petri net. The second
technique employs *process nets* representing *causal runs*. It constitutes the
causal semantics of a Petri net.

---

[*] work done within the project VIP, supported by the DFG (Deutsche Forschungsgemeinschaft)

W. van der Aalst et al.(Eds.): Business Process Management, LNCS 1806, pp. 110-128, 2000.

The main advantage of sequential semantics is formal simplicity. Sequential semantics generalizes well-known concepts of sequential systems: Every occurrence sequence can be viewed as a sequence of global system states and transformations leading from a state to a successor state. One of the main advantages of causal semantics is its explicit representation of causal dependency, represented by paths of directed arcs in process nets. Consequently, concurrent events are events that are not connected by a path in a process net.

Causal semantics of Petri nets has been studied in Petri net theory since a very long time, starting with the work of Carl Adam Petri in the 70ies (see [1]) for an overview). More recently, variants of causal semantics are used for efficient verification algorithms [8]. Applications of Petri nets, however, mostly restrict to sequential semantics, and so do most Petri net tools.

In the majority of applications, Petri nets are used for the specification, documentation and communication of planned or existing systems. They can be executed, i.e., runs can be generated, and thus the behavior of the system can be simulated and visualized. The aim of simulation is to validate the model with respect to its behavioral properties. So, in contrast to verification of correctness with respect to a formal specification, the user can check if the desired behavior is reflected in simulated runs of the model. The issue of our work is to employ causal semantics also for simulation. We will show that, despite some formal overhead, there are a number of important advantages of causal semantics compared to sequential semantics in the application area of information systems and business processes.

The remaining part of this chapter is organized as follows: In Section 2, we discuss some principles of causal semantics and provide a Petri net model that will serve as a running example in the subsequent sections. Section 3 gives some formal definitions and properties of process nets. In Section 4, we show that simulation with process nets increases expressiveness and efficiency, compared to sequential simulation. Section 5 is devoted to the construction of process nets whereas Section 6 discusses the analysis of process nets. Finally, Section 7 generalizes the approach from place/transition nets to high-level Petri nets. The chapter ends with conclusions and references.

2 Principles of Causal Semantics

In sequential semantics, a run is represented by a sequence of events such that causal dependencies are respected: If an event causally depends on another event, then these events will not appear in the converse order in a sequence. Each event is represented by the name of the respective action. These sequences are called *occurrence sequences*.

A causal run also consists of a set of events, representing action occurrences of the system. An action can only occur in certain system states, i.e. its pre-conditions have to be satisfied. The occurrence of the action leads to a new system state where some post-conditions of the action start to hold. An event is therefore causally dependent on certain pre-conditions and might lead to new

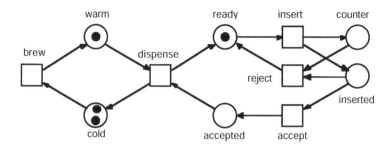

Fig. 1. A vending machine for beverages

conditions that are causal prerequisites for other events. The time and the duration of an event has no immediate influence on the system's behavior, as long as such dependencies are not explicitly modeled as actions of clocks. Combining events with their pre- and post-conditions yields the *causal structure* of a causal run of a system.

We represent the causal structure of a causal run by a particular Petri net, called *process net*. Pre- and post-conditions of events are explicitly modeled in a process net. Therefore, the immediate causal dependency is represented by the arcs of a process net. The transitive closure of this relation defines a partial order that we will call *causal order*; two events are causally ordered if and only if they are connected by a chain of directed arcs. Otherwise, they are not ordered but occur *concurrently*.

A causal run of a system model is given by a process net which is annotated by respective names of actions of the system. More formally, we define mappings from the net elements of the process net to the net elements of the net representing the system. *Causal simulation* of a system model means construction of process nets, just like traditional simulation constructs sequences of events.

Figure 1 shows a place/transition Petri net modeling a vending machine for beverages. We will use this example to demonstrate our approach. The left hand part describes a physical facility for brewing and dispensing warm beverages. At most three warm beverages can be prepared concurrently. After dispensing a beverage, cold water is filled in the respective unit, hence the place *cold* in the post-set of the transition *dispense*. The right-hand part describes the control of the machine and a counter for coins. Initially, the machine is ready for the insertion of a coin. An inserted coin will be checked; counterfeit will be rejected. When a coin is accepted, a beverage can be dispensed and the control part of the machine returns to the state *ready*.

Process nets of this system model are shown in Figures 2, 3 and 4. The relation between elements of these process nets and elements of the system net is given by annotations of the elements of the process nets. For example, each event annotated by *insert* represents one occurrence of the transition named *insert* of the system net.

The process nets shown in Figure 2 and Figure 3 describe causal runs where

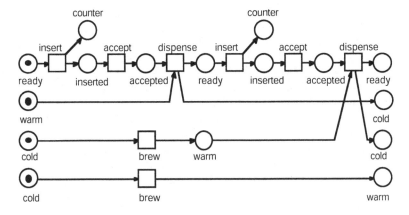

Fig. 2. A process net of the vending machine of Figure 1

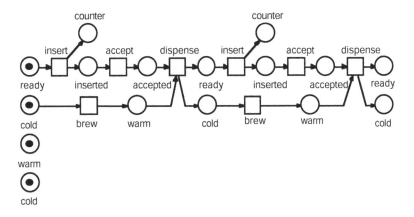

Fig. 3. A second process net of the vending machine of Figure 1

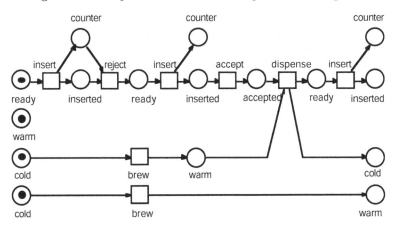

Fig. 4. A third process net of the vending machine of Figure 1

two coins are inserted, both are accepted, and two beverages are dispensed. In both runs, two beverages are brewed, and so both runs end with two tokens in *counter*, state *ready*, and two cold and one warm beverage.

In Figure 2, the beverage that was warm initially is dispensed first. The second dispensed beverage was brewed concurrently to all previous events. In Figure 3 the capacity of the brewing facility is not exploited: The second *dispense* event has to wait after the first *dispense* event at least the time necessary for brewing a beverage. Moreover, the first *dispense* does not use an initially warm beverage. So one could consider the run of Figure 2 more efficient with respect to response time. Moreover, the quality of a warm beverage might decrease after a while (this holds at least for coffee). Also according to this criterion, the run of Figure 2 shows a "better" behavior than the one of Figure 3.

The process net shown in Figure 4 describes a causal run where the first inserted coin is rejected. The second inserted coin is accepted and a beverage is dispensed. This beverage is not the one that was warm initially. Concurrently, a third beverage is brewed but not dispensed. This run ends with two tokens in *counter*, state *inserted*, and two *warm* and one *cold* beverage.

3   Formal Definitions

We follow the the standard definitions and notations of place/transition nets and process nets [12,7]. However, in contrast to the usual notion, we equip process nets with initial states, represented by markings of conditions.

A place/transition net $N = (P, T, F, M_0)$ is given by

- a finite set P of places (represented by circles),
- a finite set T of transitions satisfying $P \cap T = \emptyset$ (represented by squares),
- a relation $F \subseteq (P \cup T) \times (P \cup T)$ satisfying $F \cap (P \times P) = F \cap (T \times T) = \emptyset$ (represented by arcs), called the flow relation of the net, and
- an initial marking $M_0: P \to I\!N$ (represented by tokens in the places), where $I\!N$ is the set of nonnegative integers.

For a net element x in $P \cup T$, $^\bullet x$ (pre-set of x) denotes the set of elements y satisfying $(y, x) \in F$ and $x^\bullet$ (post-set of x) denotes the set of elements y satisfying $(x, y) \in F$. In this chapter, we restrict our considerations to place/transition nets without transitions t satisfying $^\bullet t = \emptyset$ or $t^\bullet = \emptyset$.

We do not consider arc weights or capacity restrictions, as defined in [12,7].

Given an arbitrary marking $M: P \to I\!N$, a transition t is enabled if each place p in $^\bullet t$ satisfies $M(p) \geq 1$. The occurrence of t leads to a new marking M', defined by

$$M'(p) = \begin{cases} M(p) - 1 & \text{if } (p, t) \in F \text{ and } (t, p) \notin F, \\ M(p) + 1 & \text{if } (p, t) \notin F \text{ and } (t, p) \in F, \\ M(p) & \text{otherwise.} \end{cases}$$

We denote the occurrence of t at the marking M by $M \xrightarrow{t} M'$.

The causal behavior of a system net (P, T, F, M_0) is defined by its set of process nets, representing causal runs. For the formal definition of a process net, we employ again place/transition nets: Each process net of the system net (P, T, F, M_0) consists of a place/transition net (C, E, K, S_0), together with mappings $\alpha: C \to P$ and $\beta: E \to T$, satisfying the conditions given below. The net (C, E, K, S_0) is called *process net*, its places are called *conditions*, its transitions *events* and its markings *states*. To avoid confusion, the place/transition net model (P, T, F, M_0) of the system will be called *system net*.

- Every condition c in C satisfies $|{}^\bullet c| \leq 1$ and $|c^\bullet| \leq 1$,
- the transitive closure of K is irreflexive, i.e., it is a partial order over $C \cup E$,
- for each event e, $\alpha \cap ({}^\bullet e \times {}^\bullet \beta(e))$ as well as $\alpha \cap (e^\bullet \times (\beta(e))^\bullet)$ are bijections (these intersections restrict the domain of α to the pre-set (post-set) of e and the co-domain of α to the pre-set (post-set, respectively) of the corresponding transition $\beta(e)$),
- $S_0(c) = 1$ for each condition c in C satisfying ${}^\bullet c = \emptyset$ and $S_0(c) = 0$ for any other condition c in C,
- $\alpha(S_0) = M_0$, where α is generalized to states S by

$$\alpha: (C \to I\!N) \to (P \to I\!N), \quad \alpha(S)(p) = \sum_{\alpha(c)=p} S(c).$$

A condition c in C represents the appearance of a token on the place $\alpha(c)$. An event e in E represents the occurrence of the transition $\beta(e)$. In a run, each token is produced by at most one transition occurrence, and it is consumed by at most one transition occurrence. Hence, conditions of process nets are not branched. The transitive closure of K defines the *causal relation* on events and conditions. Since no two elements can be mutually causally dependent, the causal relation is a partial order. In other words, the process net has no cycles. Since events represent transition occurrences, the pre- and post-sets of these transitions are respected. The initial state of the process net is the characteristic mapping of the set of conditions that are minimal with respect to the causal order, i.e., these conditions carry one token each and all other conditions are initially unmarked. Note that all minimal elements are conditions because, by our general assumption, every event has at least one pre-condition. Finally, the initial state of the process net corresponds to the initial marking of the system net, i.e., each initial token of the system net is represented by a (marked) minimal condition of the process net.

As mentioned before, a process net represents a single causal run of a system net. We equip a process net with an initial state S_0 so that the token game can be played for process nets as well. As will be stated in the following lemma, the sequences of event occurrences of a process net closely correspond to transition sequences of the system net. It may be worth noticing that in a process net every event can occur exactly once and that the order of these event occurrences respects the causal order given by the causal relation. Every reachable state is safe, i.e., no condition ever carries more than one token. Moreover, in every reachable state, no two marked conditions are ordered by the causal relation.

Lemma 1. [1]

Let (P, T, F, M_0) be a place/transition net. If (C, E, K, S_0) together with mappings $\alpha \colon C \to P$ and $\beta \colon E \to T$ is a process net and

$$S_0 \xrightarrow{e_1} S_1 \xrightarrow{e_2} \cdots \xrightarrow{e_n} S_n$$

is a sequence of event occurrences, then

$$M_0 \xrightarrow{\beta(e_1)} \alpha(S_1) \xrightarrow{\beta(e_2)} \cdots \xrightarrow{\beta(e_n)} \alpha(S_n)$$

is a sequence of transition occurrences of (P, T, F, M_0).
Conversely, for each sequence

$$M_0 \xrightarrow{t_1} M_1 \xrightarrow{t_2} \cdots \xrightarrow{t_n} M_n$$

of transition occurrences of (P, T, F, M_0), there is a process net (C, E, K, S_0) with mappings $\alpha \colon C \to P$ and $\beta \colon E \to T$ and a sequence of event occurrences

$$S_0 \xrightarrow{e_1} S_1 \xrightarrow{e_2} \cdots \xrightarrow{e_n} S_n$$

such that, for $1 \le i \le n$, $\alpha(S_i) = M_i$ and $\beta(e_i) = t_i$.

The first part of the lemma follows immediately from the definition of process nets because transition vicinities are respected by the mappings α and β. For proving the converse direction, we can successively construct a suitable process net by adding events with pre- and post-conditions according to the occurring transitions. However, in general this construction is not unique. For example, the occurrence sequence of transitions

$$M_0 \xrightarrow{insert} M_1 \xrightarrow{accept} M_2 \xrightarrow{brew} M_3 \xrightarrow{dispense} M_4 \xrightarrow{insert} M_5 \xrightarrow{accept} M_6 \xrightarrow{brew} M_7 \xrightarrow{dispense} M_8$$

has related occurrence sequences of events in both process nets shown in Figure 2 and in Figure 3.

Lemma 1 states that process nets respect the sequential behavior; no information about possible occurrence sequences is gained or lost when we consider process nets. Moreover, it states that reachable markings of the system net closely correspond to reachable states of its process nets. The following lemma gives another characterization of reachable states of process nets.

Lemma 2. [1]

Let (C, E, K, S_0) be a process net of a place/transition net. A state S is reachable from S_0 (by a sequence of event occurrences) if and only if S is the characteristic mapping of a maximal set of pairwise not ordered conditions.

Maximal sets of conditions that are mutually not ordered are often called *cuts*. By Lemmas 1 and 2 a marking of a system net is reachable if and only if there exists a process net with a cut that corresponds to this marking.

4   Simulation by Generation of Process Nets

The behavior of a system modeled by a Petri net is validated by simulation of the net; every run of the net gives information on the possible behavior of the system. In particular, if a run shows undesirable properties, then either the system is not correct or it is not faithfully modeled by the net. Traditionally, simulation of a net means construction of sequences of transition occurrences. The designer can analyze these sequences to investigate the system's behavior. In case of many or large simulation runs, these sequences will be constructed automatically and stored in a data base. In case of small simulation runs, the transition occurrences and the reached markings can be visualized by Petri net tools such that the user has direct control over the simulation run.

In our approach, not sequences but process nets representing causal runs are constructed. In this section, we argue that we gain two major advantages: expressiveness and efficiency.

Expressiveness

Every sequence of events, i.e. transition occurrences, defines a total order on these events. A transition can either occur after another transition because there is a causal dependency between these occurrences or the order is just an arbitrarily chosen order between concurrent transition occurrences. Hence, an occurrence sequence gives little information on the causal structure of the system run.

Consider again the following occurrence sequence of the place/transition net given in Figure 1:

$$M_0 \xrightarrow{insert} M_1 \xrightarrow{accept} M_2 \xrightarrow{brew} M_3 \xrightarrow{dispense} M_4 \xrightarrow{insert} M_5 \xrightarrow{accept} M_6 \xrightarrow{brew} M_7 \xrightarrow{dispense} M_8$$

This sequence corresponds to both process nets given in Figure 2 and 3. It is a sequential view of both causal runs because both process nets possess corresponding occurrence sequences. As argued before, the run of Figure 2 has reasonable advantages compared to the run of Figure 3. The above sequence does not distinguish between both runs. In particular, the sequence does not express important behavioral properties that are distinguished by causal runs.

The occurrence sequence given above contains no information about the causal ordering of the occurrences of the transitions *brew* and *dispense*: Either the beverage brewed first is dispensed first or the beverage which was warm initially is dispensed first. Causal runs provide full information about these causal dependencies. They clearly distinguish runs with different causal dependencies between events.

Interesting aspects of system behavior such as the flow of control, the flow of goods, possible parallel behavior etc. are directly represented in process nets, but they are hidden in sequences of events. The process net shown in Figure 2 shows very clearly the flow of control (*ready, insert, inserted, accept, ...*) and the different local states and events of the beverages (e.g., *cold, brew, warm, dispense, ...*).

Efficiency

Simulation of a system model means construction of a set of (different) runs. In general, each causal run corresponds to a nonempty set of occurrence sequences. This correspondence is formally established by Lemma 1: Taking the sequence of labels of events in occurrence sequences of process nets yields all occurrence sequences of the system net. However, since different events of a process net might have the same annotation, different occurrence sequences of the process net might relate to the same occurrence sequence of the system net.

In the example shown in Figure 2, the upper event *brew* can occur at any position before the second *dispense* event. The lower *brew* event can occur at an arbitrary position in the occurrence sequence. So the process net of Figure 2 possesses 48 maximal occurrence sequences. Some of these sequences are identical with respect to event labels, but they still represent 27 different occurrence sequences of the system net. The process net of Figure 3 exhibits 9 occurrence sequences which correspond to 9 different occurrence sequences of the system net. The process net of Figure 4 has 40 occurrence sequences, generating 25 different occurrence sequences of the system net.

The number of occurrence sequences of a single process net grows dramatically when a system exhibits more concurrency. The addition of a beverage unit to the system, and a corresponding concurrent event *brew* to the process net of Figure 2, multiplies the number of different occurrence sequences of the process net by increasing factors 9, 10, 11, ... In general, the number of occurrence sequences of a single process net grows exponentially with the number of concurrent transitions. Each of these occurrence sequences represents the very same system run. Hence, the simulation of more than one of these sequences yields no additional information on the behavior of the system. However, if a system exhibits no concurrency at all, then nothing is gained by the construction of process nets because in this case each process net has only one maximal occurrence sequence.

On the other hand, as mentioned in the previous subsection, a single occurrence sequence might correspond to more than one process. For example, the above occurrence sequence corresponds to four process nets. This only happens in case of system nets that are not safe, i.e. have more than one token on a place at a reachable marking. So the ratio between the number of process nets and the number of occurrence sequences might be slightly reduced by this fact in case of non-safe system nets.

These considerations should demonstrate that the construction of process nets is considerably more efficient than the construction of occurrence sequences. This advantage is most evident when all runs of a system can be simulated, i.e. when there is only a finite number of finite runs. In the more general case of arbitrary large runs, a set of process nets allows to represent a larger significant part of the behavior than a comparable set of occurrence sequences.

5 Construction of Process Nets

This section is concerned with the question how process nets of a system net are constructed. The core idea is to start with a set of marked conditions that correspond to the initial marking and then subsequently add suitable events, add arcs to their pre-conditions, add post-conditions, and add arcs from the new event to the post-conditions. In other words, we consider an occurrence sequence of the system net and construct a process net such that this occurrence sequence is a sequence of labels of the occurrence sequence of the process net. The existence of a suitable process net is guaranteed by Lemma 1. As an example, the process net of Figure 2 could have been constructed by starting with the four marked conditions and then adding eight events labeled by

$$insert, accept, brew, dispense, insert, accept, brew, dispense.$$

This procedure relates to the following occurrence sequence of the system:

$$M_0 \xrightarrow{insert} M_1 \xrightarrow{accept} M_2 \xrightarrow{brew} M_3 \xrightarrow{dispense} M_4 \xrightarrow{insert} M_5 \xrightarrow{accept} M_6 \xrightarrow{brew} M_7 \xrightarrow{dispense} M_8.$$

As stated before, this process net possesses a corresponding occurrence sequence, but it also represents several more different occurrence sequences.

Problems during the construction of process nets are concerned with *fairness*, *alternatives* and *termination conditions*.

Fairness

In general, a marking of a system net can enable more than one transition. Accordingly, at any stage of the construction of a process, there might be several ways to continue. Transition occurrences can either exclude each other – because they use the same input token – or they can be concurrent. During the construction of a process net, we have to distinguish these phenomena:

- The addition of a new event can exclude another event. Then, adding one or the other event leads to different process nets.
- In case of concurrent events, the events can be added in an arbitrary order, yielding the same process net.

As an example, consider again the process net shown in Figure 2. The first *insert* event (together with its post-conditions *counter* and *inserted*) can be added at the beginning of the process. The two *brew* events occur concurrently. These three events can be added in an arbitrary order. After addition of the *insert* event, there is a choice to continue with *accept* (as in the process net of Figure 2) or to continue with *reject* (as in the process net of Figure 4). These events exclude each other.

Fairness issues concern both alternative and concurrent events. We only consider fairness of concurrent events. Therefore, we have to ensure that an event that can be added to a process net constructed so far will eventually be added, provided no alternative event is added to the process net. In our example, this means that we do not construct arbitrary large process nets where one beverage remains cold forever; otherwise the transition *brew* would be persistently enabled and hence it will eventually occur and an according event will be added.

A fair construction ensures that every concurrent part of the system is reflected in the run. Fairness can be guaranteed by scheduling the process net construction stochastically. Then, the probability of the occurrence of a persistently enabled event increases with the size of the constructed process net.

The fairness problem is not specific for causal simulation. The same problem appears when only sequences of events are constructed in sequential simulation. However, for sequential runs, a clear distinction between concurrent events and alternative events is impossible.

Alternatives

As mentioned above, transition occurrences can exclude each other. More precisely, at some reachable marking, the occurrence of a transition might disable another transition and vice versa. During the construction of a process net, this means that there is an alternative between two events that can be added to a process net constructed so far, and both events have a common pre-condition. Remember that in process nets we cannot add both events, because conditions of process nets are not branched.

Consider again the example process net of Figure 2. After the addition of *insert*, there is an alternative to continue with *accept* or with *reject*. These choices lead to different process nets. Another alternative appears after the addition of the events *insert*, *accept* and *brew*. In this situation, one enabled transition is *dispense*. We have the choice to dispense the beverage that was warm initially or to dispense the freshly brewed beverage. These are different events, that both have the condition labeled *accepted* as a pre-condition. Their respective addition leads to different process nets.

For the construction of different process nets, alternatives in process nets constructed so far have to be found. To this end, we identify reachable markings of process nets with the following property:

- The process net continues with some event e,
- the process net could also continue with some event $e' \neq e$,
- e and e' share at least one input condition, and
- no process net constructed so far coincides with the process net under consideration up to this marking, and continues with e' (more precisely, it continues with some event mapped to the same transition and using the same input conditions as e').

We then continue with the event e', i.e., we consider the process net up to the marked places (with respect to the marking considered above) and add an event e', suitable arcs from marked input conditions, suitable output conditions as well as arcs connecting e' to these output conditions.

Termination conditions

A causal run does not necessarily terminate with a marking that enables no transition. It is even often part of the system specification that every reachable marking enables some transition. For these systems, termination is an undesirable behavior and terminating markings are considered errors or *deadlocks*. Operating systems, elevators, plants etc. are examples for such systems. The simulation of the behavior of a system modeled by a Petri net, however, necessarily has to stop eventually. Here we discuss criteria for the termination of a single causal run.

At this point, the difference between system models for information systems and system models for process nets is important. Termination of an information system is usually undesirable because it means that the information system has reached a deadlock and no business process can continue or can be started again. In contrast, termination of a business process is highly desired because each business process should finally lead to an end. In our example of Figure 1, the information system model corresponds to the entire Petri net and an according business process model corresponds to the entire Petri net except the transition *insert*. Starting with the marking reached after the occurrence of *insert*, this business process will either stop after rejection or after accepting and dispensing a beverage. The process nets of Figure 2, 3, and 4 contain several *insert* events and hence they represent the behavior of more than one business process. Simulation of runs of single business processes is not so illustrative because the interplay between both parts of the system is only interesting when more than one business process has been started.

The simplest way to define a termination criterion is to use a bound in terms of the number of created elements or in terms of simulation time. In general this method does not lead to "good" termination situations, as will be discussed next. However, if no other criterion is applicable, simulation has to be stopped by this method.

Sometimes, the earliest reachable state of a process net after an event e corresponds to a marking of the system net that in turn corresponds to a state reached in the same process net before. Then we have entered a cyclic behavior and can stop after e without loosing any information about reachable markings. More precisely, we do not add any further events causally after e. Formally, the event e is a *cut-off event* in the terminology of [8].

Another possibility is that the earliest reachable state of a process net after an event e corresponds to a marking that also corresponds to a state of another process net constructed before. Then, a possible continuation can be constructed from this other process net, too. In this case, we stop the construction of the current process net with all conditions that belong to the earliest reachable state after e. It might even be necessary to delete elements that are causally after these conditions.

Usually, a system model has interfaces to its environment. For example, in our vending machine example, the transition *insert* cannot occur without a corresponding action of the environment: Some user has to insert a coin. So we can distinguish *internal* transitions of the Petri net model, that are forced to occur when they are enabled and *external* transitions, that are allowed to occur when they are enabled but might remain enabled forever without occurring. In a causal run we expect that a system does not terminate as long as internal transitions are enabled. If only external transitions are enabled, then the system may terminate, and we might stop simulation. In our simulation approach, we start with the occurrence of internal and external transitions. After a while, we stop the occurrences of external transitions and continue with internal events only. For systems that require repeated interaction with the environment, the simulation run will eventually terminate. In our example, the vending machine will eventually stop in the state *ready* with all beverages warm and some number of coins in *counter*, provided that the external transition *insert* is stopped eventually.

6   Analysis of Process Nets

When large and/or many process nets are constructed, inspection by visualization is no longer feasible. Instead, the model has to be validated by automatic analysis of the process nets. The user has to identify certain desired or undesirable properties every run has to satisfy, and a computer tool checks whether these specifications hold for the generated process nets. In our approach, the specification of the properties can be done in the (graphical representation of the) system model. We distinguish three classes of properties.

Facts

A *fact* is an invariant property that holds for all reachable markings of a system model. We can check intended facts in simulation runs by analyzing all reached states. This is simple for sequential simulation runs, because the markings reached during a run can explicitly be represented. We show how facts can be checked more efficiently using causal semantics.

Here, we only consider properties of markings requiring that not all places of a given set of places are marked simultaneously. A typical example is *mutual exclusion* of critical sections of parallel programs: Two places representing the critical sections should never be marked together. In our example, the set {*ready*, *accepted*} is a fact, because there is no reachable marking where these two places are both marked. The set {*ready*, *counter*} is not a fact because there is a reachable marking that marks *ready* as well as *counter*.

Simulation can help to identify violations of intended facts (facts cannot be proved by simulation, as long as not all process nets of a system are constructed). The process net of Figure 2 can be used to show that {*ready*, *counter*} is not a fact. For this purpose, it is not necessary to play the token game. It rather suffices to find conditions labeled by *ready* and *counter*, respectively, that are not ordered, i.e., not connected by a directed path. In fact, the condition *counter* in the post-set of the first *insert* event and the second condition *ready* are not ordered. Every set of unordered conditions is a subset of a cut (i.e., a maximal set of unordered conditions). Every cut corresponds to a reachable state of the process net by Lemma 2. Every state of the process net corresponds to a reachable marking of the system net by Lemma 1. Hence, the two unordered conditions prove that there is a reachable marking of the system net that marks both places.

This example proved that causal simulation allows a very efficient way to identify violations of facts; we only have to investigate conditions that are accordingly labeled and mutually not causally dependent. Using sequential simulation instead, a fact violation is only recognized if the order of concurrent events in an occurrence sequence is chosen in such a way that a marking disproving the fact is actually reached. This is a particular drawback when system components are modeled at different levels of abstraction. Consider e.g. two concurrent system components, one modeled by two subsequent transitions and the other one by, say, 100 subsequent transitions. Now consider the marking reached after the occurrence of the first transition of the first component and after the first 50 transitions of the second component. Assume that this and only this marking violates a given fact. This violation is easily recognized by construction of the corresponding unique process net. Using sequential simulation, it is only recognized if the second transition of the first component does not occur before the 50 transition occurrences of the second component. Using any stochastic strategy to chose among concurrent transitions, recognition of the fact violation turns out to be not very likely. Even using different weights for the occurrence probability of transitions does not help much because there is in general no a priori knowledge on the granularity of different components.

Facts can be specified in the system by so-called fact-transitions. A fact transition can be viewed as a special transition which does not belong to the system and which should never become enabled. The following fact-transition represents the fact that, at no reachable marking, both places a and b are marked.

As shown above, the analysis of process nets w.r.t. facts reduces to searching a set of appropriately labeled mutually unordered conditions. This can be viewed as a simple pattern in the process:

The pattern is interpreted as follows: there are two conditions in the process, labeled by a and b respectively, such that there is no order between them. We will show next that other system properties can be reduced to a pattern searching problem in a similar way.

Causal Chains

The next property under consideration is based on immediate causal dependencies. For example, we might be interested in runs of our vending machine where two subsequently dispensed beverages use the same brewing facility; then the second user has to wait until the beverage is brewed while there might be two available warm beverages that could be dispensed immediately. In such a run, unnecessary delay occurs. Sequential simulation cannot identify such runs because the beverages are not distinguished by occurrence sequences. In causal semantics, a corresponding process net is shown in Figure 3. In general, we are looking for process nets exhibiting the following pattern:

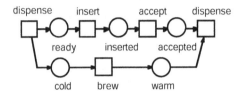

More abstractly, the user can specify that two *dispense*-events have a distance of only four subsequent arcs, which means that some path with only for directed arcs connecting the events exists.

Goals

The last property we like to discuss refers to the eventual occurrence of certain transitions. For example, one could require that after insertion of a coin either the coin is rejected or a beverage is dispensed. More generally, given two sets of transitions A and B, we require that every occurrence of an A-transition is eventually followed by an occurrence of a B-transition. In terms of process nets, this means that for every event labeled by an A-transition we find a causally subsequent event that is labeled by a B-transition. Notice that this property can only be checked when a simulation is not terminated artificially after some A-transition. Usually, goals should be reached even if external transitions do not occur. Hence, the termination criterion of the previous section using internal and external transitions respects goals.

As the other properties, a goal can be checked by searching respective patterns in process nets. In the above example, for every *insert* event we have to find a directed path that either leads to a *reject* event or to a *dispense* event.

Goals can be specified at the system level by special goal-places:

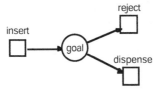

Filter

Simulation combined with analysis of process nets can be used to find out if the system model exhibits undesired behavior. Another application of the same concept is to filter process nets and then validate or analyze the remaining causal runs. For example, one could be interested in those runs of the example system net shown in Figure 1 not containing any *reject* event or in those runs not containing a causal chain pattern as described in the previous section. Using this approach, it is possible to visualize and validate only runs with certain behavior. This can be useful if only a specific feature of a system has to be checked. It is also possible to assume some properties which are not implemented in the model yet. So one can begin with a rough model together with some behavioral specification, generate causal runs of the model, ignore those runs which do not satisfy the specification and continue validation and analysis with the remaining runs. In this sense, the method supports an incremental system design, where specifications are successively implemented in the system model.

7   High-Level Petri Nets

High-level Petri nets allow to use individual tokens instead of indistinguishable tokens of place/transition nets. They allow a much more compact representation of systems. In industrial applications, high-level nets have great advantages compared to place/transition nets because they combine the graphical representation of Petri nets with the possibility to capture data. In this section, we sketch how our approach works for high-level Petri nets. First, we need some definitions.

Given a set A, a *multiset* over A is a mapping from A to $I\!N$. Multisets generalize sets but a multiset can contain several identical copies of an element. As an example, a marking of a place/transition net can be viewed as a multiset over its set of places where the number of tokens on a place defines its multiplicity. We call a multiset over A finite if only finitely many elements of A are not mapped to 0. The set of multisets over A is denoted by $\mathcal{M}(A)$. The sum (and difference, if applicable) of two multisets is defined element-wise for each element of A.

A *high-level Petri net* is given by

- sets P, T and F, defined as in the definition of a place/transition net,
- a set A of *individual tokens* and a domain $A_p \subseteq A$ for each place p in P,
- an *initial marking* M_0, where an arbitrary *marking* $M : P \to \mathcal{M}(A)$ assigns to each place p in P a finite multiset $M(p)$ in $\mathcal{M}(A_p)$,
- a set of modes μ_t for each transition t in T,
- for each pair (p, t) in $F \cap (P \times T)$, an input-mapping $i_{(p,t)} : \mu_t \to \mathcal{M}(A_p)$ specifying the tokens on the place p necessary for the occurrence of t in mode $m \in \mu_t$,
- for each pair (t, p) in $F \cap (T \times P)$, an output-mapping $o_{(t,p)} : \mu_t \to \mathcal{M}(A_p)$.
- When a transition t occurs in mode $m \in \mu_t$ at a marking M, then a successor marking M' will be reached, defined by

$$M'(p) = \begin{cases} M(p) - i_{(p,t)}(m) & \text{if } (p,t) \in F \text{ and } (t,p) \notin F \\ M(p) + o_{(t,p)}(m) & \text{if } (p,t) \notin F \text{ and } (t,p) \in F \\ M(p) - i_{(p,t)}(m) + o_{(t,p)}(m) & \text{if } (p,t) \in F \text{ and } (t,p) \in F \\ M(p) & \text{if } (p,t) \notin F \text{ and } (t,p) \notin F \end{cases}$$

The inscription of places by elements of their domains denotes the initial marking.

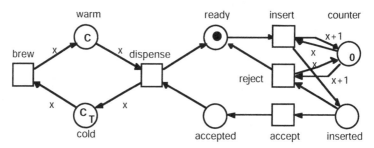

Fig. 5. A high-level Petri net model of the vending machine

For an example of a high-level Petri net, consider Figure 5. The set A of individual tokens is $\{C, T, \bullet\} \cup I\!N$. The domain of the places *warm* and *cold* is $\{C, T\}$ (for coffee and tea, respectively), the domain of *counter* is $I\!N$, and the domain of each other place is $\{\bullet\}$. Initially, all places are marked by sets, as shown in the figure. The transitions *brew* and *dispense* can occur in two different modes each, moving either a C- or a T-token. After the occurrence of *brew* in mode C, the place *warm* carries two C-tokens, i.e. its marking is $\{(C, 2), (T, 0)\}$. The transitions *insert* and *reject* can occur in each mode $n \in I\!N$. The input- and output-mappings are given by the annotations of the arcs. For example, the mode C of *dispense* associates the value C to the arcs $(warm, dispense)$ and $(dispense, cold)$ and the value $\bullet$ to $(accepted, dispense)$ and $(dispense, ready)$. Any mode $n \in I\!N$ of *insert* associates $n + 1$ to $(insert, counter)$ and n to $(counter, insert)$ and $\bullet$ to the other two adjacent arcs. Hence, the first occurrence

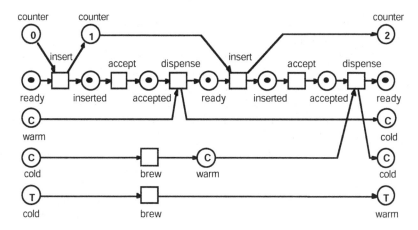

Fig. 6. A process net of the vending machine of Figure 4

of *insert* can only happen for the mode 0. Then, the 0 is removed from *counter* and replaced by 1.

A process net of this high-level net is shown in Figure 6. The inscription of the nodes does not represent the initial marking anymore but rather specifies for each condition which kind of token it represents. Process nets of high-level nets are defined very much like process nets of place/transition nets. Formally, these process nets are place/transition nets where the initial state marks the minimal conditions. All simulation concepts demonstrated in the previous sections can be applied to high-level Petri nets and their process nets, too.

8   Conclusions

The approach described in this chapter is the main aim of a current project called VIP (Verifikation von Informationssystemen durch Auswertung halbgeordneter Petrinetz-Abläufe), supported by the DFG (Deutsche Forschungsgemeinschaft). In the VIP-project, we apply the simulation concept to high-level Petri net models of systems. For an implementation of the concepts suggested in this contribution, see http://www.aifb.uni-karlsruhe.de/InfoSys/VIP/overview/vip.html.

We conclude this contribution by giving some references to related work, in particular to work done within the VIP-project.

As mentioned in the introduction, causal semantics and process nets belong to the standard concepts of Petri net theory. For process nets of condition/event systems, the textbook [12] can be consulted. Roughly speaking, condition/event systems are a subclass of place/transition nets. Process nets of place/transition nets have been defined at different places, [1] is a good reference. The way we define process nets as particular place/transition nets is unusual. However, it allows to formulate the results given in Lemma 1 and Lemma 2 in a particularly simple way. Similar results can be found in [1]. Our definition of high-level Petri nets is a simplified version of the definition given in [11]. Process nets of high-level Petri nets generalize process nets of place/transition nets in a canonical way. The graphical representation of facts is taken from [10]. The concept of internal and external transitions is adopted from [13].

The paper [4] concentrates on the principle goals of our project. In [2], it is shown how all process nets of a system net can be constructed. In [5], the user interface is emphasized. [3] deals with the algorithms for the analysis of process nets. Visualization of process nets employs graph-drawing algorithms. In [9] it is shown how process nets are visualized in the tool developed within the VIP-project, using a modified version of the so-called Sugiyama-Algorithm.

The VIP-approach can be easily extended to analysis of business processes with respect to time and cost [6]. The evaluation of a system model is based on the evaluation of its causal runs. The explicit representation of causality and concurrency in causal runs allows to apply OR-methods for calculation of optimal time and cost parameters.

References

1. E. Best and C. Fernandez C: Nonsequential Processes. Springer-Verlag (1988)
2. J. Desel, A. Oberweis and T. Zimmer: Simulation based analysis of distributed information system behavior. 8th European Simulation Symposium ESS96, Genua, pp. 319-323 (1996)
3. J. Desel, T. Freytag and A. Oberweis: Prozesse, Simulation und Eigenschaften netz-modellierter Systeme. Entwurf komplexer Automatisierungssysteme, Braunschweig, pp. 141-161 (1997)
4. J. Desel, T. Freytag and A. Oberweis: Causal semantic based simulation and validation of high-level Petri nets. 11th European Simulation Multiconference, Istanbul, pp. 826-830 (1997)
5. J. Desel, T. Freytag, A. Oberweis and T. Zimmer: A partial-order based simulation and validation approach for high-level Petri nets. 15th IMACS World Congress, Berlin. Volume 4. Wissenschaft und Technik Verlag Berlin, pp. 351-366 (1997)
6. J. Desel and T. Erwin: Modeling, simulation and analysis of business processes. In this volume.
7. J. Desel and W. Reisig: Place/transition Petri nets. Lectures on Petri Nets I: Basic Models, Lecture Notes in Computer Science Vol. 1492, pp. 122-173, Springer-Verlag (1999)
8. J. Esparza: Model checking using net unfoldings. Science of Computer Programming 23, pp. 151-195 (1994)
9. T. Freytag: Ablaufvisualisierung durch topologisch angeordnete Kausalnetze. 6. Workshop Algorithmen und Werkzeuge für Petrinetze, Oktober 1999, Institut für Wirtschaftsinformatik der Universität Frankfurt / Main, pp. 18-23 (1999)
10. H.J. Genrich and G. Thieler-Mevissen: The Calculus of Facts. Mathematical Foundations of Computer Science, Springer-Verlag, pp. 588-595 (1976)
11. K. Jensen: Coloured Petri Nets, Vol.1: Basic Concepts. 2nd edition, Springer-Verlag (1995)
12. W. Reisig: Petri Nets – An Introduction, Springer-Verlag (1985)
13. W. Reisig: Elements of Distributed Algorithms, Springer-Verlag (1998)

Modeling, Simulation and Analysis of Business Processes

Jörg Desel[1], Thomas Erwin[2]

[1] Lehrstuhl für Angewandte Informatik
Katholische Universität Eichstätt, Germany
Joerg.Desel@ku-eichstaett.de
[2] Institut für Angewandte Informatik und
Formale Beschreibungsverfahren,
Universität Karlsruhe, Germany
Thomas.Erwin@aifb.uni-karlsruhe.de

Abstract. Building and analyzing models of business processes has gained increased importance for any activity that requires a close examination of the business processes involved, e.g., Business Process Reengineering efforts. In this chapter we introduce a Petri net based approach to support such activities. Business processes are modeled using standard place/transition nets enhanced with some notions needed to integrate all aspects of business processes that are relevant with respect to analysis purposes, e.g., the notion of time and costs. The Petri net models of business processes are simulated by generating partially ordered runs. We will show how these runs can then be used for performance analysis of important key indicators such as throughput time.

All introduced concepts are summarized in a 3-step approach that supports users to base their decision between possible alternatives for the design of a business process on facts.

1   Introduction

Since the beginning of the 1990's business processes and their design have gained increased importance for almost any business. The ability to streamline one's business processes in a way as efficient and flexible as possible has become one of the most critical factors for the success of today's companies. The need to deal with business processes has caused an increased need for suitable techniques and tools for their identification, analysis and simulation. The basis for all this are *models* of business processes.

Business process models play an important role in all different phases of business process (re-)design regardless of the framework used. As a result these models are used in phases of early designs of *Business Process Reengineering* (revolutionary approach) as well as during the repetitive design circles of *Continuous Process Improvement* (evolutionary approach)[1].

---

[1] see [2, 14] and Figure 1

W. van der Aalst et al.(Eds.): Business Process Management, LNCS 1806, pp. 129-141, 2000.

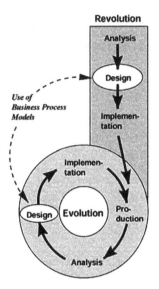

Fig. 1. Revolutionary and evolutionary phases of Business Process Reengineering [14]

Errors made in early design phases will spoil any (re-)design efforts that might follow. Hence the need for methods that support a profound evaluation of process design quality in early design phases emerges as a must - otherwise choices between alternative designs of a business process have to be based on opinions or feelings. Although this appears to be common practice these days it is clearly desirable to support these important decisions with some facts by building and evaluating business process models instead.

However, in order to be able to conduct any evaluations, quite some requirements have to be met by the formalism used for building the models. Especially results with respect to quantitative criteria such as *throughput time* or *costs* will in most cases be based on *simulations* of the model. By asking the model to support simulation one directly asks for formal syntax and semantics. Otherwise the model would not be executable by a simulation engine. This is one of the main reasons why Petri nets and related formalisms (such as *event-driven process chains (EPC)* [16]) have become a popular choice for modeling business processes. The suitability of Petri nets for the modeling of business processes has been examined and discussed extensively (e.g., see [1, 6, 10, 13]). Because they are directly executable, Petri net models can easily be used to examine behavioral aspects of the modeled system during simulation.

In this chapter we present an approach for simulating business processes in order to gain helpful information for design decisions, especially during the important early (revolutionary) phases of (re-)design (see Figure 1). To this end we first briefly introduce the way we build a model for a business process using Petri nets. By adopting the simulation approach based on *causal runs* from [5] we get a set of runs for our business process model that we can then use for a qualitative and quantitative analysis of what we have modeled. Finally we integrate all the introduced techniques into a 3-step approach that allows us to repeatedly examine (models of) business processes with respect to key performance indicators in an interactive way (see Figure 2). Throughout the chapter we will use a small example from the field of car manufacturing to illustrate our concepts.

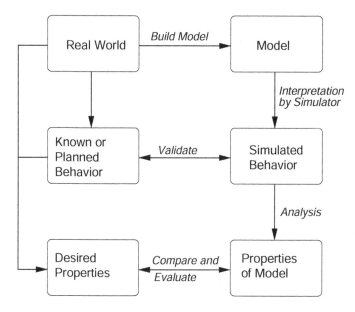

Fig. 2. A 3-step approach to support the design of business processes

2   Modeling

In this section we briefly explain what kind of business processes we aim to model within the scope of this chapter and which characteristics of these processes we consider for analysis. We then introduce some basic concepts for building business process models with Petri nets.

2.1   Business Processes

A business process can be described as a set of *activities* that are being executed according to certain *rules* with respect to certain *objectives*. The *execution* of a business process describes the execution of the corresponding activities such that the rules are obeyed and the objectives are met. During execution of a business process an activity can be executed multiple times, once or never. The execution of a business process usually involves decisions on alternative routings, i.e., *choices* between the execution of alternative activities have to be made.

During execution of business process, activities have to be coordinated. *Resources* have to be provided where needed for the execution of activities. A *business process specification* describes which activities have to be executed in what order (including concurrent execution) and what resources are needed for execution of these activities. Such a specification can contain different aspects of business processes. Depending on the modeling objectives, *functional* (concentrating only on activities and their order) or *organizational* (including the organizational context in which activities are to be carried out) aspects can be emphasized [16, 19]. In this chapter we focus on functional aspects. With respect to the type of business processes we will limit ourselves in this chapter to *production workflow* or *administrative workflow* [2], i.e., we only consider business processes which can be executed according to a given process specification.

There are many characteristics of business processes that are used for analysis purposes [11, 17, 19]. In this chapter we will concentrate on *performance analysis* of business processes with respect to key indicators from the areas *time* and *costs*. With respect to time indicators we differentiate between *activity time* and *waiting time*. Activity time is regarded as deterministic and non-variable, i.e., we assume that we can describe the time needed for the execution of an activity by using target values or estimates based on previous experiences [4][2]. On the other hand, waiting time can vary with the execution of alternative routings within the business process specification (we will see an example for this in Section 3). Costs of an activity are regarded as a function of the activity. Similar to time values we assume non-variable *activity costs* and variable *waiting costs*, each being values directly dependent on the corresponding time values.

Performance analysis of business processes often involves determining *average throughput times* or *costs of executions* of business processes as key indicators for the quality of the process design [15]. A prerequisite for the calculation of these and other indicators is the determination of all time and cost values for single activities that result from the execution of the business process, i.e., from executing activities or remaining in waiting states. In Section 3 we will see how to calculate these values by simulating the business process models. But first we will show how to build Petri net models of business processes.

2.2   Modeling Business Processes with Petri Nets

In this chapter we will use place/transition nets [7] as a Petri net class for modeling business processes. Place/transition nets are the class of Petri nets best

---

[2] Note that the approach is not limited to the use of fixed values but can easily be adopted to stochastic values.

known and most extensively examined. Since most of the relevant basic concepts have already been introduced in [5] we will just point out some basic constructs that are important with respect to *alternative routings*(see Section 2.1) during execution of a business process. A *forward branching place*, i.e., a place that has more than one transition in its post-set, models a *choice* or *OR-branch* if it carries only one token. On the other hand, *backward branching transitions*, i.e., transitions that have more than one place in their pre-sets, model *synchronization* or *AND-joins* if the pre-set places do not branch forward. A synchronizing transition can only occur if there is at least one token in each of its pre-set places. Therefore, the arrival of tokens in pre-set places at different points of time causes waiting time.

Example: Figure 3 shows a simplified process from a car manufacturing plant modeled as a place/transition net. Note that although this specific model does not contain any cycles we do not exclude cyclic business processes.

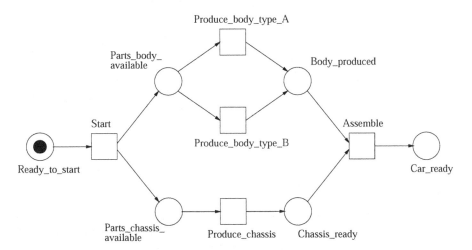

Fig. 3. A business process model for car manufacturing

The behavior of a Petri net can be described using *sequential* or *causal semantics*. We will use causal semantics and causal nets for the representation of the behavior of the modeled business processes. As introduced in [5] we will refer to an execution of a business process specification as a *causal run*. The firing of a transition, i.e., the execution of the activity modeled by the transition, is displayed by an *event*. An event is a transition in the *causal net* representing the corresponding run. Likewise, *conditions*, i.e., places in the causal net, model the states that hold between the execution of activities. We will slightly modify this interpretation of events and conditions (which is the one commonly used for runs of classical place/transition nets) as we introduce the concept of *activity transitions* in the remainder of this section.

Example (Continued): Figure 4 shows the two (maximal) runs of the business process model from Figure 3. Note that the names from Figure 3 have been abbreviated due to readability reasons.

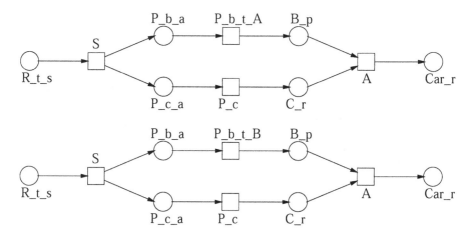

Fig. 4. Possible runs of the business process model from Figure 3

Details on the generation of runs and their analysis with respect to desired or unwanted (qualitative) properties can be found in [5].

Although they are important for the actual execution of a business process, technical (or organizational) details usually do not matter for the analysis of the structure of a business process. In most cases, by modeling too many details the expressiveness of the model with respect to the underlying structure of the business process is spoiled. Therefore it is of great value for the modeler to have a choice between several levels of abstraction. This enables him to emphasize different views of the model which might be on a more *detailed* or on a more *conceptual* level. In our approach we introduce *activity transitions* for modeling sequences of *(part-)activities* that have to be performed for the execution of an activity as a whole.

Activity transitions allow for the representation of activities in both, a detailed and an abstracting view. An example for the corresponding graphical representation is given in Figure 5, where the model from Figure 3 has been supplemented by activity transitions (as well as by time and cost inscriptions to which we will refer later). Places that are within the detailed view of an activity transition

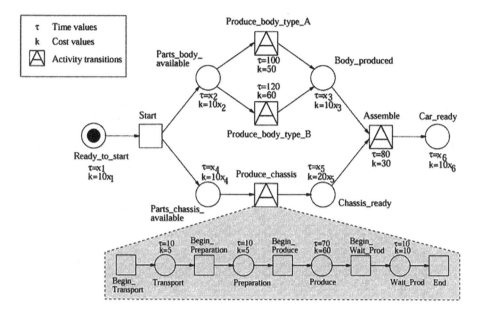

Fig. 5. Business process model including inscriptions for time and costs

are called *internal* places (e.g., place 'Produce' in Figure 5), all other places are referred to as *external* (e.g., place 'Chassis_ready' in Figure 5). Note that the execution of the (part-)activities is modeled by internal places. A marked internal place p_{int} can be interpreted as a (local) state where the system is in the state of carrying out the (part-)activity that is modeled by p_{int}. External places model the states between the execution of activities, i.e., non-planned waiting states. The concept of activity transitions can be easily mapped on the runs of a business process model. Figure 6 shows a run of the enhanced business process model from Figure 5.

A notion of *time* is a mandatory prerequisite for answering any questions related to the performance of real systems. The integration of time into Petri nets has been discussed extensively [2, 3, 12, 18]. Time-related performance indicators such as *throughput time* have become key indicators for the quality of business process design. The basic idea of the time concept we introduce in this chapter is to link time to the places of a place/transition net. Time is not consumed by the firing of transitions (as in most other approaches) but *between* firings of transitions. The firing itself does not consume any time. This timing concept corresponds to the idea of modeling (part-)activities by internal places of activity transitions. That way our approach is completely *state-based* [1], i.e., the state of the modeled business processes can be completely determined by the marking of places. This, for example, allows us to distinguish between the enabling and the actual execution of (part-)activities which in return is a mandatory prereq-

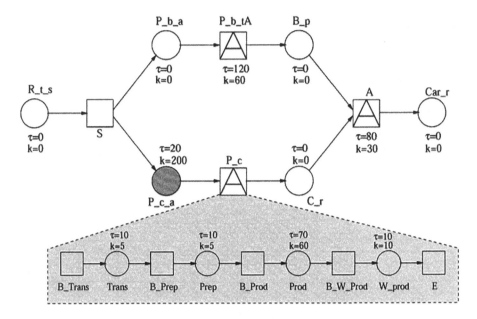

Fig. 6. An example for the cost optimal distribution of waiting time

uisite for the modeling of waiting time[3]. Time values can be fixed or variable. For analysis purposes with respect to the dynamic behavior of the model they can be transferred to runs and then be interpreted there.

Hence in our approach time is linked to the places of the business process model with an explicit distinction between time values for internal and external places. Internal places are inscribed with a fixed *activity time* value which corresponds to the target value for the time needed to execute the (part-)activity that is modeled by the place (e.g., the value '70' for place 'process' in Figure 5). Waiting time is linked to external places. Waiting time results from the synchronization of (sequences of) concurrent activities that differ with respect to the time needed for execution. If there are alternative activities with different respective activity times, the values for waiting time can be different from run to run. Hence, when building a model of a business process we use variables for waiting time (e.g., 'x_5' for place 'Chassis_ready' in Figure 5). Waiting time can only be determined for a single run.

The behavior of a modeled business process is described by a set of *time-inscribed runs*. Each time-inscribed run is a run of the business process model where conditions have a natural number as an inscription[4]. This number reflects the life-span

---

[3] More details on the advantages of state-based models can be found in [1, 2, 8]

[4] Note, that for the generation of runs for a business process model any notion of time is ignored (see Section 3).

of a condition, i.e., the amount of time the condition holds (which corresponds to the amount of time a token remains at the corresponding place). For internal places this value corresponds to the time inscriptions (the activity time) of this place. Conditions that have no successor and therefore "hold forever" have no associated number as they represent final states of the business process execution. In addition to this we require that the sum of life-spans of conditions for each pair of paths that lead to an event be equal. Furthermore the sum of life-spans of conditions on maximal paths has to be equal as well. This sum is the throughput time of the time-inscribed run.

For a single run there may exist several time-inscribed runs, for which only the time inscriptions for conditions that correspond to external places may differ. This is due to the assumption that only waiting time is variable. However, according to the above requirement, for all possible values of waiting time variables, the sum of time values has to be equal for all paths that lead to a synchronizing event. In most cases the sum of time values is fixed (by the path that is maximal with respect to this sum, at least if one wishes to determine the minimal throughput time) but the time values for conditions that correspond to tokens on external places can be varied in an arbitrary way. In other words, the total amount of waiting time is known, but one can still decide where to wait (see the example in Section 3).

The integration of *costs* into our models is accomplished using an approach similar to the one used for time. As we assume costs to be a function of time we use fixed values for *activity costs* and variable values for *waiting costs*, which are assigned to internal and external places, respectively (for an example, see cost value inscriptions for places in Figure 5).

3   Simulation and Analysis

Having built the Petri net model of the business process we can now simulate its behavior. This is done by generating runs using simulation concepts developed within the *VIP* project[5]. Since for real-life processes it is very expensive or even impossible to simulate the complete behavior we do not attempt to generate *all* runs. Instead, the generation of runs depicting the *standard behavior* of the business process (including regular exceptions) is emphasized. Recall that time and costs are ignored during simulation.

With runs generated it is possible to transfer the values for time and costs from the process model to these runs. Conditions that are mapped on internal places get the values of the activity time associated with these places. Conditions that are mapped on external places first get the variable time value that corresponds

---

[5] *Verification of information systems by evaluating partially-ordered Petri net runs*, see [9] for details on generation of runs.

to possible waiting time. Since during the generation of runs all decisions with respect to choices between alternative (sequences of) activities have been made, it is now possible to calculate (combinations of) waiting times for each run. In the following we will only consider time assignments that are minimal with respect to the total throughput time of the run. For these assignments the time values for conditions corresponding to external places are equal to zero for at least one (*critical*) path. On these places no waiting time can occur without prolonging the total throughput time of the run (hence violating our claim for minimal throughput time). A suitable algorithm that calculates the total throughput time for a time-inscribed run can be found in [8].

In case waiting time causes costs (e.g., storage costs), it may be interesting to distribute waiting time over conditions in a way that is optimal with respect to these waiting costs. Often it is reasonable not to assign waiting time to a condition in the immediate pre-set of a synchronizing event but to shift it to some earlier occurring condition.

Example (Continued): Figure 6 shows a run of the business process model from Figure 5, including the values for time and costs. If we consider the cost functions for the conditions (represented by) x_{cond} and y_{cond} we realize that total costs for the run are minimal if we wait with producing the chassis for 20 time units (which enables us to assemble chassis and body of a car directly).

In case the cost functions of conditions are linear with respect to time, the cost optimal distribution of waiting time within a run can be expressed as a linear optimization problem [8]. Having determined all variable values for time and cost it is now possible to calculate other key performance indicators such as *throughput time* or *total costs*.

4   An Interactive Analysis Approach

4.1   A 3-Step Approach

With all the concepts introduced in the previous sections we propose a 3-step approach for the simulation and analysis of business process within reengineering projects.

In a *first* step the business process is modeled as a Petri net. At this stage values for time and costs are not considered. The modeling should concentrate on building an appropriate *logical structure*, i.e., identifying necessary activities and putting them in a meaningful order. That way discussions of detailed problems like 'What should the execution of this activity cost?' can be avoided at this (early) stage of the (re-)design process. No decisions have to be made with respect to estimated or target values that are to be used for the model. Activity transitions can either be specified in detail or left as a top-level building block.

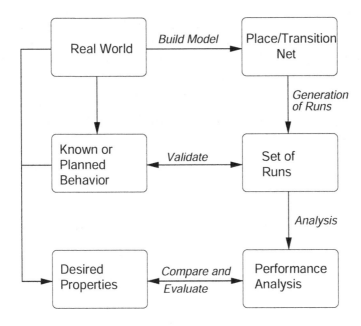

Fig. 7. Using the concepts and techniques from the previous chapters for our 3-step approach (see Figure 2)

In a *second* step a relevant set of runs of the business process model is generated and stored for later analysis. This (in most cases) time-consuming procedure can be performed independently from any values chosen for time and costs. The generation of runs can be done automatically or interactively. The corresponding simulation concept contains methods for the selection of runs that are to be generated as well as criteria for stopping the generation of a run (*cut-off criteria*) [5]. The second step only has to be repeated if the structure of the business process is changed. As long as this is not the case, all analysis steps can be performed for the set of runs generated once.

Since runs can be graphically displayed using causal nets (see Section 2.2 and [5]), they can be used for validating the behavior of a business process. A big advantage especially during discussions is the fact that the flows of documents, information and products can be represented explicitly by paths in these causal nets.

The *third* step of our approach starts with transferring time and cost values from the business process model to the generated runs (see Section 2.2). Now the generated runs can be used for performance analysis of the business process. Since the analysis techniques use runs that have already been generated, the time consumed by analysis is significantly reduced. The effects of values chosen for time and costs can be examined immediately. Since rather little time is needed for repeating this step for all kinds of time and cost values (compared to generating a new set of runs each time) this step can be easily be performed numerous times in order to experiment with different value estimates for time and costs.

The three steps are performed iteratively until the model is valid and satisfies desired properties.

4.2   So What?

Our analysis approach enables the user to *interactively* examine the business process model and its behavior by using generated runs. What advantages does this approach have?

Any 'efficiency claims', e.g., statements such as 'This design will cause much higher costs.' or 'This design will never work with our time constraints.' can be checked immediately. Especially when discussing alternative process designs it is of great importance that design decisions can be based on more objective criteria.

The dependencies between the measured quality of the business process model and estimated or target values used for time and costs can be examined. When introducing time and cost values to the business process model, the values used will either have to be based on assumptions or experiences from business practice. Since these values might significantly differ from values that occur once the business process model is put to practice, it is certainly a good idea to examine the relation between chosen values and analysis results. This is especially important in case decisions between design alternatives have to be made. Depending on the concrete scenario (and the willingness of decision makers to take risks) either the alternative with the best average results for all tested time and cost values or the alternative with the best value for one time and cost combination can be chosen.

The risk of severe mistakes caused by faulty assumptions for time and cost values is reduced. Being able to test all kinds of values for time and costs quite quickly, one can avoid situations where decisions have to made based on few (possibly faulty) values for time and costs.

In summary, the risk of wrong decisions with respect to the design of a business process can be reduced significantly. Since efficiency claims and 'But what if..'-scenarios can be checked immediately the discussion on alternative designs can be based on facts rather than on opinions. By creating the opportunity to interactively *play* with the process model the motivation and the level of active participation on behalf of the persons involved will be increased.

References

1. van der Aalst, W.M.P.: Three Good reasons for Using a Petri-net-based Workflow Management System. In: T. Wakayama et al. (eds.): Information and Process Integration in Enterprises: Rethinking documents. The Kluwer International Series in Engineering and Computer Science, pages 161–182. Kluwer Academic Publishers, Norwell, 1998
2. van der Aalst, W.M.P.: The Application of Petri Nets to Workflow Management. The Journal of Circuits, Systems and Computers, 8(1):21–66 (1998)
3. Ajmone Marsan, M., Bobbio, A., Donatelli, S.: Petri Nets in Performance Analysis: An Introduction. In: Reisig, W., Rozenberg, G.: Lectures on Petri Nets I: Basic Models, pages 211-256. Lecture Notes in Computer Science, Vol. 1491. Springer-Verlag, Berlin, Heidelberg, New York, Tokyo (1999)
4. Berkau, C., Hirschmann, P. (eds.): Kostenorientiertes Geschäftsprozessmanagement: Methoden, Werkzeuge, Erfahrungen. Vahlen, München (1996)
5. Desel, J.: Validation of Process Models by Construction of Process Nets. In this volume.
6. Desel, J., Oberweis, A.: Petri-Netze in der Angewandten Informatik - Einführung, Grundlagen und Perspektiven. Wirtschaftsinformatik, 38:359–368, (July 1996)
7. Desel, J., Reisig, W.: Place/Transition Petri Nets. In: Reisig, W., Rozenberg, G.: Lectures on Petri Nets I: Basic Models, pages 122-173. Lecture Notes in Computer Science, Vol. 1491. Springer-Verlag, Berlin, Heidelberg, New York, Tokyo (1999)
8. Erwin, T.: Leistungsbewertung von Geschäftsprozessen durch Auswertung halbgeordneter Petrinetz-Abläufe. Diploma thesis, Karlsruhe (1998)
9. Freytag, T.: Simulation halbgeordneter Petrinetz-Abläufe. In: Desel, J., Oberweis, A., Kindler, E. (eds.): 3. Workshop Algorithmen und Werkzeuge für Petrinetze, RR341, pages 14–20. Institut AIFB, Universität Karlsruhe (1996)
10. Gruhn, V., Kampmann, M.: Modellierung unternehmensübergreifender Geschäftsprozesse mit FUNSOFT-Netzen. Wirtschaftsinformatik, 38:369–381 (1996)
11. Hammer, M., Champy, J.: Reengineering the corporation. Nicolas Brealey Publishing, London (1993)
12. Jensen, K.: Coloured Petri Nets, Volume 2: Analysis Methods. Monographs in Theoretical Computer Science. Springer-Verlag, Berlin, Heidelberg, New York, Tokyo (1995)
13. Oberweis, A.: Modellierung und Ausführung von Workflows mit Petri-Netzen. Teubner-Reihe Wirtschaftsinformatik. Teubner, Stuttgart, Leipzig (1996)
14. Österle, H.: Business in the Information Age - Heading for New Processes. Springer-Verlag, Berlin, Heidelberg, New York, Tokyo (1995)
15. Scheer, A.-W.: Modellunterstützung für das kostenorientierte Geschäftsprozessmanagement. In: Berkau, C., Hirschmann, P. (eds.): Kostenorientiertes Geschäftsprozessmanagement: Methoden, Werkzeuge, Erfahrungen. Vahlen, München (1996)
16. Scheer, A.-W.: Business Process Engineering - Reference Models for Industrial Enterprises. 2nd ed., Springer-Verlag, Berlin, Heidelberg, New York, Tokyo (1994)
17. Schmidt, G.: Prozessmanagement - Modelle und Methoden. Springer-Verlag, Berlin, Heidelberg, New York, Tokyo (1995)
18. Starke, P.: Analyse von Petri-Netz-Modellen. Leitfäden und Monographien der Informatik. Teubner, Stuttgart, Leipzig (1990)
19. Vossen, G., Becker, J. (eds.): Geschäftsprozessmodellierung und Workflow-Management. International Thomson Publishing, Bonn, Albany (1996)

Using Formal Analysis Techniques in Business Process Redesign

Kees M. van Hee and Hajo A. Reijers

Faculty of Mathematics and Computing Science
Eindhoven University of Technology
P.O. Box 513, NL-5600 MB, Eindhoven, The Netherlands
{wsinhee, hreijers}@win.tue.nl

Abstract. Formal analysis techniques can deliver important support during business process redesign efforts. This chapter points out the (potential) contribution of these formal analysis techniques by giving an outline on the subject first. Next, a specific, newly developed formal technique is discussed.

1 Formal Techniques in Business Process Redesign

A thorough analysis of several redesign alternatives can help to make the choice for the most effective solution. Also, analyzing the design of a new business process may point out whether once set redesign targets are still realistic. In this paragraph we will give a short background on business process redesign, so that the role of analysis techniques in general can be explained.

1.1 Business Process Redesign

'Panta rhei' is the famous adage of the ancient Greek philosopher Heraclitus: everything is always changing. Business processes are prime examples of this statement. Everywhere around the world, in almost every industry, processes are being fine-tuned, downsized, re-engineered, value-added and re-aligned.

Drivers behind this phenomenon are manifold. In the first place, companies feel the increasing pressure of a globalising market. Cost reduction has become prevalent to survive. Secondly, the historically strong position of suppliers in many markets is becoming less dominant compared to that of the customer. To keep customers coming back, companies have to please them by shortening their production time or increasing their product quality. The last major change driver is technology. Technology offers a wide variety of new possibilities to manage business process better. The widespread application of Enterprise Resource Planning Systems and Workflow Management Systems in industry is a strong example on this note.

A business process re-engineering effort (to use one of the many possible labels) may aim at stabilizing, reducing, or improving one or more, different and often dependent entities (e.g. cost, production time, service quality, efficiency). Many business processes changes are put in motion without an accurate picture of the

W. van der Aalst et al. (Eds.): Business Process Management, LNCS 1806, pp 142-160, 2000
© Springer-Verlag Berlin Heidelberg 2000

expected earnings at forehand, but rather on a 'gut feeling'. There may be a well-understood positive or negative effect of the process change on entities such as the throughput time or production cost, but a reliable quantitative estimate is often lacking.

1.2   Phases in Redesign

The redesign of a business process is a complex activity. Specialists from different disciplines are involved, new technology is introduced, staff is confronted with drastic change, and money and time are in short supply. To handle this complexity, a redesign effort is often carried out in the form of a project. This means, among other things, that during the effort distinct *phases* are distinguished in which different activities are planned. We will describe a generally applicable model to distinguish such phases within a redesign project, based on the IPSO methodology as described in [3]. The six phases are:

1. *Create vision*:
   A vision is created on the desired and necessary changes within an organization to improve its performance. A proper recognition of the organization's *Critical Success Factors* (CSF's) is required: which organizational issues determine success or failure of the organization? For these (or some) CSF's redesign targets are set. Next, it has to be established which *business processes* contribute mostly to the development of these CSF's. This determines the scope of the redesign. Lastly, the new organizational principles and technology have to be identified that will be the backbone of the redesign. In essence, the result of phase 1 is a *conceptual design* of the change.
2. *Diagnosis*:
   A thorough analysis of the selected processes is carried out to obtain an understanding of their current performance. This performance is usually expressed in terms of rates on *key performance indicators* (KPI's) such as the throughput time, customer satisfaction, product quality, etc. Next, the causes of low scores on KPI's within the current processes are determined, if possible. This knowledge can be applied in phase 3.
3. *Process redesign*:
   For the selected scope of the redesign, targets of the most important KPI's are set, in line with the desired development of the CSF's. Then, alternative process redesigns are developed in the form of *models*. The alternative models are to be analyzed and compared. Eventually, one of the models is selected as the definite redesign, after which it is detailed. The definite redesign is to be analyzed to ensure that set goals can be satisfied. From the detailed process design the requirements follow on the necessary supporting technology and information systems within the processes. At this point, there is a *detailed design* of the change.
4. *System design and construction*:
   On basis of the requirements of the definite process design, an outline of the technology components must be made, as well as their interaction patterns. This is the architecture of the new process. Furthermore, (information) systems and applications have to be designed that enable the new process to function in

correspondence with its detailed design. Finally, both the technology architecture and the applications have to be actually constructed and tested.

5. *Transfer and implementation*:
   The newly designed process in combination with the supporting technology is integrated and transferred to the organization. New procedures, system functionality, communication structures, and responsibilities have to be communicated and explained to the relevant parties (e.g. employees, management, and customers). Feedback is generated to fine-tune the new process, after which it can be taken into full operation.

6. *Evaluation*:
   After implementation, a continuous phase of monitoring starts. The KPI's that have been determined in the diagnosis phase will be measured on regular intervals. This will usually trigger gradual adjustment and improvements of the new process(es). On basis of this information it can be determined whether the redesign effort is a success.

1.3   Formal Analysis Techniques for Business Processes

In general, there are two different categories of formal analysis techniques that can be used in the context of redesigning business process: *qualitative* and *quantitative* techniques. Qualitative techniques focus on the question whether a process design meets a specific property. Quantitative techniques are used to calculate or approximate the size or level of a specific property. For example, whether a process design meets the demand that a bank employee never can validate a cash transfer that he has initiated himself is a qualitative question. To determine how long customers have to wait before their telephone call is responded to by the call-center typically a quantitative analysis is required.

Quantitative techniques can be categorized into *simulation* and *analytical techniques*. If one compares these two types of techniques, it can be said that simulation is an approximation technique, where analytical techniques deliver exact numbers. During a simulation of a business process, at specified intervals *cases* (e.g. new orders) are generated for the model in execution. In response, each of the components within the model will behave in accordance with its specification. For instance, on receipt of a new order the computer will simulate an employee inspecting the order on completeness. The actions performed by the model in execution are realistic, but are not necessarily exactly the same or take place at the same moment as in a real-life situation. During execution, information is gathered on items that result from the interaction of the modeled components. For example, the frequency of message exchanges between two specific components is measured or the accumulation of work in front of an overloaded resource.

An analytical technique, on the other hand, is based on an *algorithm* that yields an exact result on basis of both the formal model and some well-understood relationships between the specified components. For example, a business process can be modeled as a network of nodes connected to each other by arcs, expressing precedence relations. On basis of such a network model, the shortest path leading from a new order to fulfillment can be calculated. Popular formalisms and mathematical theories to model and analyze business processes in this analytical way are, for example, Markov chains, queuing theory, CPM, PERT and GERT (e.g. [6], [7], and [9]).

Often, an exact result is preferred over an approximated result. However, the complexity of a specific business process model can be such that a quantitative, simulation approach is the only feasible means of analysis. Given a specific process model, there are several aspects that determine whether a qualitative or quantitatively analytical approach is feasible at all and, if so, preferable over simulation. For example, if both the synchronization structures within a process (e.g. parallelism) and the behavior of resources is too complex, no known general analytical techniques are available to determine the throughput patterns of work packages. Although simulation is a very flexible technique suited to investigate almost any type of business process, a common disadvantage is that, in non-trivial situations, numerous and lengthy simulation runs have to be carried out to obtain reliable results.

For all types of analysis, qualitative or quantitative, holds that a formal model of the business process underlies the analysis. Depending on the set of properties that is taken into consideration in the redesign effort, elements of the real business process are incorporated in the model. If, for example, the redesign effort is primarily concerned with the optimization of the *logistics* of the process, elements typically found in a process model are buffers, resources, routings of jobs, service times, and order arrivals. If, for example, the accent is on *cost reduction*, elements such as labor time, material costs, and depreciation factors will be part of the model.

1.4   Relevance of Formal Techniques

On basis of the phases within a process redesign project we have distinguished in paragraph 1.2 and the outline of techniques in paragraph 1.3, we can now pinpoint the places in the redesign process where analysis techniques can be useful. More in specific, whether a qualitative or quantitative is useful. As it turns out, the diagnosis and the redesign phases are best served by applying formal analysis techniques.

Diagnosis phase
As the first phase in a redesign project, the vision phase, is concerned creating prescriptive targets and means, it is not very suitable to apply formal analysis methods. During the subsequent, diagnosis phase it is paramount to come to a clear conception of the current process operations in practice. It can be argued that this could be established for a great deal on basis of observation and data gathering alone. Nonetheless, there are at least two situations when applications of analysis techniques are useful. In the first situation, it turns out to be difficult to understand the relations between different entities within a process by observation alone. For example, although historic information on resource availability and service quality at a specific work center is known, it is unclear how these two are related. The use of, for instance, a simulation model may indicate which of the alternative interaction patterns is most suited to explain current operations. It is rather awkward to interfere in the day-to-day operations to establish such a relation without a simulation.

The second situation occurs when one is interested in the *future* operations of a process. Clearly, this cannot be established by observing current processes alone. A future analysis can be performed by constructing a formal model of the current business process, and experiment with changes in the context of the process by inserting (partly) imaginary data, and analyze it accordingly. For example, a foreseen rise in demand can be projected on the model of the current business process, while keeping resources stationary. Simulation runs, then, may indicate where and in which sequence overload of capacity will occur. Qualitative analysis may point out whether dangerous or unwanted situations may occur.

Redesign phase
The subsequent phase, the redesign phase, is primarily a creative process aimed at developing new designs. Once developed, the alternative models have to be compared and the optimal solution is modeled in detail. There are three areas, normally dealt with in consecutive order during this phase, in which formal techniques can be useful:
1. Design construction,
2. Performance analysis,
3. Verification of design.

Ad 1. The design of a new process is primarily a creative process, which is likely to incorporate some level of human ingenuity for some time to come. Nonetheless, formal analytical techniques can offer support during the creation of a new design. On basis of desired properties of the process model on the one hand and characteristics of the elementary design blocks on the other hand, a formal technique may suggest (near) optimal design constructions or indicate the boundaries that the process design should stay within. For example, suppose there is a number of machines, each with a known capability. On basis of the characteristics of the desired end product, an algorithm can be used to, first, determine the required machine capabilities and, next, to indicate the alternative sets of machines that should be minimally available within the process. The designer makes the ultimate decision about which machines are chosen and at what locations within the process the machines are placed. In paragraph 2 we will describe in more detail an algorithm that can be used within this area.

Ad 2. Having created several designs, performance analyses are useful to compare these designs on how well they perform in different fields. Simulation can be used in much the same way such as described in the diagnosis phase. However, the creation of detailed simulation models and the subsequent lengthy simulation runs themselves may take too much time when roughly considering many alternatives redesigns. Analytical approaches that aim at measuring specific aspects of the designs in efficient ways are much more useful at this time. Depending on the performance indicator that is of prime interest, specific algorithms are applied. An example of such an algorithm, the computation of the throughput time, is treated in more detail in paragraph 2. In the end, when the preferred process design is established it may become much more interesting to develop a full simulation model to achieve an accurate view of the expected outcomes of the redesign effort. This may lead to tuning the goals to realistic levels.

Ad 3. Before the detailed process design is actually transferred to subsequent phases, such as the system construction, it should be established that the design is *correct*. This is very important considering the cost involved in developing a new process only to change it directly when it has been established. Although simulations used to assess the performance may have indicated no errors, this cannot be taken as that the process incorporates no faults. After all, simulations cover only a finite number of situations.

Analytic, qualitative techniques may be used to determine important properties of the design, such as the absence of dead-locks or the eventual termination of the process once work is taken on.

2. Throughput Analysis

In this paragraph, we will describe a recently developed formal technique that can be used when redesigning business processes ([4]). It focuses on the computation of the throughput time of a specific business process model. We start by introducing the throughput concept. Next, we will describe the construction of business process models within this approach and the algorithm to compute the throughput time of the business process modeled in such a fashion.

2.1   Throughput Time

One of the most important performance indicators in industry is the *throughput time*. Although authors from different disciplines use different terminology for this concept such as *passage*, *cycle* and *traversing time*, we stick to our term for reasons of popularity in the field of workflow management from which our approach originates. The throughput time of a *specific job* is the total amount of time spent from the moment that the handling of the job started until the moment it is completed. The throughput time of a job is the sum of its *service time* and its *waiting time*. Waiting time for a job is created when no task can be executed due to the unavailability of resources. When there is at least one task processing a job, this counts as service time.

The wide-spread use of the throughput performance indicator can be explained from the fact that it is concerned with the 'flowing' of work through the business process, rather than with the exact manipulations that take place. Very often, a low or stable throughput time is a desirable or even necessary characteristic of a business process. Imagine, for instance, a government agency that handles tax forms and decides whether they are valid. National regulations may be violated when the processing of a job takes over one year.

The throughput time *of a process* can be expressed in several ways. This is caused by the fact that jobs that undergo the same processing often do not share the same throughput time. In other words, there is throughput variance. An ordinary cause for this phenomenon is that resources do not deliver constant productivity. Another cause may be fluctuations in market demand, possibly flooding the system, leading to waiting time. A very common approach is to express the throughput time of a process as the average throughput time of the jobs it handles. Although this may be fine as an approximation, this average is not always a good reflector of the performance of the process. For example, if minimum and maximum throughput times of jobs are far apart, the average throughput time is hardly suitable to give customers guarantees about delivery times. An alternative sometimes used, is to declare the throughput time of a process by means of a fraction percentage and a cut-off value. For example, 90 % of the jobs going through a specific business process is finished within 6 weeks. If the throughput of jobs varies, the most detailed expression of the throughput time is as a histogram or a probability distribution of the job throughput times.

Regardless of the exact definition used, the computation of the throughput time for a business process already in action is straightforward. Actual throughput figures on job throughput times can be used to express the throughput time following either definition. A problem arises, when the throughput time is to be determined of a newly designed process. Depending on historic information only puts the designer in an awkward position. He cannot design a process with desirable throughput characteristics without putting the process to work first. Especially when design alternatives are to be compared, such as required in the redesign phase sketched in paragraph 1.2, this is not very practical.

A proper alternative, propagated in this chapter, is to apply formal quantitative techniques on a model of the designed business process. One of the possible approaches is to apply simulation. As argued before, simulation can be time consuming. An analytical approach that is time-efficient and yet powerful to yield reliable results (by being exact) would therefore be preferable in this situation. In the next paragraph we will explain the basics of such an approach.

2.2   Elements of the Process Model

When choosing an analytical approach, it is important to incorporate those aspects within the formal model that determine the throughput time of the process. Bringing back in mind the distinction between service time and waiting time, the following aspects are relevant:

1. the *structure* of the business processes: a business process is a set of tasks that have to be completed in some kind of order (possibly differing for each new job); the possible routes through the process, leading to the execution of individual tasks, is essential for determining the throughput time,
2. the *resource schedule*: the way how resources are distributed over the different tasks within the process; both the available type of resources and the number of resources may determine the flow of jobs through specific points in the process,
3. the *service characteristics* of the resources active within the process: differences in service productivity per resource influence throughput time,
4. the *arrival rate* of new jobs: the balance between new arrivals and available resources determine whether waiting time arises.

When starting to model a business process, it is generally up to the modeler how accurate each of these aspects is modeled. There are, however, practical limits to this accuracy. Usually it is not feasible to model the characteristics of each individual job or resource. Instead, *classes* of different jobs and resources are modeled. A certain pattern of behavior, then, holds for each member of a class.

A second practical limitation is that the exact chain of cause and effect *underlying* specific behavior is unknown or perhaps irrelevant. For example, the arrival of new orders may depend on the price level of a competitive product. That price strategy may be unknown.

Moreover, the exact cause for, for example, a resource to work slower at some times is less relevant than accurately modeling the phenomenon itself. A stochastic approach is then the answer. This means that, given a specific component of the model, relevant patterns of behavior are distinguished. Each pattern is assigned a probability weight, instead of modeling the specific cause. For example, fluctuations in the arrival of new orders are expressed by a probability distribution. A common characteristic to model an arrival pattern of new cases is a standard Poisson distribution.

Similarly, to model changes in the productivity of a resource, a distribution is used that asserts probabilities to each possible service time that resource may deliver. Realistic behavior is induced even more when stochastic processes are modeled to be dependent on each other. Specific resource behavior may be dependent on the resource behavior shown earlier. On the other hand, to simplify calculations, many times standard stochastic distributions are used, or even deterministic behavior. More realism can be achieved by using arbitrary or mixed distributions.

Even when (3) the service characteristics and (4) the arrival rate are modeled stochastically, analytical analysis is not straightforward. Both (1) a complex process structure or (2) a complex resource schedule may trouble the analysis. An example of a difficult resource schedule is the use of so-called "butter flies", resources that are not assigned to a fixed task within the process, but wander around. Difficult process structures are those in which other relations can be applied than mere sequential orderings of tasks, for example by allowing the parallel execution of tasks.

General applicable analytical techniques to compute the performance of a business process model with an arbitrary, independent stochastic arrival pattern, with arbitrary, independent stochastic service characteristics, with a complex resource schedule, and with a complex process structure are not available. Reduction of complexity of the model is therefore required. Many existing performance analysis techniques concentrate on omitting complex process structures from the model, such as the choice, parallel, and cycle constructions. In addition, stochastic resource behavior or stochastic arrival patterns are modeled using standard probabilistic distributions, such as normal distributions or negative-exponential distributions.

In the approach presented in this paragraph, we will apply reductions in another dimension, allowing for greater realism in two other dimensions. Our approach comes down at assuming a liberal resource schedule. No matter the number or types of resources required for the execution of a task, we will assume that sufficient resources are always available when there is a job to process by that task. In other words, the resource capacity is infinite; no waiting time can occur due to the lack of resources. The throughput time of a job under these conditions is equal to the total service time spent. In a real business process, of course, this situation will hardly ever occur. It means that the process is either in expensive excess of capacity or in a terrible lack of orders. On the other hand, this assumption allows for more accurate modeling in two other dimensions, typically neglected in other approaches. In the first place, there is a great set of possibilities to investigate the effect of complex process structures on the throughput time. It is possible to apply choice, parallel, *and* cycle constructions. Secondly, its is possible to achieve a much higher level of accuracy when modeling the service characteristics by using arbitrary (yet independent) probability distributions. Note that the exact arrival pattern has become irrelevant, because handling of a specific job cannot influence the throughput of another job.

In the next paragraph we will start the formal description of the approach. The basic framework of the model used are high-level stochastic Petri Nets.

2.3   Petri Nets

To create the structure of a business process, we will use classical Petri nets. For a formal definition, the reader is referred to [2] or [5]. A Petri net is a triple (P, T, F) that consists of two node types called *places* and *transitions*, and a flow relation between them. We will use places to model milestones reached within a business process and transitions as the individual tasks within the business process to execute. Places are represented by circles; transitions are represented by rectangles. The process constructions that can be applied in our approach to build a business process are the so-called *blocks*. These are: sequence, choice, parallelism, and iteration. The blocks that express these constructs are depicted as Petri nets in Figure 1.

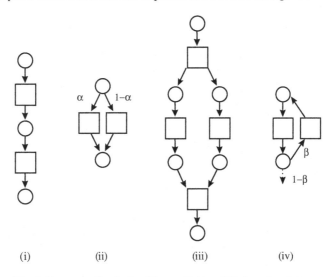

(i)   (ii)   (iii)   (iv)

Fig. 1. Sequence (i), choice (ii), parallelism (iii), iteration (iv).

The first block, the sequence block, represents a process construction that puts two tasks in sequential order. The first task has to be completed before the second can be started. The second, choice block represents a construction in which exactly one of two alternatives is carried out. The third block shows how two tasks can be modeled such that they can be executed simultaneously. The last block, the iteration block, represents the process construction in which the execution of a task can be repeated.

Arc labels occur in the choice (ii) and iteration (iv) blocks. They represent the values of a Bernoulli-distributed random variable that is associated with these blocks. An independent draw from such a random variable determines the route of the flow. Each new application of such a block is accompanied by the introduction of a new, independent random variable.

As the starting point of each Petri net model construction we will take a simple start net. This net is depicted in Figure 2. We will refer to this specific Petri net as *SN*, for start net.

Fig. 2. The start net *SN*.

The next step is to extend the original net, by subsequently applying blocks on parts of the model that are similar to the start net. We shall clarify this replacement rule informally. In Figure 3 the creation of business process model is depicted as the result of successive applications of blocks. The initial start net is extended by applying the construction rule with the sequential block. Both within the upper and the lower half, constructions similar to the start can be distinguished. The upper half of the resulting net is transformed into a choice construction. On the lower half, the parallel composition is applied. Finally, the right path of the parallel construction is modified with the iteration block.

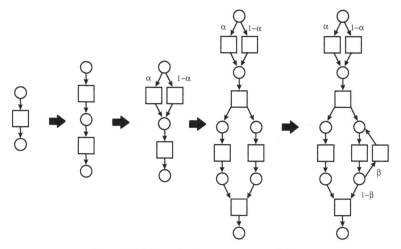

Fig. 3. Building a business process model.

The next step in building the business process model is to assign the service characteristics to the constructed model. In our approach, all service times for one specific task - a timed transition - are independently sampled on basis of the same probability distribution. We will call this distribution the *service distribution*. Its matching probability density is the *service density*. The time which is taken by a service of transition t is called the service time. The service time is a discrete random variable $\underline{t}$. Its matching probability density $f_t : \mathbb{N} \rightarrow \mathbb{R}$ is called the service density;

$$f_t(k) = \mathbb{P}(\underline{t} = k) \text{, for } k \in \mathbb{N}.$$

Its matching probability distribution $F_t : \mathbb{N} \rightarrow \mathbb{R}$, is called the service distribution;

$$F_t(k) = \mathbb{P}(\underline{t} \leq k) \text{, for } k \in \mathbb{N}.$$

The service time $\underline{t}$ is bounded: there is an upper bound $u_t \in \mathbb{N}$ which is the smallest value such that for all $j \in \mathbb{N}$ and $j \geq u_t$ holds that $f_t(j) = 0$.

Our assumption of the service time to be discrete is no real constraint: for practical purposes it is always possible to find an appropriate representation. As we will see, we do need the boundedness of the service time to perform some of the computations to come.

2.4   Blocks

In this paragraph it will be shown how the *throughput time* can be computed of a business process model that is constructed in the presented fashion. The throughput time of a business process is defined as the time that elapses between the arrival of a token at the source place and the corresponding arrival of a token in the sink place. Similar to the service time notions, it is possible to distinguish the throughput distribution and throughput density of a process. Assuming the service densities to be known of each of the transitions within a block, we will show how the throughput density of an entire block can be computed. Each of the blocks requires a specific algorithmic approach.

Sequence block
Consider the sequence block B in Figure 4 with two transitions s and t. Transition t can only be executed when s is completed.

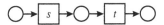

Fig. 4. Sequence block.

The throughput density f_B, given f_s and f_t, can be computed as follows:

Let $y \in \mathbb{N}$

$$f_B(y)$$
= { all possible combinations over transitions s and t; y non-negative }

$$\sum_{i=0}^{y} \mathbb{P}(\underline{s} = i \wedge \underline{t} = y - i)$$

= { $\underline{s}$ and $\underline{t}$ probabilistically independent }

$$\sum_{i=0}^{y} \mathbb{P}(\underline{s} = i)\mathbb{P}(\underline{t} = y - i)$$

= { definition convolution; represent f_s and f_t as vectors, service density in i is the ith coefficient of the vector }

$$f_s \otimes f_t(y)$$

A straightforward computation of the convolution $f_s \otimes f_t$ would require at least $u_s u_t$ multiplications (product of the upper bounds), a quadratic number. To make the computation more efficient, the Fast Fourier Transform (*FFT*) is applied. The FFT is an algorithm that computes the Discrete Fourier Transform (*DFT*) of a vector in $\theta(n \log n)$ steps. Computing a convolution of two vectors, then, comes down at multiplicating the Fourier Transforms of those vectors, after which this product has to be transformed back in a normal vector representation. Using the Fast Fourier transform, a vector representation of $f_s \otimes f_t$ can be computed in $\theta(n \log n)$ time, with n the smallest power of two that is at least twice as large as the maximum of the upper bounds of tasks s and t. For a thorough explanation of the Fourier Transform the reader is referred to [1].

Parallel block
The block we will consider next is the parallel block. Consider the parallel block B in Figure 5 with transitions $k, l, m,$ and n.

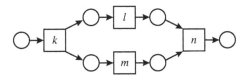

Fig. 5. Parallel block.

Due to the structure of B, transitions l and m can be executed in parallel. That is, there is no precedence constraint between transitions l and m. When both transitions l and m have ended, transition n can be executed. We want to compute throughput density f_B, given $f_k, f_l, f_m,$ and f_n. Without loss of generality we assume that $f_k(0) = 1$ and $f_n(0) = 1$ (they are *logical* transitions).

Let $y \in \mathbb{N}$,
$$f_B(y)$$
= { structure block; k and n instantaneous }
$$\mathbb{P}(\underline{l} \max \underline{m} = y)$$
= { definition max }
$$\mathbb{P}((\underline{l} = y \wedge \underline{m} \leq y) \vee (\underline{m} = y \wedge \underline{l} < y))$$
= { independent random variables }
$$f_l(y) \sum_{i=0}^{y} f_m(i) + f_m(y) \sum_{j=0}^{y-1} f_l(j)$$
= { definition service distribution; distinguish cases $y = 0$ and $y > 0$ }
$$\begin{cases} f_l(y) F_m(y) + f_m(y) F_l(y-1), y > 0 \\ f_l(y) f_m(y), \qquad\qquad y = 0 \end{cases}$$

The computation of the distribution function F_m can be done in u_m steps, just as the distribution function F_l can be computed in u_l steps. Therefore, the total computation of f_B can be done in $\theta(t)$ time, with t equal to the maximum of upper bounds u_l and u_m.

Choice block
The next block we will consider is the choice block. The choice block B is depicted in Figure 6.

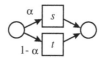

Fig. 6. Choice block.

The block B consists of two transitions s and t. Initiating block B results in either the execution of transition s or transition t, with respective chances α and 1 - α. When the selected transition is completed, the block itself is completed. We would like to compute throughput density f_B, given f_s and f_t.

Let $y \in \mathbb{N}$

$\qquad f_B(y)$

= { structure block; introduce random variable $\underline{I}$ which determines whether transition s or transition t is executed }

$\qquad \mathbb{P}((\underline{I} = s \wedge \underline{s} = y) \vee (\underline{I} = t \wedge \underline{t} = y))$

= { $\mathbb{P}(\underline{I} = s) = \alpha$; $\mathbb{P}(\underline{I} = t) = 1 - \alpha$; $\underline{I}$, $\underline{s}$, and $\underline{t}$ are independent }

$\qquad \alpha f_s(y) + (1 - \alpha) f_t(y)$

From the last expression follows that we can compute f_B in $\theta(n)$ time, with n equal to the maximum of u_s and u_t.

Iteration block
The final and most complex block is the iteration block, depicted in Figure 7. It consists of transitions t and u. The choice for either transition u or termination after completion of transition t is a matter of chance. After each firing of transition t transition u will fire with probability α.

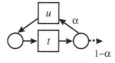

Fig. 7. Iteration block.

The throughput density f_B, given f_t and f_u, can be computed as follows:

Let $y \in \mathbb{N}$,

$$f_B(y)$$

= { t will always be executed one time more than u; define random variable $\underline{n}$ as the number of times that transition u is executed }

$$\sum_{n=0}^{\infty} \mathbb{P}\left(\sum_{j=1}^{n+1} \underline{t}_j + \sum_{j=1}^{n} \underline{u}_j = y \wedge \underline{n} = n \right)$$

= { $\underline{n}$ has geometrical distribution with $\mathbb{P}(\underline{n} = n) = (1 - \alpha)\, \alpha^n$; random variables independent }

$$\sum_{n=0}^{\infty} (1-\alpha)\alpha^n \mathbb{P}\left(\sum_{j=1}^{n+1} \underline{t}_j + \sum_{j=1}^{n} \underline{u}_j = y \right)$$

= { definition of service density f; service times are based on same service density;

definition convolution; introduce notation $\displaystyle\bigotimes_{j=1}^{n} a_j = a_1 \otimes a_2 ... \otimes a_n$ }

$$\sum_{n=0}^{\infty} (1-\alpha)\alpha^n \mathbb{P}\left(\bigotimes_{j=1}^{n+1} f_t \otimes \bigotimes_{j=1}^{n} f_u(y) \right)$$

At this point we realize that a more suitable computational approach is to derive the Discrete Fourier Transform of the vector representation of f_B from the transforms of $\vec{t}$ and $\vec{u}$. Doing so, it is possible to use an inverse transformation to actually compute $\vec{B}$ - the vector representation of f_B. Leaving undecided yet what is the proper length of $\vec{B}$ we denote the index of the DFT with l.

$$DFT_l(\vec{B})$$

= { recall derivation of $f_B(y)$; use · for pointwise vector multiplication and + for pointwise addition }

$$DFT_l\left(\sum_{n=0}^{\infty} (1-\alpha)\alpha^n \left(\bigotimes_{j=1}^{n+1} \vec{t} \otimes \bigotimes_{j=1}^{n} \vec{u} \right) \right)$$

= { DFT distributes over multiplication and addition }

$$\sum_{n=0}^{\infty} (1-\alpha)\alpha^n DFT_l\left(\bigotimes_{j=1}^{n+1} \vec{t} \otimes \bigotimes_{j=1}^{n} \vec{u} \right)$$

= { convolution theorem; convolution is associative }

$$\sum_{n=0}^{\infty} (1-\alpha)\alpha^n DFT_l^{n+1}(\vec{t})\, DFT_l^n(\vec{u})$$

= { calculus }

$$\frac{(1-\alpha)DFT_l(\vec{t})}{1-\alpha DFT_l(\vec{t})DFT_l(\vec{u})}$$

Obviously, we can not expect f_B to have an upper bound. After all, t and u could be executed infinitely often if α is non-zero. So by choosing n as proposed we may end up with a vector representation of f_B that is too short. That is, there may be interesting values of f_B that will not be represented. We will show how a relevant, estimated length of $\vec{B}$ can be determined before actually computing $\vec{B}$. We would be most pleased to find a value v such that for some very small ε holds:

$$\mathbb{P}(\underline{B} \geq v) \leq \varepsilon \tag{i}$$

We are looking for an estimation of v that takes the distribution of values within f_t and f_u into account. For this purpose we will use Chebyshev's inequality, that we present without proof (see [8]). This inequality is often used to find a rough upper bound in mostly theoretical applications.

Theorem (Chebyshev's inequality) For any random variable $\underline{x}$ for which $E\underline{x}^2$ exists:

$$\mathbb{P}(|\underline{x} - E\underline{x}| \geq c) \leq \frac{\operatorname{var}\underline{x}}{c^2}$$

With this inequality in the one hand, and the mean and variance of the throughput density f_B in the other, it can be determined which probability part of the density falls before or after a hypothetical border. As the service time for any transition t is denoted by $\underline{t}$ we will denote its mean by $E\underline{t}$ and its variance by var $\underline{t}$.

$E\underline{B}$
$= \{$ structure block$\}$
$\qquad E\underline{t} + \alpha(E\underline{u} + E\underline{B})$
$= \{$ calculus $\}$
$\qquad \dfrac{E\underline{t} + \alpha E\underline{u}}{1 - \alpha}$

The computation of the variance of the iteration block is as follows.

var $\underline{B}$
$= \{$ structure block; definition variance $\}$
$\qquad \alpha \operatorname{var}(\underline{t} + \underline{u} + \underline{B}) + (1 - \alpha) \operatorname{var}\underline{t} + \alpha(1 - \alpha)(E(\underline{t} + \underline{u} + \underline{B}) - E\underline{t})^2$
$= \{$ calculus; previous result for $E\underline{B}$ $\}$
$\qquad \dfrac{\operatorname{var}\underline{t} + \alpha \operatorname{var}\underline{u}}{1 - \alpha} + \alpha\left(\dfrac{E\underline{u} + E\underline{t}}{1 - \alpha}\right)^2$

With Chebyshev's inequality we can determine a relevant part of vector $\vec{B}$ by modifying our original requirement (i) with:

$$\mathbb{P}(\underline{B} \geq v \vee \underline{B} \leq -v) \leq \varepsilon \tag{ii}$$

This is only apparently a stronger requirement than (i), as $\underline{B}$ can never be negative and the sum of positive values of f_B is 1. Immediate application of Chebyshev on equation (ii) is possible and yields the following:

$$v \geq c + E\underline{B}$$

and

$$\varepsilon = \frac{\text{var } \underline{B}}{c^2}.$$

From these equalities we can derive that:

$$v \geq E\underline{B} + \sqrt{\frac{\text{var } \underline{B}}{\varepsilon}}.$$

Concluding, given f_t and f_u, we can compute a vector representation of f_B for the iteration block by using the *DFT*:

$$DFT_v(\vec{B}) = \frac{(1-\alpha)DFT_v(\vec{t})}{1 - \alpha DFT_v(\vec{t})DFT_v(\vec{u})}$$

with

v is the smallest power of two such that $v \geq E\underline{B} + \sqrt{\dfrac{\text{var } \underline{B}}{\varepsilon}}$, and

$$\text{var } \underline{B} = \frac{\text{var } \underline{t} + \alpha \text{ var } \underline{u}}{1-\alpha} + \alpha \left(\frac{E\underline{u} + E\underline{t}}{1-\alpha} \right)^2.$$

With the *FFT* we can compute a vector representation of f_B in ($v \log v$) time, with v as specified. To appreciate its efficiency we have to establish the computing time of calculating f_B in a straightforward manner. The complexity of this calculation depends on the maximal number of successive times that transitions t and u can be executed. We know that if both $f_t(0)$ and $f_u(0)$ are equal to zero, at most v executions of these transitions are of interest. Any more executions of transitions u and t would result in throughput times that we do not take into consideration. As a result, a straightforward approach requires the convolution of v times the function f_t and f_u. This is an operation requiring $\theta(n^v)$ time, with n the maximum of upper bounds of transitions t and u. A comparison with the $\theta(v \log v)$ time required by our newly found computation method illustrates the efficiency of the latter.

2.5   Overall Computation

Suppose we have constructed a business process model from the start model *SN* with n subsequent applications of the construction rule. Then, for $n > 1$ we can distinguish the intermediate models $W_1, W_2, \ldots, W_{n-1}$. W_1 is the result of the application of the construction rule using one of the blocks on the start model S; W_n results from the nth

application of the construction rule on intermediate model W_{n-1}. For each of the other intermediate models W_i holds that it is the result from the ith application of the construction rule on intermediate model W_{i-1}. Note that we can represent all intermediate process models hierarchically in a derivation tree. It is, in fact, this derivation tree that we will step through during our computation.

To compute the total throughput time of the constructed process model W we assume that the service density of each of its transitions is known. In addition, all probability distributions that involve choices or iterations are known too. Now we take the opposite direction of the construction route. Starting at the end, we consider the last application of the construction rule that leads from W_{n-1} to W. We know which part of W_{n-1} is replaced by which specific block. We call this part S_{n-1} and the block B_{n-1}. Recall that S_{n-1} is isomorphic with the start model. B_{n-1} is the part of which we compute its throughput density t_{n-1}. This is feasible, as we know all relevant service densities in W.

The resulting throughput density t_{n-1} is a fair characterization of the time that it takes B_{n-1} to process a job. What is more, the block can be seen as a detailed specification of the behavior of S_{n-1} that it has replaced. Therefore, the resulting throughput density is a fair characterization of the service time that it takes S_{n-1} to process a job as well. When the only transition in S_{n-1} should have a service density that is equal to t_{n-1}, the total throughput time of W_{n-1} would exactly be the same as that of W. S_{n-1} can be seen as a "black box" for the applied block. The effort of computing the throughput time of W has now become the effort to compute the throughput time of W_{n-1}.

We can repeat this approach for each of the n transformations. When we ensure that we follow the construction route in opposite direction, we can be confident that all relevant data is available to compute the throughput time of each start model that has been replaced. Finally, we end up with the start block SN. This block will have only one transition of which its service density characterization is exactly the throughput characterization of the entire process model W. And this is exactly the throughput density we were looking for.

2.6   Numerical Experience

To give an indication of the efficiency of the presented algorithm to analyze the throughput time of a business process model in the above way, we have computed the throughput density of the rightmost process model depicted in Figure 3. As tool for these calculations we have used the mathematical software package Maple V® running on a Pentium 100 MHz computer. Each of the seven transitions in the process model has been modeled to behave in accordance with distinct service densities. These service densities, together with the process model under consideration, are depicted in Figure 8. The service densities in this example are bounded by 64 time units.

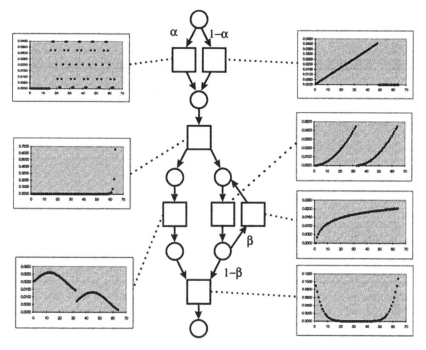

Fig. 8. Numerical example.

The probabilities α and β of the model have been set on 0.3 and 0.15 respectively. For the computation of the throughput density of the iteration block an inaccuracy (ε) of 1 percent has been allowed. The resulting throughput density for the entire net is depicted in Figure 9.

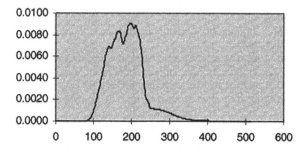

Fig. 9. Outcome throughput time.

The computation of the throughput density of the example net has been performed for several sizes of the throughput density domain. These results can be found in Table 1.

Table 1. Computation time for example

Bound (service time units)	64	128	256	512	1024	2048
Computation time (seconds)	13	28	64	152	377	990

As can be seen, the computation time increases somewhat faster than linearly in the bound dimension. It can be easily verified that the same relation exists between the number of transitions and the computation time.

3. Conclusion

In this chapter we have made a case for the application of formal analysis techniques during the redesign of business processes. We have identified the phases in a redesign project where formal techniques can be applied. On a more detailed level, we have shown how an analytical technique can be used to establish the throughput time of a business process model. This analysis technique is only one of the many possible quantitative analytical techniques that can offer support in this field. A redesign tool that incorporates these kinds of techniques, presenting relevant analytical characteristics of a business process can be a valuable asset to designers. In this way, redesign measures formerly only justified by "gut feeling" can be rationalised. Considering the money, time and stakes involved with BPR we would embrace an increased rationality of the redesign process that may be acquired with the use of a redesign tool.

References

1. Cormen, T. H., Leiseron, C.E., Rivest, R.L.: Introduction to Algorithms. The MIT Press, Cambridge (1990).
2. Hee, van, K.M.: Information Systems Engineering: a Formal Approach. Cambridge University Press (1994).
3. Hee, van, K.M., Aalst, van der, W.M.P.: Workflow Managament: Modellen, Methoden en Systemen. Academic Service, Schoonhoven (1997) [In Dutch]
4. Hee, van, K.M., Reijers, H.A.: An Analytical Method for Computing Throughput Times in Stochastic Workflow Nets. Proceedings of the 7th Analytical and Numerical Modelling Techniques Conference (1999) [Forthcoming]
5. Jensen, K: Coloured Petri Nets. Basic Concepts, Analysis Methods and Practical Use, Vol. 1, Basic Concepts. Springer-Verlag, Berlin (1992).
6. Levin, R., Kirkpatrick, C.: Planning and control with PERT/CPM. McGraw-Hill, New York (1966).
7. Neuman, K., Steinhardt, U.: GERT Networks, vol. 172 of Lecture Notes in Economic and Mathematical Systems. Springer-Verlag, Berlin (1979).
8. Thomasian, A.J.: The structure of Probability Theory with Applications. McGraw-Hill Book Company, New York (1969).
9. Tijms, H. C.: Stochastic Models: an Algorithmic Approach. John Wiley & Sons, New York (1994).

Workflow Verification: Finding Control-Flow Errors Using Petri-Net-Based Techniques

W.M.P. van der Aalst

Eindhoven University of Technology, Faculty of Technology and Management, Department of Information and Technology, P.O. Box 513, NL-5600 MB, Eindhoven, The Netherlands.
w.m.p.v.d.aalst@tm.tue.nl

Abstract. Workflow management systems facilitate the everyday operation of business processes by taking care of the logistic control of work. In contrast to traditional information systems, they attempt to support frequent changes of the workflows at hand. Therefore, the need for analysis methods to verify the correctness of workflows is becoming more prominent. In this chapter we present a method based on Petri nets. This analysis method exploits the structure of the Petri net to find potential errors in the design of the workflow. Moreover, the analysis method allows for the compositional verification of workflows.

1 Introduction

Workflow management systems (WFMS) are used for the modeling, analysis, enactment, and coordination of structured business processes by groups of people. Business processes supported by a WFMS are *case-driven*, i.e., tasks are executed for specific cases. Approving loans, processing insurance claims, billing, processing tax declarations, handling traffic violations and mortgaging, are typical case-driven processes which are often supported by a WFMS. These case-driven processes, also called *workflows*, are marked by three dimensions: (1) the control-flow dimension, (2) the resource dimension, and (3) the case dimension (see Figure 1). The control-flow dimension is concerned with the partial ordering of tasks, i.e., the workflow *process*. The tasks which need to be executed are identified and the routing of cases along these tasks is determined. Conditional, sequential, parallel and iterative routing are typical structures specified in the control-flow dimension. Tasks are executed by resources. Resources are human (e.g., employee) and/or non-human (e.g., device, software, hardware). In the resource dimension these resources are classified by identifying roles (resource classes based on functional characteristics) and organizational units (groups, teams or departments). Both the control-flow dimension and the resource dimension are generic, i.e., they are not tailored towards a specific case. The third dimension of a workflow is concerned with individual cases which are executed according to the process definition (first dimension) by the proper resources (second dimension).

Managing workflows is not a new idea. Workflow control techniques have existed for decades and many management concepts originating from production and logistics are also applicable in a workflow context. However, just recently, commercially available generic WFMS's have become a reality. Although these systems have been

W. van der Aalst et al. (Eds.): Business Process Management, LNCS 1806, pp. 161-183, 2000.

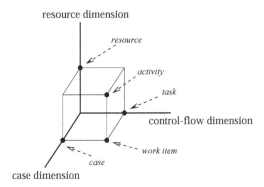

Fig. 1. The three dimensions of workflow.

applied successfully, contemporary WFMS's have at least two important drawbacks. First of all, today's systems do not scale well, have limited fault tolerance and are inflexible. Secondly, a solid theoretical foundation is missing. Most of the more than 250 commercially available WFMS's use a vendor-specific ad-hoc modeling technique to design workflows. In spite of the efforts of the Workflow Management Coalition [25], real standards are missing. The absence of formalized standards hinders the development of tool-independent analysis techniques. As a result, contemporary WFMS's do not facilitate advanced analysis methods to determine the correctness of a workflow.

As many researchers have indicated [11, 18, 26], Petri nets constitute a good starting point for a solid theoretical foundation of workflow management. In this chapter we focus on the control-flow dimension. We use Petri nets to specify the partial ordering of tasks. Based on a Petri-net-based representation of the workflow, we tackle the problem of verification. We will provide techniques to verify the so-called *soundness property* introduced in [2]. A workflow is sound if and only if, for any case, the process terminates properly, i.e., termination is guaranteed, there are no dangling references, and deadlock and livelock are absent.

This chapter extends the results presented in [2]. We will show that in most of the situations encountered in practice, the soundness property can be checked in polynomial time. Moreover, we identify suspicious constructs which may endanger the correctness of a workflow. We will also show that the approach presented in this chapter allows for the compositional verification of workflows, i.e., the correctness of a process can be decided by partitioning it into sound subprocesses. To support the application of the results presented in this chapter, we have developed a Petri-net-based workflow analyzer called *Woflan* [4, 5, 23, 24]. Woflan is a workflow management system independent analysis tool which interfaces with some of the leading products at the Dutch workflow market.

2   Workflow Perspectives

This chapter uses the soundness property as the criterion for correctness. It is clear that this property does not capture all possible errors because it primarily focuses on the control flow. Before we focus on techniques to verify soundness, we discuss the usefulness of a control-flow-based criterion for correctness.

The primary task of a workflow management system is to enact case-driven business processes by joining several perspectives. The following perspectives are relevant for workflow modeling and workflow execution: (1) *control flow* (or process) perspective, (2) *resource* (or organization) perspective, (3) *data* (or information) perspective, (4) *task* (or function) perspective, (5) *operation* (or application) perspective. These perspectives are similar to the perspectives given in [16] and the control flow and resource perspectives correspond to the first two dimensions shown in Figure 1. The third dimension reflects the fact that workflows are case-driven.

In the control-flow perspective, *workflow process definitions* (workflow schemas) are defined to specify which *tasks* need to be executed and in what order (i.e., the routing or control flow). A task is an atomic piece of work. Workflow process definitions are instantiated for specific *cases* (i.e., workflow instances). Since a case is an instantiation of a process definition, it corresponds to the execution of concrete work according to the specified routing. In the *resource* perspective, the organizational structure and the population are specified. The organizational structure describes relations between roles (resource classes based on functional aspects) and groups (resource classes based on organizational aspects). Thus clarifying organizational issues such as responsibility, availability, and authorization. Resources, ranging from humans to devices, form the organizational population and are allocated to roles and groups. The data perspective deals with *control* and *production data*. Control data are data introduced solely for workflow management purposes, e.g., variables introduced for routing purposes. Production data are information objects (e.g., documents, forms, and tables) whose existence does not depend on workflow management. The task perspective describes the elementary operations performed by resources while executing a task for a specific case. In the operational perspective the elementary actions are described. These actions are often executed using applications ranging from a text editor to custom build applications to perform complex calculations. Typically, these applications create, read, or modify control and production data in the information perspective.

This chapter addresses the problem of workflow verification. Although each of the perspectives is relevant, we focus on the control flow perspective. In fact, we focus on the life cycle of one case in isolation. In the remainder of this section, we will motivate why it is reasonable to abstract from the other perspectives when verifying a workflow.

We abstract from the resource perspective because, given today's workflow technology, at any time there is only one resource working on a task which is being executed for a specific case. In today's workflow management systems it is not possible to specify that several resources are collaborating in executing a task. Note that even if multiple persons are executing one task, e.g., writing a report, only one person is allocated to that task from the perspective of the workflow management system: This is the person that selected the work item from the in-basket (i.e., the electronic worktray). Since a person is working on one task at a time and each task is eventually executed by one person (although it may be allocated to a group a people), it is sufficient to check whether all resources classes have at least one resource. In contrast to many other application domains such a flexible manufacturing systems, anomalies such as a deadlock resulting from locking problems are not possible. Therefore, from the viewpoint of verification, i.e., analyzing the logical correctness of a workflow, it is reasonable to abstract from resources. However, if in the future collaborative features are explicitly supported by the workflow management system (i.e., a tight integration of groupware and workflow technology), then the resource perspective should be taken into account.

We partly abstract from the data perspective. The reason we abstract from production data is that these are outside the scope of the workflow management system. These data can be changed at any time without notifying the workflow management system. In fact their existence does not even depend upon the workflow application and they may be shared among different workflows, e.g., the bill-of-material in manufacturing is shared by production, procurement, sales, and quality control processes. The control data used by the workflow management system to route cases are managed by the workflow management system. However, some of these data are set or updated by humans or applications. For example, a decision is made by a manager based on intuition or a case is classified based on a complex calculation involving production data. Clearly, the behavior of a human or a complex application cannot be modeled completely. Therefore, some abstraction is needed to incorporate the data perspective when verifying a given workflow. The abstraction used in this chapter is the following. Since control data (i.e., workflow attributes such as the age of a customer, the department responsible, or the registration date) are only used for the routing of a case, we incorporate the routing decisions but not the actual data. For example, the decision to accept or to reject an insurance claim is taken into account, but not the actual data where this decision is based on. Therefore, we consider each choice to be a non-deterministic one. There are other reasons for abstracting from the workflow attributes. If we are able to prove soundness (i.e., the correctness criterion used in this chapter) for the situation without workflow attributes, it will also hold for the situation with workflow attributes (assuming certain fairness properties). Last but not least, we abstract from triggers and workflow attributes because it allows us to use ordinary Petri nets (i.e., P/T nets) rather than high-level Petri nets. From an analysis point of view, this is preferable because of the availability of efficient algorithms and powerful analysis tools.

For similar reasons we (partly) abstract from the task and operation perspectives. We consider tasks to be atomic and abstract from the execution of operations inside tasks. The workflow management system can only launch applications or trigger people and monitor the results. It cannot control the actual execution of the task. Therefore, from the viewpoint of verification, it is reasonable to focus on the control-flow perspective. In fact, it suffices to consider the life cycle of one case in isolation. The only way cases interact directly is the competition for resources and the sharing of production data. (Note that control data are strictly separated.) Therefore, if we abstract from resources and data, it suffices to consider one case in isolation. The competition between cases for resources is only relevant for performance analysis.

3   Petri Nets

This section introduces the basic Petri net terminology and notations. Readers familiar with Petri nets can skip this section.[1]

The classical Petri net is a directed bipartite graph with two node types called *places* and *transitions*. The nodes are connected via directed *arcs*. Connections between two nodes of the same type are not allowed. Places are represented by circles and transitions by rectangles.

Definition 1 (Petri net). *A Petri net is a triple* (P, T, F)*:*

- *P is a finite set of places,*
- *T is a finite set of transitions ($P \cap T = \emptyset$),*
- *$F \subseteq (P \times T) \cup (T \times P)$ is a set of arcs (flow relation)*

A place p is called an *input place* of a transition t iff there exists a directed arc from p to t. Place p is called an *output place* of transition t iff there exists a directed arc from t to p. We use $\bullet t$ to denote the set of input places for a transition t. The notations $t\bullet$, $\bullet p$ and $p\bullet$ have similar meanings, e.g., $p\bullet$ is the set of transitions sharing p as an input place. Note that we do not consider multiple arcs from one node to another. In the context of workflow procedures it makes no sense to have other weights, because places correspond to conditions.

At any time a place contains zero or more *tokens*, drawn as black dots. The *state*, often referred to as marking, is the distribution of tokens over places, i.e., $M \in P \to \mathbb{N}$. We will represent a state as follows: $1p_1 + 2p_2 + 1p_3 + 0p_4$ is the state with one token in place p_1, two tokens in p_2, one token in p_3 and no tokens in p_4. We can also represent this state as follows: $p_1 + 2p_2 + p_3$. To compare states we define a partial ordering. For any two states M_1 and M_2, $M_1 \leq M_2$ iff for all $p \in P$: $M_1(p) \leq M_2(p)$

The number of tokens may change during the execution of the net. Transitions are the active components in a Petri net: they change the state of the net according to the following *firing rule*:

(1) A transition t is said to be *enabled* iff each input place p of t contains at least one token.
(2) An enabled transition may *fire*. If transition t fires, then t *consumes* one token from each input place p of t and *produces* one token for each output place p of t.

Given a Petri net (P, T, F) and a state M_1, we have the following notations:

- $M_1 \xrightarrow{t} M_2$: transition t is enabled in state M_1 and firing t in M_1 results in state M_2
- $M_1 \to M_2$: there is a transition t such that $M_1 \xrightarrow{t} M_2$
- $M_1 \xrightarrow{\sigma} M_n$: the firing sequence $\sigma = t_1 t_2 t_3 \ldots t_{n-1}$ leads from state M_1 to state M_n via a (possibly empty) set of intermediate states $M_2, \ldots M_{n-1}$, i.e., $M_1 \xrightarrow{t_1} M_2 \xrightarrow{t_2} \ldots \xrightarrow{t_{n-1}} M_n$

---

[1] Note that states are represented by weighted sums and note the definition of (elementary) (conflict-free) paths.

A state M_n is called *reachable* from M_1 (notation $M_1 \xrightarrow{*} M_n$) iff there is a firing sequence σ such that $M_1 \xrightarrow{\sigma} M_n$. Note that the empty firing sequence is also allowed, i.e., $M_1 \xrightarrow{*} M_1$.

We use (PN, M) to denote a Petri net PN with an initial state M. A state M' is a *reachable state* of (PN, M) iff $M \xrightarrow{*} M'$.

Let us define some standard properties for Petri nets. First, we define properties related to the dynamics of a Petri net, then we give some structural properties.

Definition 2 (Live). *A Petri net (PN, M) is live iff, for every reachable state M' and every transition t there is a state M'' reachable from M' which enables t.*

A Petri net is *structurally live* if there exists an initial state such that the net is live.

Definition 3 (Bounded, safe). *A Petri net (PN, M) is bounded iff for each place p there is a natural number n such that for every reachable state the number of tokens in p is less than n. The net is safe iff for each place the maximum number of tokens does not exceed 1.*

A Petri net is *structurally bounded* if the net is bounded for any initially state.

Definition 4 (Well-formed). *A Petri net PN is well-formed iff there is a state M such that (PN, M) is live and bounded.*

Paths connect nodes by a sequence of arcs.

Definition 5 (Path, Elementary, Conflict-free). *Let PN be a Petri net. A path C from a node n_1 to a node n_k is a sequence $\langle n_1, n_2, \ldots, n_k \rangle$ such that $\langle n_i, n_{i+1} \rangle \in F$ for $1 \le i \le k - 1$. C is elementary iff, for any two nodes n_i and n_j on C, $i \ne j \Rightarrow n_i \ne n_j$. C is conflict-free iff, for any place n_j on C and any transition n_i on C, $j \ne i - 1 \Rightarrow n_j \notin \bullet n_i$.*

For convenience, we introduce the alphabet operator α on paths. If $C = \langle n_1, n_2, \ldots, n_k \rangle$, then $\alpha(C) = \{n_1, n_2, \ldots, n_k\}$.

Definition 6 (Strongly connected). *A Petri net is strongly connected iff, for every pair of nodes (i.e., places and transitions) x and y, there is a path leading from x to y.*

Definition 7 (Free-choice). *A Petri net is a free-choice Petri net iff, for every two transitions t_1 and t_2, $\bullet t_1 \cap \bullet t_2 \ne \emptyset$ implies $\bullet t_1 = \bullet t_2$.*

Definition 8 (State machine). *A Petri net is state machine iff each transition has exactly one input and one output place.*

Definition 9 (S-component). *A subnet $PN_s = (P_s, T_s, F_s)$ is called an S-component of a Petri net $PN = (P, T, F)$ if $P_s \subseteq P$, $T_s \subseteq T$, $F_s \subseteq F$, PN_s is strongly connected, PN_s is a state machine, and for every $q \in P_s$ and $t \in T$: $(q, t) \in F \Rightarrow (q, t) \in F_s$ and $(t, q) \in F \Rightarrow (t, q) \in F_s$.*

Definition 10 (S-coverable). *A Petri net is S-coverable iff for any node there exist an S-component which contains this node.*

See [10, 20] for a more elaborate introduction to these standard notions.

4   WF-Nets

In Figure 1 we indicated that a workflow has (at least) three dimensions. The control-flow dimension is the most prominent one, because the core of any workflow system is formed by the processes it supports. In the control-flow dimension building blocks such as the AND-split, AND-join, OR-split, and OR-join are used to model sequential, conditional, parallel and iterative routing (WFMC [25]). Clearly, a Petri net can be used to specify the routing of cases. *Tasks* are modeled by transitions and causal dependencies are modeled by places and arcs. In fact, a place corresponds to a *condition* which can be used as pre- and/or post-condition for tasks. An AND-split corresponds to a transition with two or more output places, and an AND-join corresponds to a transition with two or more input places. OR-splits/OR-joins correspond to places with multiple outgoing/ingoing arcs. Moreover, in [1] it is shown that the Petri net approach also allows for useful routing constructs absent in many WFMS's.

A Petri net which models the control-flow dimension of a workflow, is called a *WorkFlow net* (WF-net). It should be noted that a WF-net specifies the dynamic behavior of a single case in isolation.

Definition 11 (WF-net). *A Petri net $PN = (P, T, F)$ is a WF-net (Workflow net) if and only if:*

   (i) *There is one source place $i \in P$ such that $\bullet i = \emptyset$.*
  (ii) *There is one sink place $o \in P$ such that $o\bullet = \emptyset$.*
 (iii) *Every node $x \in P \cup T$ is on a path from i to o.*

A WF-net has one input place (i) and one output place (o) because any case handled by the procedure represented by the WF-net is created when it enters the WFMS and is deleted once it is completely handled by the WFMS, i.e., the WF-net specifies the life-cycle of a case. The third requirement in Definition 11 has been added to avoid 'dangling tasks and/or conditions', i.e., tasks and conditions which do not contribute to the processing of cases.

Given the definition of a WF-net it is easy derive the following properties.

Proposition 1 (Properties of WF-nets). *Let $PN = (P, T, F)$ be Petri net.*

 – *If PN is WF-net with source place i, then for any place $p \in P$: $\bullet p \neq \emptyset$ or $p = i$, i.e., i is the only source place.*
 – *If PN is WF-net with sink place o, then for any place $p \in P$: $p\bullet \neq \emptyset$ or $p = o$, i.e., o is the only sink place.*
 – *If PN is a WF-net and we add a transition t^* to PN which connects sink place o with source place i (i.e., $\bullet t^* = \{o\}$ and $t^*\bullet = \{i\}$), then the resulting Petri net is strongly connected.*
 – *If PN has a source place i and a sink place o and adding a transition t^* which connects sink place o with source place i yields a strongly connected net, then every node $x \in P \cup T$ is on a path from i to o in PN and PN is a WF-net.*

Figure 2 shows a WF-net which models the processing of complaints. First the complaint is registered (task *register*), then in parallel a questionnaire is sent to the complainant (task *send_questionnaire*) and the complaint is evaluated (task *evaluate*). If the

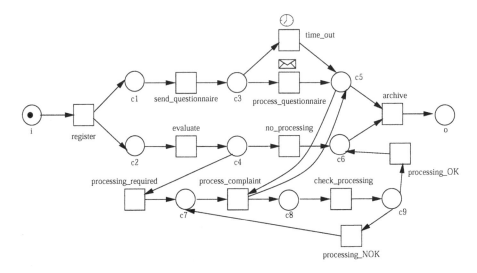

Fig. 2. A WF-net for the processing of complaints.

complainant returns the questionnaire within two weeks, the task *process_questionnaire* is executed. If the questionnaire is not returned within two weeks, the result of the questionnaire is discarded (task *time_out*). Based on the result of the evaluation, the complaint is processed or not. The actual processing of the complaint (task *process_complaint*) is delayed until condition $c5$ is satisfied, i.e., the questionnaire is processed or a time-out has occurred. The processing of the complaint is checked via task *check_processing*. Finally, task *archive* is executed. Note that sequential, conditional, parallel and iterative routing are present in this example.

The WF-net shown in Figure 2 clearly illustrates that we focus on the control-flow dimension. We abstract from resources, applications, and technical platforms. Moreover, we also abstract from *case variables* and *triggers*. Case variables are used to resolve choices (OR-split), i.e., the choice between *processing_required* and *no_processing* is (partially) based on case variables set during the execution of task *evaluate*. The choice between *processing_OK* and *processing_NOK* is resolved by testing case variables set by *check_processing*. In the WF-net we abstract from case variables by introducing non-deterministic choices in the Petri-net. If we don't abstract from this information, we would have to model the (unknown) behavior of the applications used in each of the tasks and analysis would become intractable. In Figure 2 we have indicated that *time_out* and *process_questionnaire* require triggers. The clock symbol denotes a time trigger and the envelope symbol denotes an external trigger. Task *time_out* requires a time trigger ('two weeks have passed') and *process_questionnaire* requires a message trigger ('the questionnaire has been returned'). A trigger can be seen as an additional condition which needs to be satisfied. In the remainder of this chapter we abstract from these trigger conditions. We assume that the environment behaves fairly, i.e., the liveness of a transition is not hindered by the continuous absence of a specific trigger. As a result, every trigger condition will be satisfied eventually.

5   Soundness

In this section we summarize some of the basic results for WF-nets presented in [2]. The remainder of this chapter will build on these results.

The three requirements stated in Definition 11 can be verified statically, i.e., they only relate to the structure of the Petri net. However, there is another requirement which should be satisfied:

> *For any case, the procedure will terminate eventually and the moment the procedure terminates there is a token in place o and all the other places are empty.*

Moreover, there should be no dead tasks, i.e., it should be possible to execute an arbitrary task by following the appropriate route though the WF-net. These two additional requirements correspond to the so-called *soundness property*.

Definition 12 (Sound). *A procedure modeled by a WF-net $PN = (P, T, F)$ is sound if and only if:*

(i) *For every state M reachable from state i, there exists a firing sequence leading from state M to state o. Formally:[2]*

$$\forall_M (i \xrightarrow{*} M) \Rightarrow (M \xrightarrow{*} o)$$

(ii) *State o is the only state reachable from state i with at least one token in place o. Formally:*

$$\forall_M (i \xrightarrow{*} M \wedge M \geq o) \Rightarrow (M = o)$$

(iii) *There are no dead transitions in (PN, i). Formally:*

$$\forall_{t \in T} \exists_{M, M'} i \xrightarrow{*} M \xrightarrow{t} M'$$

Note that the soundness property relates to the dynamics of a WF-net. The first requirement in Definition 12 states that starting from the initial state (state i), it is always possible to reach the state with one token in place o (state o). If we assume a strong notion of fairness, then the first requirement implies that eventually state o is reached. Strong fairness means in every infinite firing sequence, each transition fires infinitely often. The fairness assumption is reasonable in the context of workflow management: All choices are made (implicitly or explicitly) by applications, humans or external actors. Clearly, they should not introduce an infinite loop. Note that the traditional notions of fairness (i.e., weaker forms of fairness with just local conditions, e.g., if a transition is enabled infinitely often, it will fire eventually) are not sufficient. See [3, 17] for more details. The second requirement states that the moment a token is put in place o, all the other places should be empty. Sometimes the term *proper termination* is used to describe the first two requirements [14]. The last requirement states that there are no dead transitions (tasks) in the initial state i.

---

[2] Note that there is an overloading of notation: the symbol i is used to denote both the *place i* and the *state* with only one token in place i (see Section 3).

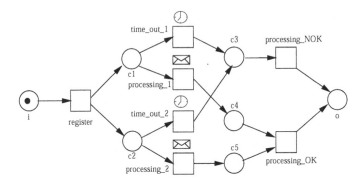

Fig. 3. Another WF-net for the processing of complaints.

Figure 3 shows a WF-net which is not sound. There are several deficiencies. If *time_out_1* and *processing_2* fire or *time_out_2* and *processing_1* fire, the WF-net will not terminate properly because a token gets stuck in *c4* or *c5*. If *time_out_1* and *time_out_2* fire, then the task *processing_NOK* will be executed twice and because of the presence of two tokens in *o* the moment of termination is not clear.

Given a WF-net $PN = (P, T, F)$, we want to decide whether PN is sound. In [2] we have shown that soundness corresponds to liveness and boundedness. To link soundness to liveness and boundedness, we define an extended net $\overline{PN} = (\overline{P}, \overline{T}, \overline{F})$. $\overline{PN}$ is the Petri net obtained by adding an extra transition t^* which connects o and i. The extended Petri net $\overline{PN} = (\overline{P}, \overline{T}, \overline{F})$ is defined as follows: $\overline{P} = P$, $\overline{T} = T \cup \{t^*\}$, and $\overline{F} = F \cup \{\langle o, t^* \rangle, \langle t^*, i \rangle\}$. In the remainder we will call such an extended net the *short-circuited* net of PN. The short-circuited net allows for the formulation of the following theorem.

Theorem 1. *A WF-net PN is sound if and only if $(\overline{PN}, i)$ is live and bounded.*

Proof. See [2].   □

This theorem shows that standard Petri-net-based analysis techniques can be used to verify soundness.

6   Structural Characterization of Soundness

Theorem 1 gives a useful characterization of the quality of a workflow process definition. However, there are a number of problems:

- For a complex WF-net it may be intractable to decide soundness. (For arbitrary WF-nets liveness and boundedness are decidable but also EXPSPACE-hard, cf. Cheng, Esparza and Palsberg [8].)
- Soundness is a minimal requirement. Readability and maintainability issues are not addressed by Theorem 1.
- Theorem 1 does not show how a non-sound WF-net should be modified, i.e., it does not identify constructs which invalidate the soundness property.

These problems stem from the fact that the definition of soundness relates to the dynamics of a WF-net while the workflow designer is concerned with the static structure of the WF-net. Therefore, it is interesting to investigate structural characterizations of sound WF-nets. For this purpose we introduce three interesting subclasses of WF-nets: free-choice WF-nets, well-structured WF-nets, and S-coverable WF-nets.

6.1   Free-Choice WF-Nets

Most of the WFMS's available at the moment, abstract from states between tasks, i.e., states are not represented explicitly. These WFMS's use building blocks such as the AND-split, AND-join, OR-split and OR-join to specify workflow procedures. The AND-split and the AND-join are used for parallel routing. The OR-split and the OR-join are used for conditional routing. Because these systems abstract from states, every choice is made *inside* an OR-split building block. If we model an OR-split in terms of a Petri net, the OR-split corresponds to a number of transitions sharing the same set of input places. This means that for these WFMS's, a workflow procedure corresponds to a free-choice Petri net (cf. Definition 7).

It is easy to see that a process definition composed of AND-splits, AND-joins, OR-splits and OR-joins is free-choice. If two transitions t_1 and t_2 share an input place ($\bullet t_1 \cap \bullet t_2 \neq \emptyset$), then they are part of an OR-split, i.e., a 'free choice' between a number of alternatives. Therefore, the sets of input places of t_1 and t_2 should match ($\bullet t_1 = \bullet t_2$). Figure 3 shows a free-choice WF-net. The WF-net shown in Figure 2 is not free-choice; *archive* and *process_complaint* share an input place but the two corresponding input sets differ.

We have evaluated many WFMS's and just one of these systems (COSA [21]) allows for a construct which is comparable to a non-free choice WF-net. Therefore, it makes sense to consider free-choice Petri nets in more detail. Clearly, parallelism, sequential routing, conditional routing and iteration can be modeled without violating the free-choice property. Another reason for restricting WF-nets to free-choice Petri nets is the following. If we allow non-free-choice Petri nets, then the choice between conflicting tasks *may* be influenced by the order in which the preceding tasks are executed. The routing of a case should be independent of the order in which tasks are executed. A situation where the free-choice property is violated is often a mixture of parallelism and choice. Figure 4 shows such a situation. Firing transition *t1* introduces parallelism. Although there is no real choice between *t2* and *t5* (*t5* is not enabled), the parallel execution of *t2* and *t3* results in a situation where *t5* is not allowed to occur. However, if the execution of *t2* is delayed until *t3* has been executed, then there is a real choice between *t2* and *t5*. In our opinion parallelism itself should be separated from the choice between two or more alternatives. Therefore, we consider the non-free-choice construct shown in Figure 4 to be improper. In literature, the term *confusion* is often used to refer to the situation shown in Figure 4.

Free-choice Petri nets have been studied extensively (cf. Best [7], Desel and Esparza [10, 9, 12], Hack [15]) because they seem to be a good compromise between expressive power and analyzability. It is a class of Petri nets for which strong theoretical results and efficient analysis techniques exist. For example, the well-known Rank Theorem (Desel and Esparza [10]) enables us to formulate the following corollary.

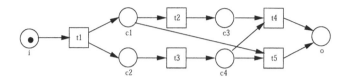

Fig. 4. A non-free-choice WF-net containing a mixture of parallelism and choice.

Corollary 1. *The following problem can be solved in polynomial time.*
Given a free-choice WF-net, to decide if it is sound.

Proof. Let PN be a free-choice WF-net. The short-circuited net $\overline{PN}$ is also free-choice. Therefore, the problem of deciding whether $(\overline{PN}, i)$ is live and bounded can be solved in polynomial time (Rank Theorem [10]). By Theorem 1, this corresponds to soundness. □

Corollary 1 shows that, for free-choice nets, there are efficient algorithms to decide soundness. Moreover, a sound free-choice WF-net is guaranteed to be safe (given an initial state with just one token in i).

Lemma 1. *A sound free-choice WF-net is safe.*

Proof. Let PN be a sound free-choice WF-net. $\overline{PN}$ is the Petri net PN extended with a transition connecting o and i. $\overline{PN}$ is free-choice and well-formed. Hence, $\overline{PN}$ is S-coverable [10], i.e., each place is part of an embedded strongly connected state-machine component. Since initially there is just one token $(\overline{PN}, i)$ is safe and so is (PN, i). □

Safeness is a desirable property, because it makes no sense to have multiple tokens in a place representing a condition. A condition is either true (1 token) or false (no tokens).
     Although most WFMS's only allow for free-choice workflows, free-choice WF-nets are not a completely satisfactory structural characterization of 'good' workflows. On the one hand, there are non-free-choice WF-nets which correspond to sensible workflows (cf. Figure 2). On the other hand there are sound free-choice WF-nets which make no sense. Nevertheless, the free-choice property is a desirable property. If a workflow can be modeled as a free-choice WF-net, one should do so. A workflow specification based on a free-choice WF-net can be enacted by most workflow systems. Moreover, a free-choice WF-net allows for efficient analysis techniques and is easier to understand. Non-free-choice constructs such as the construct shown in Figure 4 are a potential source of anomalous behavior (e.g., deadlock) which is difficult to trace.

6.2   Well-Structured WF-Nets

Another approach to obtain a structural characterization of 'good' workflows, is to balance AND/OR-splits and AND/OR-joins. Clearly, two parallel flows initiated by an AND-split, should not be joined by an OR-join. Two alternative flows created via an OR-split, should not be synchronized by an AND-join. As shown in Figure 5, an AND-split should be complemented by an AND-join and an OR-split should be complemented by an OR-join.

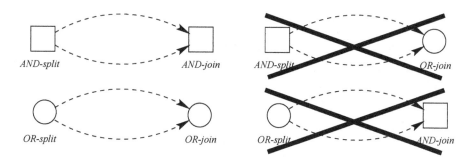

Fig. 5. Good and bad constructions.

One of the deficiencies of the WF-net shown in Figure 3 is the fact that the AND-split *register* is complemented by the OR-join $c3$ or the OR-join o. To formalize the concept illustrated in Figure 5 we give the following definition.

Definition 13 (Well-handled). *A Petri net PN is well-handled iff, for any pair of nodes x and y such that one of the nodes is a place and the other a transition and for any pair of elementary paths C_1 and C_2 leading from x to y, $\alpha(C_1) \cap \alpha(C_2) = \{x, y\} \Rightarrow C_1 = C_2$.*

Note that the WF-net shown in Figure 3 is not well-handled. Well-handledness can be decided in polynomial time by applying a modified version of the max-flow min-cut technique described in [5]. A Petri net which is well-handled has a number of nice properties, e.g., strong connectedness and well-formedness coincide.

Lemma 2. *A strongly connected well-handled Petri net is well-formed.*

Proof. Let PN be a strongly connected well-handled Petri net. Clearly, there are no circuits that have PT-handles nor TP-handles [13]. Therefore, the net is structurally bounded (See Theorem 3.1 in [13]) and structurally live (See Theorem 3.2 in [13]). Hence, PN is well-formed. □

Clearly, well-handledness is a desirable property for any WF-net PN. Moreover, we also require the short-circuited $\overline{PN}$ to be well-handled. We impose this additional requirement for the following reason. Suppose we want to use PN as a part of a larger WF-net PN'. PN' is the original WF-net extended with an 'undo-task'. See Figure 6. Transition *undo* corresponds to the undo-task, transitions $t1$ and $t2$ have been added to make PN' a WF-net. It is undesirable that transition *undo* violates the well-handledness property of the original net. However, PN' is well-handled iff $\overline{PN}$ is well-handled. Therefore, we require $\overline{PN}$ to be well-handled. We use the term *well-structured* to refer to WF-nets whose extension is well-handled.

Definition 14 (Well-structured). *A WF-net PN is well-structured iff $\overline{PN}$ is well-handled.*

PN':

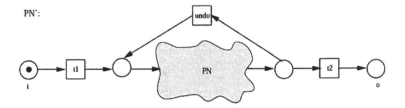

Fig. 6. The WF-net PN' is well-handled iff $\overline{PN}$ is well-handled.

Well-structured WF-nets have a number of desirable properties. Soundness can be verified in polynomial time and a sound well-structured WF-net is safe. To prove these properties we use some of the results obtained for *elementary extended non-self controlling nets*.

Definition 15 (Elementary extended non-self controlling). *A Petri net PN is elementary extended non-self controlling (ENSC) iff, for every pair of transitions t_1 and t_2 such that $\bullet t_1 \cap \bullet t_2 \neq \emptyset$, there does not exist an elementary path C leading from t_1 to t_2 such that $\bullet t_1 \cap \alpha(C) = \emptyset$.*

Theorem 2. *Let PN be a WF-net. If PN is well-structured, then $\overline{PN}$ is elementary extended non-self controlling.*

Proof. Assume that $\overline{PN}$ is not elementary extended non-self controlling. This means that there is a pair of transitions t_1 and t_k such that $\bullet t_1 \cap \bullet t_k \neq \emptyset$ and there exist an elementary path $C = \langle t_1, p_2, t_2, \ldots, p_k, t_k \rangle$ leading from t_1 to t_k and $\bullet t_1 \cap \alpha(C) = \emptyset$. Let $p_1 \in \bullet t_1 \cap \bullet t_k$. $C_1 = \langle p_1, t_k \rangle$ and $C_2 = \langle p_1, t_1, p_2, t_2, \ldots, p_k, t_k \rangle$ are paths leading from p_1 to t_k. (Note that C_2 is the concatenation of $\langle p_1 \rangle$ and C.) Clearly, C_1 is elementary. We will also show that C_2 is elementary. C is elementary, and $p_1 \notin \alpha(C)$ because $p_1 \in \bullet t_1$. Hence, C_2 is also elementary. Since C_1 and C_2 are both elementary paths, $C_1 \neq C_2$ and $\alpha(C_1) \cap \alpha(C_2) = \{p_1, t_k\}$, we conclude that $\overline{PN}$ is not well-handled. □

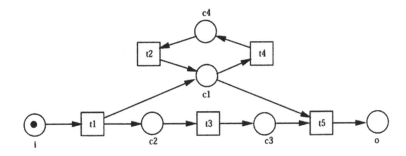

Fig. 7. A well-structured WF-net.

Consider for example the WF-net shown in Figure 7. The WF-net is well-structured and, therefore, also elementary extended non-self controlling. However, the net is not free-choice. Nevertheless, it is possible to verify soundness for such a WF-net very efficiently.

Corollary 2. *The following problem can be solved in polynomial time. Given a well-structured WF-net, to decide if it is sound.*

Proof. Let PN be a well-structured WF-net. The short-circuited net $\overline{PN}$ is elementary extended non-self controlling (Theorem 2) and structurally bounded (see proof of Lemma 2). For bounded elementary extended non-self controlling nets the problem of deciding whether a given marking is live, can be solved in polynomial time (See [6]). Therefore, the problem of deciding whether $(\overline{PN}, i)$ is live and bounded can be solved in polynomial time. By Theorem 1, this corresponds to soundness.   □

Lemma 3. *A sound well-structured WF-net is safe.*

Proof. Let $\overline{PN}$ be the net PN extended with a transition connecting o and i. $\overline{PN}$ is extended non-self controlling. $\overline{PN}$ is covered by state-machines (S-components), see Corollary 5.3 in [6]. Hence, $\overline{PN}$ is safe and so is PN (see proof of Lemma 1).   □

Well-structured WF-nets and free-choice WF-nets have similar properties. In both cases soundness can be verified very efficiently and soundness implies safeness. In spite of these similarities, there are sound well-structured WF-nets which are not free-choice (Figure 7) and there are sound free-choice WF-nets which are not well-structured. In fact, it is possible to have a sound WF-net which is neither free-choice nor well-structured (Figures 2 and 4).

6.3   S-Coverable WF-Nets

What about the sound WF-nets shown in Figure 2 and Figure 4? The WF-net shown in Figure 4 can be transformed into a free-choice well-structured WF-net by separating choice and parallelism. The WF-net shown in Figure 2 cannot be transformed into a free-choice or well-structured WF-net without yielding a much more complex WF-net. Place $c5$ acts as some kind of milestone which is tested by the task *process_complaint*. Traditional workflow management systems which do not make the state of the case explicit, are not able to handle the workflow specified by Figure 2. Only workflow management systems such as COSA [21] have the capability to enact such a state-based workflow. Nevertheless, it is interesting to consider generalizations of free-choice and well-structured WF-nets: *S-coverable WF-nets* can be seen as such a generalization.

Definition 16 (S-coverable). *A WF-net PN is S-coverable if the short-circuited net $\overline{PN}$ is S-coverable.*

The WF-nets shown in Figure 2 and Figure 4 are S-coverable. The WF-net shown in Figure 3 is not S-coverable. The following two corollaries show that S-coverability is a generalization of the free-choice property and well-structuredness.

Corollary 3. *A sound free-choice WF-net is S-coverable.*

Proof. The short-circuited net $\overline{PN}$ is free-choice and well-formed. Hence, $\overline{PN}$ is S-coverable (cf. [10]).   □

Corollary 4. *A sound well-structured WF-net is S-coverable.*

Proof. $\overline{PN}$ is extended non-self controlling (Theorem 2). Hence, $\overline{PN}$ is S-coverable (cf. Corollary 5.3 in [6]).   □

All the sound WF-nets presented in this chapter are S-coverable. Every S-coverable WF-net is safe. The only WF-net which is not sound, i.e., the WF-net shown in Figure 3, is not S-coverable. These and other examples indicate that there is a high correlation between S-coverability and soundness. It seems that S-coverability is one of the basic requirements any workflow process definition should satisfy. From a formal point of view, it is possible to construct WF-nets which are sound but not S-coverable. Typically, these nets contain places which do not restrict the firing of a transition, but which are not in any S-component. (See for example Figure 65 in [19].) From a practical point of view, these WF-nets are to be avoided. WF-nets which are not S-coverable are difficult to interpret because the structural and dynamical properties do not match. For example, these nets can be live and bounded but not structurally bounded. There seems to be no practical need for using constructs which violate the S-coverability property. Therefore, we consider S-coverability to be a basic requirement any WF-net should satisfy.

Another way of looking at S-coverability is the following interpretation: S-components corresponds to *document flows*. To handle a workflow several pieces of information are created, used, and updated. One can think of these pieces of information as physical documents, i.e., at any point in time the document is in one place in the WF-net. Naturally, the information in one document can be copied to another document while executing a task (i.e., transition) processing both documents. Initially, all documents are present but a document can be empty (i.e., corresponds to a blank piece paper). It is easy to see that the flow of one such document corresponds a state machine (assuming the existence of a transition t^*). These document flows synchronize via joint tasks. Therefore, the composition of these flows yields an S-coverable WF-net. One can think of the document flows as threads. Consider for example the short-circuited net of the WF-net shown in Figure 2. This net can be composed out of the following two threads: (1) a thread corresponding to the processing of the form (places i, $c1$, $c3$, $c5$ and o) and (2) a thread corresponding to the actual processing of the complaint (places i, $c2$, $c4$, $c5$, $c6$, $c7$, $c8$, and $c9$). Note that the tasks *register* and *archive* are used in both threads.

Although a WF-net can, in principle, have exponentially many S-components, they are quite easy to compute for workflows encountered in practice (see also the above interpretation of S-component as document flows or threads). Note that S-coverability only depends on the structure and the degree of connectedness is generally low (i.e., the incidence matrix of a WF-net typically has few non-zero entries [5]). Unfortunately, in general, it is not possible to verify soundness of an S-coverable WF-net in polynomial time. The problem of deciding soundness for an S-coverable WF-net is PSPACE-complete. For most applications this is not a real problem. In most cases the number of tasks in one workflow process definition is less than 100 and the number of states is less than 200,000. Tools using standard techniques such as the construction of the coverability graph have no problems in coping with these workflow process definitions.

6.4   Summary

The three structural characterizations (free-choice, well-structured and S-coverable) turn out to be very useful for the analysis of workflow process definitions. Based on our experience, we have good reasons to believe that S-coverability is a desirable property any workflow definition should satisfy. Constructs violating S-coverability can be detected easily and tools can be build to help the designer to construct an S-coverable WF-net. S-coverability is a generalization of well-structuredness and the free-choice property (Corollary 3 and 4). Both well-structuredness and the free-choice property also correspond to desirable properties of a workflow. A WF-net satisfying at least one one of these two properties can be analyzed very efficiently. However, we have shown that there are workflows that are not free-choice and not well-structured. Consider for example Figure 2. The fact that task *process_complaint* tests whether there is a token in *c5*, prevents the WF-net from being free-choice or well-structured. Although this is a very sensible workflow, most workflow management systems do not support such an advanced routing construct. Even if one is able to use state-based workflows (e.g., COSA) allowing for constructs which violate well-structuredness and the free-choice property, then the structural characterizations are still useful. If a WF-net is not free-choice or not well-structured, one should locate the source which violates one of these properties and check whether it is really necessary to use a non-free-choice or a non-well-structured construct. If the non-free-choice or non-well-structured construct is really necessary, then the correctness of the construct should be double-checked, because it is a potential source of errors. This way the readability and maintainability of a workflow process definition can be improved.

7   Composition of WF-Nets

The WF-nets in this chapter are very simple compared to the workflows encountered in practise. For example, in the Dutch Customs Department there are workflows consisting of more than 80 tasks with a very complex interaction structure (cf. [1]). For the designer of such a workflow the complexity is overwhelming and communication with end-users using one huge diagram is difficult. In most cases hierarchical (de)composition is used to tackle this problem. A complex workflow is decomposed into subflows and each of the subflows is decomposed into smaller subflows until the desired level of detail is reached. Many WFMS's allow for such a hierarchical decomposition. In addition, this mechanism can be utilized for the reuse of existing workflows. Consider for example multiple workflows sharing a generic subflow. Some WFMS-vendors also supply reference models which correspond to typical workflows in insurance, banking, finance, marketing, purchase, procurement, logistics, and manufacturing.

Reference models, reuse and the structuring of complex workflows require a hierarchy concept. The most common hierarchy concept supported by many WFMS's is *task*

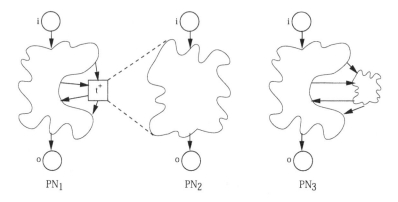

Fig. 8. Task refinement: WF-net PN_3 is composed of PN_1 and PN_2.

refinement, i.e., a task can be refined into a subflow. This concept is illustrated in Figure 8. The WF-net PN_1 contains a task t^+ which is refined by another WF-net PN_2, i.e., t^+ is no longer a task but a reference to a subflow. A WF-net which represents a subflow should satisfy the same requirements as an ordinary WF-net (see Definition 11). The semantics of the hierarchy concept are straightforward; simply replace the refined transition by the corresponding subnet. Figure 8 shows that the refinement of t^+ in PN_1 by PN_2 yields a WF-net PN_3.

The hierarchy concept can be exploited to establish the correctness of a workflow. Given a complex hierarchical workflow model, it is possible to verify soundness by analyzing each of the subflows separately. The following observation is important for compositionality.

Lemma 4. *Let $PN = (P, T, F)$ be a sound WF-net. For any $t \in T$, (i) if $t \in i\bullet$, then $\bullet t = \{i\}$, and (ii) if $t \in \bullet o$, then $t\bullet = \{o\}$.*

Proof. We prove (i) by contradiction. If $t \in i\bullet$ and $\bullet t \neq \{i\}$, then there exists a $p \in (\bullet t) \setminus \{i\}$. Clearly, t is dead because i and p cannot be marked at the same time. The proof of (ii) is similar.   □

The following theorem shows that the soundness property defined in this chapter allows for modular analysis.

Theorem 3 (Compositionality). *Let $PN_1 = (P_1, T_1, F_1)$ and $PN_2 = (P_2, T_2, F_2)$ be two WF-nets such that $T_1 \cap T_2 = \emptyset$, $P_1 \cap P_2 = \{i, o\}$ and $t^+ \in T_1$. $PN_3 = (P_3, T_3, F_3)$ is the WF-net obtained by replacing transition t^+ in PN_1 by PN_2, i.e., $P_3 = P_1 \cup P_2$, $T_3 = (T_1 \setminus \{t^+\}) \cup T_2$ and*

$$
\begin{aligned}
F_3 = & \{(x, y) \in F_1 \mid x \neq t^+ \,\wedge\, y \neq t^+\} \,\cup\, \{(x, y) \in F_2 \mid \{x, y\} \cap \{i, o\} = \emptyset\} \,\cup \\
& \{(x, y) \in P_1 \times T_2 \mid (x, t^+) \in F_1 \,\wedge\, (i, y) \in F_2\} \cup \\
& \{(x, y) \in T_2 \times P_1 \mid (t^+, y) \in F_1 \,\wedge\, (x, o) \in F_2\}.
\end{aligned}
$$

For PN_1, PN_2 and PN_3 the following statements hold:

1. *If PN_3 is free-choice, then PN_1 and PN_2 are free-choice.*
2. *If PN_3 is well-structured, then PN_1 and PN_2 are well-structured.*
3. *If (PN_1, i) is safe and PN_1 and PN_2 are sound, then PN_3 is sound.*
4. *(PN_1, i) and (PN_2, i) are safe and sound iff (PN_3, i) is safe and sound.*
5. *PN_1 and PN_2 are free-choice and sound iff PN_3 is free-choice and sound.*
6. *If PN_3 is well-structured and sound, then PN_1 and PN_2 are well-structured and sound.*
7. *If $\bullet t^+$ and $t^+ \bullet$ are both singletons, then PN_1 and PN_2 are well-structured and sound iff PN_3 is well-structured and sound.*

Proof.

1. The only transitions that may violate the free-choice property are t^+ (in PN_1) and $\{t \in T_2 \mid (i,t) \in F_2\}$ (in PN_2). Transition t^+ has the same input set as any of the transitions $\{t \in T_2 \mid (i,t) \in F_2\}$ in PN_3 if we only consider the places in $P_3 \cap P_1$. Hence, t^+ does not violate the free-choice property in PN_1. All transitions t in PN_2 such that $(i,t) \in F_2$ respect the free-choice property; the input places in $P_3 \setminus P_2$ are replaced by i.

2. $\overline{PN_1}$ $(\overline{PN_2})$ is well-handled because any elementary path in $\overline{PN_1}$ $(\overline{PN_2})$ corresponds to a path in $\overline{PN_3}$.

3. Let (PN_1, i) be safe and let PN_1 and PN_2 be sound. We need to prove that $(\overline{PN_3}, i)$ is live and bounded. The subnet in $\overline{PN_3}$ which corresponds to t^+ behaves like a transition which may postpone the production of tokens for $t^+ \bullet$. It is essential that the input places of t^+ in $(\overline{PN_3}, i)$ are safe. This way it is guaranteed that the states of the subnet correspond to the states of $(\overline{PN_2}, i)$. Hence, the transitions in $T_3 \cap T_2$ are live (t^+ is live) and the places in $P_3 \setminus P_1$ are bounded. Since the subnet behaves like t^+, the transitions in $T_3 \cap (T_1 \setminus \{t^+\})$ are live and the places in $P_3 \cap P_1$ are bounded. Hence, PN_3 is sound.

4. Let (PN_1, i) and (PN_2, i) be safe and sound. Clearly, PN_3 is sound (see proof of 3.). (PN_3, i) is also safe because every reachable state corresponds to a combination of a safe state of (PN_1, i) and a safe state of (PN_2, i).

   Let (PN_3, i) be safe and sound. Consider the subnet in PN_3 which corresponds to t^+. X is the set of transitions in $T_3 \cap T_2$ consuming from $\bullet t^+$ and Y is the set of transitions in $T_3 \cap T_2$ producing tokens for $t^+ \bullet$. If a transition in X fires, then it should be possible to fire a transition in Y because of the liveness of the original net. If a transition in Y fires, the subnet should become empty. If the subnet is not empty after firing a transition in Y, then there are two possibilities: (1) it is possible to move the subnet to a state such that a transition in Y can fire (without firing transitions in $T_3 \cap T_1$) or (2) it is not possible to move to such a state. In the first case, the places $t^+ \bullet$ in PN_3 are not safe. In the second case, a token is trapped in the subnet or the subnet is not safe the moment a transition in X fires. (PN_2, i) corresponds to the subnet bordered by X and Y and is, as we have just shown, sound and safe. It remains to prove that (PN_1, i) is safe and sound. Since the subnet which corresponds to t^+ behaves like a transition which may postpone the production of tokens, we can replace the subnet by t^+ without changing dynamic properties such as safeness and soundness.

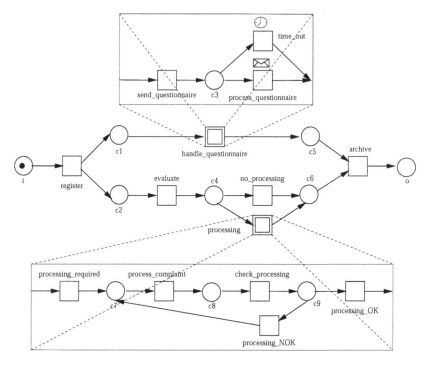

Fig. 9. A hierarchical WF-net for the processing of complaints.

5. Let PN_1 and PN_2 be free-choice and sound. Since $(\overline{PN_1}, i)$ is safe (see Lemma 1), PN_3 is sound (see proof of 3.). It remains to prove that PN_3 is free-choice. The only transitions in PN_3 which may violate the free-choice property are the transitions in $T_3 \cap T_2$ consuming tokens from $\bullet t^+$. Because PN_2 is sound, these transitions need to have an input set identical to $\bullet t^+$ in PN_1 (cf. Lemma 4). Since PN_1 is free-choice, PN_3 is also free-choice.
   Let PN_3 be free-choice and sound. PN_1 and PN_2 are also free-choice (see proof of 1.). Since (PN_3, i) is safe (see Lemma 1), PN_1 and PN_2 are sound (see proof of 4.).

6. Let PN_3 be well-structured and sound. PN_1 and PN_2 are also well-structured (see proof of 2.). Since (PN_3, i) is safe (see Lemma 3), PN_1 and PN_2 are sound (see proof of 4.).

7. It remains to prove that if PN_1 and PN_2 are well-structured, then PN_3 is also well-structured. Suppose that PN_3 is not well-structured. In this case, there is a pair of nodes x and y such that one of the nodes is a place and the other a transition and such that there are two disjoint elementary paths leading from x to y in $\overline{PN_3}$ (cf. Definitions 13 and 14). Since PN_1 is well-structured, at least one of these paths runs via the refinement of t^+. However, because t^+ has precisely one input and one output place and PN_2 is also well-structured, this is not possible.

□

Theorem 3 is a generalization of Theorem 3 in [22]. It extends the concept of a block with multiple entry and exit transitions and gives stronger results for specific subclasses.

Figure 9 shows a hierarchical WF-net. Both of the subflows (*handle_questionnaire* and *processing*) and the main flow are safe and sound. Therefore, the overall workflow represented by the hierarchical WF-net is also safe and sound. Moreover, the free-choice property and well-structuredness are also preserved by the hierarchical composition. Theorem 3 is of particular importance for the reuse of subflows. For the analysis of a complex workflow, every safe and sound subflow can be considered to be a single task. This allows for an efficient modular analysis of the soundness property. Moreover, the statements embedded in Theorem 3 can help a workflow designer to construct correct workflow process definitions.

8   Conclusion

In this chapter we have investigated a basic property that any workflow process definition should satisfy: the soundness property. For WF-nets, this property coincides with liveness and boundedness. In our quest for a structural characterization of WF-nets satisfying the soundness property, we have identified three important subclasses: free-choice, well-structured, and S-coverable WF-nets. The identification of these subclasses is useful for the detection of design errors.

If a workflow is specified by a hierarchical WF-net, then modular analysis of the soundness property is often possible. A workflow composed of correct subflows can be verified without incorporating the specification of each subflow.

The results presented in this chapter give workflow designers a handle to construct correct workflows. Although it is possible to use standard Petri-net-based analysis tools, we have developed a workflow analyzer which can be used by people not familiar with Petri-net theory [4, 5, 23, 24]. This workflow analyzer interfaces with existing workflow products such as Staffware, COSA, METEOR, and Protos.

Acknowledgements
The author would like to thank Marc Voorhoeve and Twan Basten for their valuable suggestions and all the other people involved in the development of Woflan, in particular Eric Verbeek and Dirk Hauschildt.

References

1. W.M.P. van der Aalst. Three Good Reasons for Using a Petri-net-based Workflow Management System. In S. Navathe and T. Wakayama, editors, *Proceedings of the International Working Conference on Information and Process Integration in Enterprises (IPIC'96)*, pages 179–201, Camebridge, Massachusetts, Nov 1996.
2. W.M.P. van der Aalst. Verification of Workflow Nets. In P. Azéma and G. Balbo, editors, *Application and Theory of Petri Nets 1997*, volume 1248 of *Lecture Notes in Computer Science*, pages 407–426. Springer-Verlag, Berlin, 1997.
3. W.M.P. van der Aalst. The Application of Petri Nets to Workflow Management. *The Journal of Circuits, Systems and Computers*, 8(1):21–66, 1998.

4. W.M.P. van der Aalst. Woflan: A Petri-net-based Workflow Analyzer. *Systems Analysis - Modelling - Simulation*, 35(3):345–357, 1999.
5. W.M.P. van der Aalst, D. Hauschildt, and H.M.W. Verbeek. A Petri-net-based Tool to Analyze Workflows. In B. Farwer, D. Moldt, and M.O. Stehr, editors, *Proceedings of Petri Nets in System Engineering (PNSE'97)*, pages 78–90, Hamburg, Germany, September 1997. University of Hamburg (FBI-HH-B-205/97).
6. K. Barkaoui, J.M. Couvreur, and C. Dutheillet. On liveness in Extended Non Self-Controlling Nets. In G. De Michelis and M. Diaz, editors, *Application and Theory of Petri Nets 1995*, volume 935 of *Lecture Notes in Computer Science*, pages 25–44. Springer-Verlag, Berlin, 1995.
7. E. Best. Structure Theory of Petri Nets: the Free Choice Hiatus. In W. Brauer, W. Reisig, and G. Rozenberg, editors, *Advances in Petri Nets 1986 Part I: Petri Nets, central models and their properties*, volume 254 of *Lecture Notes in Computer Science*, pages 168–206. Springer-Verlag, Berlin, 1987.
8. A. Cheng, J. Esparza, and J. Palsberg. Complexity results for 1-safe nets. In R.K. Shyamasundar, editor, *Foundations of software technology and theoretical computer science*, volume 761 of *Lecture Notes in Computer Science*, pages 326–337. Springer-Verlag, Berlin, 1993.
9. J. Desel. A proof of the Rank theorem for extended free-choice nets. In K. Jensen, editor, *Application and Theory of Petri Nets 1992*, volume 616 of *Lecture Notes in Computer Science*, pages 134–153. Springer-Verlag, Berlin, 1992.
10. J. Desel and J. Esparza. *Free Choice Petri Nets*, volume 40 of *Cambridge Tracts in Theoretical Computer Science*. Cambridge University Press, Cambridge, UK, 1995.
11. C.A. Ellis and G.J. Nutt. Modelling and Enactment of Workflow Systems. In M. Ajmone Marsan, editor, *Application and Theory of Petri Nets 1993*, volume 691 of *Lecture Notes in Computer Science*, pages 1–16. Springer-Verlag, Berlin, 1993.
12. J. Esparza. Synthesis rules for Petri nets, and how they can lead to new results. In J.C.M. Baeten and J.W. Klop, editors, *Proceedings of CONCUR 1990*, volume 458 of *Lecture Notes in Computer Science*, pages 182–198. Springer-Verlag, Berlin, 1990.
13. J. Esparza and M. Silva. Circuits, Handles, Bridges and Nets. In G. Rozenberg, editor, *Advances in Petri Nets 1990*, volume 483 of *Lecture Notes in Computer Science*, pages 210–242. Springer-Verlag, Berlin, 1990.
14. K. Gostellow, V. Cerf, G. Estrin, and S. Volansky. Proper Termination of Flow-of-control in Programs Involving Concurrent Processes. *ACM Sigplan*, 7(11):15–27, 1972.
15. M.H.T. Hack. Analysis production schemata by Petri nets. Master's thesis, Massachusetts Institute of Technology, Cambridge, Mass., 1972.
16. S. Jablonski and C. Bussler. *Workflow Management: Modeling Concepts, Architecture, and Implementation*. International Thomson Computer Press, London, UK, 1996.
17. E. Kindler and W.M.P. van der Aalst. Liveness, Fairness, and Recurrence. *Information Processing Letters*, 1999 (to appear).
18. G. De Michelis, C. Ellis, and G. Memmi, editors. *Proceedings of the second Workshop on Computer-Supported Cooperative Work, Petri nets and related formalisms*, Zaragoza, Spain, June 1994.
19. W. Reisig. *Petri Nets: An Introduction*, volume 4 of *EATCS Monographs in Theoretical Computer Science*. Springer-Verlag, Berlin, 1985.
20. W. Reisig and G. Rozenberg, editors. *Lectures on Petri Nets I: Basic Models*, volume 1491 of *Lecture Notes in Computer Science*. Springer-Verlag, Berlin, 1998.
21. Software-Ley. *COSA User Manual*. Software-Ley GmbH, Pullheim, Germany, 1998.
22. R. Valette. Analysis of Petri Nets by Stepwise Refinements. *Journal of Computer and System Sciences*, 18:35–46, 1979.
23. E. Verbeek and W.M.P. van der Aalst. Woflan Home Page. http://www.win.tue.nl/~woflan.

24. H.M.W. Verbeek, T. Basten, and W.M.P. van der Aalst. Diagnosing Workflow Processes using Woflan. Computing Science Report 99/02, Eindhoven University of Technology, Eindhoven, 1999.
25. WFMC. Workflow Management Coalition Terminology and Glossary (WFMC-TC-1011). Technical report, Workflow Management Coalition, Brussels, 1996.
26. M. Wolf and U. Reimer, editors. *Proceedings of the International Conference on Practical Aspects of Knowledge Management (PAKM'96), Workshop on Adaptive Workflow*, Basel, Switzerland, Oct 1996.

Compositional modeling and verification of workflow processes

M. Voorhoeve

Eindhoven University of Technology,
POB 513, 5600MB Eindhoven
wsinmarc@win.tue.nl

Abstract. Workflow processes are represented as Petri nets with special entry and exit places and labeled transitions. The transition labels represent actions. We give a semantics for such nets in terms of transition systems. This allows us to describe and verify properties like *termination*: the guaranteed option to terminate successfully. We describe the composition of complex WF nets from simpler ones by means of certain operators. The simple operators preserve termination, giving correctness by design. Only the advanced communication operators are potentially dangerous. A strategy for verification of other properties is described.

1   Introduction

Workflow management is an important new development in the computerized support of human work. As such, it is an emerging market with scores of commercially available products, not to mention research prototypes at universities. A workflow management system (WFMS) focuses on *cases* flowing through the organization, while *tasks* are executed for them. We assume the reader to be familiar with these notions (c.f. [11], [1]).

In this chapter we limit ourselves to the *process* of a single case. Such a process has a large number of *states* and *actions* move the process from state to state. For this aspect of workflow, Petri net models are often used. Petri nets (c.f. [7]) combine expressive power (to a degree) with a formal semantics that allows analysis. Although it is focused towards actions, there is a clear notion of *state*, which is essential as argued by [1].

A WF net is a Petri net describing the flow of a single case. A source place marks its initial state and a sink place its terminal state. The transitions are labeled; labels correspond to tasks.

In Figure 1, such a net is shown, modeling the process of travel arrangement. A travel request initially enters the process and three parallel activities are started. A budget check is performed and the hotel and travel requirements are studied. If necessary, hotel and travel information is obtained. After obtaining enough information and receiving a budget approval, travel and hotel accommodation

W. van der Aalst et al.(Eds.): Business Process Management, LNCS 1806, pp. 184-200, 2000.

is booked, the travel documents and budget approval are assembled and sent to the client.

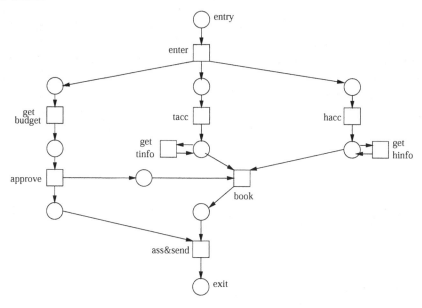

Fig. 1. A WF net: travel department

Models such as the one in Figure 1 can be built intuitively, as illustrated above. However, in order to analyze and discuss these models, we need a formal notion of workflow processes and the way in which they are modeled by nets. Assume that two different WF nets have been presented based on an informal description of one and the same process. One immediately asks whether these WF nets represent the same process, and, if not, in which respect they differ. Such questions need an answer; if not, one cannot be sure whether one's intentions are modeled correctly.

Such a formal semantics of WF nets allows verification. Every WF net should be *terminating*, i.e. from every state that can be reached (by executing tasks) from the initial state, it is possible to reach the terminal state. In [1] the *soundness* property of WF nets is introduced; one of the propertiues that a sound WF net should satisfy is that it is terminating. More specific properties can be formulated and subjected to verification; e.g. that before termination a certain task t should be executed.

It is a good thing to be able to make models, more or less intuitively, and verifying them afterwards. The verification should point out which parts of the model contain erroneous or dangerous constructions and hint at possible improvements. The tool Woflan (WOrkFLow ANalyzer, c.f. [8]) assesses the net's soundness and even supports the modeler by indicating dangerous constructs.

It is even better to create models in an organized way, by combining predefined building blocks in certain prescribed ways. Such models can be verified compositionally, leading to correctness by construction. Often, intuitive and rigorous modeling approaches are combined.

In the sections to come, we introduce transition systems as our basic process model for workflow systems. Then, we define WF nets. We define two ways, called *firing rules* that convert a WF net into a transition system. Next, we introduce operators to compose WF nets, starting with some predefined building blocks. Finally, we treat verification and present some consequences of both our semantics and the compositional approach.

The results presented in this chapter are far from conclusive. Our presentation focuses on the ideas behind them, which we hope the reader will appreciate.

2   Definitions

This section starts with introducing *processes* and the bisimilarity equivalence relation. Then we define the class of Petri nets we call WF nets. Finally, we treat two *firing rules* that generate a process from a net.

2.1   Processes

A process consists of *states* and *events*. There are two special states: the *initial* and *terminal* state. To each state corresponds a set of events that can *occur* in it. When an event has occurred in some state, another state is reached. The reached state depends on both the old state and the event that has occurred. No events can occur in the terminal state; other states in which no events can occur are called *deadlocks*.

A process (or *transition system*) can be depicted as a *directed graph* with labeled edges. The nodes are states and the edges connect the old state to the new one, where the edge labels denote the events. Two special nodes indicate the initial and terminal states. In Figure 2, such a process is shown. The thick incoming/outgoing arrow indicates the initial/terminal state, the edges are indicated by solid lines.

We say that a state s' can be *reached* from another state s if there is a sequence of events leading from s to s'. In the graph, this corresponds to a directed path as indicated by the dashed line in Figure 2. In a process, we assume that all states are reachable from the initial state, so the state σ and edge g in the figure must be removed.

The internal states (neither initial nor terminal) can only be distinguished from one another by the events that they allow and the states that are reached by them. This means that we can divide the states into groups (e.g. by coloring them) of indistinguishable (or *bisimilar*) states. This coloring algorithm starts with three colors (initial, terminal and internal). If a pair of states having the same color can be distinguished (i.e. one state has an a-labeled edge leading to a d-colored state and the other not), one of the two receives a new color. This

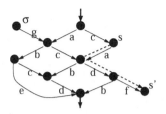

Fig. 2. The graph of a process

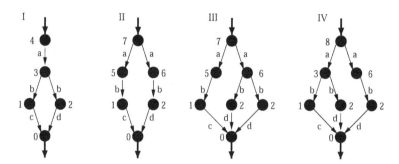

Fig. 3. Process colorings

is repeated until all states have different colors or states having the same color cannot be distinguished.

In Figure 3, the coloring result is shown for four processes. Processes like II and III, that can be colored with exactly the same set of colors are called equivalent or *bisimilar*. Bisimilarity is an equivalence relation. [1] Processes that cannot be colored the same, like I and IV can be distinguished by describing their states; IV has a state in which event b followed by d is possible, but b followed by c is impossible (the state with color 6), but I does not have such a state. Similarly, II and III have a state (with color 5) that IV and I do not possess.

In some cases, we distinguish *visible* and *invisible* events and we want to call processes equivalent if their visible behavior is the same. We represent invisible events by unlabeled edges (often the label τ is used instead). One cannot tell the difference between a real a-labeled edge and a virtual one, i.e. a sequence of zero or more unlabeled edges, an a-labeled one and then again unlabeled ones. Neither can one tell the difference between a sequence of unlabeled edges and no edge at all.

Our coloring algorithm then must be adapted: if an a-labeled edge leads from one c-colored state to a d-colored state and no real *or virtual* a-labeled edge exists from another c-colored state to a d-colored state, one of the c-colored edges must be recolored. Processes that can be colored with the same colors

---

[1] This definition of bisimilarity induces the same equivalence relation as in process algebra literature (see e.g. [6]). The above presentation highlights its essence.

are called *weakly bisimilar*. The previous notion is called "strong" bisimilarity in contrast. If all events are visible, the two notions coincide.

Given a process, one can formulate and verify properties it is supposed to have. The logic HML (c.f. [5]) can be used to this end. Bisimilar processes are characterized by the fact that any HML formula that holds for one process also holds for the other and vice versa. If processes are not bisimilar, there is a HML formula that holds for one process but not for the other. Compare the statement we used to distinguish between I and IV in Figure 3.

We want all workflow processes to be *terminating*. This means that every state of the process (that is reachable from the initial state) can reach the terminal state. A terminating process thus cannot reach a deadlock. Termination can be formulated in HML, so if a process is terminating, all (weakly) bisimilar processes are terminating too.

2.2   WF Nets

Simple workflow processes can be modeled directly as transition systems. However, more advanced processes with a lot of parallelism do not allow such an approach, due to an enormous number of states. Petri nets (c.f. [7]) allow a more concise representation.

A net consists of *nodes*, connected by directed edges. Nodes are divided into *places*, depicted as circles and *transitions*, depicted as squares. The transitions are labeled; a transition label corresponds to a *task* in the workflow system. Edges connect places to transitions and vice versa. No edges are allowed between two places or two transitions.

A WF net has an entry place without incoming edges and a exit place without outgoing edges. Each node must lie on at least one directed path from the entry place to the exit place. For technical reasons, we will allow several entry and exit places. In this general case, we require that every node lies on a directed path between some entry and exit place. An example WF net is depicted in Figure 1.

Given a transition t, the set of edges leading to t are called *input arcs* of t and the places these arcs lead from are called *input places* of t. Similarly, the set of edges leaving t are called *output arcs* of t and the places these arcs lead to are called *output places* of t.

A Petri net is a natural and concise way of representing a process. The key idea behind Petri nets is that tasks can occur whenever certain objects (materials, resources or permissions) are present. When a task starts, these objects are consumed. Upon termination, new objects are produced, that may allow new tasks to start.

Each place of a net contains certain objects (called *tokens*). Transitions correspond to certain tasks. The required objects for this tasks reside in its input places, and the result objects in its output places. The execution of an task corresponds to the *firing* of a corresponding transition, consuming tokens for its input places and producing tokens for its output places.

For the sake of simplicity, we assume that only one token per place is consumed or produced when a transition fires. This assumption is not unreasonable for modeling workflow. Without it, the definition of a Petri net and the descriptions below get slightly more complicated. However, this complication is only technical.

2.3   Firing Rules

The conversion of a Petri net into a process is formalized by so-called *firing rules*. These firing rules thus define the behavior of a net. There do exist algorithms that allow us to decide whether the process of a WF net is terminating, and, if so, compute this process. However, a *combinatorial explosion* may occur that makes this decision and computation infeasible. So the firing rules given below are not meant to be a guideline for computing a process but rather serve as a means to derive properties (like termination) of a WF net's process without having to compute it.

The simplest firing rule is the *interleaving* rule. We assume a net N and derive from it a process I_N. A state s of I_N corresponds to a *marking* of N, a function that assigns to every place p of N a nonnegative integer $s(p)$. The events of I_N correspond to the transition labels of N. We denote by $i_t(p)$ the number of input arcs (zero or one) leading from place p to transition t and by $o_t(p)$ the number of output arcs leading from t to p. Given a transition t of N with label a and a state s of I_N, there is an edge with label a connecting s to a state s' whenever $s(p) > i_t(p)$ and $s'(p) = s(p) - i_t(p) + o_t(p)$ for every place p.

The initial state of I_N is the marking where the (each) entry place of N contains one token and the other places none. Similarly, the terminal state of I_N is the marking where the (each) exit place of N contains one token and the other places none.

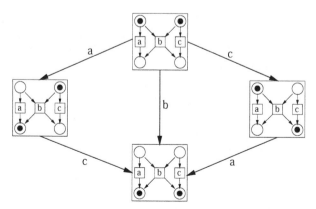

Fig. 4. The interleaving process of a net

In Figure 4, the derivation of a process from a Petri net by the interleaving rule is shown. The tokens are indicated by dots; counting the dots in each place yields the state of the net.

The interleaving rule allows us to study most properties of a WF net. In some cases, however, this rule is not completely adequate. Consider the nets in Figure 5 for instance. Each net is mapped to the same process by the interleaving rule, but there is an intuitive difference between e.g. nets I and IV. In net I, tasks b and c can be executed simultaneously (or *concurrently*) after a. In net IV, b and c can both be executed after a, but if one is busy, the other must wait (this behavior is called *sequential*). As a consequence, the flow modeled by net I is more efficient and will show e.g. lower resource idle times than net IV.

A slightly more subtle difference exists between nets I and III. In net III it is possible to start task b (the transition in the middle) such that task c must wait, although this need not be the case due to the other b-labeled transition. This phenomenon cannot happen in I. However, there is no clear difference between nets I and II. If task b has terminated and c not yet started, a second possibility for executing c becomes manifest in net II, but one cannot distinguish between the c transitions firing. [2]

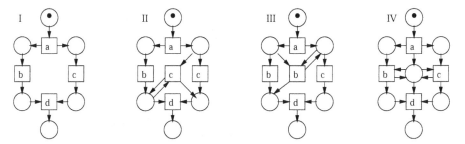

Fig. 5. Concurrent versus sequential behavior

A firing rule that discriminates between concurrent and sequential behavior is the *ST firing rule* (c.f. [4] and [9]). Although the ST rule assumes that tasks are not instantaneous, it is not based on an explicit notion of time, thus allowing to derive properties of WF nets without having to provide e.g. information about the duration of tasks. Most properties of the interleaving process of a net (like termination) carry over to the its ST process.

We define the ST process S_N of a net N as follows. A state of S_N consists of two parts, a marking (as in I_N) and a (possibly empty) list of "busy" transitions. The order of the transitions in this list corresponds to the order in which they started. For net I in Figure 5, S_I contains two distinct states where both transitions are busy: either transition could have started first.

---

[2] A difference arises when examining the *causal* dependencies between tasks. It seems that we can neglect causality when modeling and verifying workflow processes.

The events of S_N are the starting of a transition and the termination of a busy transition. The labels of these events are a^+ for starting an a-labeled transition and a_n^- for termination of the n-th transition of the busy list, where a is its label. The initial (terminal) state of S_N is composed of the initial (terminal) marking of I_N and the empty busy list. A state s of S_N with marking m_s and busy list b_s is connected to state s' with marking $m_{s'}$ and busy list $b_{s'}$ by an edge with label a^+ if and only if there exists a transition t with label a such that $m_{s'}(p) = m_s(p) - i_t(p)$ for every place p and $b_{s'}$ is b_s with t added to its tail. s is connected to s' by an edge with label a_n^- if and only if b_s contains at its n-th position a transition t with label a such that $m_{s'}(p) = m_s(p) + o_t(p)$ for every place p.

In Figure 6, the derivation of a process from a Petri net by the ST firing rule is shown. Markings are shown by dots as in Figure 4 and the busy list is depicted by adding numbers to busy transitions.

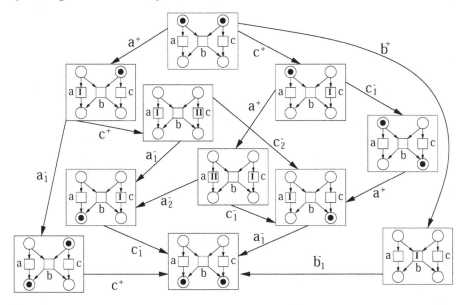

Fig. 6. The ST process of a net

We conclude this section by pointing out the correspondences between the two processes of a net N. The states of I_N correspond to the set E of states of S_N with an empty busy list and an a-labeled edge connects two states of I_N if and only if the corresponding states in S_N are connected via a^+ and then a_1^-. From each state of S_N a state in E can be reached by terminating all busy transitions. States in E can reach one another in S_N if and only if the corresponding states in I_N can reach one another. Hence S_N is terminating if and only if I_N is terminating.

We call two WF nets N, M *I-equivalent* if I_N and I_M are bisimilar processes and *ST-equivalent* if S_N and S_M are bisimilar. It is easy to show that ST-equivalence implies I-equivalence, but not vice versa.

We recommend the use of the ST firing rule and ST-equivalence as equivalence relation between WF nets. The above correspondence indicates that many properties of the ST process can be deduced from the interleaving process. Adopting the ST approach does not rule out the use of interleaving-based analysis tools.

3   Construction and Verification

Having defined the semantics of WF nets, we investigate the ways in which to construct them. We advocate a compositional approach that allows for both top-down and bottom-up modeling. We then turn to verification, showing how it can profit from the compositional approach. We conclude by presenting the construction of our travel example.

3.1   Construction

It is perfectly possible to construct WF nets from intuition, guided by some ad-hoc principles. In fact, the example in Figure 1 has been presented in this vein. However, for large nets more rigor is needed in the net's construction process. We propose here an approach based on building blocks that can be combined in certain prescribed ways into larger nets. The building blocks are themselves WF nets that are well understood and thoroughly verified and validated.

It is of great importance for organizations to create and maintain a set of standard procedures to be aplied in specific situations. Such a "procedure base" is one of the main assets of an organization. The process part of such procedures can be modeled as WF nets and used as building blocks.

We will not further investigate the way to obtain an adequate set of building blocks. Instead, we stress the ways in which WF nets can be combined, i.e. the WF net *operators*. These operators have one or more nets as *operands*; the application of an operator to its operand(s) gives a *result* net. This result then can serve as operand to a new operator. In this way we can build *expressions* that represent nets. This approach is inspired by PBC, the Petri Box Calculus [3].

Most operators are based upon the notion of place fusion. Fusing a set A of places to another set B of places means adding a new place for every pair (a, b) of places from $A \times B$, adding an edge to the place corresponding to (a, b) iff there exists a similar edge to a or b and then removing the places in A and B and edges from or to them. If A and B are singleton sets, this is equivalent to "gluing" the places onto one another. If A or B is empty, it becomes removal of places and edges. In other cases a kind of "weaving" occurs, as illustrated in Figure 7. In the figure, place identifiers are added to illustrate the correspondence between the original and the new places.

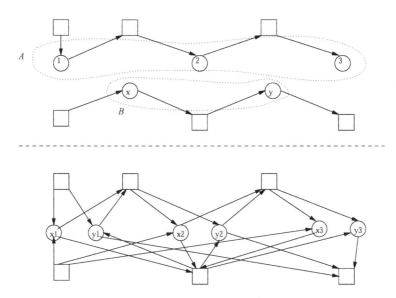

Fig. 7. Place fusion

We will fuse entry and/or exit places and strive for singleton such places, so fusion of singleton places will occur most often. The complicated weaving of the figure (where both sets have cardinality greater than one) is not likely to occur.

The operators we propose are sequencing, choice, iteration, free merge, synchronous communication, asynchronous communication and refinement. We describe the intended processes, followed by a net-based explanation. These net-based definitions are similar to [4] and [10].

The sequencing and choice operators have two operands. Putting two processes in sequence means that the first one is executed and upon termination of the first the second one. A choice between two processes means that either process can be executed; the first event determines which one. Graphically, sequencing fuses the exit places of the first operand net to the entry places of the second. Choice fuses the entry and exit places of its operands so that they only share the initial and terminal marking.

Iteration has three operands. The first process is executed; upon termination either the second one or third one can be executed. If the second one is chosen and it terminates, the iterated process has the same state as when the first one terminated, so the choice between the second and third recurs. If the third is chosen and terminates, the iterated process terminates. Graphically, the exit places of the first are fused with the entry and exit places of the second and the entry places of the third, thus creating a loop.

The free merge operator has two operands. Both operand processes can execute independently. Graphically, the two nets are juxtaposed. Since the result of the free merge has more than one entry and exit place, the sequencing operator is often used to add an initial task (the *and-split* of a case into two ot more parallel streams) and a terminal one (the *and-join*).

In Figure 8, the above operators are given when applied to the simplest processes, i.e. isolated tasks (*a*, *b* and *c*).

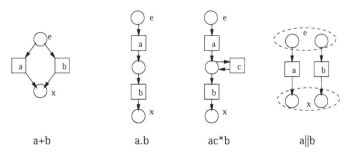

a+b   a.b   ac*b   a‖b

Fig. 8. Workflow net operators

Refinement has one operand and a parameter function f that maps tasks onto processes. In the operand, any transition denoting a task t in the domain of f is replaced by the process $f(t)$. Graphically, another place fusion occurs: the entry places of $f(t)$ are fused with the input places of t. Likewise, the output places of the t are fused to the exit places of $f(t)$. A special case is *relabeling*, where $f(t)$ is a single transition.

We can use refinement to formally define the result of the operators in Figure 8 when applied to arbitrary WF nets. For example, the choice $A + B$ between WF nets A and B is obtained by consecutively refining task a and b in the net $a + b$ with A and B respectively. From this observation it is clear that the place fusions from the descriptions above are related. In Figure 9, the net $a(d‖e) * b$ is shown that is obtained by refining c with $d‖e$ in $ab * c$ from Figure 8. This is a case where weaving cannot be avoided.

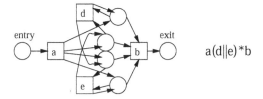

$a(d‖e)*b$

Fig. 9. Iterated merge

The above operators are the "neat" ones. They are however not sufficient to model all possible processes. Subprocesses that run more or less independently in different parts in an organization (initially modeled by means of the free merge operator) may influence one another at some points: tasks at one side may need information or await decisions from the other side and vice versa. For this phenomenon, "dirty" communication operators are needed. We define synchronous (two-way) and asynchronous (one-way) communication.

Tasks that communicate synchronously must be executed together. This simultaneous execution of these tasks can be seen as a single one. The synchronous communication operator has one operand net and a parameter function f that maps task sets onto tasks. The simultaneous execution of a set A of tasks in the domain of f amounts to executing $f(A)$.

Graphically, synchronous communication amounts to transition fusion and relabeling the transitions thus synchronized. Note that one and the same transition might communicate with several other transitions. If this is the case, another "weaving" (this time with transitions instead of places) will occur.

Asynchronous communication means that a task has to wait until another task has occurred in another stream. There is one operand and a parameter set R that consists of pairs of task sets. If a pair (A, B) is in R, then any task from B has to wait until a task from A occurred. Graphically, this amounts to adding a place for every pair (A, B) in R, that serves as an output place for the transition(s) in A and as input place for the transition(s) in B.

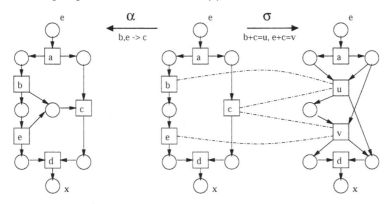

Fig. 10. Communication operators

In Figure 10, the communication operators are illustrated. The process $X = a.(b.e||c).d$ is shown in the middle. To its left is $\alpha_R(X)$, where the task c must wait for b or e. The set $R = \{(\{b\}, \{c\})\}$ is a singleton pair. To its right is $\sigma_f(X)$, where the task pairs b, c and e, c communicate synchronously and the communication results are u and v respectively. So the domain of f is the set of sets $\{\{b, c\}, \{e, c\}\}$, whereas $f(\{b, c\}) = u$ and $f(\{e, c\}) = v$.

3.2 Properties of Operators

We like our operators to have the property that combining equivalent operand nets leads to an equivalent result. This means that if nets N and N' are equivalent then replacing N by N' in an expression leads to an equivalent result net. Such a property allows us to prove that two nets are equivalent without having to compute their processes. An operator is called an *ST-congruence* if the above property holds for ST-equivalence and an *I-congruence* if it holds for

I-equivalence. Another desirable property is termination preservation, i.e. that the result is terminating if and only if the operands are terminating.

The table in Figure 1 shows a list of properties of the operators. Figure 10 shows that the communication operators are not termination preserving. The original process is clearly terminating, whereas the derived processes are not. The right-hand process cannot reach the terminal state (a *deadlock* occurs), whereas the left-hand process can produce a token in the exit place, but in doing so an extra is token left behind, so it also cannot reach the terminal state. It seems interesting to investigate conditions that are sufficient or necessary for termination preservation of the communication operators.

Table 1. Operator properties

operator	I-congruence	ST-congruence	termination preserving
sequencing	yes	yes	yes
choice	yes	yes	yes
iteration	yes	yes	yes
free merge	yes	yes	yes
refinement	no	yes	yes
sync. comm.	no	yes	no
async. comm.	yes	yes	no

The fact that all operators but the synchronizations are termination (and even soundness) preserving can be used when checking the termination of nets resulting from expressions. The refinement operator is very important, as it allows a hierarchical approach to net construction. The fact that the refinement operator is an ST-congruence and not an I-congruence is one of the main reasons for embracing the ST firing rule.

The construction operators can be incorporated in an editor for workflow processes. This editor could contain a soundness checker that can be invoked for suspect processes that result from the application of dirty operators.

3.3   Verification and Reduction

The primary reason for modeling workflow is the possibility to control and monitor the work by means of a WFMS. These models will be tested (validated) to create confidence in them. The existence of a formal model also allows for verification. As models become more complex, the need for verification will grow.

There are various properties that need verification. Soundness is a property that all processes must have, but other, more specific properties come to mind, like the need for approval of specific tasks, or protocol conformance. Verification of a large process may become computationally infeasible. The compositional construction of processes allows for compositional verification: defining properties for the operand processes in a certain construct, verifying them and proving that these properties and the given construction yield the desired property of the complete process.

Another property that can be verified is that a certain WF net represents the same process as another given WF net, i.e. their processes are equivalent. As indicated, the congruence properties of the operators allow this to be done compositionally, and even calculationally, using laws from process calculi (or algebra's) like CCS [6] or ACP [2]. Here, we present the *reduction* of a WF net by removing places and/or transitions.

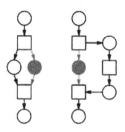

Fig. 11. Redundant places

The simplest reduction is achieved by removing *redundant* places. A place p is redundant iff every transition t with p as input place has other input places and whenever these other places contain a token, then p contains a token too. Figure 11 shows a few (grey) redundant places. The black net (with the grey arcs and places removed) is the reduced net. The original and reduced nets are ST-equivalent (and thus I-equivalent).

Another reduction consists of removing *inert* transitions. A transition is inert iff it does not represent a real task (i.e. it is unlabeled) and its firing does not remove any options for continuation. This will be the case when the transition does not share any of its its input places with another transition. Removing the inert transition implies fusing its input and output places. Again, the nets are equivalent, this time by weak bisimilarity.

An inert transition can also be *added* in order to simplify complicated place weavings. In Figure 12, this unweaving by adding an inert transition is depicted.

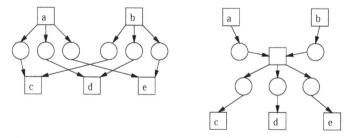

Fig. 12. Adding and removing an inert transition

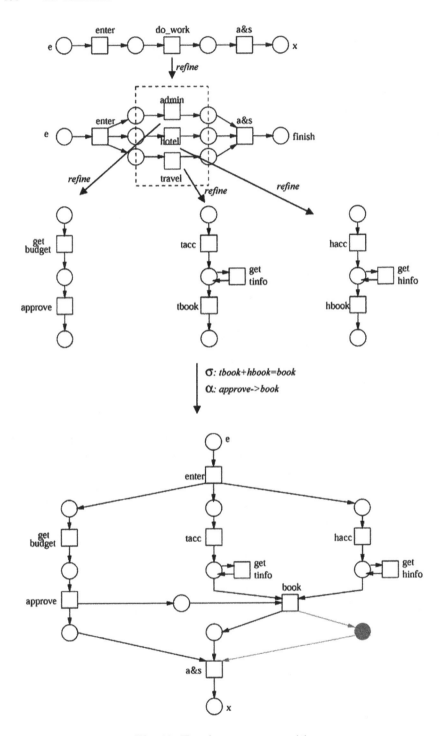

Fig. 13. Top-down net composition

3.4   Example Construction

As an example, we show the construction of our trip planning example, illustrated in Figure 13. By sequential composition of three actions, the first net is arrived at. Now the middle action do_work is refined into the parallel composition (merge) of administration, travel and hotel actions. These actions on their turn are refined into nets involving sequencing and iteration. Asynchronous communication causes the hotel and travel booking to wait for budget approval. The hotel and travel booking is performed synchronously (as they influence one another). By removing a redundant place, we obtain the net in Figure 1.

4   Conclusions and Further Work

This chapter treats the semantics of processes in a workflow context. We combine theoretical notions from Petri nets and process algebra. We hope that we have shown to the non-expert that it is worthwhile to investigate the meaning of the diagrams that represent workflow processes. Backed-up by these investigations, we can construct, discuss, verify and simplify our process models.

It seems worthwhile to further investigate the ST firing rule, since it can be used to assess the net models in terms of efficiency without the need to quantify task durations. The rule also supports refinement, which is important for structured modeling.

Conditions that allow the "dirty" operators to become "cleaner" are an interesting subject. Also, many WFMS systems allow the "rollback" of tasks that are being executed. Incorporating this notion in the firing rules will give yet another process equivalence. The difference between such equivalence notions may be marginal and of theoretical interest only, but it has to be investigated before one can be really sure.

References

1. W.M.P. van der Aalst. Verification of Workflow Nets. In *Application and Theory of Petri Nets 1997, 18th. International Conference, Proceedings*, volume 1248 of *Lecture Notes in Computer Science*, Toulouse, France, 1997. Springer–Verlag, Berlin, Germany.
2. J.C.M. Baeten and C. Verhoef. Concrete Process Algebra. In A. Abramsky, D.M. Gabbay, and T.S.E. Maibaum, editors, *Handbook of Logic in Computer Science*, volume 4, pages 149–268. Oxford University Press, Clarendon, UK, 1995.
3. E. Best, R. Devillers, and J. Hall. The Petri Box Calculus: a New Causal Algebra with Multilabel Communication. In G. Rozenberg, editor, *Advances in Petri Nets 1992*, volume 609 of *Lecture Notes in Computer Science*, pages 21–69. Springer–Verlag, Berlin, Germany, 1992.
4. R.J. van Glabbeek and U. Goltz. Equivalence Notions for Concurrent Systems and Refinement of Actions. In A. Kreczmar and G. Mirkowska, editors, *Mathematical Foundations of Computer Science 1989, 14th. International Symposium, Proceedings*, volume 379 of *Lecture Notes in Computer Science*, pages 237–248. Springer–Verlag, Berlin, Germany, 1989.
5. M. Hennesy and R. Milner. Algebraic Laws for Nondeterminism and Concurrency. *Journal of the ACM*, 32(1):137–161, 1985.
6. R. Milner. *Communication and Concurrency*. Prentice–Hall, London, UK, 1989.
7. W. Reisig. *Petri Nets*. Springer–Verlag, Berlin, Germany, 1985.
8. H.M.W. Verbeek, T. Basten, and W.M.P. van der Aalst. Diagnosing Workflow Processes using Woflan. Computing Science Reports 99/02, Eindhoven University of Technology, 1999.
9. W. Vogler. Bisimulation and Action Refinement. *Theoretical Computer Science*, 114(1):173–200, 1993.
10. M. Voorhoeve. State Event Net Equivalence. Computing Science Reports 98/02, Eindhoven University of Technology, 1998.
11. WFMC. Workflow Management Coalition Terminology and Glossary. Technical Report WFMC-TC-1011, Workflow Management Coalition, Brussels, 1996.

A Workflow Change is a Workflow

Clarence A. Ellis and Karim Keddara

Collaboration Technology Research Group
Department of Computer Science,
University of Colorado,
Boulder, CO 80309-0430, USA.
skip|karim@colorado.edu

Abstract. Organizations that are geared for success within today's business environments must be capable of rapid and continuous change. This business reality is boosting the popularity of various types of workflow systems. However, current workflow systems are not yet capable of facing the ever-changing nature of their business environment. Part of the answer to the challenge, in our view, lies in change understanding, communication, implementation, and analysis. In this chapter, we present an overview of our work on modeling dynamic change within workflow systems. This work was recently completed by the introduction of $\mathcal{ML\text{-}DEWS}$, a Modeling Language to support Dynamic Evolution within Workflow Systems. We firmly believe the thesis put forth in this chapter that a change is a process that can be modeled, enacted, analyzed, simulated and monitored as any process.

1   Introduction

A 1998 issue of Information Systems News featured an article headlined "Organizations Which Cannot Dynamically Change Cannot Survive." This is now a well-known theme in the business literature. The article notes that there are many kinds of change (e.g. organizational, social, ...) and that change is often done in an ad hoc manner. Thus, the ramifications of change, particularly complex changes within large organizations, are frequently not well understood, sometimes resulting in surprising negative side effects.

Organizations must frequently make changes such as consolidating systems and procedures, improving business processes, complying with new regulations and restructuring their work forces. To accommodate such changes, the specification and execution modules of a worklow system must be tightly interwoven. For example, it should be possible to edit the workflow model of a procedure and thereby dynamically and safely change how the steps of the procedure are being executed.

In the context of this work, the emphasis is put on dynamic procedural change, simply referred to herein as *process change*. Other types of change such as

W. van der Aalst et al.(Eds.): Business Process Management, LNCS 1806, pp. 201–217, 2000.

change of organizational structures, change of social structures, albeit important, are beyond the scope of this work. The term *dynamic* means that we are making the change "on the fly" in the midst of continuous execution of the changing procedure. Dynamic procedural change is challenging, and sometimes produces "dynamic bugs" which can be very obscure and elusive in large workflows.

A process change has two facets; namely *schema change* and *instance change*. A schema change occurs when a process definition is modified. An instance change occurs when a process execution changes. For example, an *exception* represents a form of instance change; it occurs when a case deviates from its specification as the result of an enactment error (e.g. a constraints violation) or an unexpected situation (e.g. a workers strike).

The underlying philosophy of our work on workflow change is based on the following key observations:

1. A process change is a process that can be modeled, enacted, analyzed, coordinated and monitored as any other process.
2. Change specification is a, albeit complex, process specification which describes the steps of the change, the flow of data and control among these steps, the participants involved in the change, and the change rules.
3. Schema changes, in general, yield to some form of instance changes.
4. Instance changes such as exceptions, frequently, may be assimilated to *temporary* schema changes.

The Collaboration Technology Research Group (CTRG) at the University of Colorado has been performing research in the groupware and workflow areas for the last eight years. Our prior work has considered issues of correctness and consistency of process change [9, 10] in workflow systems, and has been recently complemented by the introduction of $\mathcal{ML\text{-}DEWS}$ [11], a modeling language for the specification of change. $\mathcal{ML\text{-}DEWS}$ facilitates the examination and change of workflow schemas. It represents a structure within which a modeler can analyze notions of temporal evolution, dynamic change, and exceptions.

The rest of this chapter is organized as follows: First, a short overview of related work is given in the next section. Followed by a discussion on the various change modalities. Then, we illustrate some of the features of $\mathcal{ML\text{-}DEWS}$ using a simple example. The reader is referred to [11] for a detailed description of the modeling language and more complex examples of change. We assume that the reader has a basic understanding of the workflow concepts and terminology.

2   Related Work

There has been a large volume of work addressing workflow systems, but until recently, very little work concerned with the rigorous specification of dynamic change within workflows. There are many workflow products currently on the market, as well as research prototypes systems reported in the literature [15]. A lot of good work has been done in the areas of workflow architectures, workflow models, and pragmatic workflow studies [14].

The first work in the literature which carefully motivated and mathematically articulated the issues of dynamic workflow change was a 1995 paper by Ellis, Keddara and Rozenberg at the Organizational Computing Conference [9]. This paper began with justification for the investigation of dynamic change via examples of "dynamic bugs" which can yield surprising chaotic results if the change is done without care and precision. It presented a Petri net abstraction for modelling dynamic change. It showed that change to workflow procedures can be accomplished dynamically without shutting down the system, and without aborting or restarting work in progress. The paper rigorously defined the notion of dynamic change, and the notion of change correctness.

Recent follow-up has included work by van der Aalst [1, 2], by Agostini and DeMichelis [4], and by Ellis, Keddara and Wainer [10]. Other highly related recent work includes the work reported in [15], in [19], in [16], and in [7]. Some workflow prototype efforts have recently emerged to deal with flexibility in workflow systems including ADEPT [16] and Milano [4].

Ellis, Keddara, and Wainer improve on gradual case migration using flow jumpers and hybrid flow nets. The authors also introduce timed flow nets as a model for analysis of workflow change which incorporates specification of temporal constraints. A similar approach to case migration has been independently introduced by Agostini and DeMichelis in [4] based on linear jumps.

A formal foundation to support the dynamic structural change of workflow processes is presented by Reichert and Dadam in [16]. The workflow model, referred to therein as ADEPT, supports a graph-based representation of workflow processes. Based on ADEPT, a set of modification primitives which preserve a restricted form of control flow consistency similar to the soundness property of van der Aalst, and a newly introduced data flow consistency. The authors also deal with another change modality; namely the change lifetime, and provide a framework to support permanent and temporary change with the possibility of undoing temporary changes only and change composition.

In [7], Casati et al. present systematic approach to management of dynamic workflow evolution and case migration. In particular, various policies to support progressive case migration are discussed. For example, *migration to final workflow* is a policy which requires a case to be compliant with the new workflow, or to be brought to compliance (using rollback mechanism) before the case migration to the new workflow proceeds. The authors discuss also a strategy for managing case migration which uses case *segmentation* based on the selected migration policy.

Most of current workflow systems have some support for process versionning whereby multiples versions of a process may be active at the same time. A few workflow products (e.g. Inconcert [13] and Ensemble [12]) provide a basic support for dynamic change on a single case basis: Each case keeps a private copy of its definition that may be modified independently. This approach is suitable to deal with ponctual changes (e.g. workflow exceptions), but fails to address the issue of case migration from one process definition to another. A number of commercial products incorporate support for flexibility through ad-hoc workflows. For example, Inconcert supports ad hoc worflows by using Process Design by Discovery, a method which allows customers to deploy workflow without a preliminary design phase: The process is built by doing the tasks, may be changed on the fly by users, and saved as a template when completed.

As a final note concerning related work, we emphasize that dynamic process change is an important issue within numerous other domains such as software engineering [5, 8].

3   Modalities of Change

When one specifies a change, there are many factors which must be taken into account. Many of these factors can be considered as pre-conditions and post-conditions for change to happen. These pre- and post-conditions may be expressed as functions of time, application data, organizational context, process data, history, personnel data, state of the work-case, state of the total system, resource availability, and other exogenous information.

The concept of "change specification roll-out time" denotes the date and time when the change begins. This time specification acts as an anchor for other times which can be specified in absolute time, or in relative time. Relative is always with respect to the change specification roll-out time.

We next identify and explain several modalities of change that are important elements in any change specification. The lack of specification of these elements frequently leads to ambiguity - the manager distributes a statement of change, and the employees misinterpret the statement, and the change is mis-implemented.

3.1   Change Duration: Instantaneous vs Time Interval vs Indefinite

One factor is the specification of whether the change is to happen quickly (instantaneously) or over a noticeably long (but finite and well specified) time period or an unspecified amount of time ("as long as it takes for the old stuff to change"). Frequently change that is immediate and instantaneous is desired by management, but sometimes an indefinite time period for change is preferred. An example of the latter (ongoing, indefinite time) is a change by introducing a new version of a software package. Some customers will immediately switch to the new version, and others may switch at a later time. Frequently there is an expressed commitment to maintain the old version for as long as customers are using the old version. Thus, the amount of time for all customers to switch from the old to the new version may be indefinitely long.

3.2   Change Lifetime: Permanent vs Temporary

Another factor is the amount of time that the change is in effect (with respect to the change specification roll-out time). If this time is specified as forever, then the lifetime is permanent. However, many changes are put in place for a specific and finite period of time. For example, a new set of procedures may be in effect for the next two weeks while the head manager is away on vacation only. Of course the nature of the temporary lifetime can be conditioned upon many factors such as customer satisfaction or time of new employee hire.

We believe that the notion of exception handling can fruitfully be considered as a special case of dynamic change whose lifetime is temporary, and whose filters may select one and only one work-case. Thus if it is decided that one particular customer must skip the time consuming credit approval activity, then we make a dynamic change to the procedure by omitting the credit approval step. This change is not permanent, but temporary; and we specify a filter which enables the change to be applicable only to this one customer.

3.3   Change Medium: Manual vs Automatic vs Mixture

Most changes require different data and/or routing to occur for some number of customers (or work-cases). When the number of work-cases that must change is small, it is frequently done by a human who uses a medium such as pen and paper to make changes (and perhaps explanatory notes). On the other hand, if there are thousands or millions of work-cases which are affected by the change, then a computer program is typically written to allow the work-cases which fit within the filter to be automatically updated. There are other media which have been used for change, and the media possibilities will continue to grow in the future.

3.4   Change Time-frame: Past vs Present vs Future

In considering the work-cases to which a change is applicable, one typically restricts consideration to work-cases which are currently in progress (where current typically refers to the change specification roll-out time). This is an aspect in which ordinary English language specifications of change are sometimes unclear. It must be remembered that there are situations in which one must specifically exclude work-cases which have not yet begun, or specifically include work-cases which have already terminated. Thus we find change notifications which are retroactively applicable to old work-cases - e.g.: "this ruling applies to all jobs completed in 1998 and after". This type of change may require that certain old work-cases be updated.

3.5   Change Continuity: Preemptive vs Integrative

Every change requires some planning and some implementation work. Every change thus embodies a migration strategy. In the case of exception handling, the planning may necessarily be short in duration, and it may be highly intertwined with implementation at workflow enactment time. Nevertheless, we always must decide the various modalities, including whether we will somehow disrupt (or preempt) currently running work-cases, or whether we will somehow allow the current work-cases to continue for some time in a smooth fashion. Preemptive strategies include abort schemes, rollback schemes, restart schemes, checkpoint schemes, and flush schemes. Non-preemptive strategies, which we define as integrative strategies, include versioning, SCOC [9], and other gradual work-case migration schemes. In general, the specific requirements and desires and capabilities of an organization, and of a specific change dictate the choice between preemptive versus integrative continuity.

3.6   Change Agents

This is a specification of which participants play which organizational roles within the change process. For example, it specifies who has the right to specify, enact, and authorize what types of changes. This is an important vehicle for *participatory change*.

Every change requires someone to specify and do it. The change agents specification details which participants play which roles within the change process. Note that activities may involve multiple roles and/or multiple agents. Besides agents who perform the activities, there are customers of the activity, overseers, responsibles, clients, and other stakeholders. These should all be explicitly declared. For example, manager may have privilege to see ALL data, and responsibility to be held accountable for its timeliness and accuracy, although he does not actually do the detailed data processing work. Notions of change agent are frequently implemented by an organizational model which specifies which people play which roles.

Especially within change processes, it is important to identify who will play which roles, and who has which responsibilities. Questions which must be answered within the change process specification include the following. Who has final authority to say that a change MUST be done? Once it is authorized, who actually disseminates and implements the change? Who is the "blamee" that takes responsibility for correct timely implementation (getting the praise for success, and the blame for failure of the change)? Who are the actors who must do their jobs differently after the change?

3.7   Change Rules

Every change comes to life to achieve a set of business goals. The change rules guide a change process in its pursuit of meeting these goals. There are various kinds of rules: *Participatory rules* define the participation aspect of a change process. *Integrity rules* define the various constraints of a change including temporal constraints (e.g. scheduling), data integrity constraints, and flow constraints. *Situated rules* define how to react in the face of exceptional situations such as constraint violation, or a system failure, or the occurrence of an external condition such as delays in a software release.

Every change is also based on a set of assumptions and predictions that are typically validated based on past behavior or forecasting analysis. However, a business environment may be highly volatile and unpredictable. Thus, a change design must clearly identify these assumptions, incorporate checkpoints to verify their validity, and offer course of actions in case of violations. We believe that situated rules may be used to provide such support.

3.8   Change Migration

A procedure may have a large number of work-cases in progress at any given time. When a change is specified, it is also necessary to specify the subset of the work-cases to which the change is applicable. *Filtering* refers to the ability to specify this subset. For example, a change of top management approval may be instituted for all work-cases involving more than 10,000 dollars. In general, subset selection may be a complex function.

Migration refers to the ability to bring the filtered-in cases into *compliance* with the new procedure in *accordance* with the migration policies *agreed upon* by the change designers. Frequently, these cases, by the end of migration, barely resemble to the new procedure. Any aspect of a migrating case may change *because of* the migration, including its state, data, flow, rules, and participants.

Frequently, the migration modalities (i.e *which, what, how, when, who*) are complex enough that a *migration process* is warranted. In essence, the migration process *realizes* case migration. Note that the migration process is different from the change process: Migration is one aspect of the change. Other aspects include change analysis, change monitoring, change simulation, change coordination, etc.

Finally, a side note to conclude our discussion on change modalities. Sometime, the change modalities are not known ahead of time or the actual change circumstances make it impractical to spend the extra effort to plan for a change. *Ad hoc changes* fit into the former description and exceptions fit into the latter description. $\mathcal{ML}$-$\mathcal{DEWS}$ provides support for *incomplete change specification*. This topic will be further developed later.

4   Change Specification Using $\mathcal{ML}$-$\mathcal{DEWS}$

$\mathcal{ML}$-$\mathcal{DEWS}$ is a special purpose meta-language geared toward the specification of workflow changes. In order to specify a change, there must be an existing specification of the workflow before the change. As mentioned in the introduction, a change is a process that is specified and enacted as any other process in a wokflow system. This *reflexive view* entails that $\mathcal{ML\text{-}DEWS}$ is also used for process specification.

$\mathcal{ML\text{-}DEWS}$ is a visual modeling language designed to specify, visualize, and construct the artifacts of a process. $\mathcal{ML\text{-}DEWS}$ is an extension of the *Unified Modeling Language* (abbreviated to UML) [6]. $\mathcal{ML\text{-}DEWS}$ is simple, powerful and extensible. The language is based on a small number of core concepts as proposed by the Workflow Management Coalition (WfMC) [18], that most workflow modelers in general, and object oriented modelers in particular, can easily apply. All workflow model elements such as processes, activities, rules, events and flow are modeled as classes. Object oriented behavioral and structural modeling artifacts such as attributes, operations, association, and generalization are thusly supported. In particular, we take the view that a process is an object whose behavior is partly described by its control and data flow.

4.1   The Process Meta Model

A process class describes a process. It includes the process medium that indicates if the process is manual or automated, the process category that indicates if the process is structured or ad hoc, the process pre-conditions that define when the process may start, the process parameters that describe the process input/output data, and the process signals that define the process-specific events that may be triggered within the process including its exceptions.

An activity class describes a step within a process. The activity category indicates if the activity is a macro or an elemental activity. A macro activity refers to another process that is executed when the activity starts. The priority of the activity is used in conflict resolution. The activity parameters define the input/output data.

The $\mathcal{ML\text{-}DEWS}$ event model is similar to the UML event model. Several kinds of events are thusly supported: A time event indicates the passage of time. It is specified using the keyword `After` followed by a time expression; e.g. `After(3 * Day)`, or `After(startTime + 2 * Hour)`. A change event represents a change in an object attribute value or the satisfaction of some condition. It is specified using the keyword `When` followed by some condition; e.g. `When(Clock = '11:59')`, or `When(state = Completed)` (here, `Clock` is a macro which is expanded to reflect the current system time). A call event represents the invocation of an operation on a object. A signal event represents a named object that is sent asynchronously by one object and then received by other objects. For example, `CaseCompleted` is a predefined signal that is triggered when a work-case is completed and `TaskCompleted` is a predefined signal that is triggered when a task is completed. Both call and signal events are specified using the keyword `On` followed by the name of an operation or a signal; e.g. `On TaskCompleted` or `On setBalance`. Optionally, a parameter binding may be specified; e.g. `On evt:TaskCompleted`.

Events are mainly used in the specification of guards (e.g. the pre- or post-conditions of a process or an activity). A modeler may use <u>active guards</u>. An active guard has an event-part and a condition-part. When an <u>event</u> as specified by the event part occurs, the condition part is evaluated. The condition part is written using the Object Constraint Language (OCL), a standard language used in UML modeling. For example, the expression: `On evt:TaskCompleted` `(evt.sender.isInstanceOf(Shipping)` may be used to flag the completion of a `Shipping` activity.

A <u>rule class</u> models a process rule. In particular, *active rules* may be defined using a simple textual representation of the form:

$$[Rule\ Name\ Priority\ Guard\ Body]$$

the optional priority is used by the rule manager to determine the next rule to be triggered. For example, the following process rule causes an exception to be raised 3 days after the process has started:

```
[  Rule  Rule_72H
     When (Clock = (startTime + 72 * Hour))
     Exception :: instantiate(Constraint_Violation).throw()
]
```

A <u>flow net class</u> models the control and data flow of a process. Flow nets are a class of high level Petri Nets with a single entry place, a single exit place, and extra connectivity properties. Each transition in the flow net represents an activity of the process that is executed whenever the transition fires. Tokens flowing through the flow net are either control or data tokens. Data tokens carry the information exchanged between activities. Control tokens are used for synchronization purposes; to indicate when an activity starts and completes.

Example 1. Consider the flow of the order processing procedure depicted in Figure 1. When a customer requests by mail, or in person, an electronic part, this is the beginning of a work-case. An order form is filled out by the clerical staff (`OEntry` activity). The order form is routed in parallel to the finance department for customer credit check (`Credit` activity), and to the inventory department (`Inventory` activity). The finance agent files a customer credit report with the collection agency, records its findings in the order form and sends the order form to the sales department. The inventory agent checks the availability of the goods, and records the availability status in the order form.

After evaluating the reports (`Evaluation` activity), the order may be either sent to a manager for approval (`Approval` activity), or the order is rejected and a rejection letter is sent to the customer (`Rejection` activity). Upon approval, the order is sent to the billing department, and then to the shipping department. The shipping department will actually cause the parts to be sent to the customer (`Shipping` activity), the billing department will see that the customer is sent a bill, and that it is paid (`Billing` activity). Finally, a log with a description of the order processing is created by the system (`Archiving` activity).

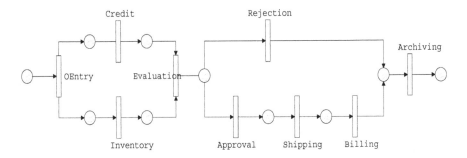

Fig. 1. The old version of the procedure for order processing

4.2   The Process Change Meta Model

A process change means that a process definition, referred to as the old process, is transformed into another process definition, referred to as the new process. A process change, frequently, may require some cases to *migrate* to the new process. Such cases are either enactments of the old process, and in a more general setting, they may be cases which have migrated, or are in the midst of migration, to the old process (*change composition*). In the context of change, an old case is either an execution of, has migrated to, or is migrating to, the old process.

A change process class describes a process change in a form which can be understood and used by all parties involved in the change, to communicate, and carry out their responsibilities. change process definition includes change *roll-out time* to indicate when the change begins, and the change expiration time that indicates when the change ends (indefinite by default). Unless specified otherwise, all in-progress case migrations are allowed to proceed as planned after the expiration time is reached, however, no new case migration is initiated afterwards. The *change filter* specifies the subset of old cases that are allowed to migrate to the new process. The *migration process* (yet another process) encapsulates the migration modalities of the filtered in old cases. For the purpose of this work, we assume that each change process may be associated with one migration process at the most.

The change filter is an OCL expression that is used to specify the old cases that are allowed to migrate to the new procedure. Filtering varies from one change to another. For example, in some situations, it may be desirable to *filter-in* the old cases which are already completed (e.g. recalling defective parts). In other situations, it may be necessary to *filter-out* the old cases to which a previous change has been applied (e.g. irreconcilable changes). Complex filtering policies may be defined based on the state, the data, the (execution and the change) history and the participatory aspects of the old case.

Example 2. In the context of our running example, the manager decides to speed up the order processing by introducing new billing and shipping systems. The shipping and the billing activities must be done in parallel. Also, all current orders with a value of 1000 dollars and which have not been yet shipped must switch to the new system.

The new version of the procedure is depicted in Figure 2. The change filter is expressed as follows:

$(isOpen()$ and $(balance >= 1000)$ and $not(isCompleted(Shipping))$

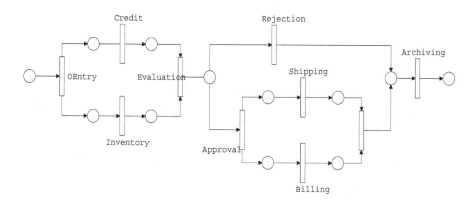

Fig. 2. The new version of the procedure for order processing

The migration process specifies how the filtered-in old cases migrate to the new process. Each enactment of the migration process, also called a migration case, refers to a single old case; this reference is noted *oldCase*. The migration policies, as specified in the migration process, may express the various properties that a migration case ought to fulfill in the course of its lifetime; including constraints. Yet, in other situations, a migration policy may modify the rules of the old case; e.g. scheduling or integrity constraints may need to be readjusted.

Example 3. In the context of our running example, the goal of the change is to achieve a three-fold processing time improvement. Therefore, the temporal constraint of the old case is adjusted as follows:

```
[ Rule  MigRule
    On CaseStarted
    {
        oldCase.remove(Rule_72H);
        oldCase.insert(Rule_24H);
    }
]
```

[*Rule Rule_24H*
   When $(Clock = (startTime + 24 * Hour))$
   $Exception :: instantiate(Constraint\_Violation).throw()$

]

The definition of the migration process may specify a *migration flow*. The *migration activities*, reflect the steps to be carried out during the migration; these steps may be *out-of-band*, in the sense that they are part of neither the old process nor the new process.

A migration activity may be a meta-activity that includes one or more actions, each action represents a non interruptible operation to be performed on the old case. These operations may alter various aspects of an old case, including its state, data, flow, rules, history, participants, rules and business goals. Of particular interest are the flow operations which may change the marking of the old case; e.g. a token may be *moved* from one place to another, a new token may be *injected* into a place, or an existing token may be *removed* from a place. Flow operations may also change the flow of the old case; e.g. a flow element (i.e. a place, transition or a connector) or a region (i.e. a sub-net) may be *added* or *deleted*.

Example 4. The migration process for our example of change is depicted in Figure 3. First, the migration case undergoes a registration phase for book-keeping purposes (`MigrationRegistry` activity). Then, the old case is momentarily suspended (`SuspendOldCase` activity). Next, a test is performed to check if the old case is being shipped. If no, the flow of the old case is changed on the fly by the `AutoEdit` activity, and then resumed by the `ResumeOldCase` activity. If yes, then billing is blocked within the old case by the `BlockBillingOldCase` activity, then the old case is resumed. Upon Completion of shipping within the old case, and billing within the migration case, the old case skips billing and proceeds to archiving (`SkipBillingOldCase` activity). Finally, the migration case is archived (`MigrationArchiving` activity).

The change process is also a process, and as such it has its own structure with a *change flow, change activities, change rules* and *change agents*. The enactment of a change process, also called a change case, may have at any time many migration cases which are in progress. Every change requires some preliminary *preparation* before deployment: A change notification may be sent to all parties concerned with the change (e.g. agents or customers), a Request For Comment or Request For Proposal may be issued to get various inputs on change policies and change implementation, or new systems and procedures must be put in place to support the change. Every change also necessitates some post-change planning: For temporary change, the modalities to revert back to the old process must also be defined. Close monitoring is also an essential step, at least at early stage of deployment, to ensure a smooth transition and readiness to react to any unexpected situation.

Example 5. For our example of change, the change manager opts for a gradual and smooth transition. The change steps are as follows: A change notification is

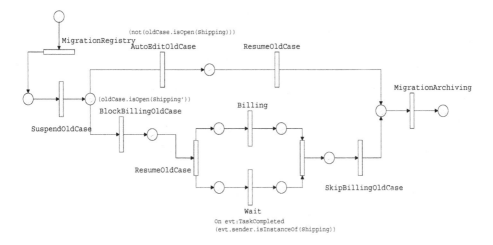

Fig. 3. The migration process

sent to all employees, the notification reads as follows: "Notice to all employees - Effective at the beginning of the work day on November 1st, 1999: Our company will do shipping and billing in parallel (concurrently). Also, a new computer system has been installed. The new shipping and billing software will be up and working soon. All employees of shipping and billing should try out the new system on a few of your orders before October 15, 1999. The transition to the new process should complete before the beginning of the Christmas shopping period - 11/28/1999." On November 1st, the old process is deactivated and the new process is activated, this also marks the beginning of the migration of "big-dollar" orders.

The change roll-out time is assumed to be October 1st, 1999 (the date at which it is specified). The change expiration time is November 28, 1999. The change process is depicted in Figure 4. The activity NotifyAllEmployees sends the notification to all employees. The activity CheckFew checks if all employees have successfully tried the new system before October 15th. The activity ActivateNewProc is used to activate the new process definition. The activity MigrateOldCases sees that the old cases migrate in accordance with the change filter and the migration process described earlier.

4.3   The Predefined Change Schemes

$\mathcal{ML}$-$\mathcal{DEWS}$ supports a variety of pre-defined change schemes; including the *Synthetic Cut Over Change* (*SCOC*) scheme, the *Abort* scheme, the *Defer* scheme, the *Edit* scheme, and the *Ad-hoc* scheme.

SCOC applies to changes in the flow of a process. It is based on the principle of change locality: The set of changes that a flow net undergoes may be localized

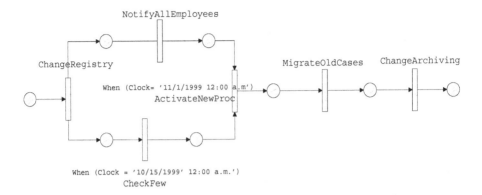

Fig. 4. The change process

within a region of the flow net, referred to as the change old region. The change is viewed as a net-replacement; the change old region is replaced with another region, referred to as the change new region.

The specification of *SCOC* consists of the selection of the change regions and the definition of flow jumpers, a class of Petri Net transitions, that are used to connect old region to the new region. The basic functions of the migration process in the context of *SCOC* is to change the flow of the old case as follows:

- sever the old region from the flow so that no new tokens are allowed in the old region.
- insert a copy of the new change region in place of the old change region.
- maintain the old change region part of (but separate from) the flow of the old case as long as it is active.
- set up the specified jumpers.

The idea here is that work evolving outside the change regions is not disrupted by the change. Work inside of the old change region is allowed to proceed *as if the change did not take place yet*, however, flow jumpers are used to *gradually migrate* this work to the new change region. In addition to its role as a token migrator, a flow jumpers may be used to support *corrective migration* whereby a sub-process attached to the jumper is started when the jumper is initiated.

The selection of the change regions and the definition of the jumpers may be done manually, or *computed* by the system based on a set of *correctness criteria*. For example, Agostini and De Michelis propose an automated method based on minimal critical specification [4]. Whereas Voorhoeve and van der Aalst [17] propose a set of rules based on Petri Nets branching semantics.

Example 6. Figure 5 depicts the selection of the change regions and the flow jumpers for our running case.

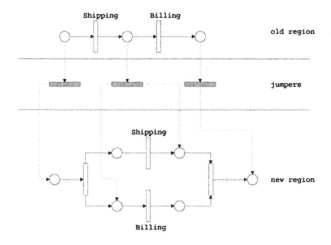

Fig. 5. The SCOC method

The *Abort* Scheme is a disruptive migration strategy in which the old case is simply aborted. The tasks which have already been carried out may or may not be *undone*. The old case may or may not be *resubmitted* for execution according to the new process.

The *Defer* scheme allows an old case to proceed according to the old process, and at completion a set of corrective steps may be executed to bring the old case into compliance with the new process.

In many situations such as exceptions, the migration modalities of an old case are not known ahead of time. The *Edit* Scheme may be used to allow a modeler to define the migration modalities using a *case editor*. The case editor is invoked by the migration process on the old case.

The *Ad-hoc* scheme is introduced to support ad-hoc changes whose components are not all fully specified in advance. The idea here is to precisely complete the change specification at run time when the change process is enacted. For example, a collaborative sub-process may be started by the change process. The participants in the collaborative sub-process define the missing change components, and then the change process resumes its execution fully specified. One may also imagine a scenario in which the change design is an ongoing incremental effort; the change design and enactment either alternate or are done in parallel.

5   Conclusions

We have presented a modeling language for the specification of dynamic process change. A process change is viewed as a process that can be modeled and enacted as a process. Various change modalities, change composition, ad hoc change, participatory change and exception are conveniently handled within the framework presented in this chapter.

$\mathcal{ML}$-$\mathcal{DEWS}$ is an on-going research effort dedicated to bring practical solutions to the problem of dynamic change within workflow systems. Currently we are investigating the issue of change enactment to support our reflexive view. In particular, gradual case migration is a challenging proposition, and requires some innovative workflow architectural design to deal with concurrency control, scalability, coordination, replication, security, recovery and interoperability. Yet another appropriate question is: How can we model workflows that may be easily and dynamically changed? The organizational and the social aspects of (change in) workflow systems are increasingly important. For example: How do workflow change and the social fabrics of an organization affect each other? is a crucial question to address.

References

1. Aalst W.M.P. van der (1997): Verification of Workflow Nets.*In P. Azema and G. Balbo, editors, Application and Theory of Petri Nets 1997,volume 1248 of Lecture Notes in Computer Science, pages 407-426. Springer-Verlag, Berlin, 1997.*
2. Aalst W.M.P. van der (1999): Finding Errors in the Design of a Workflow Process: A Petri Net Approach. In this volume.
3. Aalst W.M.P. van der , Michelis G. De, Ellis C. A. (editors,1998): Proceedings of WFM98: Workflow Management: Net-Based Concepts, Models, Techniques and Tools, PN98, Lisbon, Portugal.
4. Agostini A., Michelis G. De (1999): Improving Flexibility of Workflow Systems. In this volume.
5. Bandinelli S., Fuggetta A., Ghezzi. C. (1993): Software process model evolution in the SPADE environment. *IEEE Transactions on Software Engineering, December 1993.*
6. Booch G., Rumbaugh J., Jacobson I. (1997): *Unified Modeling Language Semantics and Notations Guide 1.0*: San Jose, CA: Rational Software Corporation.
7. Casati F., Ceri S., Pernici B., Pozzi G.(1996): Workflow Evolution. *In Proceedings of the 15th International Conference on Conceptual Modeling (OOER 96), Cottbus, Germany.*
8. Cugola G. (1998): Tolerating Deviations in Process Support Systems via Flexible Enactment of Process Models. *IEEE Transactions on Software Engineering, vol. 24, no 11, 1998.*
9. Ellis C. A., Keddara K., Rozenberg G. (1995): Dynamic Change within Workflow Systems. *In Proceedings of the Conference on Organizational Computing Systems, ACM Press, New York (1995) 10-21.*
10. Ellis C. A., Keddara K., Wainer J. (1998): Modeling Dynamic Change Using Timed Hybrid Flow Nets. In [3].
11. Ellis C. A., Keddara K. (1999): $\mathcal{ML}$-$\mathcal{DEWS}$: A Modeling Language to Support Dynamic Evolution within Workflow Systems. To appear in the Journal of CSCW, Special issue on Adaptive Workflow.
12. FileNet. Ensemble User Guide. FileNet Corp., Costa Mesa, California, 1998.
13. InConcert. InConcert Process Designer Guide. InConcert, Inc., Cambridge, Massashusets, 1997.

14. Jablonski S., Bussler C. (1996): *Workflow Management, Modeling Concepts, Architecture and Implementation.* International Thomson Computer Press (publisher) 1996.
15. Klein, M., Dellarocas C., Bernstein A. (editors, 1998): Toward Adaptive Workflow Systems. *Workshop at the ACM CSCW'98 Conference, Seattle, WA, August, 1998.*
16. Reichert M., Dadam P. (1998): Supporting Dynamic Changes of Workflows Without Loosing Control. *Journal of Intelligent Information Systems, V.10, N.2, 1998.*
17. Voorhoeve M., Aalst W.M.P. van der (1996): Conservative Adapation of Workflow. In [19]
18. WfMC (1996): Workflow Management Coalition Terminology and Glossary. Technical Report, Workflow Management Coalition, Brussels, 1996.
19. Wolf M., Reimer U. (editors.) (1996): Proceedings of the International Conference on Practical Aspects of Knowledge Management (PAKM'96), Workshop on Adaptive Workflow, Basel, Switzerland.

Improving Flexibility of Workflow Management Systems

Alessandra Agostini and Giorgio De Michelis

Cooperation Technologies Laboratory, DISCO, University of Milano "Bicocca",
Via Bicocca degli Arcimboldi, 8, 20126, Milano, Italy
agostini@cootech.disco.unimib.it; gdemich@disco.unimib.it

Abstract. In order to support both the redesign of a Business Process and its continuous improvement, the technology supporting it must be as flexible as possible. Since workflow management systems are the main technology for supporting Business Processes, they and, in particular, their modeling framework must satisfy a long list of apparently conflicting requirements: the models must be both cognitive artifacts and executable programs; they must be simple and yet able to support exceptions; they must support both static and dynamic changes. In this chapter, after briefly discussing the above requirements, we present the formal aspects of the modeling framework of the MILANO workflow management system. Its flexibility is based on a net-theoretical modeling framework which lets simple process models deliver a large class of services to its users.

1 Introduction

A turbulent market and social context as well as technological innovation force any organization to change the rules defining and/or governing its Business Processes (BPs) ever more frequently. These changes regard every dimension of a BP:

- its objectives and/or outcomes;
- the activities performed within it;
- the roles played by its actors and their professional skills;
- its data flow and integration with the corporate information system;
- its control flow;
- the way exceptions are handled;
- the technologies supporting it.

Designing a change generally impacts several of the above dimensions. Moreover, implementing a change is a complex process in itself requiring time and resources. In fact, implementing a change in a BP is a learning process within which its team continuously improves its performance, exploiting advantages while overcoming both constraints and obstacles introduced by the change [10, 12, 31]. The intertwining between designed changes and continuous improvements is bi-directional: on the one hand, as asserted above, designed changes

W. van der Aalst et al.(Eds.): Business Process Management, LNCS 1806, pp. 218-234, 2000.
© Springer-Verlag Berlin Heidelberg 2000

create new conditions for the learning process (the change has to be learned, i.e. internalized [21] by the team); on the other hand, the improvements introduced in a BP's performance by its team need sooner or later to be reflected by the rules defining and/or governing it (it has to be transformed into new rules, i.e. externalized [21] by the team).

Therefore, while the design from scratch of a new BP is a rare and non repeatable event in the life of an organization, changing existing BPs becomes ever more frequent. Moreover, the rules defining a BP must be light and open enough to leave room for the improvements its team can introduce through its learning process.

If we restrict our attention to the main technology supporting Business Processes, i.e. workflow management systems [19, 26, 34], the above observations translate into a quest for flexibility. The lack of adequate flexibility can be considered the main reason why for many years workflow management systems have been announced as the next best-selling computer application [19] but up to now have not matched the success of other packages such as productivity tools, e-mail systems, web-browsers and even groupware platforms [3].

Given that the main components of a workflow management system architecture are its modeling framework and run-time engine [37], flexibility depends primarily on the features characterizing the former. Flexibility means in fact many interrelated things: easy design and change; easy enactment of changes in the running workflow instances; good support of exceptions handling; support of all interested actors (process team, process owner, process managers/supervisors, process designers). Therefore, a workflow management system is flexible if its modeling framework offers a balanced combination of the following features:

- its models are both maps—cognitive artifacts [22] helping users to situate themselves in the process instance they are executing—and scripts—programs executable by the workflow engine to automate the flow, control and execution of routines allowing users to concentrate on sense-making tasks [27];
- it clearly separates data and control flow, the description of articulation and production work as well [28];
- it supports representing the process from the various viewpoints of the different actors participating to it;
- it supports both static and dynamic changes, respectively verifying their consistency and/or correctness and safely enacting them on the already ongoing instances [18];
- it supports exception handling, providing its users with the paths they must use for recovering them [9].

The above list is quite demanding since it contains apparently conflicting requirements: multiple views need multiple representations, but the latter may make the design of changes particularly heavy; exception handling mechanisms may render the process model very complicated; and so forth.

Over the last years, in response to the quest for flexibility, several proposals have appeared. Let us review some of them. The list is not complete, in fact, its aim is to highlight the approaches that from our viewpoint are most relevant to the creation of flexible workflow management systems. The interested reader can find an interesting and more comprehensive overview in [2].

A first group of proposals aims to support a flexible execution of the workflow: its focus is on exception handling through local changes. Some of them weakens, when it does not eliminate, the organizational control of workflows [17, 32], allowing the initiator/performer of a workflow to change it when she needs it, while other aim to anticipate exceptions trying to structure and encapsulate the run-time emergencies within 'static'—i.e. definable at design time only—mechanisms [11]. An interesting alternative solution is presented in [9]. In this approach—exploiting the main object-oriented principles—"deviations, anticipated or unanticipated" (page 67, [9]) are handled in a structured and elegant way.

A second group aims to support the design of adaptable workflows—i.e. e-volving workflows granting the correctness of the static/dynamic changes of their model. Many researchers—coming from various areas—are contributing with various relevant proposals to face the complexity of the problems. Without commenting two promising related areas—machine learning and schema evolution in database—let us recall two general solutions for the change of workflow models which are based on transformation rules granting the desired consistency relation between the two models [30, 33], even if they do not take into account the dynamicity of changes. Focussing on the treatment of dynamic changes (that is, the application of the change to the model during the execution of the model itself), the proposal by [18], which has deeply influenced our work, is the most representative solution to the problem. In fact, both the consistency of the new model is preserved and the changes are automatically enacted in the running instances.

In conclusion, we think that the above recalled solutions to the flexibility problem, even if they contain original ideas, are still inadequate because each one of them has some limits. In fact, either they are easy to manage by end users but they do not grant the correctness of exception handling processes and/or static and dynamic changes, or they offer effective means to grant their correctness but they are based on complex modeling formalisms (they have complicated graphs and/or they are based on higher order theories). On the contrary, flexibility requires both easy management techniques and powerful correctness verification methods and therefore it needs to escape from the above polarization.

We argue in this chapter that, contrary to what appears as commonsense, formal theory-based models can contribute to bridge the gap between easiness and correctness if they are conceived from a different perspective. Good algebra, in fact, offers effective tools for creating a process modeling environment exhibiting the following properties:

- it allows us to simulate the process before its execution;
- it allows formal verification of some workflow properties;
- it supports an unambiguous graphical representation of the workflow;

- it allows us to use a minimal input for redundant outputs, through the algorithmic completion of the model;
- it supports multiple views of the process, through synthesis algorithms and model conversions;
- it allows the automatic derivation of exceptional paths from the acyclic normal flow of the process, when needed;
- it automatically enacts model changes on the running instances of a workflow, protecting them from undesired outcomes.

What is needed in order to get all these services from algebraic theory is to keep workflow models as simple as possible, i.e. to use a *divide et impera* approach to the workflow. This means treating the following in a distinct way: the execution of the tasks embedded in the workflow steps, the data flow, the control flow, the latter being the only issue to be handled directly by the workflow management system.

In this chapter we present the prototype of the workflow management system we are developing within the MILANO system—a groupware platform which supports its users while concurrently performing various cooperative processes. In particular, we discuss how the theory it embodies provides the above services to its users. Throughout the chapter we illustrate our approach with a simple example of order processing procedure [18].

2   The Workflow Management System of Milano

In 1994 at the Cooperation Technology Laboratory the authors together with Maria Antonietta Grasso and several students initiated development of the prototype of a new CSCW system called MILANO [4, 6, 15]. MILANO is a CSCW platform supporting its users while performing in cooperative processes [13, 14]. MILANO is based on a situated language-action perspective [31, 35, 36] supporting the users so that they can keep on to the history they share with the actors they are cooperating with. It offers them a set of strictly integrated tools designed expressly for experiencing that history: in particular, a multimedia conversation handler and a workflow management system. Without adding more details about MILANO's other components (for a fuller account the interested reader can refer to [4, 6]), let us spend some more words on its workflow management system and in particular on its specification module.

The MILANO workflow management system is a new generation workflow management system [3]: its aim is to support its users not only while performing in accordance with the procedure described in its model, but also when needing either to follow an exceptional path or to change the workflow model. Within MILANO the workflow model is therefore not only an executable code but also a cognitive artifact. It is in fact an important part of the knowledge its different users (the initiator of a workflow instance, the performer of an activity within it, the supervisor of the process where it is enacted and, finally, the designer of the workflow model) share while performing within a cooperative process.

Thus the model must support not only the execution of several workflow instances but also the enactment of any model change on all the ongoing instances (dynamic changes). On the other hand, its cognitive nature requires that a workflow model supports all its users so that they can understand their situation, make decisions, perform effectively. The workflow model is not merely a program to be executed and/or simulated by the execution module with a graphical interface making it readable by its users. Rather, it is a formal model whose properties allow the user to get different representations of the workflow, to compute exceptional paths from the standard behavior, to verify if a change in the model is correct with respect to a given criterion and to safely enact a change on the ongoing instances.

Widely used in process modeling for over twenty years, Petri Nets offer moreover the kind of theoretical framework we are looking for [16]. Both High Level and Basic (Elementary, 1-Safe, etc.) Petri Nets have been used to model workflows respectively focusing on their expressiveness and on their simplicity. As we will better explain in the Conclusion, we think that simple models are preferable because they induce a clear separation between the control and the data flow. For this reason the specification module of the MILANO workflow management system is based on the theory of Elementary Net Systems (ENS) [25]. In fact ENS has some nice mathematical properties that appear suitable for providing the above services. For instance, using ENS, we can compute and classify forward- and backward-jumps linking their states; there is a synthesis algorithm from Elementary Transition Systems (ETS) to ENS [20]; the morphisms in ENS (ETS) preserve some important behavioral properties. Moreover, since MILANO is based on the idea that workflows must be as simple as possible, its workflow models constitute a small subcategory of ENS: namely, Free-Choice Acyclic Elementary Net Systems, whose main properties are computable in polynomial time, allowing an efficient realization of the specification module.

3   Modeling Workflows in Milano

Let us introduce in the following the main definitions and facts about modeling workflows in MILANO. We will illustrate them using an hypothetical order procedure; for more complete and concrete examples of the use of our modeling framework please refer to [6]. To avoid repetitions, for the main definitions on Elementary Net Systems and Elementary Transition Systems we refer to [8, 20, 25]. As mentioned above, the specification module offers two different representations of a workflow model: the first, called Workflow Net Model, is based on Elementary Net Systems; the second, called Workflow Sequential Model, is based on Elementary Transition Systems.

Definition 1 (Workflow Net Model). *A Workflow Net Model is a contact-free Elementary Net System, $\Sigma = (B, E, F, c_{in})$, such that the following hold:*

a) Σ is structurally acyclic (there are no cycles in the graph);
b) Σ is extended Free-Choice (all conflicts are free).

The class of Workflow Net Models is called WNM.

Definition 2 (Workflow Sequential Model). *A Workflow Sequential Model is an Elementary Transition System $A = (S, E, T, s_{in})$, such that the following hold:*

a) A is acyclic (there are no cycles in the graph);
b) A is well structured (all diamonds have no holes and the transitions with the same name are parallel lines in a diamond).

The class of Workflow Sequential Models is called WSM.

Figure 1 shows the Workflow Net Model (on the left) and the Workflow Sequential Model (right) of a hypothetical order procedure (for a real example please refer to [6]). While the Workflow Net Model (Fig. 1, left) is a local state representation making explicit, for example, the independence between the actions of *Inventory Check* and *Compile Reference*, the Workflow Sequential Model (Fig. 1, right) is a global state representation where the path followed during the execution of an instance is made immediately visible.

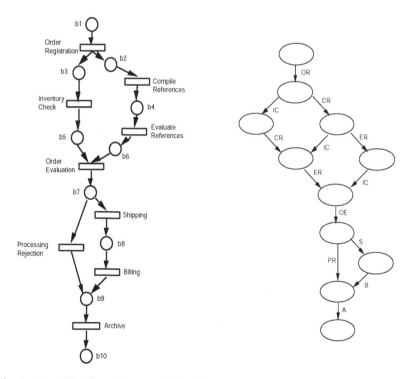

Fig. 1. The Workflow Net Model (left) and the Workflow Sequential Model (right) representing a hypothetical order procedure

It is well known that the sequential behavior of an ENS can be represented as an ETS; and, conversely, given an ETS it is possible to synthesize an ENS whose sequential behavior is equivalent to the source ETS [20]. It is easy to show that the above relation between ENS and ETS restricts itself to a relation between WNM and WSM.

The algorithm to build the ENS corresponding to ETS is based on the computation of Regions (subsets of S uniformly traversed by action names). While the algorithm presented in [20] generates a saturated ENS, having a place for each region of the source ETS, Luca Bernardinello [8] introduced a synthesis algorithm generating an ENS having a place for each Minimal Region of the source ETS, that is not a minimal representation of an ENS having the behavior described in the source ETS. The latter has some nice properties (e.g. it is contact-free and state-machine decomposable) making it very readable and well structured. We have therefore decided to normalize each WNM to its Minimal Regional representation and to associate to each WSM its Minimal Regional representation.

Proposition 1. *The sequential behavior of a WNM can be represented as a WSM; and conversely, given a WSM there is a WNM whose sequential behavior is equivalent to it.*

Proof (outline). The proof is based on the fact that the sequential behavior of an acyclic extended free-choice Elementary Net System is acyclic and well structured and, conversely, the (Minimal) Regions of an acyclic well structured Elementary Transition System are such that the corresponding Elementary Net System is both acyclic and extended free-choice.

The synthesis algorithm for ENS has been proved to be NP-complete [7], making its use in real applications impossible. The strong constraints imposed to WNM allow a rather efficient computation of Minimal Regions, so that it is usable in the specification module of the MILANO Workflow Management System. Let us sketch the algorithm for the computation of the Minimal Regions of a WNM. Let $A = (S, E, T, s_{in})$ be a Workflow Sequential Model. The following algorithm computes the Minimal Regions of A.

```
begin
C  := {(S - {s_in}, {s_in})};
R  := ∅;
while C ≠ ∅ do
    C  := C - (S', r) with S' maximal;
    E_r := {e| e exits r};
    E'_r := {e| e ∈ E_r and ∃s ∈ S'; e exits s};
    if E_r = ∅ then
        R := R ∪ {r};
    else
        if E'_r = ∅ then
            R := R ∪ {r};
```

```
    C  :=  C  ∪  {(S″,r′)| ∃e ∈ E_r,  r′  =  {s| e enters s}
           and  S″  = {s| s ∈ S′ − r′
           and s reachable from a state of r′}};
  else
     C :=  C  ∪  {(S″,r′)| ∃e ∈ E′_r,  r′  =  r ∪ {s| e exits s}
           and  S″  =  S′ − r′};
  fi
 fi
od
end.
```

Figure 2 labels each state of the WSM in Fig. 1 (right) with the Minimal Regions containing it. It is not difficult to see that the WNM in Fig. 1 (left) has a place for each of its Regions (it is therefore the result of the synthesis algorithm applied to the WSM in Fig. 2) and that the WSM in Fig. 1 is isomorphic to it.

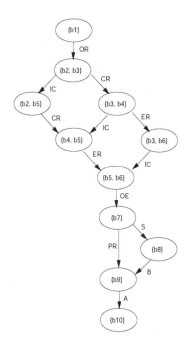

Fig. 2.

Proposition 2. *The algorithm given above is polynomial in the size of A (of its set of states, S).*

Proof (outline). The number of elements we can put in C lies between $|S|$ and $2\sqrt{|S|}$. Moreover, each step of the algorithm requires at most one observation of each element of S. □

The efficiency of the algorithm shown before grants that the switch between the two representations of a workflow model (namely WNM and WSM) can be computed whenever necessary, so that there are no constraints imposing a particular representation on the user. The problems related to the graphical visualization of the two representations (e.g. multi-dimensional diamonds will appear as intricate and difficult to read graphs) are not considered in this context.

The reader may object that the constraints imposed on WNM (WSM) are so strong that the actors are forced to follow very rigid prescriptions. This is not true, since whenever they cannot act in accordance with the model the actors can jump (either forward or backward) to another state from which execution can progress again. The freedom in the choice of the states that may be reached through jumps is not constrained by the model. But it can be constrained in accordance with the rules of the organization where the workflow is modeled. The actors are supported in the choice of an authorized jump by the possibility of computing and classifying composed paths in the graph.

Let us assume that the organization allows two different classes of jumps: strongly linear jumps (moving in the WNM only one token) not requiring any type of authorization, and weakly linear jumps (canceling two or more tokens and writing one token in the WNM) requiring authorization of the process initiator, i.e. of the person responsible for the execution of the procedure.

Let an instance of the order procedure presented in Figures 1 and 2 be in the state $\{b_2, b_5\}$. The available linear jumps from this state are represented in Fig. 3 (dashed lines). The allowed strongly linear jumps can either move the process back to the state $\{b_2, b_3\}$ or move the process forward to the states $\{b_4, b_5\}$ or $\{b_5, b_6\}$. In practice, from the state $\{b_2, b_5\}$ the backward strongly linear jump allows the employees to refine or redo the check of the inventory. In other words, when an employee needs additional information, which might have been produced previously in the process, she can directly jump backward and ask her colleague in charge for one of the previous activities. From the same state $\{b_2, b_5\}$ weakly linear jumps may either move the process back to the states $\{b_1\}$ or move forward to all possible states between $\{b_7\}$ and $\{b_{10}\}$. For instance, if an experienced manager intends to reject an order of a particular client, all she has to do is jump forward at the state $\{b_7\}$ and execute the *Processing Rejection* activity.

Here is an additional simple example of the potentiality of these jumps: every time a well-known client issues a new order, the sales manager would like to jump to the *Shipping* activity as soon as possible and avoid the client evaluation phase; therefore a weakly linear jump from state $\{b_2, b_5\}$ to state $\{b_7\}$ will be used. Of course, while strongly linear jumps can be applied directly by the employees, weakly linear jumps (like the one described above) involve the approval of a manager in charge, such as the sales manager.

The modeling framework constituted by the couple (WNM, WSM) therefore offers various services to its various categories of users. Actors, initiators, admin-

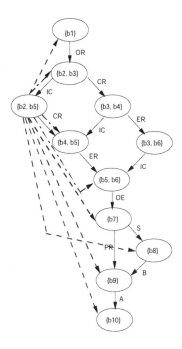

Fig. 3. The available linear jumps (dashed lines) from the state $\{b_2, b_5\}$

istrators and designers can choose between WNM and WSM to have the most effective visualization of the workflow model with respect to their current interest; actors and initiators can analyze the context in which a breakdown occurs and choose how to solve it.

From the above modeling framework administrators and/or designers also receive some services that are relevant with respect to their responsibility in regard to the model and its changes. We can assume that they are free to design the most efficient and/or effective workflow to execute a routine—provided that they satisfy those constraints characterizing what, anyhow, the procedure must do. However, they must be able to check any change with respect to those constraints.

Our modeling framework provides them with some services supporting both design change and its verification with respect to the constraints imposed on the procedure. They can in fact define a Minimal Critical Specification (see Definition 3, below) that must be satisfied by the adopted workflow model and all its changes, using it as a reference to guide changes. The theory embedded in the framework (i.e. the properties of the morphisms between WNMs and/or WSMs) allows it to support them with the automatic verification of the correctness of changes. Moreover, they can enact the change on all the already ongoing instances of the workflow, moving to the new model all the instances that are in a safe state while postponing the enactment of the change in those instances that are in an unsafe state until they reach a safe one (for the definition of safe and unsafe states see Definition 4, below). These services are based on the following:

- the class constituted by a minimal critical specification together with all the workflows that are correct with respect to it is closed under the morphisms induced by the action-labels;
- the composition of morphisms and inverse morphisms (morphisms always admit inverse, since they are injective and total) allows us to distinguish between safe and unsafe states with respect to a given change.

Let us explain the above claim with some simple examples, assuming that any workflow model must have the same set of action labels as its Minimal Critical Specification and that only changes not modifying the set of action labels are allowed.

Definition 3 (Minimal Critical Specification). *A WSM, $A = (S, E, T, s_{in})$, is correct with respect to a minimal critical specification $MCS = (S', E, T', s'_{in})$ if and only if the morphism induced by E, $g : S \rightarrow S'$, is injective and total.*

As its name suggests and its definition grants, a minimal critical specification is less constraining than any workflow model correct with respect to it, i.e. it admits a larger class of behaviors. Whenever no minimal critical specification is given, it can be assumed that the n-dimensional diamond representing the sequential behaviors of the workflow where all the n actions labels are concurrent is the implicit minimal critical specification to be taken into account.

Definition 4 (Unsafe states with respect to a change). *Let $A = (S, E, T, s_{in})$ be a WSM and $A' = (S', E, T', s'_{in})$ be a WSM being the effect of a change on it. Let both, A and A', be correct with respect to the minimal critical specification, $MCS = (S'', E, T'', s''_{in})$. Let, finally, $g : S \rightarrow S''$ and $g' : S' \rightarrow S''$ be, respectively, their morphisms on MCS induced by E; then $S - g^{-1}(g'(S'))$ is the set of unsafe states of A with respect to the given change. If a state is not unsafe with respect to a change, then it is safe with respect to it.*

$S - g^{-1}(g'(S'))$ contains all the states of A not having an image in S' (the new changed model); therefore it is impossible to move an instance being in one of them to the changed model since we cannot find univocally the state in which it will be after the change. Moreover, any choice we do for it does not allow a correct completion of the process.

Let the WSM in Fig. 4 be the effect of a change to the WSM in Fig. 2. This change makes the procedure more efficient, allowing us to perform the activities *Shipping* and *Billing* concurrently. All states of the original procedure are safe states with respect to this change; that is, all running instances can be safely moved in the new model. Let the WSM in Fig. 5, right, be the effect of a change of the WSM in Fig. 5, left. In this case the organization decided that the *Billing* of an order should be done before *Shipping* the goods to the client. Then the shaded state of the original WSM (Fig. 5, left) is its only unsafe state with respect to this change. Figure 6 summarizes the three patterns of change

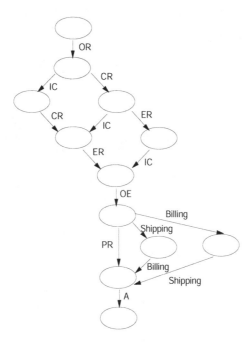

Fig. 4. A new version of the order procedure allowing a concurrent execution of the *Shipping* and *Billing* activities

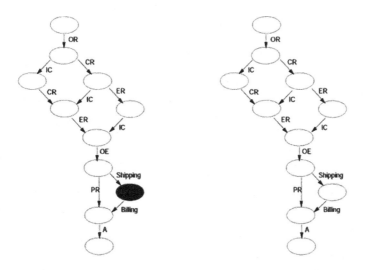

Fig. 5. A further version of the order procedure (right) with the swap between the *Shipping* and *Billing* activities

allowed by our theoretical framework: parallelization, making two sequential action labels concurrent (Fig. 6, left); sequentialization, creating a sequence with two concurrent action labels (Fig. 6, center); swapping, inverting the order of two sequential action labels (Fig. 6, right). The shaded states represent the unsafe states. The class of changes introduced above is quite small. In fact,

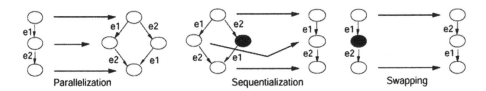

Fig. 6. The three possible category of changes allowed by the MILANO theoretical framework

originally, the minimal critical specification must contain all the action labels of any workflow model correct with respect to it. We can relax this constraint and only impose that the action labels of the minimal critical specification are contained in the set of action labels of any workflow model correct with respect to it. This would enlarge the class of allowed changes. Finally, a precise definition of action-label refinement within the above theoretical framework will further extend the class of changes supported by the specification module of the MILANO workflow management system.

4   Conclusion

It may appear paradoxical that we propose a stronger use of formal process models to increase the flexibility of workflow management systems, but we hope to have shown that what characterizes our proposal is mainly a different way of conceiving formal models of processes. While formal theories have been applied up to now mainly to get a non ambiguous semantics of the model and to attain an executable model, we apply net-theoretical concepts to obtain different (and partial, if necessary) representations of the model without requesting extra work by the model designer. If in the traditional approach formal theories could be used to claim for the objectivity of a model, for its truth, we apply net-theoretical concepts to grant mutual consistency of the different views of a model and to provide users with a fragment of a process model that can be extended as needed without losing any necessary information. Even the automatic verification of properties changes its meaning in our approach since it wants to prove not the objective correctness of the model but the correctness of a change with respect to a given minimal critical specification.

It is not by chance, therefore, that we apply net-theoretical concepts which have not been taken into consideration in process modeling up to now: Synthesis of Elementary Net Systems by means of Regions, Net Morphisms and Process Extensions of Net Systems.

One common criticism of our approach is that the models we can create are too simple to characterize real complex Business Processes. We respond to this recalling three important points.

– First, we separate the model of the control flow from both the data flow and the characterization of the activities constituting the nodes of the model. Therefore we do not need to use High Level Nets for modelling the workflow, because we model its control flow *per se*. That way users can deal with the articulation work separating it from the production work in accordance with the suggestions of various scholars who have studied coordination problems, e.g. [28]. We are convinced that even an object oriented approach to concurrency cannot be usable if it does not allow us to use this simple *divide et impera* rule.

– Second, our models are acyclic but our modeling framework allows us to add any backward (and forward) jump to them. From this point of view we can generate a very complex model, taking into account any exception handling path, from a very simple model without any loss of generality and making model changes very simple, since designers are not forced to re-trace backward jumps. Jumps are computed by the modeling framework, when necessary.

– Third, our models are free-choice, because we think that well-designed business processes are so in order to have a clear responsibility distribution and well-identified decision makers. If a business process cannot be modeled as a free-choice net system, then more than a more powerful modeling framework it needs redesigning.

If we shift our attention from business processes to other types of processes like production processes and/or system protocols, then it may be necessary to handle more complex processes. But still our approach can be applied since it has already been shown that other larger classes of net systems exist whose synthesis algorithms are polynomial time computable.

5   Acknowledgments

The authors presented the main ideas of the process modeling framework of the MILANO workflow management system at the Workshop on "Workflow Management: Net-based Concepts, Models, Techniques, and Tools" at the International Conference on Applications and Theory of Petri Nets in Lisbon, June 1998 and at the workshop on "Petri Nets and Business Process Management" in Dagstuhl July 1998 [5]. The authors thank the participants in both the above events for their various comments and suggestions, which helped us while writing this chapter. Special thanks are also due to our students, Roberto Tisi, Paolo Bertona, Pietro Nardella and Mario Manzoli, who contributed greatly to the development of the MILANO workflow management system.

References

1. van der Aalst, W.M.P.: Finding Errors in the Design of a Workflow Process. A Petri-net-based Approach. In: Workflow Management: Net-based Concepts, Models, Techniques and Tools, Computing Science Report 98/07, Eindhoven, The Netherlands: Eindhoven University of Technology (1998) 60-81
2. van der Aalst, W.M.P., Basten, T., Verbeek, H.M.W., Verkoulen, P.A.C., Voorhoeve, M.: Adaptive Workflow. On the interplay between flexibility and support. In: Proceedings of the 1st International Conference on Enterprise Information Systems, Setubal, Portugal (1999)
3. Abbott, K.R., Sarin, S.K.: Experiences with Workflow Management: Issues for The Next Generation. In: Proceedings of the Conference on Computer Supported Cooperative Work, ACM, New York (1994) 113-120
4. Agostini, A., De Michelis, G., Grasso, M.A.: Rethinking CSCW systems: the architecture of Milano. In: Proceedings of the Fifth European Conference on Computer Supported Cooperative Work, Kluwer Academic Publisher, Dordrecht (1997) 33-48
5. Agostini, A., De Michelis, G.: Simple Workflow Models. In: Workflow Management: Net-based Concepts, Models, Techniques and Tools, Computing Science Report 98/07, Eindhoven, The Netherlands: Eindhoven University of Technology (1998) 146-164
6. Agostini, A., De Michelis, G.: A light workflow management system using simple process models. Computer Supported Cooperative Work. The Journal of Collaborative Computing, (1999) (to appear)
7. Badouel, E., Bernardinello, L., Darondeau, P.: The synthesis problem for elementary net systems is NP-complete. Theoretical Computer Science, 186, 8 (1997) 107-134
8. Bernardinello, L.: Synthesis of Net Systems. In Application and Theory of Petri Nets, Lecture Notes in Computer Science, Vol. 691. Springer-Verlag, Berlin (1993) 89-105
9. Borgida, A., Murata, T.: Tolerating Exceptions in Workflows: a Unified Framework for Data and Processes. In: Georgakopoulos, D., Prinz, W., Wolf, A.L. (eds.): WACC'99. Proceedings of the International Joint Conference on Work Activities Coordination and Collaboration, San Francisco, CA, February 22-25, 1999. New York, NY: ACM Press (1999) 59-68
10. Bowers, J., Button, G., Sharrock, W.: Workflow from Within and Without: Technology and Cooperative Work on the Print Industry Shopfloor. In: Marmolin, H. Sundblad, Y., Schmidt, K. (eds.): ECSCW'95. Proceedings of the Fourth European Conference on Computer Supported Cooperative Work, Stockholm, Sweden, September 10-14, 1995. Kluwer Academic Publisher, Dordrecht (1995) 51-66
11. Casati, F., Ceri, S., Paraboschi, S. Pozzi, G.: Specification and Implementation of Exceptions in Workflow Management System, TR 98.81, Dipt. di Elettronica e Informazione, Politecnico di Milano (1998)
12. Ciborra C.: Groupware and Teamwork : Invisible Aid or Technical Hindrance?. John Wiley, New York, (1997)
13. De Michelis, G.: Computer Support for Cooperative Work: Computers between Users and Social Complexity. In C. Zucchermaglio, S. Bagnara and S. Stucky (eds.) Organizational Learning and Technological Change (eds.), Springer-Verlag, Berlin, (1995) 307-330
14. De Michelis, G.: Cooperation and Knowledge Creation. In: I. Nonaka, I., Nishiguchi, T. (eds.): Knowledge Emergence: Social, Technical and Evolutionary

Dimensions of Knowledge Creation. Oxford University Press, New York, 1998 (to appear)

15. De Michelis, G., Grasso, M.A.: Situating conversations within the language/action perspective: the Milan conversation Model. In: Furuta, R., Neuwirth, C. (eds.): Proceedings of the Conference on Computer Supported Cooperative Work, ACM, New York (1994) 89-100

16. De Michelis, G., Ellis, A.C.: Computer Supported Cooperative Work and Petri Nets. In W. Reisig and G. Rozenberg (eds.): Lectures on Petri Nets II: Applications, Lectures Notes in Computer Science, Vol. 1492. Springer-Verlag, Berlin, Germany (1998) 125-153

17. Dourish, P., Holmes, J., Mac Lean, A., Marqvardsen, P., Zbyslaw, A.: Freeflow: Mediating Between Representation and Action in Workflow Systems. In: Ackerman, M.S. (ed.): CSCW'96. Proceedings of the Conference on Computer Supported Cooperative Work, Cambridge, MA, November 16-20, 1996. ACM Press, New York (1996) 190-198

18. Ellis, C, Keddara, K., Rozenberg, G.: Dynamic Change within Workflow Systems. In: Proceedings of the Conference on Organizational Computing Systems. ACM Press, New York (1995) 10-21

19. Koulopoulos, T. M.: The Workflow Imperative. Van Nostrand Reinhold, New York (1995)

20. Nielsen, M., Rozenberg, G., Thiagarajan, P.S.: Elementary Transition Systems. Theoretical Computer Science, Vol. 96, no. 1 (1992) 3-33

21. Nonaka, I., Takeuchi, H.: The Knowledge Creating Company. Oxford University Press, New York (1995)

22. Norman, D. A.: Cognitive Artifacts. In: Carroll J. M. (ed.) Designing Interaction. Psychology at the Himan computer Interface. Cambridge University Press, Cambridge, (1993) 17-38

23. Reisig, W., Rozenberg, G. (eds.): Lectures on Petri Nets I: Basic Models. Lectures Notes in Computer Science, Vol. 1491. Springer-Verlag, Berlin, Germany (1998)

24. Reisig, W., Rozenberg, G. (eds.): Lectures on Petri Nets II: Applications. Lectures Notes in Computer Science, Vol. 1492. Springer-Verlag, Berlin, Germany (1998b)

25. Rozenberg, G., Engelfriet, J.: Elementary Net Systems. In Reisig, W., Rozenberg, G. (eds.): Lectures on Petri Nets I: Basic Models. Lectures Notes in Computer Science, Vol. 1491. Springer-Verlag, Berlin, Germany (1998) 12-121

26. Schael, T.: Workflow Management Systems for Process Organizations. 2nd Edition. Lectures Notes in Computer Science, Vol. 1096. Springer-Verlag, Berlin, Germany (1998)

27. Schmidt, K.: Of maps and scripts: the status of formal constructs in cooperative work. In S. C. Hayne and W. Prinz (eds.): GROUP'97. Proceedings of the International ACM SIGGROUP Conference on Supporting Group Work, Phoenix, AR, November 16-19, 1997. New York, NY: ACM Press, (1997) 138-147

28. Schmidt, K., Bannon, L.: Taking CSCW Seriously: Supporting Articulation Work. Computer Supported Cooperative Work (CSCW). An International Journal, Vol. 1, nos. 1-2, (1992) 7-40

29. Schmidt, K., Simone, C.: Coordination mechanisms: Towards a conceptual foundation of CSCW systems design. Computer Supported Cooperative Work. The Journal of Collaborative Computing, Vol. 5, nos. 2-3, (1996) 155-200

30. Simone, C., Divitini, M., Schmidt, K.: A notation for malleable and interoperable coordination mechanisms for CSCW systems. In: Proceedings of the Conference on Organizational Computing Systems. ACM Press, New York (1995) 44-54

31. Suchman, L.A.: Plans and Situated Actions. The Problem of Human-Machine Communication. Cambridge University Press, Cambridge (1987)
32. Swenson, K.D., Maxwell, R.J., Matsumoto, T., Saghari, B., Irwin, K.: A Business Process Environment Supporting Collaborative Planning. Collaborative Computing, Vol. 1, no. 1 (1994) 15-34
33. Voorhoeve, M., van der Aalst, W.M.P.: Ad-hoc Workflow: Problems and Solutions. In Proceedings of the 8th International Workshop on Database and Expert Systems Applications. IEEE Computer Society, California (1997) 36-41
34. White, T.E., Fischer, L. (Eds.): The Workflow Paradigm, Future Strategies, Alameda, (1994)
35. Winograd, T., Flores, F.: Understanding Computers and Cognition. : A New Foundation for Design. Ablex Publishing Corp., Norwood (1986)
36. Winograd, T.: A Language/Action Perspective on the Design of Cooperative Work. Human Computer Interaction, Vol. 3, no. 1 (1988) 3-30
37. Workflow Management Coalition: Coalition Overview. TR-WMC, Brussels (1994)

Inter-operability of Workflow Applications: Local Criteria for Global Soundness

Ekkart Kindler, Axel Martens, and Wolfgang Reisig

Humboldt-Universität zu Berlin, Institut für Informatik, D-10099 Berlin, Germany*

Abstract. Automatic analysis techniques for business processes are crucial for today's workflow applications. Since business processes are rapidly changing, only fully automatic techniques can detect processes which might cause deadlocks or congestion.

Analyzing a complete workflow application, however, is much too complex to be performed fully automatically. Therefore, techniques for analyzing single processes in isolation and corresponding soundness criteria have been proposed. Though these techniques may detect errors such as deadlocks or congestion, problems arising from an incorrect inter-operation with other processes are completely ignored. The situation becomes even worse for cross-organizational workflow applications, where some processes are not even available for analysis due to confidentiality reasons.

We propose a technique which allows to detect but a few errors of workflow applications which arise from incorrect inter-operation of workflows. To this end, the dynamics of the inter-operation of different workflows must be specified by the help of sequence diagrams. Then, each single workflow can be checked for local soundness with respect to this specification. If each single workflow is locally sound, a composition theorem guarantees global soundness of the complete workflow application. This way, each organization can check its own workflows without knowing the workflows of other organizations—still global soundness is guaranteed.

Introduction

Automatic analysis techniques for business processes are crucial for today's workflow applications. Since business processes are rapidly changing (sometimes even at runtime), only automatic techniques can detect processes which might cause deadlocks or congestion.

Van der Aalst [8, 9] has proposed simple but powerful *soundness criteria* for a single workflow. These criteria can be checked fully automatically. In [10], these criteria have been extended to *global soundness* of a system of *loosely coupled workflows*. To check global soundness, one needs a model of the complete *workflow application*. This model, however, is often not available for cross-organizational workflow applications because organizations are not willing to

---

* Email: `kindler|martens|reisig@informatik.hu-berlin.de`

W. van der Aalst et al.(Eds.): Business Process Management, LNCS 1806, pp. 235-253, 2000.

disclose their workflows. Therefore we need a technique which allows to argue locally on global soundness.

This paper is a first step towards such a technique. We present a *local criterion* for single workflows which can be checked without knowing the other workflows. Of course, we need some information on the interaction with the other workflows, which will be captured by *scenarios*. The local criterion consists of two parts: *Local correctness* guarantees that the interactions of the workflow under consideration is allowed by a scenario; *local soundness* guarantees proper termination of the workflow. According to our main theorem a workflow application is globally sound if each involved workflow is locally sound and locally correct.

As mentioned above, we use *scenarios* for specifying the interaction between different workflows. A single scenario shows one possible interaction between the workflows by sending and receiving messages; a scenario abstracts from internal behavior of each workflow. A set of scenarios specifies all legal interactions. Syntactically, a possibly infinite set of scenarios can be represented by high-level Message Sequence Charts [3] or Sequence Diagrams in UML [7]. In this paper we concentrate on the semantical foundations and, therefore, we do not fix a particular representation of scenarios.

The paper is structured as follows: In Sect.1 we present the basic concepts and the basic idea by the help of an example. In Sect. 2 we give formal definitions. In Sect. 3 we present the local conditions for global soundness. At last, we indicate how the techniques presented in this paper can be mechanized—which is subject to further research.

1   Example

In this section, we introduce the basic concepts by the help of an example.

1.1   Scenarios

We choose a simple workflow application as an example. The workflow application consists of three workflows concerning three different parties (resp. organizations): A Customer, a Support department, and a Production department. The Customer may ask the Support department a question (e.g. about a particular product). Then, the Support department either answers the question directly and terminates, or the Support department requests some more detailed information from the Production department. In order to make matters more interesting, we allow the Support department may request more details several times. The Support department eventually acknowledges the receipt of all details to the Production department and compiles an answer which is sent to the Customer.

The interaction defined above is formally represented by the scenarios shown in Fig. 1. Figure 1(a) shows the scenario where the Production department is not involved at all; Fig. 1(b) represents all other scenarios. In fact, Fig. 1(b)

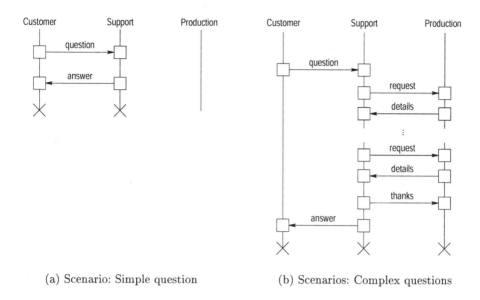

(a) Scenario: Simple question   (b) Scenarios: Complex questions

Fig. 1. A set of scenarios: A specification

represents infinitely many scenarios—one for each number of requests. A set of scenarios is called a *specification.*

Note that we explicitly represent termination of a workflow by a cross at the bottom of the corresponding workflow. In the scenario of Fig. 1(a), workflow Production is never initiated and, therefore, never (explicitly) terminated.

1.2 Workflow application

Figure 2 shows an operational model of a *workflow application* which satisfies the specification of Fig. 1. The application consists of three workflow modules Customer, Support, and Production. Each workflow module is modeled by a Petri net with distinguished input and output places which correspond to the message channels of the scenarios. Moreover, each workflow has a distinguished *start place* (indicated by a token) and an *end place* (indicated by a cross).

In order to reason about the behavior of a workflow application, we can transform it to a conventional *system net* by identifying input and output places which carry the same name. A *run* of a workflow application basically is a *non-sequential process* of this system net. Figure 3 shows the one and only run of the workflow application of Fig. 2. Figure 4 shows a representation of the run of Fig. 3 where all internal details are omitted and only the interaction between the different workflow modules is represented. We call this abstract version of a run an *abstract run* of the workflow application. This abstract run immediately corresponds to the scenario of Fig. 1(b) (with exactly one request to Production). Since all abstract runs of the workflow application correspond to a scenario of

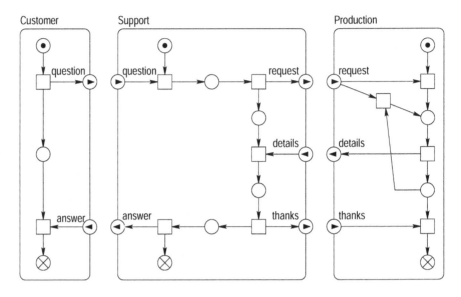

Fig. 2. A workflow application

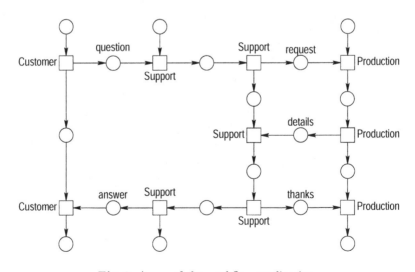

Fig. 3. A run of the workflow application

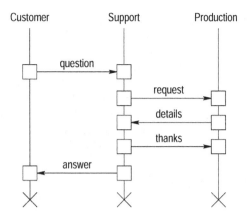

Fig. 4. The corresponding abstract run

the specification, we say that the workflow application satisfies the specification. In general, we say that a workflow application is *globally correct* with respect to a specification if each abstract run of the workflow application corresponds to a scenario of the specification. We do not require that each scenario of the specification has a corresponding abstract run in the workflow application. Our example from Fig. 2 has only one abstract run though we have infinitely many scenarios. In particular, there is no abstract run of the workflow application corresponding to the scenario from Fig. 1(a).

One might expect that even a prefix of the run shown in Fig. 4 represents an abstract runs of the workflow application too (i. e. Support department stops before sending an answer). This, however, is not true since we assume *progress* of all[1] transitions: An abstract run must not stop when further transitions are activated.

1.3   Global and local soundness

Van der Aalst [8, 9] proposes a simple *soundness* criterion for a single workflow which is modeled by a Petri net. Basically, this criterion requires that each workflow terminates and that, upon termination, the workflow net carries one token only, located at the end place. This criterion can be easily formalized and verified by the help of typical Petri net properties such as *liveness* and *boundedness*.

In [10], this idea is carried over to complete workflow applications and is called *global soundness*. This definition, however, has a subtle problem: It requires that each workflow module terminates with a token on its end place. Our example shows that there are reasonable scenarios, where one workflow module (Production in our example) is never started. In that case, it cannot and should

---

[1] Indeed, we only require progress for distinguished *progress transitions*. In our example, all transitions are progress transitions.

not terminate with a token on its end place. Therefore, we introduce a slightly modified definition of global soundness. Technically, it is different from the definition in [10]—but, it is still in its spirit. Our definition of global soundness basically says that each workflow module which was invoked (i.e. the token has been removed from the start place) will eventually terminate with a token on the end place. Upon termination, all other places including communication channels are unmarked. In combination, we call this condition *proper termination* of the workflow application. Workflow modules which never have been invoked, however, need not terminate. The workflow application in Fig. 2 is globally sound because the above conditions are met by its only run shown in Fig. 3. In this particular case, all workflow modules do terminate and no place except for the end places remains marked.

When checking global soundness, we are faced with the following problems:

1. Global soundness can only be checked if there is a model of the complete workflow application. In the context of cross-organizational workflow applications, however, different organizations might be involved which do not want to disclose their workflow modules to the other organizations. Therefore, a complete model of a workflow application is not achievable.
2. Even if we can obtain a complete model of the workflow application, this model will be too large for formal analysis.

In order to deal with these problems, we define a criterion for each workflow module separately, which is called a *local criterion*. This way, a cross-organizational workflow can be checked by each organization separately without disclosing its workflow modules.

However, we cannot expect to find a sufficiently powerful local criterion for a workflow module without knowing anything about its interaction with other workflow modules of the workflow application. This was the reason for introducing scenarios. By the help of scenarios, we are able to define the local criterion. On the one hand we require each workflow module to behave according to the scenarios as long as the other workflow modules do. We call this requirement *local correctness*. On theother hand we require the workflow module to terminate properly in a correct environment. We call this requirement *local soundness*. Both requirements are nessesary to guarantee global soundness. But they do ever more. We will see that local correctness implies global correctness. So, we pay more to prove global soundness, but global correctness comes for free.

1.4   Fairness

The definition of global soundness requires that each run of a workflow application terminates. In order to guarantee proper termination, we sometimes need a fairness assumption in the operational model of a workflow module. For example, consider the workflow module Support shown in Fig. 5.

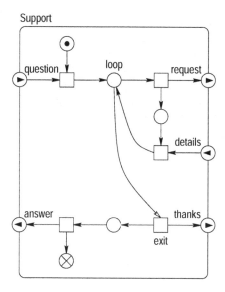

Fig. 5. A workflow which needs fairness

If this workflow module is replaced for the workflow module Support in the workflow application from Fig. 2, the following infinite behavior is possible: After a question, the module Support infinitely often sends a request to the module Production and receives details—it never sends a thanks to the module Production and never terminates. This behavior is outlined by the abstract run shown in Fig. 6.

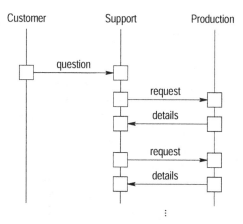

Fig. 6. An infinite abstract run

Clearly, this behavior is not desirable and is not allowed by the specification of Fig. 1. In practice, this infinite behavior will not occur because the number of check-backs with the production is limited by some *business rule*. In our model, we abstract from a concrete business rule by introducing a fairness assumption in the model of the workflow module. The recurrent conflict between the transition sending requests and transition exit should eventually be resolved in favor of transition exit. We denote this assumption by a distinguished arc with a white arrowhead from place loop to transition exit in the workflow module (cf. Fig. 5): a so-called *fair arc* [5].

1.5   Summary of concepts

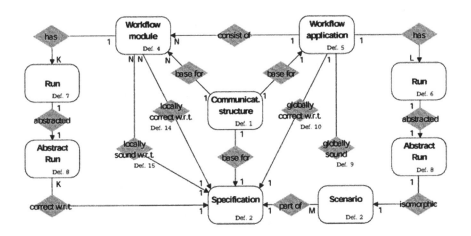

Fig. 7. E-R-Diagram for the main concepts

Figure 7 shows an Entity-Relationship-Diagram of the notions defined above. It illustrates the relations among the concepts which were used for the formalization of a local criterion for global soundness. On the one hand there is the workflow application which consists of several workflow modules; on the other hand there is the specification of the interaction between the workflow modules—represented by a set of scenarios. Both sides use the same naming conventions which are fixed in the *communication structure*. According to our main theorem, a workflow application is globally sound and globally correct if each involved workflow module is locally sound and locally correct. Global correctness means that each run—represented in its abstract form—is isomorphic to a scenario of the specification (the rightmost path in Fig. 7). This property can locally be checked by local correctness with respect to the specification which is defined for each abstract run (the leftmost path in Fig. 7). Local soundness in combination with local correctness of each workflow module guarantees global soundness.

2   Formal model

In this section, we formalize scenarios, workflow modules, workflow applications, as well as global soundness and global correctness.

2.1   Basic definitions

We start with a brief summary of concepts and notations from Petri net theory and concurrency theory (cf. [1]).

The basic concept of this paper are *partial orders*. For some set Q, a binary relation $<$ on Q is a *partial order* if $<$ is *irreflexive* and *transitive*. Throughout this paper, we only consider partial orders $(Q, <)$ such that, for each $q \in Q$, the set of the predecessors of q is finite. For $q \in Q$, the set ${}^\bullet q$ represents the *immediate predecessors* and the set $q^\bullet$ represents the *immediate successors* of q with respect to $<$. For a partial order $(Q, <)$, we denote the *set of minimal elements* (elements without predecessors) by ${}^\circ Q$ and we denotes the *set of maximal elements* (elements without successors) by Q°.

A *Petri net* $N = (P, T, F)$ consists of a set of *places* P, a set of *transitions* T, and a set of *arcs* $F \subseteq (P \times T) \cup (T \times P)$. The sets P and T must be disjoint. Since the transitive closure of F can be considered as a partial order relation (the *flow relation*), we also use the notation ${}^\bullet x$ and $x^\bullet$ for elements $x \in P \cup T$. Then, ${}^\bullet x$ is called *preset* and $x^\bullet$ is called *postset* of x. Throughout this paper, we only consider Petri nets with ${}^\bullet t \neq \emptyset$ and $t^\bullet \neq \emptyset$ for each transition $t \in T$.

An *occurrence net* $K = (B, E, \lessdot)$ is a special Petri net such that the transitive closure of $\lessdot$ (denoted by $<$) is a partial order and for each place $b \in B$ we have $|{}^\bullet b| \leq 1$ and $|b^\bullet| \leq 1$. The set of minimal elements of this order is denoted by ${}^\circ K$ and the set of maximal elements of this order is denoted by K°—by slight abuse of the above notation.

Moreover, for a mapping $f : A \to B$ and some set $X \subseteq A$, we denote the restriction of f to X by $f|_X$.

2.2   Scenarios

Basically, a *scenario* is a partial order of *events* which send and receive *messages* via distinguished *channels*. Each event is executed by some *agent*. Before defining scenarios, we fix the underlying *communication structure*. The communication structure represents the set of the involved *agents* I as well as the connection of the agents along communication *channels* C. Each communication channel $ch \in C$ has a fixed *sender agent* $s(ch)$ and a fixed *receiver agent* $r(ch)$. In order to describe explicit termination, we introduce one *termination channel* for each agent. The set of termination channels is denoted by X. We assume that an agent sends a message on its termination channel upon termination. This message is not received by any agent.

Definition 1 (Communication structure). *A communication structure $\mathcal{C} = (I, C, X, s, r)$ consists of a finite set of agents I, a finite set of channels C and* termination channels $X \subseteq C$, and two mappings $s : C \to I$ and $r : C \setminus X \to I$ such that $s|_X$ is bijective and $s(ch) \neq r(ch)$ for each $ch \in C \setminus X$.

A *scenario for some communication structure* C is a partial order $\prec$ of events E and messages M. Each event $e \in E$ is associated with an agent $l(e)$ and each message $m \in M$ is associated with a channel $c(m)$. These associations must respect the communication structure. Moreover, events of different agents must not be immediate successors because events of different agents may only synchronize by sending and receiving messages.

In the context of workflow applications, we additionally assume that each scenario is finite.

Definition 2 (Scenario). *Let* $C = (I, C, X, s, r)$ *be a communication structure. A scenario* $S = (E, M, \prec, l, c)$ *consists of two finite and disjoint sets* E *and* M, *a partial order* $\prec$ *on* $E \cup M$ *and two mappings* $l : E \to I$ *and* $c : M \to C$ *such that:*

1. *For each event* $e \in E$, *we have* $|(^\bullet e \cup e^\bullet) \cap M| = 1$ *and for each event* $e' \in {}^\bullet e \cap E$ *we have* $l(e) = l(e')$ *(i.e. each event sends or receives exactly one message and immediate predecessor events belong to the same agent).*
2. *For each message* $m \in M$, *we have* $^\bullet m = \{e\}$ *for some* $e \in E$ *with* $l(e) = s(c(m))$ *and for each* $m \in M$ *with* $c(m) \in C \setminus X$ *we have* $m^\bullet = \{e\}$ *for some* $e \in E$ *with* $l(e) = r(c(m))$ *(i.e. the sending event belongs to the sending agent and the receiving agent belongs to the receiving agent of the channel).*
3. *For each event* $e \in E$, *we have a termination message* $m \in M$ *with* $c(m) \in X$ *and* $s(c(m)) = l(e)$ *(i.e. each agent which ever executes an event terminates explicitly).*
4. *For each message* $m \in M$ *with* $c(m) \in X$, *we have:*
   (a) $m^\bullet = \emptyset$ *(i.e. a termination message is not received by any agent).*
   (b) *For each event* $e \in E$ *with* $l(e) = s(c(m))$, *we have* $e \prec m$ *(i.e. each event of an agent happens before its termination).*

A set of scenarios S *for a given communication structure* C *is called a* specification *for* C.

In Sect. 3.3, we will impose a further restriction on specifications.

2.3 Workflow modules and applications

In this section, we define workflow modules and workflow applications and their (non-sequential) runs. A workflow module for some agent of a communication structure C is modeled by a Petri net with a distinguished *start place* and a distinguished *end place* as proposed in [9]. We use a slightly refined version of Place/Transition-Systems which are equipped with *external transitions* and *fair arcs*. We call this version *system net*. For technical reasons, we fix a set P of possible places for all workflow modules.

Definition 3 (System net). *A* system net $\Sigma = (P, T, F, T^e, F^f, \mu)$ *consists of a set of* places $P \subseteq \mathcal{P}$, *a set of* transitions T *disjoint from* $\mathcal{P}$, *and a set of arcs* $F \subseteq (P \times T) \cup (T \times P)$. *Moreover,* $T^e \subseteq T$ *is a distinguished set of* external *transitions,* $F^f \subseteq F \cap (P \times T)$ *is a set of distinguished* fair arcs, *and* $\mu : P \to \mathbb{N}$ *is the* initial marking.

A transition $t \in T \setminus T^e$ is called *progress transition*. In a *workflow module* for some agent $i \in I$ of some communication structure, we additionally distinguish one *start* and one *end* place, and *input* and *output* places which correspond to the channels of agent i in the communication structure.

Definition 4 (Workflow module). *Let* $\mathcal{C} = (I, C, X, s, r)$ *be a communication structure and let* $i \in I$ *be an agent. A* workflow module $L = (\Sigma, \alpha, \omega, P^I, P^O)$ *for agent* i *consists of*

1. $\Sigma = (P, T, F, T^e, F^f, \mu)$, *a system net*
2. $\alpha \in P$, *a distinguished* start place, *such that* $^\bullet\alpha = \emptyset$ *and* $\mu(\alpha) = 1$ *and* $\mu(p) = 0$ *for all* $p \in P$ *with* $p \neq \alpha$,
3. $\omega \in P \cap X$, *a distinguished* end place, *such that* $\omega^\bullet = \emptyset$ *and* $s(\omega) = i$,
4. $P^I = \{p \in P \cap C \mid r(p) = i\}$, *a distinguished set of* input places, *such that* $^\bullet p = \emptyset$ *for each* $p \in P^I$, *and*
5. $P^O = \{p \in P \cap C \mid s(p) = i\}$, *a distinguished set of* output places, *such that* $p^\bullet = \emptyset$ *for each* $p \in P^O$.

A *workflow application* for some communication structure $\mathcal{C}$ consists of one workflow module for each agent of the communication structure.

Definition 5 (Workflow application). *Let* $\mathcal{C} = (I, C, X, s, r)$ *be a communication structure. A family* $\mathcal{A} = (L_i)_{i \in I}$ *of workflow modules* L_i *for each agent* $i \in I$ *is a* workflow application *if, for each two agents* $j \neq k$ *of* $\mathcal{C}$, *we have* $T_j \cap T_k = \emptyset$ *and* $P_j \cap P_k \subseteq C$, *where* T_i *and* P_i *denote the transitions and places of workflow module* L_i.

The corresponding system net $\Sigma_\mathcal{A}$ *is defined as the union of all system nets:*

$$\Sigma_\mathcal{A} = (\bigcup_{i \in I} P_i, \bigcup_{i \in I} T_i, \bigcup_{i \in I} F_i, \bigcup_{i \in I} T_i^e, \bigcup_{i \in I} F_i^f, \mu)$$

where $\mu(p) = \mu_i(p)$ *for each agent* $i \in I$ *and each place* $p \in P_i$.

Basically, a *run* of a workflow application $\mathcal{A}$ is a non-sequential process [1] of the system net $\Sigma_\mathcal{A}$ with some additional requirements concerning progress transitions and fair arcs. A non-sequential process is a labeled *occurrence net* K. A labeling ρ of places of the occurrence net establishes the correspondence to the places of the system net. A labeling λ of the transitions of the occurrence net establishes the correspondence to the agents of the workflow application. Figure 3 shows an example of a run of the workflow application of Fig. 2.

We additionally require a run not to terminate with an enabled progress transition $t \in T \setminus T^e$, conflicts are to be resolved in a fair way with respect to fair arcs (see [5] for details).

Definition 6 (Run of a workflow application).
Let $\mathcal{A} = (L_i)_{i \in I}$ be a workflow application for some communication structure $\mathcal{C}$ and let $\Sigma_\mathcal{A} = (P, T, F, T^e, F^f, \mu)$ be the corresponding system net. An occurrence net $K = (B, E, <)$ along with two mappings $\rho : B \to P$ and $\lambda : E \to I$ is a run of $\mathcal{A}$, if the following conditions are satisfied:

1. $\rho|_{{}^\bullet e}$ and $\rho|_{e^\bullet}$ are injective for each $e \in E$.
2. For each $e \in E$, there exists a transition $t \in T_{\lambda(e)}$ of the workflow module for agent $\lambda(e)$ such that $\rho({}^\bullet e) = {}^\bullet t$ and $\rho(e^\bullet) = t^\bullet$ (i.e. each event has a corresponding transition in the corresponding workflow module).
3. For each $p \in P$, we have $\mu(p) = |\{b \in {}^\circ K \mid \rho(b) = p\}|$ (i.e. the initial marking of the system net corresponds to the initial state of the labeled occurrence net).
4. For each $t \in T \setminus T^e$, we have ${}^\bullet t \not\subseteq \rho(K^\circ)$ (Progress).
5. For each fair arc $(p, t) \in F^f$, we have: If $\rho(K^\circ) \supseteq {}^\bullet t \setminus \{p\}$ and $\{b \in B \mid \rho(b) = p\}$ is infinite, then $\{e \in E \mid \rho({}^\bullet e) = {}^\bullet t \wedge \rho(e^\bullet) = t^\bullet\}$ is also infinite (Fairness).

A run of a workflow module for some agent $i \in I$ can be defined analogously to a run of a workflow application. Since we do not know the behavior of the other workflow modules of the application, we allow unrestricted behavior for all agents $j \neq i$. We only require that the other agents respect the direction of the communication channels of the underlying communication structure. Since we do not even know the places of the other workflow modules, the labeling is now into our fixed domain $\mathcal{P}$ of places. Altogether, the runs of a workflow module represent the behavior of a workflow module in an arbitrary environment.

Definition 7 (Run of a workflow module).
Let $L = (\Sigma, \alpha, \omega, P^I, P^O)$ be a workflow module for some agent $i \in I$ of some communication structure $\mathcal{C} = (I, C, X, s, r)$ as defined in Def. 4.

An occurrence net $K = (B, E, <)$ along with two labelings $\rho : B \to \mathcal{P}$ and $\lambda : E \to I$ is called a run of L for module i if the following conditions are satisfied:

1. $\rho|_{{}^\bullet e}$ and $\rho|_{e^\bullet}$ are injective for each $e \in E$.
2. For each $e \in E$ with $\lambda(e) = i$, there exists a transition $t \in T$ of the workflow module L such that $\rho({}^\bullet e) = {}^\bullet t$ and $\rho(e^\bullet) = t^\bullet$ (i.e. each event corresponding to agent i has a corresponding transition in the workflow module).
   For each event $e \in E$ with $\lambda(e) \neq i$, we have $\rho({}^\bullet e) \cap P \subseteq P^O$ and $\rho(e^\bullet) \cap P \subseteq P^I$ (i.e. events corresponding to other workflow modules respect the communication structure).
3. For each $p \in P$, we have $\mu(p) = |\{b \in {}^\circ K \mid \rho(b) = p\}|$
4. For each $t \in T \setminus T^e$, we have ${}^\bullet t \not\subseteq \rho(K^\circ)$.
5. For each fair arc $(p, t) \in F^f$ we have: If $\rho(K^\circ) \supseteq {}^\bullet t \setminus \{p\}$ and $\{b \in B \mid \rho(b) = p\}$ is infinite, then $\{e \in E \mid \rho({}^\bullet e) = {}^\bullet t \wedge \rho(e^\bullet) = t^\bullet\}$ is also infinite.

There is a simple relation between the runs of a workflow application and the runs of its workflow modules: The set of runs of a workflow application is the intersection of sets of runs of all its workflow modules.

Theorem 1 (Compositionality). *Let $\mathcal{A} = (L_i)_{i \in I}$ be a workflow application and let $\Sigma_\mathcal{A} = (P, T, F, T^e, F^f, \mu)$ be the corresponding system net. Let $K = (B, E, <)$ be an occurrence net, and let $\rho : B \to \mathcal{P}$ and $\lambda : E \to I$ be labelings. Then, (K, ρ, λ) is a run of the workflow application $\mathcal{A}$ if and only if (K, ρ, λ) is a run of each workflow module L_i for agent $i \in I$ and $\rho(B) \subseteq P$.*

This result guarantees that the set of runs of a workflow application can be deduced from the set of runs of its workflow modules—this is one of the key arguments in the forthcoming Theorem 2. The proof of Theorem 1 is similar to the proof given in [6].

In order to relate runs of a workflow application or a workflow module to a specification, we define the abstract version of a run—*abstract run* for short. In an abstract run, we omit all internal details and only keep the events which send or receive messages, the messages themselves, and the partial order on the elements. Thus, an abstract run lives in the same mathematical domain as scenarios: It only represents the interaction between workflow modules and no internal behavior.

Definition 8 (Abstract run). *Let (K, ρ, λ) be a run with occurrence net $K = (B, E, <)$. The corresponding abstract run $\sigma = (E', M, \prec, l, c)$ consists of $M = \{b \in B \mid \rho(b) \in C\}$, $E' = \{e \in E \mid (^\bullet e \cup e^\bullet) \cap M \neq \emptyset\}$, $l = \lambda|_{E'}$, $c = \rho|_M$, and $\prec = <|_{E' \cup M}$.*

From a mathematical point of view, abstract runs and scenarios are the same. This allows to relate the behavior of a workflow application (a set of abstract runs) to the specification (a set of scenarios). For a clear separation of the specified behavior from the system's behavior, we use different names for scenarios and abstract runs.

2.4   Global soundness

Based on the runs of a workflow application, we define *global soundness* of a workflow application.

Definition 9 (Global soundness). *Let $\mathcal{A}$ be a workflow application for some communication structure, and let α_i and ω_i be the start place resp. end place of the workflow module for each agent $i \in I$. The workflow application $\mathcal{A}$ is globally sound if for each run (K, ρ, λ) of $\mathcal{A}$ the following conditions hold:*

1. *K is finite.*
2. *For each $i \in I$, we have $|\{b \in K^\circ \mid \rho(b) = \alpha_i \vee \rho(b) = \omega_i\}| = 1$.*
3. *$\rho(K^\circ) \subseteq \bigcup_{i \in I} \{\alpha_i, \omega_i\}$.*

Soundness states that each started workflow module properly terminates with all its places unmarked—including its message channels. Therefore, soundness of a workflow application does not involve a particular specification. It is a minimal requirement which should hold true for each workflow application. In contrast, correctness requires a specification.

Definition 10 (Global correctness). *Let C be a communication structure, let S be a specification for C, and let A be a workflow application for C. The application A is* globally correct with respect to specification S *if each abstract run of A is isomorphic[2] to a scenario of S.*

Note again that global correctness does not require that there is an abstract run of the workflow application for each scenario of the specification. The specification may have more runs. The requirement that something must happen in a workflow application is expressed by the fact that the specification is not prefix-closed. Therefore, the workflow application must continue a run until it reaches a scenario of the specification. This is the usual way to specify *liveness* in *linear-time semantics*.

3   Local criteria

Up to now, we have a soundness and a correctness condition for a complete workflow application. Since these conditions can only be applied if all workflow modules of the workflow application are known, we call these conditions *global*.

In this section, we present *local* criteria for soundness and correctness. These criteria can be applied to a single workflow module without knowing the other workflow modules of the application. Moreover, if all workflow modules satisfy the local criteria, the complete workflow application satisfies the global criteria.

3.1   Informal presentation

Before formalizing the local criteria in Sect. 3.2 and Sect. 3.3, we informally introduce the employed concepts.

As mentioned before, we cannot expect to have a local criterion for soundness without any information on the interaction with other workflow modules. This information is captured in the specification. Basically, a workflow module is *locally sound with respect to a specification* if, in each run of the workflow module which corresponds to a scenario of the specification, the workflow module properly terminates (if started at all).

Unfortunately, local soundness for each workflow module does not guarantee global soundness. The reason is that local soundness guarantees proper termination only if the complete workflow application behaves according to the specification (i.e. if it is globally correct). Fortunately, we can give a local criterion for correctness, too.

The basic idea of local correctness for a workflow module is the following: First, each workflow module behaves according to the specification as long as its environment does. Second, the workflow module does not indefinitely ignore a message in its mailbox (i.e. in its input places) and does not indefinitely defer a message which could be sent according to the specification over and over again.

---

[2] *Isomorphisms* between runs and scenarios will be formally defined in Def. 11.

The first condition can be formalized by the help of prefixes of an abstract run. We say a prefix of an abstract run *satisfies a specification* if there exists a scenario of the specification with the same prefix. Otherwise we say that the prefix *violates the specification*. Now, the first condition can be expressed in the following way: Let σ be an abstract run of the workflow module and let Q be some prefix of σ which satisfies the specification. Then, each prefix Q' of σ which only adds events of the workflow module under consideration to the prefix Q must also satisfy the specification.

The second condition can be formalized by a fairness requirement: If we can find infinitely many prefixes of an abstract run at which some message could be sent or received by the workflow module, then this message must be sent or received eventually.

With these definitions, we basically get the following results:

1. If each workflow module of a workflow application is locally correct, the workflow application is globally correct.
2. If each workflow module of a workflow application is locally sound and locally correct, then the workflow application is globally sound (and correct).

3.2   Prerequisites

In this section, we define the prerequisites for the definition of local soundness and local correctness. First, we define the *prefix* of an abstract run and we define when a *prefix satisfies a specification*. This is formalized by the help of *prefix homomorphisms* from abstract runs to scenarios.

Definition 11 (Prefix). *Let C be a communication structure, and let $\sigma = (E, M, \prec, l, c)$ be an abstract run.*

1. *A set $Q \subseteq E \cup M$ is a* prefix *of σ if, for each $q \in Q$, we have $^\bullet q \subseteq Q$ and, for each $e \in Q \cap E$, we have $e^\bullet \cap M \subseteq Q$.*
2. *Let $S = (E', M', \prec', l', c')$ be a scenario for C, and let $Q \subseteq E \cup M$ and $h : Q \to E' \cup M'$ be an injective mapping such that the following conditions are satisfied:*
   (a) Q and $h(Q)$ are prefixes of σ and S, respectively.
   (b) For each $m \in Q \cap M$, it holds $h(m) \in M'$ and $c(m) = c'(h(m))$.
   (c) For each $e \in Q \cap E$, it holds $h(e) \in E'$, $l(e) = l'(h(e))$, $h(^\bullet e) = {}^\bullet h(e)$, and $h(e^\bullet \cap M) = h(e)^\bullet \cap M'$.
   Then, Q is also called a prefix *of S, and h is called a* prefix homomorphism *from Q to S. If $Q = E \cup M$ and h is bijective, we call σ and S isomorphic.*
3. *Let S be a specification for C. A prefix Q of σ* satisfies *S if it is a prefix of some scenario $S \in S$. Otherwise, we say that Q* violates *S.*

Next we define fairness of a run with respect to some specification. We distinguish two cases: fairness with respect to sending messages and fairness with respect to receiving messages. For simplicity we rather define unfairness. Basically, an abstract run is not *send fair* with respect to some channel if a message on this channel could be sent with respect to the specification at infinitely many positions of the run, but is not. Similarly, a run is not *receive fair* if a message on a channel could be received at infinitely many positions but it is never received.

Definition 12 (Fairness with respect to a specification). *Let S be a specification for some communication structure $C = (I, C, X, s, r)$, let $ch \in C$ be some channel, and let $\sigma = (E, M, \prec, l, c)$ be an abstract run.*

1. *σ is not send fair with respect to channel ch and specification S if σ is not isomorphic to a scenario of S and the following two condition are satisfied:*
   (a) *For each finite prefix Q of σ, there exists a finite prefix $Q' \supseteq Q$ of σ which is a also a prefix of some scenario $S = (E', M', \prec', l', c') \in S$ with a prefix homomorphism $h : Q' \to E' \cup M'$, and there exists an event $e \in E' \setminus h(Q')$, and a message $m \in e^\bullet \cap M'$ such that $^\bullet e \subseteq h(Q')$ and $c'(m) = ch$.*
   (b) *The set of messages $\{m \in M \mid c(m) = ch\}$ is finite.*
2. *σ is not receive fair with respect to channel ch and specification S if σ is not isomorphic to a scenario of S and the following two condition are satisfied:*
   (a) *For each finite prefix Q of σ, there exists a finite prefix $Q' \supseteq Q$ of σ which is also a prefix of some scenario $S = (E', M', \prec', l', c') \in S$ with prefix homomorphism $h : Q' \to E' \cup M'$, and there exists an event $e \in E' \setminus h(Q')$ and a message $m \in {}^\bullet e \cap M'$ such that $^\bullet e \subseteq h(Q')$ and $c'(m) = ch$.*
   (b) *There exists a message $m \in M$ with $c(m) = ch$ and $m^\bullet = \emptyset$*
3. *Let $i \in I$ be some agent. The abstract run σ is i-fair (fair for agent i) with respect to S if σ is send fair for each channel $ch \in C$ with $s(ch) = i$ and σ is receive fair for each channel $ch \in C$ with $r(ch) = i$.*
4. *σ is fair with respect to S if σ is i-fair with respect to S for each agent $i \in I$.*

In this paper, we restrict ourselves to fairness-closed specifications. This restriction allows us to give simple local arguments for global liveness properties—in particular for termination. Without this restriction, a sophisticated mechanism for specifying liveness properties in a rely/guarantee-style [4] would be necessary.

Definition 13 (Fairness-closed specification). *A specification S is called* fairness-closed *if for each abstract run σ one of the following conditions is satisfied:*

1. *σ has a finite prefix which violates S.*
2. *σ is not fair with respect to S.*
3. *σ is isomorphic to some scenario $S \in S$.*

3.3   Local correctness and soundness

Basically, an abstract run is locally correct for some agent $i \in I$ with respect to some specification if each event of agent i corresponds to some scenario as long as the events of the environment do. Moreover, the run must be i-fair.

Definition 14 (Local correctness). *An abstract run* $\sigma = (E, M, \prec, l, c)$ *of a workflow module for agent* $i \in I$ *is correct with respect to some specification* $\mathcal{S}$ *if the following two conditions are satisfied:*

1. *For each prefix* Q *of* σ *which satisfies* $\mathcal{S}$, *each prefix* $Q' \supseteq Q$ *of* σ *with* $l(Q' \setminus Q) = \{i\}$ *also satisfies* $\mathcal{S}$.
2. σ *is i-fair with respect to* $\mathcal{S}$.

A workflow module L *for some agent* $i \in I$ *is correct with respect to a specification* $\mathcal{S}$ *if each abstract run of* L *is correct for* i *with respect to* $\mathcal{S}$.

In contrast to global soundness, local soundness must be defined with respect to some specification. Local soundness requires proper termination for all correct runs.

Definition 15 (Local soundness). *A workflow module* $L = (\Sigma, \alpha, \omega, P^I, P^O)$ *for some agent* $i \in I$ *and with places* P *is locally sound with respect to some specification* $\mathcal{S}$ *if, for each run* (K, ρ, λ) *with an abstract run isomorphic to some scenario in* $\mathcal{S}$, *it holds:* $\rho(K^\circ) \cap P \subseteq \{\alpha, \omega\}$ *and* $|\{b \in K^\circ \mid \rho(b) = \alpha \vee \rho(b) = \omega\}| = 1$.

Now, we can formalize the relation between local and global correctness and local and global soundness.

Theorem 2. *Let* $\mathcal{S}$ *be a fairness-closed specification for some communication structure* $\mathcal{C}$, *and let* $\mathcal{A} = (L_i)_{i \in I}$ *be a workflow application for* $\mathcal{C}$.

1. $\mathcal{A}$ *is globally correct if each workflow module* L_i *is locally correct for agent* $i \in I$ *and specification* $\mathcal{S}$.
2. $\mathcal{A}$ *is globally sound if each workflow module* L_i *is locally sound and locally correct for agent* $i \in I$ *and specification* $\mathcal{S}$.

In a nutshell, this theorem guarantees that a cross-organizational workflow application is sound and correct if each organization checks soundness and correctness locally. It is not necessary to know the workflow modules of the other organizations—it is only necessary to agree on the specification of their interaction.

4 Outlook

In the previous sections, we defined global soundness and global correctness for a (cross-organizational) workflow application. Then, we have shown that global soundness and global correctness can be checked by a local condition for each workflow separately.

Up to now, the local soundness and the local correctness conditions are defined purely semantically. An automatic checker for these conditions is subject to future research. Here, we can only present a first idea. First of all, an automatic checker requires a syntactical representation of specifications, e.g. in terms of high-level Message Sequence Charts [3]. Given a specification, a checker can proceed in two steps for checking the local conditions for an agent i:

1. Reducing the set of scenarios to the ones which are relevant for agent i. For example, for checking soundness of agent **Customer** for the specification of Fig. 1, it is sufficient to consider scenario 1(a); from the **Customer**'s point of view all other scenarios reduce to this scenario.

2. Constructing a workflow module which exhibits all the behavior of the environment which is allowed by the remaining scenarios. We call this net the *environment net* for agent i. The composition of the workflow module and this environment net can be checked for local correctness and soundness by automatic techniques: either model checking or standard techniques from Petri net theory as used in [8, 9]. The construction of the environment net is similar to the construction of [2]—but only those parts which belong to the environment are constructed.

Conclusion

This paper is a first step towards an automatic technique for checking soundness of a workflow application locally. Even when the steps discussed in Sect. 4 are taken, the techniques presented in this paper need further refinement, subject to further research.

1. Up to now, the communication structure is static. We do not yet know how to deal with dynamically changing communication structures and dynamic creation and deletion of workflows.

2. Up to now, workflow modules only communicate asynchronously by sending and receiving messages. Synchronous communication (as well as other constructs from Message Sequence Charts) can be incorporated into the formalism—but the formal definitions will become more involved.

3. Moreover, some constructs of Message Sequence Charts such as lost and found messages, FIFO-channels, gates, and timers are still missing in scenarios.

References

1. Eike Best and César Fernández. *Nonsequential Processes, EATCS Monographs on Theoretical Computer Science* 13. Springer-Verlag, 1988.
2. Peter Graubmann, Ekkart Rudolph, and Jens Grabowski. Towards a Petri net based semantics definition for message sequence charts. In O. Færgemand and A Sarma, editors, *SDL '93 Using Objects, proceedings of the Sixth SDL Forum*, pages 415–418. North-Holland, October 1993.
3. ITU-T Recommendation Z.120. Message sequence charts (MSC). ITU, 1996.
4. Cliff. B Jones. Specification and design of (parallel) programs. In R.E.A Mason, editor, *Information Processing*, pages 321–332. IFIP, Elsevier Science Publishers B.V. (North Holland), 1983.
5. Ekkart Kindler and Wolfgang Reisig. Algebraic system nets for modelling distributed algorithms. *Petri Net Newsletter*, 51:16–31, December 1996.

6. Ekkart Kindler. A compositional partial order semantics for Petri net components. In Pierre Azéma and Gianfranco Balbo, editors, *Application and Theory of Petri Nets, 18th International Conference, LNCS* 1248, pages 235–252. Springer-Verlag, June 1997.

7. James Rumbaugh, Ivar Jacobsen, and Grady Booch. *The Unified Modeling Language Reference Manual.* Object Technology Series. Addison Wesley, 1999.

8. W.M.P. van der Aalst. Exploring the process dimension of workflow management. Computing Science Reports 97/13, Eindhoven University of Technology, September 1997.

9. W.M.P. van der Aalst. Verification of workflow nets. In P. Azéma and G. Balbo, editors, *Application and Theory of Petri Nets, LNCS* 1248, pages 407–426. Springer-Verlag, June 1997.

10. W.M.P van der Aalst. Interorganizational workflows: An approach based on Message Sequence Charts and Petri nets. *Systems – Analysis – Modelling – Simulation,* 34 (3):335–367, 1999.

Object Oriented Petri Nets in
Business Process Modeling

Daniel Moldt and Rüdiger Valk

Universität Hamburg, Fachbereich Informatik, Vogt-Kölln-Straße 30, D-22527
Hamburg, {moldt, valk}@informatik.uni-hamburg.de

Abstract. Business systems have to adapt to changing requirements
coming from their environment. The rate is continuously increasing and
leads to massive use of computer based systems. To specify the systems
in a way that allows for adaptability and flexibility adequate techniques
are necessary.
The disadvantages using traditional modeling techniques are partially
overcome by Business Process Petri nets (BPP-nets) which are informally introduced in this contribution. The key concepts are an object
oriented structure of the net models, allowing to partition the model
according to an application and also to follow a process centered approach. Workflows within the system can be modeled in separate objects
and thus allow the dynamic adaptation of the system if the environment
requires a behavioral change.

1 Introduction

The modeling of business systems becomes increasingly difficult, due to the growing demands on the flexibility of the implemented business processes and also
due to the wide use of the Internet and intranets. Especially the problem of
distributed and concurrent execution is of interest when modeling the business
processes.

From the numerous concepts and tools used for business process engineering,
object oriented modeling and Petri nets are of particular importance. Comparing statements concerning the goals and advantages of both techniques, similar
and occasionally identical assertions are found: software development by abstraction of objects, building a language independent design, better understanding
of requirements, clearer design and better maintainable systems. Furthermore,
there are also complementary benefits: while research in object oriented modeling has concentrated more on structuring objects and their relations, little has
been done with respect to process description and dynamic behavior, which is
the traditional domain of Petri nets. In this contribution we will focus our work
on combining the fields in order to profit from both.

We will describe an object oriented static structure with a process oriented
behavior which is again encapsulated within objects. This allows to introduce
physical and logical functional units which may be nested and which execute
objects, agents or workflows in a flexible way.

W. van der Aalst et al.(Eds.): Business Process Management, LNCS 1806, pp. 254-273, 2000.

The following sections introduce the Object Oriented Coloured Petri Net formalism, the Object Petri Net formalism, the informal integration of them, a small case study to illustrate the modeling approach, and the conclusions.

2   Object Oriented Coloured Petri Nets

The approach to *Object Oriented Coloured Petri Nets* (OOCP-nets) (see [BM93], [Mol96] and [MW97]) has introduced objects, classes and methods known from object oriented programming to Coloured Petri nets. Structural building blocks in this methodology are *class nets* that communicate with the environment by a specific interface and contain *methods* to perform different actions. The formalism has been used to translate object oriented notions into the field of Petri nets. Though in [MW97] an extension to multi-agent systems was proposed, contrary to the object systems from [Val98] no mobility was included.

The general structure of an Object Oriented Coloured Petri net of [Mol96] can be seen in Figure 1. The figure shows the central aspects of the structure of a

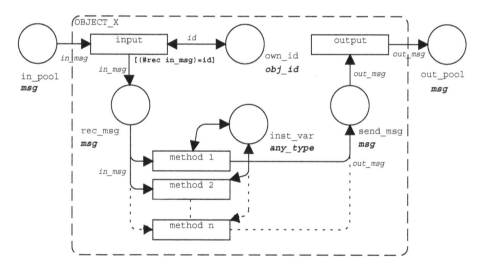

Fig. 1. The object oriented net structure from [Mol96]

net which represents an object. It has a place for incoming messages (eventually shared with other objects). The **input** transition filters all messages according to the object identifier **id**. Internally the methods again pick up the right message according to their names. No complex action is shown in the example. A refinement for more complex actions is possible e.g. by the refinement of the method transitions. Internal states are represented by the place **inst_var**. The transition **output** then puts the outgoing messages into the place **out_pool** which can be the pool for incoming messages of other objects.

In general objects can be folded to classes by keeping the structure and adding relevant functionality for classes. The methods, attributes (inst_var), and the identifiers (own_id) are easily introduced by the net inscriptions. The main idea is to fold similar structures of nets, what actually is one of the central ideas of coloured Petri nets. The given net in Figure 1 can be seen as a folding to coloured places with respect to the traditional Place/Transition-nets (see e.g. [Rei92]). Classes again can be seen as foldings of objects, however, keeping the net structure by introducing tuples to allow the selection of single objects within the class net.

In the following all systems, functional units, business processes, workflows, and agents are considered to be special objects each represented by an OOCP-net with specific properties.

An extension of the usual Coloured Petri nets has been developed by [CH92]. For the adoption of the original definitions to object oriented nets see [MM99], [Ren] [Kum98] or [Kum99]. Synchronous channels can be seen as a shorthand notation of a protocol which is based on message passing. However, some semantics allow a more powerful abstraction that can not be reached with message passing, due to the synchronization aspect. For more details see e.g. [Kum99]. The net structure of an OOCP-net changes when using only synchronous channels (see Figure 2). Incoming and outgoing places for messages are no more neces-

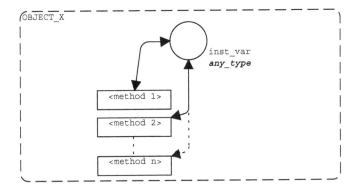

Fig. 2. The object oriented net structure with synchronous channels

sary. The notation for the naming of the synchronous channels used here are brackets around a string, e.g. <method 1>. In Figure 2 only the pure version of called methods via synchronous channels is shown. This means that even the object identifier is not needed here and the net gets a very simple structure. The calling object must know the object and then calls one of the methods via the synchronous channels. In this contribution we use the traditional message passing of OOCP-nets in addition with synchronous channels as it seems appropriate to support a direct modeling of synchronous and asynchronous communication between objects. This implies that the net structure from Figure 1 and Figure 2 are merged. Some of the transitions are not connected to other nets via the places but by synchronous channels.

3 Object Petri Nets

In the approach to *Object Systems* (see [JV87], [Val91] and [Val98]) structure has been added to tokens of Petri nets in order to consider them as dynamic objects. Being subject to migration and interaction in a surrounding system called *system net*, they are modeled as Petri nets themselves. To better distinguish both types of nets, the former are usually called *object nets*. In this contribution we are using the notion of *token nets* to emphasize the character of the net being a token in the context of a system net. The original motivation was to model workflow in a system of functional units, thus adding resources to traditional workflow models. Token nets can be seen as specifications of workflow processes that are executed in a system of human beings, machines, software systems, or organizational units. In Figure 3 an *Elementary Object Net* [Val98] is given, containing the system

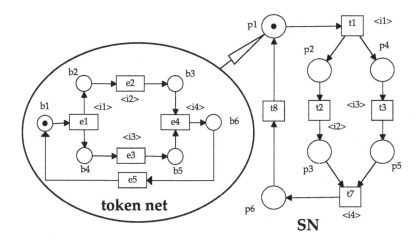

Fig. 3. Object System from [Val98]

net on the right hand side and the token net (*object net*) on the left. The token net can be thought of to lie in place p_1 of the system net and is moved like a standard token. When being displaced, however, it can reach different internal states by changing its marking. Such internal changes are synchronized with transitions of the system net by common labels (e.g. i_1 in Figure 3). For more details see [Val98], where also a more realistic example from workflow modeling is contained. The resulting formal model is used for investigating basic properties, the design of graphical representations (e.g. graphic tools) or for analysis in general (e.g. performance analysis for a given workload). Various case studies have shown that object systems are capable of integrating two different sights on business process models, i.e. the more static sight of system structure with the more dynamic sight of processes in such a system.

4   Business Process Petri Nets

The Petri nets introduced in the following will provide modelers with the means to structure a business system specification in a modular way. A set of well adjusted Petri net classes is presented and called *Business Process Petri nets* (BPP-nets). Each of them has specific features which allow to cover a certain kind of information, relevant for a specific view on a whole system. The integration of all views results in the overall system specification.

4.1   Some basic notions and assumptions

The goal for us is to provide a set of adequate techniques to allow an intuitive way of modeling of business applications. There are some basic assumptions for the following techniques:

- The notion of system here is that a system is something which is mainly determined by its kind of input and output and the kind of function it performs on the input. It has an internal state and a set of operations it can perform on the input. The system can either be fixed in its static structure or can be flexible. For the following we assume a static structure. However, as will be discussed in the Section 5, there is a very natural way to extend the given set of techniques to allow a flexible structure.
- A system consists of a set of functional units (see Section 4.3). These are the execution engines.
- By the functional units objects can be executed. These objects can be functional units, again.
- A trigger is a kind of external event that reaches the system border and contains the request to fulfill a certain system function, meaning i.e. a business process.
- Business processes describe the control and object flow for a set of objects to handle one single specific trigger.
- Objects can be seen as *concrete* parts, that can be represented separately using their own identity. This is very useful for business processes, since it allows to use the metaphor of splitting objects into object (parts) and gluing object parts together to objects.
- System specifications should be executable. Petri nets with an appropriate semantics are therefore a good candidate for the modeling technique.
- There is some kind of communication or transportation mechanism that connects the functional units. In terms of Object Oriented Coloured Petri nets one can think of fusion places for the input and output places. Each two fusion places can be seen as two graphical representations of the same place. There can be different sets of fusion places with different scopes.

– The idea of our Petri net models is that objects flow through our system model. Each object itself can be a system again, therefore it can be active while moving inside a system. Therefore, we do not restrict the level of nesting systems.

The set of net classes allows to structure a system in a modular way, one could also say in components (see [Szy98]). The system modeler can build the models in an object oriented style using a technique for which the models can be executed: Petri nets. At the same time the concepts of mobility and process orientation are integrated. Each mobile part of a system can be modeled as a separate net model. This allows to encapsulate the *local* information. In order to make the nets readable the nets should be structured in an uniform way. Each net model represents one object and can have the net structure as shown in Figure 1, described in Section 2.

4.2   Objects

In the context of programming languages, e.g. Smalltalk, there is the view "Everything is an object". This allows to have an uniform view on a system. The same is applied here, therefore we say "Everything is an object oriented Petri net". The main question is how to map application objects to object oriented Petri nets. To keep it simple: each application object is modeled as an object in OOCP-nets. In Section 2 the net structure has been shown.

Not only functional units can be seen as objects, but also the resources and services or workflows within a system. Processes are special objects, hence they can be assigned all characteristics of an object: identification, behavior, and attributes.

Each specialized object fulfills its determined purposes. Therefore, they have to be described separately in different classes. In the context of Business Process Management especially business processes (see Subsection 4.4) are of interest. One main difficulty can be seen in the integration of all models or views (see Subsection 4.5).

This very specific view leads to a distinction into passive and active objects. The active objects are nets which represent nets as tokens and show dynamic behavior, while passive objects do not have a dynamic behavior on their own, like simple data structures including black tokens. Objects (and classes) represent the basic structure in our approach.

4.3   Systems and functional units

Systems, as seen in this contribution, consist of a certain number of physical functional units (FUs). These FUs build the basic set of processors for the system. Each FU may be connected somehow to the other FUs. Here it can be assumed that there is a global transportation system for "things" flowing in the system. Things that can flow are materials or data. On a more abstract level one could say objects or information. FUs can again be seen as systems, the notion is more or less a matter of abstraction and of the context. This allows a homogeneous description of both.

It is important to notice that the notion of functional units can also be used for logical functional units. This allows to look at basic software programs of a system e.g. operating systems as functional units. Therefore, in the following we consider also logical FUs, which is mainly a matter of perspective and level of abstraction, hence operating systems are often counted to the environment of a program even if they consist of software. Virtual machines running on this operating system again can be seen as the environment for programs running on these virtual machines. Therefore, we model those objects as FUs which are some kind of execution engine for other objects.[1]

In Figure 4 the FUs of a system are represented by transitions. This kind of

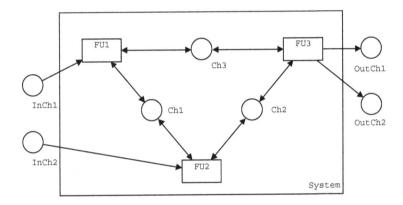

Fig. 4. The system seen as a channel/agency-net.

nets from the Figure 4 is called channel/agency nets in [Rei92]. The communication media are represented as channels. The communication is asynchronous. Synchronous communication would require a transition fusion as defined in [CH92]. This implies that only within the FUs activities take place. Whereas refinements of transitions are considered, places are not refined here. The channel/agency nets are extended in two ways. First we extend them to Coloured Petri nets (see [Jen92]) and more precisely to OOCP-nets with synchronous channels. Second we introduce dynamic behavior by adding tokens and furthermore we use also active tokens, which are again (Coloured) Petri nets (see Figure 3 in

---

[1] When two objects synchronize, this does not mean that one has to be the execution engine for the other. However, even when they are logically on the same level they need at least one FU and a communication channel to be executed.

Section 3). If tokens are nets they can be active (occur) if there is no restriction to synchronize the activity to a functional unit on this level of abstraction.[2]

By FUs some functions or tasks are performed. More abstract: methods are executed. The executed objects must conform to the interface of the FUs, otherwise objects can not be executed correctly. In terms of nets this means that the synchronous channels or the transitions of the token net must be matched with the necessary resources from the FU net. In terms of objects the methods that can be accessed from the outside can be seen as the interface. For asynchronous communication the messages that match a method inside of a net and for synchronous communication the synchronous channels of the nets can be considered to be the interface of the net (or object or FU).

To make the description and the understanding more easy, each FU can be seen as an object. A FU can have methods, attributes, and identifiers. Resources are modeled as attributes of FUs. These attributes can be any kind of object, passive and active ones. This allows to represent physical or logical discrete resources as well as references to resources and to encapsulate the behavior of the resources.

When modeling a FU, a single Object Oriented Coloured Petri Net model (see Section 2) is used for the specification. Of course, complex object models can be refined or split into several models. Transition refinement is an adequate means for this.

Objects have, according to [EMNW00], an interface. The behavior of a FU can be characterized by its interface(s). When implemented as active tokens the interfaces of a FU (or any other object) can again be active. This means that the interface does not only represent the static interface (list of methods and parameters), but also some kind of behavior. Explicitly applied in the OOCP-net models it is used to allow for polymorphism and code reuse (reuse of model components).

From the explanations above some properties of a system or a functional unit in combination with Petri nets can be derived:

- The active parts are methods. The parameters of the methods are control values, data values and active / passive objects or references to them.
- There is an object pool which contains objects or references to objects. These objects can again be seen as data or as control algorithms. The data pool contains local values or resources. The control algorithm pool contains those descriptions which are used to control the actual behavior of the system or functional unit.
- There is a communication interface which represents the externally visible behavior. The static interface can be seen as a list of the methods which can be called from the environment. An interface for the dynamic behavior also represents when a method can be called. Communication can be synchronous by synchronous channels or asynchronous by message passing

---

[2] Otherwise we need to refine also the channels and map them to some FUs or the tokens are physical FUs themselves. This is not considered here for the sake of simplicity.

(with or without waiting at the caller side). The interface instance(s) can be seen as the sensors to the environment.

- A part of the system or functional unit can be active without external resources from the environment under the assumption that there is some kind of physical or logical processor inside the system of functional unit. This is only possible for active tokens (active objects).

4.4   Business Processes

A business process (BP) is a holistic view on that set of activities that is necessary and sufficient to fulfill one specific request concerning the system under observation. Activities are methods of objects. A business process starts as soon as a physical FU connected to the environment receives an input (trigger). Triggers can be any kind of objects, depending on the kind of system and FU. The trigger is directly forwarded to an object running on that FU. The object then classifies the input and one of the methods of the object related to that event is called.

Concerning the control structure a business process can be seen as a partially ordered set of activities, represented by an occurrence net. The causal order of the activities is represented by an object that just covers the control (structure) of this BP. Different kinds of such partial ordered sets for similar cases can be folded to coloured occurrence nets. In [Mol96] also refinement and (finite) loops are added as a shorthand for a finite set of different occurrence nets. This family of nets is called *Scenario nets*. These nets are very similar to the Workflow nets by van der Aalst (see [Aal97]). However, the Scenario nets are specially designed to support the incremental building of whole system models and are not restricted to workflows.

To view business processes (BPs) just as partially ordered sets is too simple. Additional dependencies between the different activities not directly related to the causal order come from resource sharing. This can even be true within one BP, when there are two or more branches competing for the same resource. Therefore, means to model these dependencies are necessary and if possible means to investigate the properties of the system. In this chapter we concentrate on the modeling and the informal inscription of the technique itself.

4.5   Method and Integration

The basis for our approach is that all application objects are mapped to objects of an OOCP-net. Objects can be either systems, functional units, business processes, or any kind of application object which can be identified in the application. Each object is represented by an object of an OOCP-net with synchronous channels, while they are based on the Coloured Petri net definition of Kurt Jensen (see [Jen92]). The uniform background allows to use an uniform communication architecture and mechanism. By this, different parts of a system can be integrated in a reasonable manner. All objects must be assigned to FUs. Finally all FUs must be mapped onto physical FUs. Activities are mapped to methods of objects. Business processes represent the abstract behavior of abstract objects. Each single BP can be represented as a single object (class). This is the kind of protocol that is used in the example (see especially Figure 13 in scenario 3). A protocol can be included by another object to represent the behavior of this other object[3]. The use of active tokens, like protocols, is one of the special aspects of our approach.

The way to proceed when building the models is quite complex. Roughly speaking, without implying any strict order on the different tasks, the method is as follows:

- The boundary between system and environment is determined.
- The main FUs and objects are characterized.
- The containment relationship between systems, FUs, workflows, and objects is modeled.
- Each object (system, FU, etc.) is modeled with an OOCP-net with synchronous channels with the specific restrictions for BPP-nets. The communication is modeled by message passing or with synchronous channels.
- The activities within an object are checked. Either they can be static, which means that they can not be changed at the execution phase of the system. Or otherwise, the dynamic parts of the control of the object are distilled and modeled in a separate object, called protocol. Between the object and its protocol exists a special aggregation relationship. This allows to restrict the specific elements that are needed to draw the models, and hence makes the models easier to read.
- Each model can be tested separately by direct execution. The integration happens according to the application specific scenarios. A problem, not covered here, is to avoid further possible behaviors which are not specified. This requires to check the models formally, hence this can not be ensured by tests. A business process is the integrating object for a related set of activities.
- New objects can be introduced as appropriate at each level of abstraction.

The strict separation into separated systems allows to use an object oriented structure for the model but also allows to follow a process centered approach. Further business processes can easily be added. If they require new FUs, these have to be added. Otherwise they are assigned to already existing ones. If necessary, new object instances can be introduced with respect to resource restrictions. If an object needs additional new behavior or attributes (incl. resources), then these can be added. The nets allow an executable specification model and provide therefore the necessary means for software engineers.

---

[3] This is some kind of aggregation. There is a local instance of such a protocol which is strictly bound to the object using the protocol. If protocol instances are shared then it is an object of itself and represents a shared resource between the using objects. Formally, there is no restriction of the usage, however, a good application architecture makes this sharing of resources explicit by providing a specific object for each resource.

4.6   Example

The example chosen here is used to demonstrate the essential new features of our formalism. General ideas for object oriented modeling are assumed to be present to the readers. UML (Unified Modeling Language) as the standardized version of the Object Management Group (OMG) (see [UML]) is a good background for this (see [BRJ99], [JRB99], and [RJB99] which are the three standard books for UML).

The system for which we demonstrate our approach is a shop which sells technical goods. There are people to handle customer requests and people to test and configure a technical system. The goods can be passive like cable or can be active like a walkman[4]. The system resources are money, cables, and walkman. Paper e.g. for receipts, tools to configure the goods, rooms, tables, electricity etc. are explicitly not modeled.

Now we describe some scenarios and how to model the system. These scenarios represent some specific processes that can happen in a system. All scenarios here should be seen in isolation, since it is not intended that they should be integrated. Furthermore, they can be seen as isolated possibilities which show the different kinds of processes and the proposed solutions.

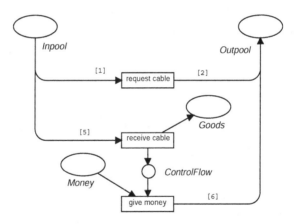

Fig. 5. Customer purchases a cable (asynchronous version). The numbers [1] to [6] show the message flow (see also Figure 6).

Scenario 1: A Customer buys a cable

In this scenario the simplest case is shown. It is used to demonstrate the concepts of asynchronous and of synchronous communication via messages and syn-

---

[4] Active means that some internal behavior of the walkman does not depend on the environment. It can be "active" while it is passed from a shopman to a customer. In terms of nets this means, that the Petri net of the walkman contains a Petri net as a token which is not always blocked from the environment.

chronous channels respectively. In the following we use an approach which uses both kinds of communication. A customer arrives and requests a cable. The shopman picks up a cable from the store and delivers the cable. The customer pays and leaves with the cable.

This first scenario illustrates the here proposed use of object oriented concepts in combination with Petri nets. The two main objects are modeled, customer and shopman. The focus is put on the control flow within the objects. Figure 5 and Figure 6 show the general structure of the nets. Several inscrip-

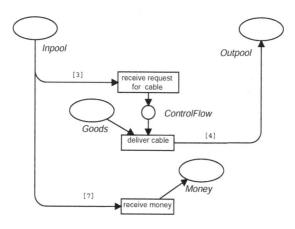

Fig. 6. Shopman sells a cable (asynchronous version).

tions have been dropped for better readability. The nets presented here can be seen as a shorthand notation for our formalism. An exact syntax has not been developed completely. However, with reference nets we have the basic formalism which has a precise semantics and an available tool. Reference nets need to be specified in more details, since they have to be executed. To introduce our main ideas we use the shorthand notation. In Figure 9 we show how a synchronous channel has to be formally specified. Figure 5 and Figure 6 contain some numbers (see e.g. [1]). The numbers in these square brackets represent the control flow and therefore the sequence of messages from [1] to [7] between the customer and the shopman. The main methods of the customer and the shopman relevant for this scenario are shown. Something or somebody tells the customer to request a cable (see flow [1]). If the customer is an autonomous object (or agent), it would be a local decision to perform a request. Here it is modeled by a message, without showing from where this message is coming. Similar assumptions will be made for the other following models. [2] shows the request going to the shopman. In Figure 6 [3] shows the incoming message. Internal control flow is not numbered, resulting in [4] as the outgoing message. It should be mentioned that now the "message" contains the cable, meaning that the message can be quite complex. [5] and [6] show the control flow for the customer and [7] indicates that the shopman finally receives his money. Due to the underlying asynchronous communication the messages from [1] to [7] can be followed easily.

There are several possibilities to realize the communication. In [MW97] a message identifier is used within the messages themselves to handle the proper assignment of messages to objects. Other possibilities are to use method invocation instances (see e.g. [EMNW00]) where an instance of a method waits for a reply. The structure of the messages is more complex than a single color. It is a tuple which describes the sender, receiver, the method called, the calling method, parameters, and some content for the proper assignment of message and the sequencing of messages. The original definitions are extended here to allow the modeling of the transfer of goods, money etc. to be covered by messages. However, these are details which are not discussed here.

The nets for the cable (goods) and for the money are not shown. In this example it is sufficient to consider them as passive objects. On the abstraction level used here the objects could also be ordinary tokens of Coloured Petri nets. Between the **receive cable** and **give money** in Figure 5 obviously the information about the amount has to be transferred as well as a reference to the receiver. Again this is suppressed to concentrate on the central issues. In Figure 9 all details are given for the synchronous case as described below.

The synchronization is done as shown for the synchronized action in Figure 7 and Figure 8 where an example for a fully synchronized action between the cus-

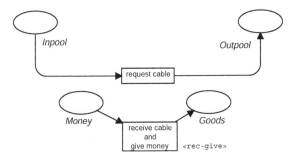

Fig. 7. Customer purchases a cable – the cable and the money are synchronously exchanged.

tomer and the shopman is shown, while the first interactions are asynchronous. The synchronous channel <rec-give> is only represented by a transition inscription according to the approach in [Val98] (see Section 3). The other inscriptions to assure the right synchronization of the right objects, like messages and their parameters, are not shown here, but in Figure 9. In Figure 9 two nets can be seen: the customer (a) and the shopman (b). The customer knows the shopman. Additionally the synchronous channels, the references, and the arc inscriptions are inserted. The reference of the shopman to the pricetable might be deduced from other parts of the specification. Here it allows to fix the price for the cable.

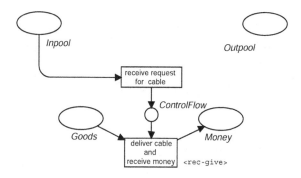

Fig. 8. Shopman sells a cable – the cable and the money are synchronously exchanged.

An implementation of the concept of synchronous channels is used in the tool Renew [Ren]. This tool has been developed in our group and implements the main characteristics of the nets used here.

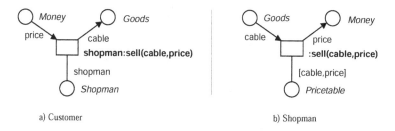

Fig. 9. Reference net for Figure 7 and Figure 8 showing the synchronous cable and money exchange.

Scenario 2: A Customer buys a walkman

A customer arrives and requests a walkman. The shopman picks up a walkman from the store and starts playing the walkman. The customer tests the walkman by listening to the music and pays for the walkman.

This scenario shows the use of a fixed workflow for a functional unit. Furthermore the transfer of an active token to another functional unit is presented.

The diagrams in Figure 10, 11 and 12 show the (simplified) model for the purchase of a walkman. The central point here is to show that a walkman is a separate object and communicates with the shopman and the customer. The communication is presented in the traditional Petri net way. The token is withdrawn from the place and moves together with the control token (which is no more explicitly modeled). The action of starting the walkman to play is done via a synchronous channel. An alternative communication has been discussed in

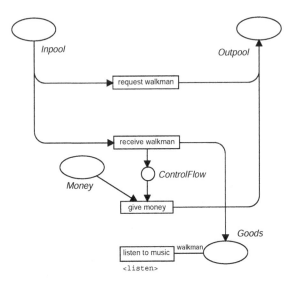

Fig. 10. Customer purchases a walkman.

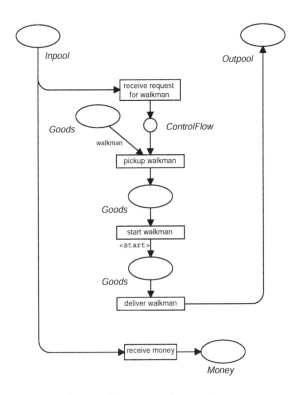

Fig. 11. Shopman sells a walkman.

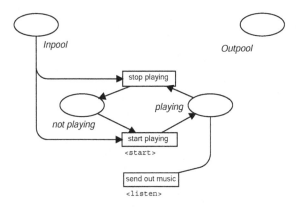

Fig. 12. Walkman which is sold.

the cable example. The listening of the customer is modeled via a synchronous channel. Further actions are hidden in the method listening. If a customer really has the intention to listen to the music, is not shown here. The arc without an arc head represents a test arc. As long as there is a token on the related place the connected transition is activated, assuming that no other place is restricting the transition. In general test arcs allow the concurrent access to the same token, here the access to the walkman is modeled as a concurrent access, even if the specific example does not require this. Inside the walkman diagram one can see that there is no message going out to the Outpool. However, the synchronous channel allows a continuos access to the music, while the music is made available via a method with a synchronous channel. The handling of the walkman by the shopman is modeled explicitly, with the workflow being fixed. In the next scenario a protocol is introduced for the separation of the shopman and his behavior.

Scenario 3: A Customer buys a walkman and the shopman follows a protocol

From an application point of view the same requirements are given as in scenario 2. However, scenario 2 is now extended by the introduction of a protocol for the behavior of the shopman.

The diagram in Figure 13 shows how the workflow which has to be performed by the shopman is represented by a separate object in another net (see Figure 14). The connections between the two nets are shown by the place *Behavior*. All actions of the shopman have to be synchronized with a protocol that is assigned to each of his transitions via a test arc to the *Behavior* place where the protocols are put. Synchronization is again realized by synchronous channels <P1> to <P5>. The proper use of the assignment of the channels is not shown by the arc and channel inscriptions. The protocol restricts the shopman in his possible actions stronger than the net structure in Figure 11. This can easily

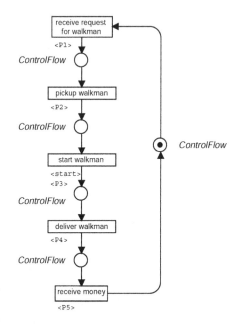

Fig. 13. Protocol for the shopman in Figure 14 to trigger his behavior.

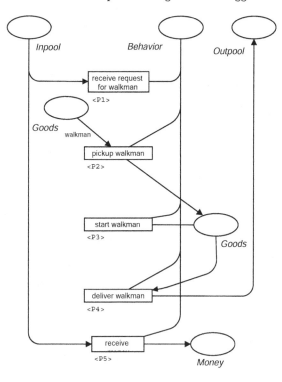

Fig. 14. Shopman sells a walkman according to the protocol in Figure 13.

be overcome by a more sophisticated protocol. Even if the structure of the two nets are very similar, it should be clear that both net structures can be modified independently to add some more actions or to modify the structure in a way to coordinate each net with other nets.

Scenario 4: Customer brings back a walkman for repair

A customer arrives with a defective walkman. He delivers it to the shopman. The shopman gives it to the repairman. The repairman repairs the walkman. The repairman gives the walkman to the shopman. The customer receives the walkman, starts it, pays, and leaves.

Scenarios 2 or 3 are extended by a further person that is involved. This person can modify an object, of course according to its *repair interface* which is not discussed here. This requires that the nets provide the means for this. Modifying passive tokens is the traditional way. However, here active tokens can be modified. Using reference nets it is possible to do this without further operators, as long as the kind of modifications are somehow predefined. If the kind of operations are not determined before the system is executed, special operators within the nets are necessary and type checking becomes more difficult.

Scenario 5: The protocol of the shopman is exchanged

This scenario extends the scenario 3 and allows to replace the protocol of the shopman. From the application point of view different behaviors are necessary due to different business requirements. For this scenario again the nets are omitted. We give a short discussion only.

From an application point of view the exchange of a protocol means that the shopman can adapt to a new behavior. The change of the protocol can either be done according to the kind of customer, requiring that the shopman can apply different kinds of protocols, or the exchange is done by a chief of the shopman who gives different orders from time to time.

This action again has to be modeled at the appropriate level. It is obvious that the exchange of a protocol is an explicit action. Modeling this is only necessary, if it is a relevant issue of the system specification. In traditional business processes many aspects were fixed. Nowadays, more flexible structures become necessary. This can be reflected in the specifications by the BPP-nets. In general new and powerful modeling techniques are necessary. The dynamic aspects require more net components in terms of modeling with Petri nets. One goal of our work is to find appropriate abbreviations with a precise semantics still modeling the essential parts without loss of correctness.

5   Conclusions

After a short introduction into object oriented coloured Petri nets and object nets a new formalism for the modeling of business processes is presented. The main characteristics of this formalism are that

- it is based on Coloured Petri nets (see [Jen92]);
- it uses a specific net structure from [Mol96] to allow the use of object oriented features;
- it extends the objects nets (see [Val98]) to high-level Petri nets;
- it supports a process oriented view on a system specification which is built on objects, modeled in OCPN-nets;
- it allows to model the dynamic adaptation to changing workflows by adding, exchanging, and deleting token nets within a certain system net level;
- mobility can be modeled intuitively;
- it allows a natural way of abstraction for the specification of internet application and a kind.

The presented formalism of Business Process Petri nets (BPP-nets) is powerful and allows to capture especially the problems occurring in business system specification when modeling dynamic changes to those parts which are normally modeled by complex structured tokens within a Petri net. Traditional modeling techniques like UML do not cover the dynamic interface and the aspect of mobility in this direct way. By using also Petri nets for the complex tokens the formal methods available for usual Petri nets become applicable, not considering the state explosion problem which may cause some practical problems. Due to the new kind of hierarchy within the net models additional formal methods have to be developed. This will be done in the near future in the area of workflow modeling and computer integrated manufacturing with respect to the use of Inter- and intranet facilities.

References

[Aal97]   Wil van der Aalst. Verification of workflow nets. In Azéma and Balbo [AB97], pages 407–426.

[AB97]   Pierre Azéma and Gianfranco Balbo, editors. *Application and Theory of Petri Nets 1997*, number 1248 in Lecture Notes in Computer Science, Berlin, Heidelberg, New York, 1997. Springer-Verlag.

[BM93]   Ulrich Becker and Daniel Moldt. Objektorientierte Konzepte für gefärbte Petrinetze. In Scheschonk and Reisig [SR93], pages 140–151.

[BRJ99]   G. Booch, J. Rumbaugh, and I. Jacobson. *The unified modeling language user guide: The ultimate tutorial to the UML from the original designers.* Addison-Wesley object technology series. Addison-Wesley, Reading, Mass., 1999.

[CH92]   Søren Christensen and Niels Damgaard Hansen. Coloured Petri Nets Extended with Channels for Synchronous communication. Technical Report DAIMI PB–390, Computer Science Department, Aarhus University, DK-8000 Aarhus C, Denmark, April 1992.

[EMNW00] Adriana Engelhardt, Daniel Moldt, Marc Netzebandt, and Frank Wienberg. Erweiterung objektorientierter gefärbter Petrinetze um Typisierung und Schnittstellen. Fachbereichsmitteilung, University of Hamburg, Department of Computer Science, Vogt-Kölln Str. 30, 22527 Hamburg, Germany, 2000. in print.

[Jen92]   Kurt Jensen. *Coloured Petri Nets: Basic Concepts, Analysis Methods and Practical Use; Vol. 1.* EATCS Monographs on Theoretical Computer Science. Springer-Verlag, Berlin, Heidelberg, New York, 1992.

[JRB99]   I. Jacobson, J. Rumbaugh, and G. Booch. *The unified software development process: UML; The complete guide to the Unified Process from the original designers.* Addison-Wesley object technology series. Addison-Wesley, Reading, Mass., 1999.

[JV87]   Eike Jessen and Rüdiger Valk. *Rechensysteme; Grundlagen der Modellbildung.* Springer-Verlag, Berlin, Heidelberg, New York, 1987.

[Kum98]   Olaf Kummer. Simulating synchronous channels and net instances. In J. Desel, P. Kemper, E. Kindler, and A. Oberweis, editors, *5. Workshop Algorithmen und Werkzeuge für Petrinetze*, Forschungsbericht Nr. 694, pages 73–78. Fachbereich Informatik, Universität Dortmund, October 1998.

[Kum99]   Olaf Kummer. A Petri net view on synchronous channels. *Petri Net Newsletter*, (56):7–11, 1999.

[MM99]   Christoph Maier and Daniel Moldt. Object Coloured Petri Nets – a Formal Technique for Object Oriented Modelling. In G. Agha, F. De Cindio, and G. Rozenberg, editors, *Concurrent Object-Oriented Programming and Petri Nets*, Lecture Notes in Computer Science, Berlin, Heidelberg, New York, 1999. Springer-Verlag. in print.

[Mol96]   Daniel Moldt. *Höhere Petrinetze als Grundlage für Systemspezifikationen.* Dissertation, University of Hamburg, Department of Computer Science, August 1996.

[MW97]   Daniel Moldt and Frank Wienberg. Multi-Agent-Systems based on Coloured Petri Nets. In Azéma and Balbo [AB97], pages 82–101.

[Rei92]   Wolfgang Reisig. *A Primer in Petri Net Design.* Springer Compass International. Springer-Verlag, Berlin, Heidelberg, New York, 1992.

[Ren]   The Renew Home Page. WWW page at http://www.renew.de. Represents the Renew homepage.

[RJB99]   J. Rumbaugh, I. Jacobson, and G. Booch. *The unified modeling language reference manual: The definitive reference to the UML from the original designers.* Addison-Wesley object technology series. Addison-Wesley, Reading, Mass., 1999.

[SR93]   Gert Scheschonk and Wolfgang Reisig, editors. *Petri-Netze im Einsatz für Entwurf und Entwicklung von Informationssystemen*, Informatik Aktuell, Berlin, Heidelberg, New York, 1993. Gesellschaft für Informatik, Springer-Verlag.

[Szy98]   Clemens Szyperski. *Component software: Beyond object-oriented programming.* ACM Press books. Addison-Wesley, Reading, Mass., reprint edition, 1998.

[UML]   The UML Home Page. WWW page at http://www.rational.com/uml/. Represents the UML homepage hold by the originators of UML.

[Val91]   Rüdiger Valk. Modelling Concurrency by Task/Flow EN Systems. In *Proceedings 3rd Workshop on Concurrency and Compositionality*, number 191 in GMD-Studien, St. Augustin, Bonn, Germany, 1991. Gesellschaft für Mathematik und Datenverarbeitung.

[Val98]   Rüdiger Valk. Petri Nets as Token Objects: An Introduction to Elementary Object Nets. In Jörg Desel and Manuel Silva, editors, *19th International Conference on Application and Theory of Petri nets*, number 1420 in Lecture Notes in Computer Science, Berlin, Heidelberg, New York, 1998. Springer-Verlag.

Information Gathering and Process Modeling
in a Petri Net Based Approach

Wolfgang Deiters

Fraunhofer Institute for Software- and Systems Engineering
P.O. Box 520 130, FRG- 44207 Dortmund
deiters@do.isst.fhg.de

Abstract. Petri nets are seen as a suitable process modeling language since they lead to graphical process descriptions that can be understood by different people, since formal process analysis can be performed, and enaction of processes can be done on the basis of a process model described by Petri nets. We have developed a Petri net based process modeling language and applied it to various practical projects. From the experiences we have derived new concepts and techniques in order to enhance our approach. In this paper we mainly discuss two aspects (1) modeling semi-structured process parts and (2) gathering the relevant information to be put into process models.

1 Introduction

Within the last years workflow management has become a technology that is being more and more used in order to support business processes. Based on an enactable description the processes are being supported by workflow systems that usually interpret the processes, assign to the various people involved in the process the tasks they have to perform, and, provide the tools and objects that are needed to perform the tasks. Thus, workflow systems drive and monitor the business processes.

For modeling the processes Petri nets have been widely used. Petri nets are seen capable because of its following features:

- graphical description yielding in a workflow representation that can be understood by various groups of people
- formal basis - workflow models based on Petri nets can be formally analysed in order to achieve improvements of the modelled processes
- enactable models - Petri net based workflow models can be enacted

Within the last years we have intensively used a Petri net based workflow language called FUNSOFT nets [DG98]. The language has been applied in various projects w.r.t. the goals indicated above (workflow modeling, analysis as well as enaction). On the one hand side within the projects the possibility to use Petri nets has been shown. However, on the other side some points of weakness have also been shown. These experiences (as well as the improvements in order to deal with the weak points) will be discussed in the paper.

W. van der Aalst et al. (Eds.): Business Process Management, LNCS 1806, pp 274-288, 2000
© Springer-Verlag Berlin Heidelberg 2000

Among the experiences are issues that lead to questions like (1) how to model workflows where different organisations are involved in (i.e. how to model the co-ordination process of the partners while at the same time the individual partners want to behave autonomously within their workflows), (2) how to deal with process parts that have to be performed completely or not at all (i.e. the issue of workflow transactions), and (3) how to deal with exceptional cases in workflows, and, generally process parts that cannot be completely defined in advance.

Furthermore experiences have been made considering the development of workflow models based on Petri nets. Since Petri nets support a broad range of goals (modeling analysis, and enaction) its usage has a great benefit for a workflow management. However, not all people (especially non-technical people on the end-user level) "think" in terms of Petri nets. However, these people are involved in the processes, i.e. are the people that have the process knowledge to be modelled in the workflows. In order to "integrate" these people into the information gathering and workflow model development process we describe our approach for capturing workflow related information, storing and structuring it in an organisational memory information system which will be used for deriving a Petri net based workflow representation.

For the scope of this paper we want to concentrate ourselves on the questions about the definition of workflows that consist of information that is only partially available at process model build time in conjunction with the question about how to collect and structure information about processes at all. Therefore, the structure of the paper is as follows: In section 2 some basic aspects of our approach are discussed. Following that the issue of semi-structured business processes (i.e. processes that cannot be completely defined at model build time) is tackled. In section 4 we discuss how to collect and structure information that is relevant to be defined in process models and how to make this information consistent. Section 5, finally, summarises and addresses some future work to be done.

2 Some Basic Aspects of Our Process Management Approach

For developing process based IT application based on the workflow management technology different activities have to be performed. The sequence of these activity is also called process model lifecycle (c.f. Figure 1).

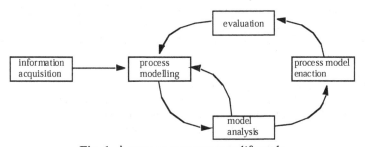

Fig. 1. A process management lifecycle

Continuous engineering of systems usually takes place in running organisations. Thus, in a first activity the information about the processes has to be gathered. Within an *information acquisition* the information about the „as is processes" is collected. This can take place by different means: document analysis (e.g. using a ISO9000 documentation if it exists in the organisation), structured interviews, workshops, etc.. This information that has been collected is fixed in the process model in an activity that is called *process modeling*, then. This process model serves as a basis for discussion about the processes. Furthermore, in a *process model analysis* activity the model can be evaluated in order to detect deficiencies of the process. A typical analysis technique is the one of simulating the process. Results of the analysis usually are suggestions for improvement that result in changes of the process model. Iterating the modeling and analysis activities usually leads to „should be process models" which are an improvement of the „as is models". Once a „should be model" has been decided upon a *process model enaction* can take place. This takes place on the basis of a workflow application where the process is driven by the workflow engine, and different services are called supporting the different process activities. According to the process state the different persons involved in the process get informed about the activities they have to perform, and they are provided with the necessary process objects and services to work upon the objects according to the activity definitions. One further important activity is the *process evaluation* in order to detect further possible process improvements during the process or a posteriori, i.e. after the process has been terminated.

Various process modeling approaches each of which focussing on a certain goal have been developed in the last years (e.g. FlowMark [IBM95], Action Workflow [MWFF92], Promet [Oest95],). A couple of the process modeling languages base on the Petri net language paradigm ([AME98, Ober96]), others exist that use programming language like notations (e.g. MOBILE [JB96]) and/or object oriented languages (e.g. SOM [FS95]).

One approach that has been developed for managing business processes in the scope that is given by the lifecycle of Figure 1 is called FUNSOFT nets [DG94], an approach basing on Petri nets. Due to the limited space of this paper we do not give a separate introduction of FUNSOFT here. For an understanding of this paper we assume that the reader is familiar with Petri nets. Further details of the FUNSOFT net approach can be found in ([DG94, DGW95]). The FUNSOFT net approach has been applied in several projects within the last years [DG98]. When applying that approach it has been shown that the main goals (1) understandability of processes by using a graphical notation, (2) analysis of process models, and (3) support for process model enaction can be achieved.

However when performing our projects we also have been faced with a couple of problems that partially occur in general when trying to manage business processes but partially also came with the application of the concrete approach we have taken. These problems can be structured into three different classes:
- Missing process modeling constructs
- Missing process structure
- Missing concepts for bringing user information into process models

Considering the problem of missing modeling constructs we have modelled processes where the user could tell us, for example, the activity schedule to be performed in the process but, furthermore, told us that certain exceptional or error situations could occur that make it necessary to undo part of the process. With the Petri net language concepts we have had so far, this "undo" of process parts was cumbersome to describe. From that experience we developed the concept of process transactions [SDL96] and extended our language by that concept. The problem denoted above by missing process structure describes the fact that processes quite often cannot be completely defined at process model build time. There are either a large variety of alternative solution paths for certain partial processes, sometimes one could indicate the different activities to be performed but could not determine the order in which these activities are to be performed. In other situations the information how to perform the process even became only be available while the process was running. In order to manage these kinds of processes, that we have started to term semi-structured processes, we have worked on different concepts for extending the process modeling language as well as for integrating different types of IT-systems (e.g. workflow, groupware, and document management systems). Concerning the last point we quite often were faced with the problem that the information we had to put into process models had been spread over various people, documents, etc. and was available at very different levels of abstraction. We therefore felt the necessity to develop conceptual means for collecting, structuring, and homogenising information to be put together into a process model. In the reminder of this paper we want to focus on the latter two problems the support for semi-structured business processes as well as the problem of gathering information to be put into process models.

3 Modeling Semi-Structured Process Parts in a Petri Net Based Approach

When modeling processes we quite often have been faced with the problem to model exceptional and error cases. We therefore introduced the concept of process transactions [SDL96] into the Petri net language we use. However, there are also cases where it is not possible to completely define processes by means of process models in advance or even not at all. In those cases we have to deal with the problem of evolution of processes that are incompletely specified.

Incomplete specification raises the question concerning the available information at model build time. In general, incomplete means, that information about some of the metamodel entities is not available when defining the model. This - what is quite often the case - can be that the activities but not the order of activities is known, it can be that the persons responsible for performing the activities are not known or the assignment of persons to activities is not known or changes quite frequently.

There are a couple of approaches classifying business processes. In the following we build up a classification scheme for business processes that spans up three dimensions distinguishing process model entities information objects, co-operating persons and solution paths (see also [LSD98], [DLS99]). One major characteristic for all these entities is whether they can be planned, i.e. whether they are known at process model build time and, thus, can be fixed in a process model or not. Using the three entities and the characteristic of plannability we can build up a scheme spanning eight different classes of business processes.

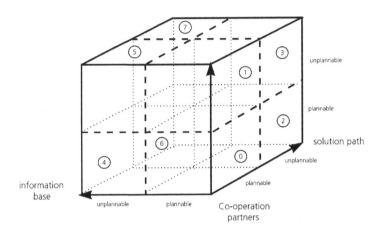

Fig. 2. A classification scheme for semi-structured process models

Within class 0 we find those business processes that are plannable with respect to all three entities information objects, co-operating persons, and solution path. We call this class of business processes ***structured business processes*** in the following. Class 7 encompasses those processes that are unplannable with respect to all three entities. We call these processes ***unstructured processes***. Those processes that belong to one of the classes 1 to 6 are called ***semi-structured processes*** in the following.

Processes belonging to class 0 are the typical application domain for workflow management applications. Here all information regarding the activities and their execution order, the persons participating in the activities, and the documents needed for performing activities or produced by the activities are known in advance and, thus, can be fixed in the process model. All semi-structured process classes have in common that at least one information entity that spans up a dimension of the classification scheme is unknown at process model build time. For these kind of processes workflow management systems usually give inappropriate support. One idea, therefore is to integrate workflow management systems with other systems supporting co-ordination, co-operation, and communication in order to support semi-structured processes. This means, for example, to support different parts of business processes using different kinds of systems (e.g. workflow management, groupware, document management, videoconferencing, joint editing) each of which supporting the corresponding process part best. Discussions on the different classes as well as on the different type of IT-support can be found in [DLS99].

In the following we concentrate on mechanisms how to deal with unplannable aspects (of classes 1 – 6) in Petri net based process modeling approaches. One major problem that yields in semi-structured business processes at process model build time results from the point of time when certain information becomes available (i.e. when plannability is given). Quite often process models must stay incomplete because some information is not available when modeling the process (i.e. at model build time) but rather becomes available only during the process (i.e. at process model run time). That means the fixed separation of building a model of the process first and, then, running the process according to the defined model afterwards quite often does not hold in practice. Process modeling and process enaction rather have to be interweaved. It must be possible to add process information to the process model that is being enacted.

Different approaches have been developed in order to enable a certain intermixing of model definition and model enaction while using a Petri net process modeling language:

For FUNSOFT nets the concept of **late modeling** has been developed. Late modeling can be applied when parts of the process are known at build time but others have to be added during run time of the process. Upon occurrence of certain events during a process the models that have been partially fixed so far become completed. An example for this is given in Figure 3. There a cut out of a process model is sketched for checking the capacity of certain parts that are needed in an assembly activity. At first a *capacity_check[1]* is performed in order to determine whether enough parts for assembling are available. If this activity ends up positive the assembly takes place otherwise new parts have to be get. However, at process model build time it is still unclear how to get new parts (e.g. whether they should be bought or fabricated). Therefore, the activity *get_new_parts* has been modelled as a black box. A modification triggering event exists (in the example the channel *amount_not_ok* associated with a flag) triggering the modeling of the black box. In case a token is put into that channel the black box *get_new_parts* becomes subject of change (i.e. can be replaced by a net) while the remaining net remains under enaction. This mechanism holds whenever the *amount_not_ok* channel is filled, i.e. different events can result in different specifications of *get_new_parts*. Different models can be implemented defining who is allowed to change the model [Herr95].

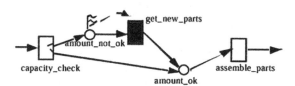

Fig. 3. The concept of late modeling

In the HOON approach [CHW97, HHSW96] the Petri net paradigm has been extended in order to arrange Petri nets, e.g. FUNSOFT nets, and their surrounding

---

[1] In that example the FUNSOFT net agency *capacity_check* has a so called DET-OUT firing behavior (indicated by the small switch symbol) saying that one of the two channels in its postset is filled with a token upon firing the agency. For further details on firing behaviors of agencies in FUNSOFT see [DG94, DGS95].

environment and to model the interfaces towards the environment explicitly in process models. For modeling the interfaces between process models and the environment external to the model special places so called *interface places* have been introduced. Through these interface places information can be dynamically exchanged between the process models and the external environment. By that resources are directly encapsulated as distributed objects or correspond to devices of distributed objects. As a result the management of process resources is excluded from the process model and is realised by the workflow environment which runs in the background. This workflow environment can bring information into the process model even during run time of the process, thus, it becomes possible to interweave modeling and enaction of process models.

In Figure 4 an example demonstrating the effect of *resource tokens* is given. In that example a business process activity *edit_report* is modelled by a Petri net agency. It operates on an input called *abstract* specifying what the report should be about. The result of the activity, of course, is the *report* that has to be edited. Beside the activity its input and its output an interface place called *editor_licences* is introduced. This interface place models that for performing the edit operation an editor is needed for which tool licences are needed. A licence for the editor is associated with a token that is put into the interface place. The activity can only be started when at least one licence is put into the corresponding channel. Upon firing of the agency *edit_report*, i.e. upon performing the edit the licence token is read from the interface channel, it is put back again when having finished the edit.

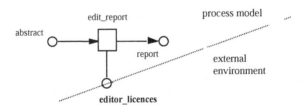

Fig. 4. The concept of resource tokens [CHW97]

Now, let us assume that the company has, say, three licences for the editor. Furthermore let us assume that in the model (resp. in different process models) more than three activities are defined the performance of which needs an editor. Each of the four editing activities, of course, is connected to an interface place associated with editor licence tokens. In this case three edit activities can start, the fourth one would be prohibited from starting since its resource place would own no licence token for an editor. Its execution would be delayed until the termination of one of the other three editing activities. However, the amount of resources (in this example the editor licences) is managed outside the process model. If the company would decide, for example, to buy 5 more licences the external environment would create the resp. number of token and would induce them into the resource place. By that resource places act as interface between external environment and process model.

The concept can be exploited further on for a dynamic process model modification at run time of the business process. If we consider the notion of resources that is associated with the resource places in a broad sense regarding process models as one kind of resource it becomes possible to identify complete process models by resource tokens. Now, if we associate refined agencies with resource places the token in the resource place identifies the subnet to be executed when performing the refined agency. By that it becomes possible to model different nets at process model build time each of which is a candidate refinement for the refined agency (of course, the nets have to be semantically correct refinements. For further details see [CHW97]). This is graphically depicted in Figure 5. In that figure we have modelled a refined agency a1 and three possible refinements ref1 to ref3. Which of the possible refinements is to be executed when starting a1 is addressed by the token in the resource place for a1. The content of this token has not to be defined at build time but is put into the resource place at run time by the workflow environment prior to the execution of a1. Even the set of refinement candidates has not necessarily to be specified during model build time. New nets being potential refinement candidates can be added up to that point in time when the binding of refined agency and refining subnet is made by the resource token. By that it becomes possible to change and extend a process model even during run time of the process that has been instantiated from the model.

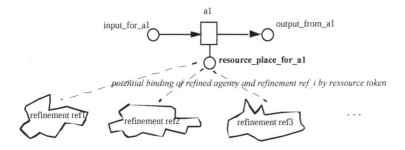

Fig. 5. Dynamically binding process model parts using the concept of resource tokens

4 Information Gathering for Building Process Model

In section 2 we have addressed major problems we were faced with when applying a Petri net language in practical industrial projects. In the last section we have addressed the issue of modeling semi-structured business process parts. In this section the second problem namely the one of gathering the information to be put into process models should be addressed. We were faced with the problem when sing our Petri net approach. However, the problem also occurs when other modeling approaches are applied.

Usually it is the goal of a process management project to improve and to support processes that are already being carried out in practice. However, only in rare cases processes are completely to be defined from anew. In most cases these processes have been carried out implicitly so far, i.e. the persons involved in the process knew their job (that means, they had in mind what to do) but no (complete) explicit description of the processes existed so far. Thus, for building process models all relevant information concerning the processes has to be acquired first. Based on this information a first model describing the "as-is" situation is build that is subject for analysis, improvement and enaction, then.

This acquisition of information is done in the information gathering phase indicated in the lifecycle that has been introduced in section 2 (cp. Figure 1). However in projects that we have carried out collecting information concerning the processes showed to be a complicated process itself due to the following issues:

• Process information is distributed among different information resources

When collecting information about the processes to model it shows that usually the information about the processes is not concentrated in one information source but rather is distributed among different information sources of different type. Among information sources are written materials e.g. handbooks of tools that are being used in the process so far, partial process descriptions that have been made so far (e.g. rule sets for handling certain activities, mission statements for certain processes, quality management documentation (e.g. ISO 9000), etc.). However most information about the processes is available in the minds of the persons performing the processes that are to be supported.

In order to capture this information different gathering techniques have to be adopted. Among these techniques are document analysis, observation and inquiry. Document analysis means collecting and studying the written material available about the processes and to mark the information relevant for building a process model. Observation means that the process modeller joins the process noting what people do in the process and how they do their job. The results are specified in observation protocols, then. Inquiry means asking people about the information they have about the process. This can take place by interviews (face to face or using telephone), workshops, questionnaires etc. As a result of applying these information gathering techniques different documents (questionnaires, protocols, interview traces) exist the content of which has to be structured and put together to yield a process model.

• Process information has to be collected, structured and consolidated

Industrial processes are quite often very complex, consisting of hundreds of activities, documents, persons involved, and tools that are used by the persons. For those processes the relevant information cannot be collected in one step. For complex processes it becomes necessary to start with an abstract process description identifying the processes' scope and to refine the abstract description in a next step. One reason for doing so is that different persons usually have different type of information. Quite often managers know the processes on an abstract level, and, know the interrelation of process parts while the persons that work in the processes know the process details (e.g. how to perform activities, know why activities are performed in a certain sequence and so on).

Since, additionally, organisations that are involved in the processes are quite often dispersed over different geographical locations it becomes impossible to bring all relevant persons together at one point in time for information gathering since (1) the relevant persons work at different places, and (2) bringing all persons together would result in workshops the size of which would lead to unproductive work and the resulting information would be too complex and unstructured to be useful. Thus, information gathering has to be performed in several steps, for example, starting with an initial workshop where the managers are interviewed about the process scope and the abstract process steps, followed by detailed interviews among the process experts, a review workshop after a first information integration, followed by a interviews for refining and completing the information set, etc. For this it becomes necessary to collect information, integrate different information sources, to mark information as being relevant or irrelevant and consistent or inconsistent, to delete unnecessary information, etc.

Doing so the organisational knowledge (i.e. the information of all persons of an organisation) about the processes is captured. Since for real-life processes this information can become very large an *organisational memory information system* is needed for managing this information. In this context we understand an organisational memory information system (OMIS) as "an enterprise-internal application independent information and assistant system. It stores large amounts of data, information and knowledge from different sources of an enterprise. These are represented in various forms, such as databases, documents and formal knowledge-bases. The OMIS will be permanently extended to keep it up-to-date and can be accessed enterprise-wide through an appropriate network infrastructure" [KA98]

For the scope of achieving the goals of information gathering sketched above an OMIS has to fulfil the following requirements:

1. storage of information objects of different type such as text, audio, video graphics

   The different information gathering techniques addressed above result in different information objects such as, for example, hand-written protocols, audio tape traces of interviews, videos from process observations. These information objects have to be stored in the OMIS, it has to be possible to structure this information, to indicate relevant information areas in the objects, and to associate the information with appropriate meta information (e.g. date of gathering, author).

2. associations between different information objects

   It must be possible to associate information objects with each other for relating information objects that give information about the same process entities (e.g. a workshop protocol where a process activity is noted with an interview giving details about that activity). These associations have to be attributed in order to give certain semantics to the associations between the information objects that are linked to each others via this associations. By that it can, for example, be expressed that an object is needed for an activity (if an association is made between an information describing an activity and another one describing a document), that an activity is predecessor of another one (two information objects each one describing an activity), consistency or inconsistency of information can be denoted (two information objects describing the same entity), etc.

3. retrieval of information

Having stored the information objects the OMIS needs to support different kinds of information inquiry. We distinguish between passive and active information supply, depending on whether the user selects the information (passive supply means the OMIS is passive) or whether the OMIS selects information and provides it to the user (active supply).

In case of a passive information supply a query interface as well as a navigation interface for information retrieval is needed. With the query interface the user can retrieve information by issuing queries like *"give me all information about all process activities in a certain process step"*. The navigation interface allows to browse through the OMIS visiting information objects along the associations between the objects.

In case of an active information provision the user gets information upon the occurrence of certain events he can specify. For example, if he specifies that he wants to be informed if new (or inconsistent) information concerning a certain process entity is put into the OMIS the system monitors this event and notifies the user upon its occurrence.

4. access rights for the OMIS

In order to achieve an acceptance of the OMIS among the participants of the organisation a dedicated access right system is needed. For example, in some cases process participants will not give all detail information how they behave in the process depending on the fact whether their superior or certain colleges get this information either. Thus, for each information object it must be possible to specify which person is allowed to view or to change the information.

Based on this requirements an OMIS called PRINCE (PRocess INformation CEnter, [Kuhl99]) has been designed and implemented. This systems allows to store different kinds of multimedia objects. Since the **information objects** usually give information about different process entities (consider e.g. a workshop protocol where all activities of a certain process step are listed) it is possible to structure the information objects in different **information areas**. The definition of information areas depends on the type of multimedia object (e.g. areas on a photo or a hand-written note, time slots in an audio or video document). Within one information area only **information** about one process entity is given (see below).

The information about the different process entities is structured according to the different entity types (e.g. activities, documents, roles, tools) of the process management approach. An illustration of this is given in Figure 6. In this Figure an information document giving a hand written workshop protocol is shown (part A of the screendump). Two information areas one for a process document "Rollkarte" another one for a process activity "Termingut_Bearbeitung" are defined. For these process entities instances are created (see for example the highlighted entry in part B of the screendump which gives an structured overview about all process entity instances for which information is available). Part C of the screendump shows some metainformation about the information object.

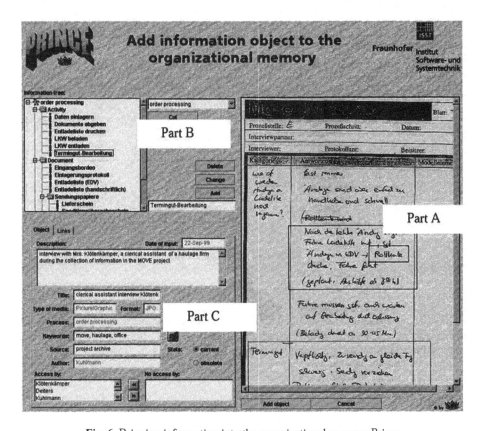

Fig. 6. Bringing information into the organizational memory Prince

PRINCE allows to retrieve information according to the requirements given above. The user can issue queries for obtaining certain information (e.g. all information that is inconsistent) or he can navigate through the graph of linked information objects given by the associations between information objects. In Figure 7 a screendump showing how to browse through the information graph is illustrated. In that figure an object called *interview_protocol* is selected. Association to five other objects exist. The user now either can open the document or he can select one of the associated ones. In this case this object becomes the selected one (i.e. moves to be the centred one) and all associations to this information object are shown. Furthermore, the user obtains information by defining so called knowledge abonements specifying upon which events he wants to become informed actively by the OMIS.

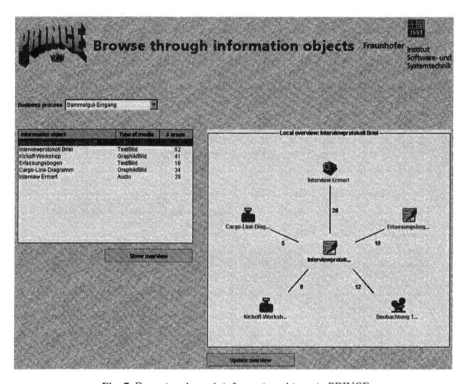

Fig. 7. Browsing through information objects in PRINCE

PRINCE has been implemented in JAVA as a Web-based application. One reason for doing so was the goal to achieve a portable system that can be used at different user places during the information gathering phase.

5 Summary

Within this paper we have discussed experiences that we have gained when managing business processes in practice based on a Petri net language paradigm. In general Petri nets have been shown a useful approach leading to graphical process descriptions that can be understood by end users from various application domains including users without a deep technical background. Furthermore Petri nets are a means for a process analysis aiming at problem detection and process improvement, and, they can be used for process enaction.

Problems we have been faced with consider the handling of exceptional process cases (for which we have introduced the concept of process transactions), the management of semi-structured processes and the gathering of information to be put into the process models. For handling semi-structured processes one approach is to define new language constructs (like it has been done, for example, in the HOON approach), another one is to integrate different types of systems (like workflow, groupware, document management). In order to manage the amount of information to be described in a process model organizational memory information systems can be used. In this paper we have described a system called PRINCE that allows to collect, structure and consolidate information objects that have been obtained applying different techniques (document analysis observation, investigation) during the process analysis phase. One next step of our work will be to generate process skeletons (i.e. Petri net skeletons) from the structured collection of information objects in PRINCE and to build up a bidirectional link between information objects in PRINCE with the corresponding process model objects (agencies and channels of Petri nets).

References

[AME98] v.d.Aalst W., Michelis G., Ellis C.: Workflow-Management: Net based concepts, models, techniques and tools (WFM98), UNINOVA, Lisboa, June 1998

[CHW97] Claßen I., Han Y., Weber H.: Towards Evolutionary and Adaptive Workflow Systems - Infrastructure Support Based on Higher Order Object Nets, in: Proc. Of the First Int. Enterprise Distributed Object Computing Workshop, EDOC 97, Gold Coast, Queensland, Australia, October 1997

[DG94] Deiters W., Gruhn V.: The FUNSOFT Net Approach to Software Process Management, Int. Journal on Software Engineering and Knowledge Engineering, Vol. 4, No. 2, June 1994

[DG98] Deiters W., Gruhn V.: Process management in practice - applying the FUNSOFT net approach to large scale processes, Automated Software Engineering, Vol. 5, Kluwer Academic Publishers, Dordrecht, NL, 1998

[DGW95] Deiters W., Gruhn V., Weber H.: Software Process Evolution in MELMAC, in: The Impact of CASE on the Software Development Life Cycle, World Scientific Publishing, Singapore, 1995

[DHLS96] Deiters W., Herrmann T., Löffeler T., Striemer R.: Identification, classification and support of semi-structured processes in process based telecooperation systems (in German), in: H. Krcmar, H. Lewe (eds.) Proc. DCSCW: Herausforderung Telekooperation, Springer, Berlin, 1996

[DLS99] Deiters W., Löffeler T., Striemer R.: Applying Workflow Management Technology To-Semi Structured Business Processes, in: C.M. Khoongh (ed.) Reengineering in Action - The Quest for World Class Excellence, World Scientific Publishing, Singapore, Spring 1999

[FS95] Ferstl O., Sinz E.J.: Der Ansatz des semantischen Objektmodells zur Modellierung von Geschäftsprozesses, Wirtschaftsinformatik, Nr. 3, 1995

[HHSW96] Han Y, Himmighöfer J., Schaaf T., Wikarski D.: Management of Workflow Ressources to Support Adaptability and System Evolution, in: Wolf M., Reimers U.: Workshop on Adaptive Workflows, Proc. of the 1st. Int. Conf. on Practicals Aspects of Knowledge Management, Vol. 1, 1996

[Herr95] Herrmann T.: Workflow Management Systems: Ensuring Organisational Flexibility by Possibilities of Adaptation and Negotiation, Conf. on Organisational Computing Systems (COOCS), ACM Press, New York, 1995

[IBM94] IBM: IBM FlowMark Programming Guide, Version 2.1, International Business Machines Corporation, 1995

[JB96] Jablonski S., Bussler C.: Workflow Management. Modeling Concepts, Architecture and Implementation, International Thomson, London, 1996

[KA98] Kühn O., Abecker A.: Corporate Memories for Knowledge Management in Industrial Practice: Prospects and Challenges, in: Borghoff U., Pareshi R. (eds.): Information Technology for Knowledge Management, Springer, Berlin, New York, Heidelberg, 1998

[Kuhl99] Kuhlmann A.: Entwurf und Einsatz eines Organisational Memories im Rahmen des Geschäftsprozeßmanagements (in German), Diploma Thesis, University of Dortmund, Dortmund, March 1999

[LSD98] Löffeler T., Striemer R., Deiters W.: A Framework for Identification, Classification and IT Support for Semi-Structured Business Processes, World Multiconference on Systemantics, Cybernetics and Informatics (SCI97), Caracas, Venezuela, July 1997, also: Knowledge and Process Management, Vol. 5, Issue 1, Wiley and Sons, London, April 1998

[MMFF92] Medina-Mora R., Winograd T., Flores R.: The action workflow approach to workflow management technology, Proc. of the 1992 Conf. on Computer Supported Cooperative Work, Toronto, ACM Press, 1992

[Ober96] Oberweis A.: Modellierung und Ausführung von Workflows mit Petri-Netzen (in German), Teubner, Stuttgart, 1996

[Oest95] Österle H.: Business Engineering - Prozeß und Systementwicklung (in German), Berlin, Springer 1995

[SDL96] Schiprowski R., Deiters W., Lindert F.: A transaction concept for FUNSOFT nets , in: Jablonski S., Groiss H., Kaschek R., Liebhart W. (eds.): Geschäftsprozeßmodellierung und Workflow-Systeme, Proc Informatik 96, Vol. 2, Klagenfurt 1996

[WfMC95] The Workflow Management Coalition, Workgroup 1a: The Workflow Reference Model, WFMC WG01-1000, February 1995

Why Modellers Wreck Workflow Innovations

Stef M.M. Joosten

Open University Netherlands
Dept. of Computer Science
P.O. Box 2960
6401 DL Heerlen
stef.joosten@ou.nl
also:
Anaxagoras Process Architects
Hengelosestraat 511
7521 AG Enschede
joosten@anaxagoras.com

Abstract. Why did ten modelers spend over a year mapping and charting business processes, and why did the workflow project still fail? Questions like this form the mortar that builds the nightmares of business managers into a brick wall that blocks successful innovations. In this chapter we discuss an approach that has demonstrated to innovate processes successfully by avoiding known pitfalls and risks. We focus on the practical questions, such as:
- how can you tell in advance whether a model will help?
- in which situations do users benefit from your models, and what can you do about it?
- when is it useful to use your workflow model for documentation purposes?
- spend plenty of time to find out how to achieve your innovation goals with the help of business process models, but don't spend a long time choosing your modelling technique.

Available evidence suggests that not the modeling techniques as such are to blame, but the way of working that modelers employ in practice. On the experience gathered in workflow projects, carried out in the financial and government sectors, we have built a framework for business process innovations that puts modeling in perspective and has shown to achieve results for the business.

1 Introduction

If a process innovation changes the way people work (i.e. the business process), then many workflow projects of the past cannot be characterized as a process innovation. A recent survey by Anaxagoras[1] among business managers showed that more than half of all workflow projects fail to contribute to business process innovation.. 84% of successful workflow projects in practice result in an information system that integrates a number of different application components, without affecting the structure of the work processed on the shop floor. Of 14 workflow projects that existed two years ago, 9 were never heard of anymore. So why is it that workflow projects fail? And how does process modeling prevent failure? In an attempt to answer these questions, we have identified risk factors that threaten the success of a

---

[1] Anaxagoras Process Architects is a Dutch consulting firm, led by the author, that specializes in process innovations for banks and insurance companies.

W. van der Aalst et al. (Eds.): Business Process Management, LNCS 1806, pp 289-300, 2000

business process innovation[2]. After a validation, these risk factors were used to design a project approach, based on the assumption that the safest route to success avoids all known pitfalls.

A business process innovation differs from an information system innovation. If an organization changes the way of doing business, i.e. changes its own way of working, we call it a business process innovation. An information system innovation introduces new technology, limiting the changes to the introduction of new. A business process innovation is meant to innovate value chains in which an organization participates. Only if an organization is prepared to change its ways of doing business, we have a business process innovation. An insurance company entering in electronic commerce on the Web, coming from a sales organization based on intermediaries, is clearly innovating its business processes. But if the changes in the way of working are limited to absorb the effects of implementing new information systems, we call it an information system innovation. Process innovations do not typically question an organization's strategy, but use strategy as a given starting point.
Early expectations that workflow management was sufficient to bring the business and technology together have not materialized. The naive view that process architects build process models have pushed the topic into the technology side of the innovation. Analysis of the problems shows that ignorance in user communities, showing up in the form of paradigm misconceptions and unsubstantiated prejudices, is a major cause. This is both good news and bad news. The good news is that ignorance will resolve as time proceeds. The bad news is that it has limited the impact of workflow management mainly to information and communication technology.

The same analysis has led to the identification of risk factors involved in business process innovations. This has produced a practical instrument to assess innovation projects, which managers in large financial businesses have used during the initial decision taking process.
Indeed, in some project plans process architects are scheduled to do nothing but the modeling of business processes, as though window dressing is needed to make an information system innovation look like a process innovation. Apparently, process modeling is seen as the core skill of process innovation.

There are many reasons that explain the slow rate of adoption of workflow technology. These reasons vary in nature: there are technological issues, methodological issues, commercial issues, lack of knowledge in user communities, and innovation issues. In order to achieve operational results in a given situation, a project manager can influence only some of those issues. There is little a practitioner can do about technological, methodological, and commercial issues. The issues that can be influenced from within a project form the basis on which Anaxagoras has developed the rainbow approach. It is developed for rapid, robust and reliable business process innovations. It allows us to focus on the things we can influence, for a large part involving innovation issues and educating user communities. Built to avoid known risks, the method has been and is still being used successfully in practical business process innovations.

---

[2] An excerpt of our risk analysis can be found on www.anaxagoras.com, which is meant to give practitioners a superficial scan of their projects for free, without spending more than 30 minutes of their time.

Definitions

Throughout this paper we use the terms business process, value chain, procedure, workflow, task, activity, innovation project in specific meanings, as defined in this section. The definitions are designed to match the most common use of terms, as identified both in practice and in the literature. The terms can therefore be used in the normal stream of a conversation, without thinking about the definitions all the time.

In a business process we distinguish five different levels of abstraction: the value chain, the procedures, the tasks, the services and the data. In the architectural thinking, a ICT architecture typically covers the latter three levels whereas a process architecture typically covers the former three levels. Overlap exists on the task level.

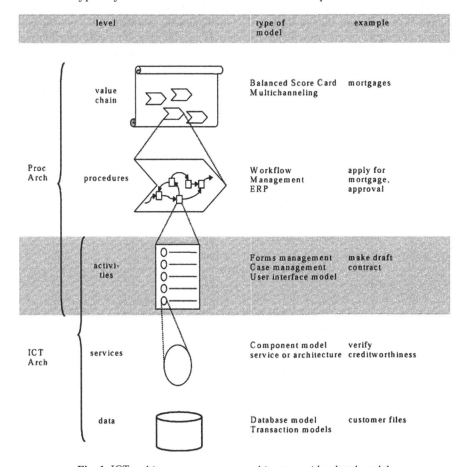

Fig. 1. ICT architecture vs. process architecture with related models

A *value chain* is a collection of activities that contribute directly to an operational goal of a business. This corresponds to the notion of supply chain, which is the integration of business processes from end-user through original suppliers that provides products, services, and information that add value to a customer" (see for example Mintzberg 83, Hammer 93). For instance, the activity of registering a new mortgage contract contributes directly to the goal of selling an X amount of new mortgages in the current year, so for that reason it belongs to the mortgage sales&handling process. On the level of value chain, models such as business score card are relevant in discussions among the people who are responsible for the running the business as a whole (typically the upper management).

At the procedure level, we use procedural models to identify for example how work is routed in a business process. A *procedure* is a collection of activities, rules that govern the order of events in those activities, and rules that identify the responsibilities of people involved, all of which belong together for the sake of realizing a specific commitment among the stakeholders in the context of a business process. For example, the procedure for approving a mortgage loan involves an account manager who is responsible for identifying the loan, the creditworthiness of the debtor, the securities involved and the risks. It may also involve the advice of a loan assessor and a decision made in a loan approval committee. The entire procedure fulfills a commitment of the bank and the prospect to identify all relevant information and take every necessary action to make a timely decision. Wherever we use the term *workflow management*, we mean to identify the support of procedures in a business process by means of computer systems that coordinate the work of people with respect to temporal order on the basis of a procedural model. For example, systems based on Staffware, MQ-workflow, COSA, and Action-Workflow are workflow

Table 1. Example of workflow tools

tool	company
workflow management system:	
Staffware	Staffware
MQSeries Workflow	IBM
COSA	Cosa Solutions BV
Action-Workflow	Action Technologies, Inc.
workflow management without process model:	
Lotus-Notes	Lotus
LinkWorks	Digital
case management :	
FlowER	Pallas Athena BV
Vectus	Hatton Blue
Activity Manager	

systems according to this definition. Systems such as Lotus-Notes and LinkWorks are not covered in this definition, because the process logic is not brought together into one coherent model, but it is distributed over various pieces of application code.
On the activity level, a model defines for example that drafting a mortgage contract involves a text template, a standard assessment of the customer coming from a credit approval application, a check by the assessor of the execution value of the mortgage

object, etc. Technically, an *activity* is an amount of work that can be performed in an uninterrupted span of time under responsibility of a single actor. Drafting a contract for a newly sold mortgage is an example of an activity, to be performed for instance by a mortgage clerk. Activity models are used to generate user interfaces that suit the needs of a specific user who has a specific role in the procedure. Such technology is known as "case management tools", such as FlowER, Vectus, and Activity Manager.

On the service level, software components are available that offer *services*. Nowadays we draw up a model for the service architecture. In a corporate infrastructure, a set of services is made available through the network. Functions such as "print", "run a commercial analysis on this client", "send a confirmation" are examples that are typically implemented as services available to many users. These services are implemented on a layer in which all corporate data persists, usually implemented by means of database systems.

On lower levels we rely on conventional models, such as data modelling and dataflow modelling. CASE tool are developed to a stage in which large parts of the implementations are generated from these models, which avoids mistakes and accellerates the development process.

2 Ignorance, Modeling and Perceived Complexity

If workflow management technology promises to make business processes more flexible, more profitable, and of better quality, how come there are so few organizations able to use this technology successfully? In this section we explore some of the reasons that workflow management has not yet delivered on its promises. The idea of translating these reasons to project risks, has led us to develop the "rainbow approach" for conducting projects that innovate business processes. This model was developed within Anaxagoras Process Architects, a Netherlands based research company which employs scientific methods to make new technology deliver on business goals.

A careful analysis of workflow projects and business process innovations shows ignorance as the main cause of failure. Technological problems alone rarely cause a project-abortion. If a workflow project is staffed by experienced, knowledgable personnel and competent project management, the project stands a fair chance of achieving its technological goals. Most problems occur when the technology is implemented in the organization, because at that moment the organization has to implement their newly designed ways of working. If the organization appears to be unwilling to change its ways, the business process innovation degenerates to an information system innovation.

Ignorance induces complexity. If an organization is unsure about the approach, a typical solution is to assemble a task force to sort it out. If that task force produces reports at a generic level of abstraction, everyone in the organization realizes that something more must be done. An organization that is aware of its lack of knowledge can prevent such scenarios by hiring the appropriate knowledge. An experienced facilitator points out the simplicity of a process, motivates people to do the right thing and prevents endless discussions that do not contribute to results. Provided with the right skills and appropriate experience, an organization needs a year or less to implement an entirely new strategy in an existing situation.

Models do not help to resolve ignorance, but the activity modeling does. For every model we make, irrespective of the type of model (see Figure 1) we try to involve the right people in drawing these models. In a situation where an organization has models readily available, we involve people by scrutinizing the available models. Available models cannot always be understood by the people who will assume responsibility for the effects of those models. If they are to understand the consequences of these models, there is no alternative than to go through a modeling activity with them. In fact, drafting a suitable model appears to be a very effective way to learn about the aspects represented in the model. If "learning by modeling" is facilitated by an experienced consultant, it can also be done in a matter of days (sometimes hours) rather than months.

Practice still suffers from ignorance, though. Last year, october 1998, an insurance company sent us the report of a business analysis, asking whether we could make a concrete proposal to implement the advice given in the report. The report, in which the word workflow occurred 137 times, was being used as a call to tender. Upon closer inspection the insurance company wanted to implement a call center. A workflow engine was projected to control the user interface. All of the functionality, such as registering a damage claim, had to be taken from existing systems, linked to the workflow layer through user dialogue emulation. In terms of Figure 1, the proposal covered the bottom three layers. To use events that occur in the call center for triggering activities elsewhere, which is the basic idea of workflow technology, was notably absent in the report. After reading the report, we concluded that this was a call-center information system rather than a workflow application. The explicit statement that the organization was not willing to reflect on (and change) its way of working, meant that this was not a business process innovation, but a technological innovation.

Tool vendors provide tools and system integrators build the applications, but in the practice of process innovations users are very much on their own to achieve their business goals. An executive at an investment bank felt cheated, even though he got everything that was sold to him: "They promised we could acquire new business with their tools, they implemented the software and left us behind telling us that we can now acquire the new business". Recent research, jointly conducted by the Department of Finance and Anaxagoras Process Architects, confirms that vendors of process tools provide little support in the innovation process, whereas users also expect assistance in working more effectively with those tools ([2]).

3 Innovation Risks

Of all workflow projects conducted in the Netherlands, we estimate that 80% is not a business process innovation, because the related changes in the ways of working are limited to absorbing the effects of using different technology. Projects that are labeled process innovation are mostly front-office renovations or implementations of an electronic archive. In cases where workflow systems are implemented and exposed to daily use, many tools show an immature nature. In one case, bank employees would interpret the status "ready" as a sign not to touch that activity. After all, the computer says it's ready! The intended meaning, however, is that the computer is ready and it is the user's turn to act. A tool that contains several of such issues irritates end users to a point where it wrecks an otherwise sound process innovation, because end users need to do banking rather than wrestle with the idiosyncrasies of tools. Yet, the technology is not the worst risk factor in workflow projects. Some failures can be predicted on the basis of the innovation plan, and are therefore avoidable. Plans have to be carefully crafted to the situation, for the very reason that an organization is prepared to change its working procedures as well as adopt new technology. An approach that works for mortgage sales and handling processes in a cooperative bank may fail radically in a centrally governed bank, even if the mortgage processes of both banks are similar.

By content analysis of twenty different workflow projects, we have developed a set of questions that identify project risks. This set is intended for use during the development of an innovation project plan. The approach has been designed from known and documented failure factors for workflow management innovations.

Our questionnaire is designed by identifying various risk categories, and formulating a few questions that characterize the risk of that category. Thus, we get a fairly complete coverage with approximately 50 questions. Every risk category bears a message for one of the seven infrastructures (Table 2). Notice that the matrix identifies few risks in the technical and information infrastructures. This corresponds to the experience of many workflow experts that the success of workflow projects usually depends on the way in which the business adopts the innovation.

The questionnaire starts with some questions about the *Organization*. In some types of organization (e.g. government) business process innovations are more difficult to bring to a successful end than in others (e.g. insurances). The category *Environment* observes the strategy of an organization and how process innovation fits into that strategy. *Commitment* is important, because a process innovation typically takes more time and effort than an information system innovation. Especially the commitment at higher management levels needs to be given in terms of action (e.g. allocation of budgets) and not just words. The category *Awareness* questions how familiar an organization is with process thinking. If "process speak" is all over the place, but people seem to be occupied mostly with ways to get their own work off their own desks, the awareness is questionable. The *Preliminary investigation* is a risk factor if it does not identify clear business goals (rather than technical goals), if it does not demarcate the scope of the innovations and of the processes to be innovated clearly.

Table 2.

risk category	innovation risks	technical risks	information risks	business risks	support risks	quality risks	social risks
Organization	✓						✓
Environment	✓			✓	✓		✓
Commitment	✓			✓			✓
Awareness				✓		✓	✓
Preliminary investigation	✓	✓	✓	✓	✓	✓	✓
Project definition	✓					✓	✓
Project management	✓			✓			✓
Complexity	✓			✓	✓	✓	✓
Means	✓					✓	
Project team	✓			✓		✓	
Adaptivity				✓	✓		✓
Standards	✓					✓	
User interface				✓			✓
Automation		✓	✓				✓
Hardware		✓					
Software			✓	✓			
System management					✓		✓
Other	✓						

Similarly the *Project definition* can be a risk, which covers the standard set of risks that are valid in all projects. Then we ask questions about how the *Project management* is arranged. As long as there are projects that suffer from flawed project management, this risk factor remains important. The *Complexity* of the innovation is estimated according to the size of the organization, the scope of the innovation and the ambitions to be achieved. Questions about allocation of people and funding are asked in the category *Means*. Similarly, the skills of the *Project team* is one risk that requires questions. The flexibility to absorb changes is assessed in the *Adaptivity* of an organization, which depends mostly on people's attitudes. Neglecting to use available *Standards*, if applicable, is seen as a risk too. Information on the involvement of users in defining the *User interface* appears to deliver valuable information on possible project risks. The level of automation and the familiarity of people with the use of information technology comes in the category *Automation*. The issues *Hardware* and *Software* are treated similarly. In order to assess whether the organization can guarantee the continuity of the innovation, questions are included about *System management*.

4 The Rainbow Approach

At Anaxagoras, we have developed and successfully applied an approach to implement business process innovations. Project experience shows that this approach eliminates a number of significant risks, accellerating the speed of innovation and enhancing the results of workflow projects in the business.

A plethora of relevant aspects in business process innovations require a systematic approach of the innovation project. In practice, one is organizing the conversion of scores of dossiers using cheap labor to scan documents, one is reporting to his management and helping it to decide about starting and stopping subprojects, one is busy motivating automation personnel to visit the shop floor, to link workflow systems with existing system, one has to negotiate with vendors, provide instruction and education, coach and monitor software construction, etcetera. This work is what we call process architecture. If an organization wants to adopt different working practices, the innovation gets too complex to do without a systematic approach. In order to maintain an overview over such innovations, we distinguish seven areas of interest, or infrastructures if you will.

The premises of this approach are:
1. robust innovation by adopting a risk oriented approach
2. fast innovation by smart distribution of project activities over the organization
3. management in control by plotting a decision trajectory in advance
4. user commitment by careful use of involvement techniques
5. design for continuity in the business rather than design for roll-out
6. integral approach with lightweight activities.

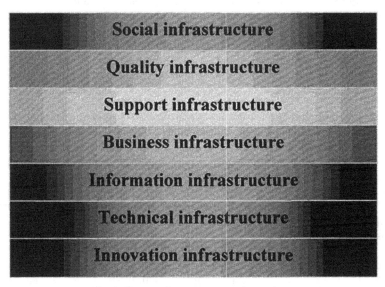

Fig. 2. Seven infrastructures in the rainbow

The rainbow houses every project activity in one of the infrastructures, and each infrastructure is populated differently. The *innovation infrastructure* is the domain of decision makers, project management, and others who bear responsibility for the innovation. It contains project activities such as the making of the project plan and the continuous monitoring of progress. The *technical infrastructure* contains project activitiess related to the basic machinery such as hardware, network and operating systems. The selection of appropriate scanners, network performance prediction, and supplying laptops to account managers who need to work "on the road" are examples of project activities in the technical infrastructure. The *information infrastructure* is designed by ICT specialists, who define the information technology necessary for a successful innovation. Development of software components, linking a workflow engine to the credit management database, installing a case management tool, and configuring the activity structure and process structure for automated support exemplify the information infrastructure. The *business infrastructure* contains the process innovations of primary processes. Redesigning the work structure in the sales department of business credits is typically performed in this infrastructure, staffed mainly by people from that department and facilitated by process architects if the required knowledge is lacking. Project activities in the business infrastructure are always run by people from the core business, because they will have to take mental ownership of the results of the innovation. The *support infrastructure* contains project activities meant to maintain the results of the innovation. Support and maintenance staff will run these activities, focusing on the continuity of the innovation's benefits. They define procedures for introducing and changing automated procedures, erect a competence center, and generally do anything to ensure a permanent effect. The *quality infrastructure* is needed to guarantee the required standards and to minimize business risks. For example, they must sign off on any automated procedure before it becomes fully operational. Controllers, auditors, and quality staff are most likely to populate this infrastructure. The *social infrastructure* contains all project activities that relate to human aspects, such as communication and education. Some of the largest project risks originate from this domain, such as effective communication about the innovation sufficiently early and with the right people in the organization.

5 Results

The rainbow approach has been used in several projects in several different ways. One of them was a smaller bank with approximately 200 staff and $1bn total balance. We were invited in December 1997. The bank had decided to increase customer orientation and reduce cost simultaneously, by doing business in a process oriented way. The rainbow approach was attractive because it minimizes the risk of innovation. After all, banks are primarily interested in providing a reliable financial service to customers on the basis of trust. Innovation may jeopardize the trust relationship with customers. In this situation, the rainbow approach has shown to limit the risks of the innovation.

When we drew the innovation plan as a whole the ambition was to cover all activities of the bank, but in a step-by-step fashion. Together with the bank, we defined results that had to be implemented in the short term: introduction of an electronic archive for all customer related documents (600000) and implementation of business processes in the mortgages segment and industrial finance segment. These steps were small enough for reliable estimation of cost and benefit, but large enough to return on their separate investments. If the total impact cannot be predicted at the start, the stepwise approach provides the required assurance in an organization not sufficiently familiar with business processes, workflow management, and document management. The rainbow approach requires that each project activity is budgeted and accounted for separately, enabling the steering committee to make separate decisions on each of the partial projects. By the end of the summer in 1998, the electronic archive was operational and most of the customer files were available electronically. By that time, the workflow engine was running the industrial finance processes. At the same time, it became clear that the higher management of the bank would change. The new management adopted a strategy of internally reorganizing rather than increasing the commercial power. The rainbow approach allowed the bank to wrap up the ongoing project activities and reap their benefits, since they were designed to return on their own investments. The approach helps to limit loss of investments due to changes in policy.

Momentarily, the rainbow approach is being used in different banks and insurance companies as a means to make process innovations more controllable and to minimize the risks involved in innovations.

6 Conclusion

We have found that the act of modeling is more important than the resulting models. This can explain for example why discussions over the choice of an appropriate modeling technique have in the past not always contributed to the progress of a project. Our findings suggest that the way of working of modelers influences the success of a project much more than the choice of a modeling technique.

The rainbow approach has shown to avoid many of the known pitfalls in business process innovations. Consequently, we are using and refining the method further.

A model can represent the shared understanding by a group of people. Especially if those people have collectively contributed to the model, scrutinized it or used it as part of familiarizing themselves with current procedures, the model "does its job".

The choice of a modeling technique should depend only on which aspects are relevant for achieving the project goals. For example, a discussion around administrative procedures should not be conducted on the basis of a data model or a dataflow model. because these techniques show aspects that are irrelevant in that context. A business procedure model that lets people discuss their work will have more success in this situation. Irrelevant models may even obscure discussions and generate a sense of difficulty in the discussion that is harmful to the attitudes of participants.

Models help to achieve success in a business process innovation if the model represents only relevant aspects that are necessary to know and if the activity of modeling has brought about the appropriate learning process with the right persons. Shared understanding is the key to successful modeling. Having a model by itself does not bring about this shared understanding, as any employee who flips through the "corporate handbook of administrative procedures" will quickly realize. If the process of modeling is essential in creating shared understanding, the modeling technique is meant to keep discussions on the right track and avoid irrelevant sidetracks in the process.

A workflow model represents the procedural aspect of a business process. It has documenting value for auditors in the business, especially in financial organizations where administrative procedures are subject to strict rules. If a workflow engine controls an administrative procedure, adhesion to the procedure in day-to-day operations is guaranteed because the workflow engine has no other option than to follow the procedure as described in the workflow model. This facilitates the work of an auditor, who will pay attention to the process model and the event logs of the workflow engine.

References

1. Dommelen, W.D. van, Joosten, S.M.M., Mol, M.C.J. de, Zwart, H. de: Vergelijkend onderzoek hulpmiddelen beheersing bedrijfsprocessen, EAP, Apeldoorn (1999)
2. Hammer, M., Champy, J.: Reengineering the corporation. Nicolas Brealey Publishing, London (1993)
3. Hee, K. van, Aalst, W. van der: Workflow Management. Modellen, methoden en systemen. Academic Service, Schoonhoven (1997)
4. Joosten, S.: De hype voorbij? Informatie, Vol. 40, December (1998) pp. 8-17
5. Joosten, S.M.M., Schipper, M.: Improving your business: Think processes. Anaxagoras, (1997)
6. Joosten, S., Aussems, G., Duitshof, M., Huffmeijer, R., Mulder, E.: WA-1 an Empirical Study about the Practice of Workflow Management. University of Twente, Enschede (1994)
7. Mintzberg, H.: Structure in fives: designing effective organizations, Prentice Hall, Englewood Cliffs (1983)

The Effects of Workflow Systems on Organizations: A Qualitative Study[1]

Peter Kueng

University of Fribourg, Institute of Informatics, 1700 Fribourg, Switzerland.
Email: peter.kueng@unifr.ch

Abstract. The introduction of new information systems has many organizational, economic, and social effects. It is generally accepted that the implementation of workflow systems (WFSs) cannot be seen just as a technological activity. However, although WFSs has been an important technology for almost a decade, there is still a lack of empirical data regarding its effects. Therefore, the field is open to speculation. For example: while one community believes that WFSs will disburden office workers from simple routine tasks, another community argues that WFSs would lead to monotonous 'chain production'. What are the main findings of the qualitative study? Through the use of WFSs the quality of output of business processes increased: documents became more uniform since processes were under closer control. The implementation of WFS led to modifications in the processes; however, business process reengineering was not carried out in any of the cases analyzed. Additionally the study revealed that overall job satisfaction was influenced positively. Interestingly, for the lower management WFSs led to a dis- empowerment. From an economic point of view it may be interesting that the use of WFSs led to a significant reduction in cycle time and an increase in productivity. Overall it can be said that the positive effects of WFSs outbalanced the negative effects.

1 Introduction

Today it is generally accepted that business processes are the basic unit of any organization. Hence, managers are confronted with the question: how should the business processes be designed and supported through information technology (IT) so that they are most effective? In the last few years, many researchers and IT suppliers have emphasized that workflow systems (WFS) should play an important role in the context of business process reengineering (BPR) and business process management. The benefits mentioned on the vendor side were mainly the following: (a) shorter cycle time – primarily achieved through a reduction of queuing time and through electronic communication; (b) faster and more accurate feedback regarding the state

---

[1] A previous version of this paper was presented on the 5th European Conference on the Evaluation of Information Technology; cf. Kueng (1998).

W. van der Aalst et al. (Eds.): Business Process Management, LNCS 1806, pp 301-316, 2000
© Springer-Verlag Berlin Heidelberg 2000

of business cases; (c) better responsiveness to customers. On the other hand, more skeptical arguments were raised by employees (the potential users of the workflow systems) and work psychologists. They fear that workflow systems might lead to a mechanical approach to office work where man is seen as an exchangeable resource (like a machine) and not as a human being. Thus, jobs would become highly specialized, fragmented and not very meaningful to the employee. A second issue has been monitoring and violation of privacy. Since workflow systems offer capabilities for collecting masses of information about handling of documents and electronic transactions (e.g. who made what when, how much, in what quality) such anxiety is understandable. Unfortunately there is very little published information regarding the impact of workflow systems on organizational and human aspects.

In short, a 'workflow system' is an IT system that supports office workers with the execution, co-ordination, and control of workflow instances. According to the Workflow Management Coalition, a workflow system can be described as "a system that defines, creates and manages the execution of workflows through the use of software, running on one or more workflow engines, which is able to interpret the process definition, interact with workflow participants and, where required, invoke the use of IT tools and applications." (WfMC, 1999). Therefore, a workflow system comprises a workflow engine (sometimes referred to as workflow management system) plus one or several applications based on the workflow engine.

Workflow systems are able to support business processes if they meet one or several of the following criteria: the business process is clearly structured and defined, the process is executed repeatedly or even frequently, the process involves several organizational roles, the process requires checking and control mechanisms that are time-consuming if done manually, input and output of the business can be stored electronically (cf. Baresi et al. 99, p. 23).

In the beginning of the 90s, workflow systems represented – for many people – the new approach to making white-collar work more efficient. "Computer industry analysts tout workflow as the «technology of the 1990s» and predict that workflow will become part of all office applications in the next decade" (Abott & Sarin, 1994, p. 113). An analysis of the current level of deployment of workflow systems suggests that the above statement was overly optimistic. Nevertheless, many companies are considering support of their full or semi-structured business processes by a workflow system. In order to decide whether the implementation of such a system would be fruitful, empirically based results are useful. As long as it is not known how behavior and working practices of organizations are affected through the use of workflow systems, the field is open to speculation and it will be hard to discuss the matter objectively. The aim of this empirical study is to provide IT managers with information to assess the appropriateness of a workflow system in their company and to take corrective action in order to reduce potential negative effects.

The purpose of this article is to provide an empirically based examination of the manifold effects of workflow systems. In section 2, an overview regarding state-of-the-art on ex-post evaluations is given. Section 3 describes the research design. In section 4, the main findings are presented in the form of eight hypotheses. Finally, the chosen approach is critically reviewed in section 5 and conclusions are outlined in section 6.

2 Ex-post Evaluations: An Overview

According to Smithson & Hirschheim (1998, p. 161), evaluations can be performed at five different levels: (1) macro level, e.g. general impact of IT on productivity; (2) sector level, e.g. impact of factory automation on manufacturing industry; (3) firm level, e.g. impact of a firm's IS on performance; (4) application level, e.g. impact of a particular application; (5) stakeholder level, e.g. impact of IT on a certain group of users.

From a conceptual point of view it is important to distinguish between pre-investment and post-investment evaluation, cf. Figure 1. In the first mode, evaluation is carried out prior to an investment (ex-ante). In the second mode, the evaluation is performed after the investment has taken place (ex-post).

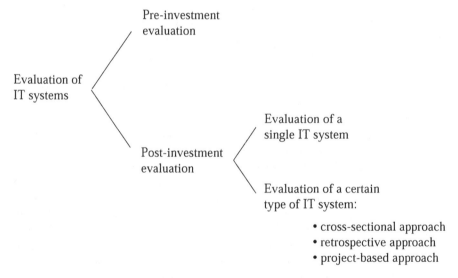

Figure 1. Types of IT evaluations

Pre-investment evaluations are usually executed on a project basis. In that case, prior to an investment, the IT manager wants to identify financial benefits and business opportunities as well as costs and potential risks of a new, particular IT system (Willcocks & Lester, 1994). To perform pre-investment evaluations various tools exists. Traditional, financially-based tools are for example: Return on investment (ROI), internal rate of return (IRR), net present value (NPV). To assess non-financial aspects, the number of instruments is not overwhelming. One of the most popular is the 'value and risk analysis', a part of the Information Economics approach proposed by Parker & Benson (1988, pp. 177). Another useful approach – encompassing the three dimensions project, system, and environment – has been presented by Boloix & Robillard (1995).

Post-investment evaluations (sometimes referred to as post-implementation reviews, PIRs) aim to examine the results achieved. The first option of a post-investment evaluation refers to a single, particular IT system put in place by an enterprise. The question to be answered is the following: "How effective towards goal fulfillment was the implementation of an IT system (say Miracle V) in the company xyz?" The second option seeks to assess a certain category of IT systems that are being used by various enterprises. The objects of such an ex-post evaluation are all types of computer-based information systems such as: Accounting information systems, executive information systems, decision support systems, enterprise resource planning systems, computer-aided software engineering tools, workflow systems, etc. The aim of this second ex-post evaluation approach is to find 'generally valid' results usable by a broader audience.

As indicated in the title of this article, the evaluation is applied to workflow systems – a certain category of IT systems. In that context, two questions are of primary interest: (1) "Was it beneficial to invest in workflow technology?" (2) "What were the main effects of workflow systems encountered in enterprises already using this technology?" In this paper, the second question is addressed.

In order to assess the effects of workflow systems ex-post, three approaches exist. The cross-sectional approach, the retrospective approach, and the project-based approach.

1 **The cross-sectional approach** involves the comparison of two groups of enterprises, those using workflow systems and those not using workflow systems. Therefore, two sets of enterprises are asked to rate performance regarding financial and non-financial criteria. Higher performance ratings from WFS-applying enterprises would stand for a positive impact of workflow systems (cf. Coupe & Onodu, 1997, p. 16). A central element of this approach is that the performance-relevant criteria are given in detail and cannot be determined by the interviewees.

2 **The retrospective approach** utilizes just a single set of enterprises, namely those using workflow systems. In this method each questioned person compares the organizational performance and behavior before and after the implementation of the workflow system (cf. Coupe & Onodu, 1997, p. 16). Based on a subjective before/after comparison, he or she should be able to identify significant effects caused by the workflow system. In contrast to the cross-sectional method, there are no detailed criteria given upon the before/after comparison.

3 **The project-based approach** is based on the assumption that the effects produced by a workflow system are predominantly determined by the goals a company wants to achieve. Applying this approach could mean that a set of enterprise-specific PIRs were collected and analyzed.

What are the main strengths and drawbacks of each approach? The *cross-sectional method* employs uniform criteria for all participating enterprises. This is both an advantage and a disadvantage. On the one hand, we get some kind of guarantee that we are not, metaphorically speaking, comparing apples with oranges. On the other hand, there is a genuine risk that the findings will be influenced by the interviewer since the criteria upon which the comparison is made are given in detail. In other words, the spectrum of potential effects is narrowed externally. Since little information is available regarding the effects of workflow systems, the cross-sectional approach is rather inappropriate. Is the *retrospective method* more suitable? A major strength of this approach is that the 'performance metrics' are not pre-defined by the investigators. It gives the informants the freedom to state aspects ('performance metrics') that they regard as important. The main drawback of the retrospective method is that it relies on the informants' memory. Additionally, the problem of labor turnover complicates the application. Despite these limitations, the retrospective method was favored in our study. The *project-based approach* was not taken into account since it would have been difficult to find companies that carried out comprehensive (i.e. considering both financial and non-financial aspects) post-implementation reviews on workflow projects. On the one hand, organizations already using workflow systems are still not very numerous (Kueng, 1997), on the other hand there is evidence that organizations "… continue to place low emphasis on post-implementation audits" (Miller, 1997, p. 53).

3 Research Design

Today, organizations are seen as complex systems encompassing technical and non-technical components. A classical and very useful view has been proposed by Leavitt (1965). In his perspective four interacting variables come into play: task (the production of goods and services), actors, structure (systems of communication, authority, workflow), and – finally – technology; cf. Figure 2.

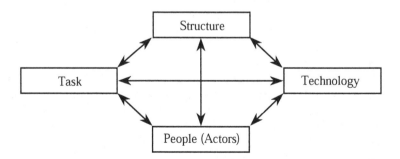

Figure 2. The four interacting variables in an organization (taken from Leavitt, 1965)

As these four components are highly interactive, the introduction of new technology "may cause changes in structure (e.g. in the communication system or decision map of the organization), changes in actors (their numbers, skills, attitudes, and activities), and changes in performance or even definition of tasks since some tasks may now become feasible of accomplishment for the first time, and others may become unnecessary."(Leavitt, 1965, p. 1145).

Essentially, this statement formed the basis of the empirical study reported here. The research design was determined by the simple purpose of finding out what kind of impact the use of a workflow system induces. The trilogy 'task', 'structure', and 'people' seemed appropriate – as it is broad and encompasses the key elements – in order to elicit the main effects of workflow systems.

Since there are few, if any, reports that analyze the impact of workflow systems in its broad sense, a two-phased approach was adopted. Phase 1: Based on a review of literature, a preliminary study was carried out. The questions in mind when contacting the informants were very broad, such as: "Did you get positive feedback from the workflow end-user?" This initial phase helped to broaden the spectrum of effects of workflow systems. Phase 2: Based on the findings of the preliminary study, a more focused principal study was designed.

In the *preliminary study*, data was gathered through interviews and recorded by hand-written notices. Eight people (mainly departmental managers and project leaders) working in eight different enterprises were interviewed face-to-face or by telephone. Each interview lasted between 30 minutes and 1 hour. The interviews were conducted in February 1997. The interview manual was little focused and contained questions about positive and negative experiences and effects of the workflow system regarding organizational structures and employees' activities and motivation. The findings were elicited through a qualitative content analysis.

The purpose of the *principal study* was to gain a deeper understanding of the changes caused by workflow systems as well as more reliable findings, i.e. better funded hypotheses. As in the preliminary study, only enterprises applying workflow systems in the operational state were included. Companies using workflow systems in a pre-operational or pilot phase were not considered in the study. Thus, all enterprises surveyed used workflow systems for more than one year. Overall, eight people working in five different companies were interviewed. One of the five companies was the same as in the preliminary study; the person interviewed was, however, not the same. The face-to-face interviews were conducted from November 1997 to January 1998. It should be noted in passing that the interviewer of the preliminary study was the author of this paper whereas the interviewer of the principal study was a student doing his diploma work and supervised by the author. As in the preliminary study, the interviewees were department managers and former workflow project leaders. Each interview lasted approximately two hours and was recorded on audiotape to be subsequently transcribed. Data analysis was done by qualitative content analysis wherein the interviewer and the interpreter were not identical. The five enterprises examined in the main study belong to the following industries: financial service, energy engineering, insurance (life), insurance (life and non-life), and pension fund.

The workflow systems utilized by the five companies were the following products: Workflow (by CSE), Lotus Notes (by Notes), and VisualWorkFlow (by FileNet).

4 The Main Findings

The findings of the preliminary and principal studies comprise many different facets. Selected aspects of the preliminary study were presented in Kueng (1997). This paper presents the main findings of the overall study in the form of eight hypotheses.

Hypothesis 1: Workflow systems increase the quality of the output produced

All interviewees agreed that the overall quality of the output of the business process increased through the support of a workflow system. As the approach of the empirical study was mainly qualitative, it is not possible to report the quality improvement in quantitative terms. However, there is evidence for hypothesis 1. The interviewees reported that information processing and the documents produced both became more uniform (at a higher level), and the potential for non-conformances declined. Using the words of the SPC community (Juran & Gryna, 1993, p. 380), business processes became more stable, and process variation declined. This, in turn, led to better prediction of process behavior. Business processes supported by workflow systems were under control (in comparison to the pre-workflow phase).

Why has the quality of the output increased? The informants mentioned three aspects. First, the implementation of a workflow system required a clear documentation of the processes; it would not have been possible otherwise to create the workflow model executed by the workflow system. Therefore, the process-related know-how (i.e. procedures and activities) was no longer the property of just a few collaborators; it had become common property shared by many. Secondly, the main rules regarding the execution of business processes were put into software; this led to the effect that 'identical' workflow instances are treated 'identically'. In other words, the degree of individual interpretation declined. Thirdly, through the use of workflow systems the flow of work has become more transparent. Each office worker (actor) is aware of the source of the documents received and the sink (consumer) into which the results are fed. Thus, employees are more aware of the responsibility upon them, and they give – consciously or not – more attention to quality aspects of their work.

To exemplify the first hypothesis, four statements, collected during the interviews, are given:
1 "The system forces people to work in a manner which has been previously defined. The system does not permit any other manipulations."
2 "The workflow system ensures that every working step (from A to Z) of a business case takes place."
3 "Without this system, I can bring four (identical) dossiers to four offices and I get four different results."

4 "The processing of a certain workflow instance no longer depends on one single person who might eventually put the needed documents in a drawer where they are not accessible by others."

Hypothesis 2: Workflow systems lead to modified processes

Within the business process reengineering (BPR) community there is a broad consensus that business processes must be reengineered prior to the implementation of IT systems, otherwise the full potential of automation cannot be realized (Hammer & Champy, 1993). There is also an accord that workflow systems are mainly useful for structured procedural processes. This raises the question of whether the companies have redesigned the dedicated processes in order to gain a stronger, unambiguous structure and a better overall performance.

The investigation showed that none of the participating enterprises extensively reengineered their processes prior to its workflow-based 'automation'. Their approach was to apply workflow systems to those processes that were already well structured. The alternative, and equally reasonable, approach of structuring a previously unstructured process in order to support it by a workflow system was not applied in the cases we analyzed. However, even though no BPR took place in advance, the implementation of workflow systems led to some differences of the processes as they were before and after. The reasons were threefold. First, the application of workflow technology required new, additional activities (e.g. scanning) whilst others became useless. Hence, a process modification was necessary. Second, the workflow system did not offer the necessary functionality to transform the business process model into a workflow model. Third, to achieve the project goals (e.g. a reduction of cycle time), a process redesign on a rather low level was required. From this it follows that process reorganization on one hand and implementation of workflow systems on the other were done concurrently.

To illustrate the extent, to which processes were modified, three statements are listed:
1 "The manual activities regarding information collection and distribution have been taken over the workflow system."
2 "Now, office workers mostly sit in front of a screen. 'Paper handling' is done electronically."
3 "The workflow has been implemented according to the process definitions created by the ISO 9000 project."

Hypothesis 3: Workflow systems increase overall job satisfaction

As mentioned in the introduction, there is a lot of speculation about the effects of workflow systems on employee job satisfaction. The first question is what is job satisfaction? According to Spector, job satisfaction is "how people feel about their jobs and different aspects of their jobs. It is the extent to which people like (satisfaction) or dislike (dissatisfaction) their jobs" (1997, p. 2). In order to assess job satisfaction, various facets should be measured, e.g.: communication, co-workers, job conditions, nature of the work, operating procedures, pay, personal growth, supervision, recognition, etc. (Spector, 1997).

It is obvious from this list that the use of a workflow system can affect job satisfaction only partially. The purpose of our study was not to assess job satisfaction holistically in all its details, but to focus on those facets that might be influenced by the application of a new IT system. It was a pragmatic attempt to gather experiences on the practical effects of workflow systems on the quality of employees' jobs.

According to the informants, the satisfaction and motivation of employees using a workflow system has increased. In general, feedback and comments from the employees was positive. If it was negative (which was rather rare) they complained about technical matters like response time or inappropriate layouts. In particular, the workflow users appreciated the user-friendly interfaces (in comparison to the previous mainframe-based applications), the fact that they no longer needed to manually transfer data from one system to another, and the faster service they could offer internal and external customers. They also emphasized that business process-internal and cross-process communication has improved in its speed and clarity. Of the negative effects, the issue that was mentioned most often was physical strain caused by more intensive screen gazing. Overall, however, employees are more satisfied since workflow systems have been adopted.

A few statements illustrate how workflow systems are perceived regarding job satisfaction:
1 "Today, nobody would do his job without the workflow system."
2 "Previously we had to enter the same data into four or five different systems – this has gone."
3 "In the past, the most difficult business cases had to be processed by the very best employees; using a workflow system, these business cases can now be processed by mediocre employees."

Hypothesis 4: Workflow systems do not lead to greater responsibility for the employees

In hypothesis 2 it was mentioned that the implementation of workflow systems led to modified processes. From this perspective the question is whether the processes were modified in such a manner that employees had to or could take on more responsibility and competencies (in the sense of authorization). The analysis of the interviews indicates that the degree of responsibility and competencies remained mainly unaltered. In several instances, the use of a workflow system led to job enlargement; i.e. the employees acquired new skills and took on additional tasks. However, the impact of workflow systems and process modification respectively was not so deep that it affected the level of responsibility of people doing the operational work in a significant way.

It was noticeable that often the respondents expressed themselves rather vaguely, and they usually hesitated to confirm or reject non-ambiguous statements. One put it in the following way: "The competencies remained the same. We are still hierarchically organized."

Hypothesis 5: On one hand workflow systems make interesting jobs even more interesting, on the other they make uninteresting jobs monotonous

The question of whether employees' jobs became more interesting (demanding, challenging) after a workflow system was implemented was answered very differently and inconsistently. Several interviewees emphasized that the workflow system disburdens the actors of non-intellectual working steps. They also mentioned that the proportion of non-value-adding activities (e.g. control activities) has declined. In contrast, others mentioned that the jobs became more monotonous. Two statements may illustrate these inconsistent views:

1 "The uninteresting routine work has gone. In general, work became more challenging."
2 "Jobs became more monotonous. The system forces the employees to work strictly according to the process definition. Through the use of the workflow system, we now have some kind of 'chain production' in the office."

How can these different perceptions be explained? What are the causes of the different viewpoints? Workflow systems are good at routine work such as collecting data from different sources, checking consistency of a well structured document, distribution of reports to a pool of people, routing of certain information to the right person, etc. For employees executing intellectual and demanding tasks, routine work is regarded as something dispensable, which can be automated. This is different to those office workers who are doing less demanding and sometimes monotonous tasks. They may regard the execution of tasks like 'data collection' and 'data distribution' as a pleasant and enjoyable change.

Hypothesis 6: Workflow systems lead to a dis-empowerment for the lower management

What are the tasks of lower managers? It is obvious that they cannot be identified precisely. However, even a short inspection shows that lower managers are partially engaged in tasks such as monitoring work in progress or assigning work (business cases) to office workers and teams. Potential questions a manager wants to answer include the following: What is the current status of a certain order or customer request? Which office worker should proceed business case xyz? What is the actual backlog and workload? It is apparent from this that some managerial tasks can be formalized and incorporated into an executable model and then performed by a workflow system.

In our empirical study we found that the lower management of the IT departments were more involved in the workflow projects than the lower managers of the operational business units where the workflow systems were being applied. Additionally, we found that the tasks of the lower management were only marginally embedded into the automated workflow. Thus it is not surprising that the implementation of a workflow system leads to the effect that the job of lower managers is regarded as less important (in comparison to the pre-workflow era) and sometimes even dispensable.

The following statements show how two informants put it:

1 "A shift in power towards the IS department takes place."
2 "Managers use primarily the archiving functionality, and they are not fully integrated in the operational workflow."

It is yet not clear what role lower management should play in an organization where processes are being substantially supported through workflow systems. While one group argues that the activities of lower managers should be taken into consideration as much as possible (i.e. embedded into the 'automated process'), an alternative view argues that workflow systems make lower managers dispensable since their original work is, too a large extent, programmable.

Hypothesis 7: Workflow systems facilitate the modification of processes

Business processes are embedded into an environment where changes and unforeseen events occur: The services desired by the customers alter, new regulations may be imposed, new tools become available, new competitors appear, etc. These few examples show that business processes and the underlying workflow models have to be modified and improved continuously. This raises the question whether workflow systems act as a facilitator or, on the contrary, as an inhibitor regarding ease of process modification.

In the enterprises considered, workflow systems had a positive impact on the ease of modification of processes. First, through the use of workflow systems, modifications in process definitions could be carried out more quickly. This is due to the fact that a considerable part of the processes was defined using a computer-based information system. Thus process definition was no longer carried out on several sheet of papers or worse in the heads of a few collaborators! Secondly, it was emphasized that modifications were put into practice (i.e. the employees act upon the new process definition) more rapidly. This was partly because the process was automated (i.e. the application becomes compulsory), and partly because the process of informing employees was much faster than before.

In enterprises where workflow systems were deployed, process models and documentation have become more influential. In these firms it is generally accepted, that the operational processes – even if they are not fully described by a workflow system – have to be in line with the process model. This shift in thinking helps to modify processes in a co-ordinated manner, and in turn leads to a faster process conversion, implementation, and institutionalization. One interviewee described the effect of workflow systems regarding the modification of processes as follows: "In the past, if an employee didn't like a new instruction, he worked according to the old one. Using the workflow system this is no longer possible."

Hypothesis 8: Workflow systems increase productivity by 50 percent

The use of workflow systems has led to a significant reduction in cycle time. This was achieved through task automation, a decrease in the manual exchange of information between human actors, a reduction in the proportion of rework (cf. hypothesis 1), and clarification of the processes which led to a better informed staff. Interestingly the benefits of speedier workflows were rarely attributed to the possibility, offered by many workflow systems, of executing activities concurrently.

All informants emphasized that business cases could be carried out faster since they are supported by a workflow system. Some statements illustrate the effects encountered by enterprises:

1 "Cycle time has been reduced by 40 percent."
2 "The customer gets his confirmation or whatever he needs within a shorter period than previously."
3 "Productivity (number of workflow instances carried out by an employee) has doubled."
4 "The volume of work has quadrupled while the number of employees has remained the same."
5 "Productivity has increased whereas the costs remained unaltered."

The statements regarding the rise in productivity attained through workflow systems are impressive. However, a closer inspection showed that the performance measures were not always taken with the necessary accuracy. For example it turned out that the processes were defined quite narrowly. In one instance, this led to the effect that the activity of 'scanning incoming mails' was not considered part of the business process. Another shortcoming was that the length of time during which performance measures were taken was short. Nevertheless, it can be concluded that workflow systems lead to a significant gain in productivity. As it was not the intention of this study to explore financial effects in detail, it is not clear whether the overall financial effect was positive. However, there is some evidence that the total cost of process execution declined.

5 Critique of the Chosen Approach

The section above gives the impression that the various effects (cf. hypothesis 1 to 8) stem solely from the use of workflow systems. Taking a positivist's world view (cf. Taylor & Bogdan, 1998), one assumes so-called 'cause/effect relationships' where a distinction between *independent* and *dependent* variables is made.[2] Applied in our domain of interest, the independent variable (i.e. the thing doing the influencing) is 'the use of a workflow system (boolean)'; dependent variables (i.e. the things being influenced) are 'the speed of execution of modifications on business processes', 'the degree of job satisfaction', etc.

However, the four variables (IT system, people, task, and structure) are highly interdependent – as stressed by Leavitt (1965) – and the effects of a new IT system are therefore the result of an interplay between many technical and non-technical, static and dynamic factors. Hence, the implementation of a workflow system may be regarded as *one* possible cause that led to a given effect. Other causes – that might lead to the same effect – may include actions on the process level (e.g. a new process manager), or actions on the enterprise level such as the introduction of a company-wide TQM programme; cf. left hand side of Figure 3. Additionally there may exist causes (influences) that are beyond the control of the enterprise, such as an increasing competition among customers and suppliers. In other words, there are many IT-related and non IT-related factors that can lead to a certain effect. It is obvious that the first-order cause cannot always be identified clearly. The findings are based on the assumption that the informants were able to distinguish between effects caused by the implementation of a workflow system and those induced by other factors.

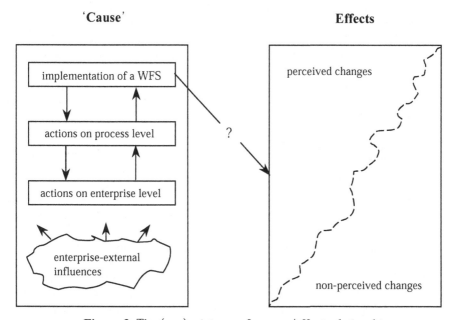

Figure 3. The (non)existence of a cause/effect relationship

There is a further aspect to keep in mind while assessing the hypotheses above. As shown in Figure 3, effects caused by the implementation of a workflow system belong to two classes: (1) perceived changes, and (2) non-perceived changes. The qualitative study reported here is based on the retrospective approach wherein the informants compared the situation before and after the implementation of the workflow system. It is obvious that interviewee sensitivity varies, i.e. while a certain change or effect (e.g. less face-to-face communication caused through the implementation of a workflow system) is perceived by one person, it may not be perceived by another. The right hand side of Figure 3 illustrates that only perceived changes (effects) were taken into consideration. The application of another evaluation approach (e.g. observational studies) could offer more insights regarding non-perceived changes.

6 Conclusions

A workflow system can be seen as a component of an information system which is embedded in a particular technical and social environment. Since the entire system evolves over time, and since the technical and non-technical components interact, it is difficult to isolate the factors that produce a certain effect. Despite these limitations, some conclusions can be drawn.

From a business perspective there is evidence that the implementation and use of a workflow system increases the competitiveness of the supported business process. In fact, major parameters such as throughput, cycle time, speed of communication, process variation and productivity improved. Due to the fact that workflow systems are not always used in crucial, core business processes, these improvements do not necessarily lead to a significant increase in the overall organizational performance.

Through the use of workflow systems, jobs become more structured and more routine. Additionally, individuals are forced to stay within given limits. Since a larger proportion of work is programmed, it becomes harder to exercise and integrate creativity and ingenuity. Using the vocabulary of Leavitt and Whisler (1958, p. 44) workflow systems lead – to a certain extent – to a depersonalization of relationships. To counterbalance such effects, organizational measures can be taken (e.g. job rotation, a redefinition of actors' roles).

Workflow systems have been criticized in the literature because of their inflexibility, i.e. their tendency to prescribe tasks and task sequencing quite rigidly (cf. Ellis & Wainer, 1994, p. 73). That aspect was not seen as a serious problem by the interviewees. This 'contradiction' (cf. hypothesis 7) may be explained by the fact that in this study the business processes supported by a workflow system did not belong to a category of office processes that are modified very frequently. However, better support of ad-hoc changes and exception handling would enlarge the potential of workflow applications considerably.

Overall, the findings of the empirical study show clearly that the introduction of a workflow system should be driven by a business and organizational perspective. This means, for example, that a purely activity-based modeling approach is not suitable.

Workflow design should be extended towards job design or even organizational design. This implies that people outside of the IT department have to play an active role from the very beginning of a workflow project. They can bring in an actor-centered perspective (clerical or managerial level) and supply the process goals sought by the company. Using the terminology of Leavitt (1965), by the act of implementing a workflow system, enterprises should re-balance the diamond "technology – task – people – structure".

Acknowledgement

I would like to thank the enterprises which participated in the empirical study. Special thanks are extended to Andy Meier who collected empirical data needed for the principal study.

7 References

Abott, Kenneth; Sarin, Sunil: Experiences with Workflow Management – Issues for the Next Generation. In: Proceedings of the Conference on Computer Supported Cooperative Work, 22-26 October 1994, Chapel Hill, USA, ACM press, pp. 113-120.

Baresi, Luciano et al.: WIDE Workflow Development Methodology. In: Proceedings of the International Joint Conference on Work Activities Coordination and Collaboration; edited by D. Georgakopoulos et al., San Francisco, 22-25 February 1999, pp. 19-28.

Bolloix, Germinal; Robillard, Pierre: A Software System Evaluation Framework. IEEE Computer, Vol. 28, No. 12 (December 1995), pp. 17-26.

Britt, David: A Conceptual Introduction to Modelling – Qualitative and Quantitative Perspectives. Lawrence Erlbaum Associates, Mahwah NJ, USA, 1997.

Coupe, Tim; Onodu, Nnadi: Evaluating the impact of CASE – an empirical comparison of retrospective and cross-sectional survey approaches. European Journal of Information Systems, Vol. 6, No. 1 (March 1997), pp. 15-24.

Ellis, Clarence; Wainer, Jacques: Goal-based models of collaboration. Collaborative Computing, Vol. 1, No. 1 (March 1994), pp. 61-86.

Hammer, Michael; Champy, James: Reengineering the Corporation – A Manifesto for Business Revolution. Nicholas Brealey Publishing, London, 1993.

Juran, Joseph; Gryna, Frank: Quality Planning and Analysis – From Product Development through Use, McGraw-Hill, New York, 1993.

Kueng, Peter: Workflow Management Systems – still few operational systems. ACM SIGGROUP Bulletin, Vol. 18, No. 3 (December 1997), pp. 32-34.

Kueng, Peter: Impact of Workflow Systems on People, Task, and Structure: a post-implementation evaluation. In: Proceedings of the 5th European Conference on the Evaluation of Information Technology; edited by A. Brown and D. Remenyi, Reading, UK, 27 November 1998, pp. 67-75.

Leavitt, Harold: Applied Organizational Change in Industry – Structural, Technological and Humanistic Approaches. In: J. March (Ed.): Handbook of Organizations. Rand McNally, Chicago, 1965, pp. 1144-1170.

Leavitt, Harold; Whisler, Thomas: Management in the 1980's. Harvard Business Review, Vol. 36, No. 1 (Nov/Dec 1958), pp. 41-48.

Miller, Keith; Dunn, Dennis: Post-implementation of information systems/technology – a survey of UK practice. Proceedings of the 4th European Conference on the Evaluation of Information Technology, edited by E. Berghout and D. Remenyi, Delft, 30-31 October 1997, pp. 47-55.

Parker, Marilyn; Benson, Robert: Information Economics – Linking Business Performance to Information Technology. Prentice-Hall, Englewood Cliffs NJ, 1998.

Smithson, Steve; Hirschheim, Rudy: Analysing information systems evaluation – another look at an old problem. European Journal of Information Systems. Vol. 7, No. 3 (September 1998), pp. 158-174.

Spector, Paul: Job satisfaction – Application, assessment, causes, and consequences. Sage Publications, Thousand Oaks, CA, USA, 1997.

Taylor, Steven; Bogdan, Robert: Introduction to Qualitative Research Methods. John Wiley & Sons, New York, 1998.

Willcocks, Leslie; Lester, Stephanie: Evaluating the feasibility of information systems investments – recent UK evidence and new approaches. In: L. Willcocks (Ed.): Information Management – The evaluation of information management systems. Chapman & Hall, London, 1994, pp. 49-80.

WfMC: The Workflow Management Coalition Specification: Terminology & Glossary. Document Number WFMC-TC-1011, Document Status: Issue 3.0, February 1999; available: http://www.aiim.org/wfmc/standards/docs.htm, accessed 15 September 1999.

On the Practical Relevance of an Integrated Workflow Management System - Results of an Empirical Study

Martin Meyer

Institute of Information Systems, Information Engineering Research Group, University of
Bern, Engehaldenstrasse 8, CH-3012 Bern, Switzerland
meyer@ie.iwi.unibe.ch

Abstract. The implementation of the integrated standard software SAP R/3 has
been fully or partially completed in many Swiss companies. Many of these
companies are now initiating follow-up projects with the aim of expanding their
use of SAP R/3. One possible area that is frequently mentioned in this context
is the use of workflow management systems (WfMS). The Information
Engineering Research Group of the Institute of Information Systems, University
of Bern, therefore conducted an empirical study among Swiss R/3 users at the
end of 1997, with the aim of obtaining a better assessment of the importance
and current status of workflow management, particularly on the basis of SAP
R/3. This survey endeavors to summarize the findings obtained with SAP
Business Workflow (SAP BWF) to date, in order to provide some ideas for
application scenarios and information about potential advantages and
disadvantages.

1   Introduction

More and more companies are attempting to improve their competitive prospects by
designing their organizational structure along flexible and process-oriented lines.
Whereas traditional organizational theory concentrated mainly on structural
organization, today there is a visible trend toward process organization.[1] The focus is
therefore on a company's process orientation. Following on from the statement
attributed to Chandler, that "structure follows strategy", the idea that "process follows
strategy" is also being discussed.[2] Current management concepts, such as Business
Process Reengineering (BPR), Total Quality Management (TQM) or Lean
Management, have been used in recent years as catalysts for the changeover to a
process organization.

This paradigm shift in organizational structure is also leading to fundamentally
changed requirements for the conversion of operational processes in a company's
information systems.[3] The issue of how individual business processes can be
adequately supported by information technology is raised. The use of *workflow
management systems* presents itself as the solution for this problem. This type of

---

[1] Cf. Nippa/Picot (1995), p. 14 ff.
[2] Cf. Osterloh/Frost (1996), p. 7.
[3] Cf. Österle (1996).

W. van der Aalst et al. (Eds.): Business Process Management, LNCS 1806, pp 317-327, 2000

system presents a technology for converting operational processes in the information systems of a company.[4] WfMS are regarded as tools for the efficient execution of business processes, which also allow the continuous evolution of processes.[5]

In this context, this paper attempts to expand on existing market studies[6], investigations[7] and progress reports[8], and to throw light upon the importance of workflow management in Swiss companies and the potential concealed behind the workflow concept. It also establishes how the frequently argued advantages and disadvantages of WfMS by (potential) users are assessed.

First, the design of the empirical study conducted at the Institute of Information Systems is presented in Section 2. A brief description of SAP Business Workflow (SAP BWF) is given in Section 3. Selected results from the study are then described in Section 4.

2   Design of the Empirical Study

The study presented in this paper is mainly descriptive in character. The workflow components of the R/3 system were deliberately chosen as the object of investigation. The reasons are: Firstly, this tool is supplied with the basic system as a standard component, and is therefore automatically available with every R/3 installation. Secondly, the investigations and studies into various aspects of the R/3 system conducted by the Institute of Information Systems of the University of Bern[9] are continued and expanded.

To date (end 1997), over 600 R/3 installations have been implemented in Switzerland. 204 companies were selected for this survey, and they were sent a four-page questionnaire at the end of 1997. Of the 204 questionnaires sent, 90 were returned. 76 of these could be evaluated. The response rate actually achieved was therefore more than 37%. The following subject areas were covered by the survey:

- **Corporate profile:** industry sector, number of employees in the company, number of employees in the R/3 environment.
- **Workflow management:** evaluation of workflow management, necessity of workflow management, importance of WfMS, knowledge of workflow management in companies.
- **SAP BWF:** existing use, planned projects, types of workflow applications, collaboration with consulting companies, knowledge in companies, importance of SAP BWF, potential areas of application, potential advantages and disadvantages.

---

[4] Cf. Becker/Vogler (1997), p. 2.

[5] Cf. Georgakopoulos/Hornick/Sheth (1995); Vogler/Jablonski (1998), p. 2.

[6] Cf. Erdl/Schönecker (1993); Derungs/Vogler/Österle (1995); Weiss/Krcmar (1996); Endl et al. (1997); Petrovic/Altenhofen (1998).

[7] Cf. Chroust/Bergsmann (1995).

[8] Cf. Galler/Scheer/Peter (1995); Meyer/Pfahrer (1997).

[9] Cf. e.g. Gerber/Knolmayer (1996); Strebi (1996); Knolmayer/von Arb/Zimmerli (1997); Meyer (1997); Meyer/Pfahrer (1997); von Arb (1997).

3   SAP Business Workflow (Brief Description)

With the workflow component available for the first time in Release 3.0 of the R/3 system, SAP AG provides a tool which enables operational procedures to be electronically processed in a standardized way.[10] The customized operation of business processes can thus be coordinated across all applications and workstations.

Workflow Management Systems may be classified as *usage-oriented, technically-oriented* or *origin-oriented*. For this purpose SAP BWF may be classified with regard to its origin: the original source of this workflow component is the R/3 system. SAP BWF thus belongs to the "derivative"[11] workflow management system category. This category of systems is characterized by heavily standardized cycles which contain constant tasks and which are highly repetitive.[12]

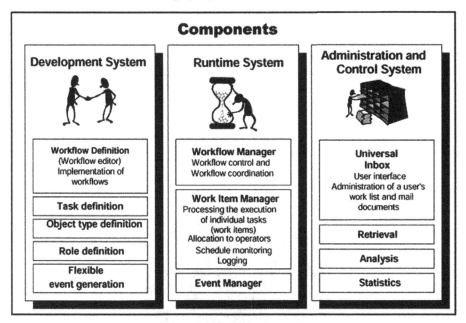

Fig. 1. Components of SAP BWF[13]

SAP BWF consists of three components: *Development System, Runtime System* and *Administration and Control System* (c.f. Fig. 1). The Development environment contains constructs for implementing a workflow definition (objects, tasks, roles, etc.) The Runtime System comprises the components Workflow Manager, which is necessary for controlling a workflow process, the Work Item Manager, which executes the individual tasks, and the Event Manager, which is responsible for event-controlled operation in SAP BWF. Numerous test tools that enable processes to be

---

[10] C.f. SAP (1996); SAP (1998).

[11] Weiss/Krcmar (1996), p. 507 ff.

[12] C.f. Erdl/Schönecker (1993), p. 18; Weiss/Krcmar (1996), p. 508.

[13] C.f. e.g. SAP (1996); SAP (1998); Berthold/Mende/Schuster (1999).

efficiently monitored and controlled are included in the Administration and Control System, which is also called the Information System by SAP. The Universal Inbox (=work list of a user) is also part of the Administration and Control System, though this is unusual since it ought rather to be interpreted as part of the Runtime System.

Selected results, focussing primarily on the application of SAP BWF, are now presented in the following section.

4   Presentation of Selected Results of the Study

4.1   Evaluation of Workflow Management

The concept of workflow management is not only the object of scientific debate, but is also increasingly being discussed for practical purposes. 58% of the companies surveyed consider that the time is *just right* for a discussion about workflow management and the related technologies. 5% however believe that it is already *too late* for a detailed discussion, and only around a third of those surveyed (30%) consider the time for discussion as being *too soon* (cf. Fig. 2).

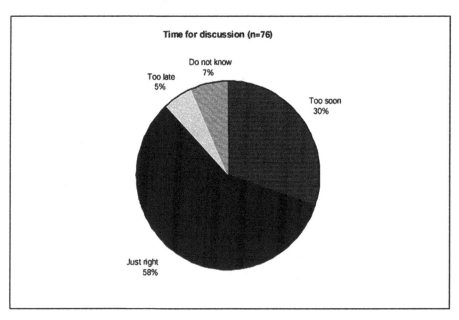

Fig. 2. Time for discussion about workflow management

The companies are clearly convinced of the great importance of using a WfMS: 60% of those surveyed considered the application of a WfMS to be *important* or *very important*. A minority (11%) considered that workflow products were of *minor* or *no* great importance. Similar results were produced in the appraisal of the *potential benefits* of a WfMS. Only 10% of those surveyed believe that WfMS are of *minor* potential benefit. The remaining companies are convinced of the positive effects of this technology (cf. Fig. 3).

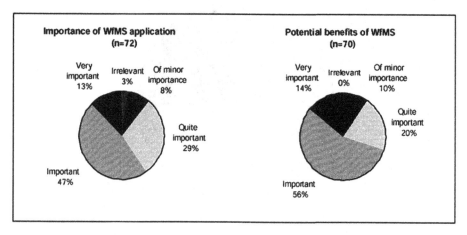

Fig. 3. Importance and potential benefits of workflow management systems

4.2   Use of SAP Business Workflow

If the level of distribution of SAP BWF is considered, it will be noticed that only 7% of those surveyed are *productively* using SAP BWF, 3% are conducting a *pilot project*, and 20% are *planning* an application. 70% of the respondents do not plan to use SAP BWF (cf. Fig. 4).

An analysis of the reasons for not using SAP BWF reveals the main arguments as being *lack of knowledge* of the technology (25%), and *time constraints* (31%) (cf. Fig. 5). It can be seen that other projects receive greater priority within the SAP environment (e.g. release upgrades or migration projects). *Lack of (product) information* (8%) or *no requirement* (9%) are also stated as arguments against using SAP BWF. *Insufficient technical development of product* (3%) is rarely given as a reason. This result is interesting because, in a survey carried out by the publication Computer Zeitung in 1997, 57% of those surveyed argued against the use of a commercial workflow tool for reasons of insufficient technical development.[14]

Other reasons stated for not using SAP BWF are summarized under the heading *Other* (24%). They include the following interesting arguments: SAP BWF not available because of obsolete release status, greater priority given to current implementation projects, greater priority given to the optimization and consolidation of the modules implemented, lack of financial resources for the implementation of a workflow project, necessity of cross-system tools, lack of willingness in the organization, and lack of implementation concepts.

---

[14] Cf. Heinrich (1997), p. 17.

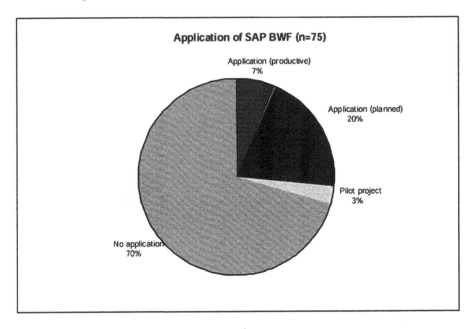

Fig. 4. Application of SAP Business Workflow

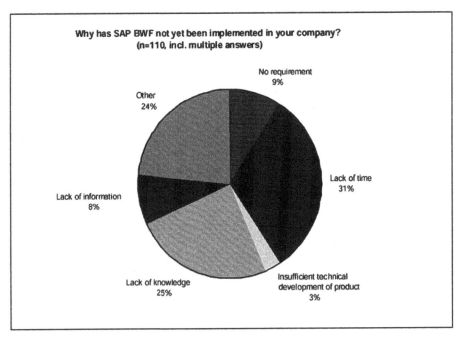

Fig. 5. Reasons against using SAP Business Workflow

An analysis of the potential areas of application shows that *control of the operational flow of information* is at the forefront (cf. Fig. 6). Thus, over 70% of the respondents use SAP BWF for the *active support of information flow* (automatic distribution of information) or for *document management* or *archiving*. It becomes clear that document handling is one of the possible sources for workflow management. This helps to explain why workflow management is also currently being equated with document management.[15] Of secondary importance is *automation of individual system activities* or *control of several interrelated transactions* (e.g. *time scheduling* or *authorization procedures*). Over 60% of the respondents use SAP BWF for these complex processes.

Over 60% said they would use SAP BWF for the *interconnection and control of distributed applications* (e.g. linking of several R/3 systems using Application Link Enabling) and for the *integration and control of desktop applications*. This percentage is still relatively high, yet the result is surprising in view of the fact that the integration of different applications along a business process represents a principle task for the application of WfMS. This task ought to have attracted a far higher rate of agreement accordingly. Of lesser importance are *automatic error handling*[16] and *automatic help*, which are to be controlled by SAP BWF.

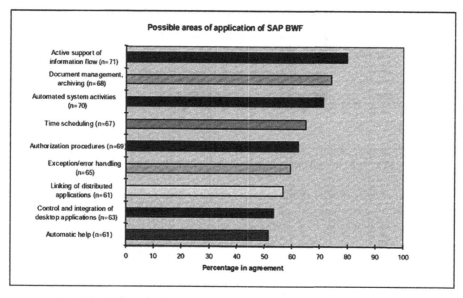

Fig. 6: Potential areas of use for SAP Business Workflow

Potential advantages as seen by the companies surveyed are shown in Fig. 7. Of these, the most popular were *operational time improvement* (e.g. reducing throughput times) and *quality improvements* in both workflow and in individual processing operations, accounting for 80% of respondents. Other studies have noted similar results.[17]

---

[15] Cf. Wenzel (1997), p. 33.

[16] Cf. e.g. Strong/Miller (1995), p. 218 ff; Kamath/Ramamritham (1998).

[17] Cf. Chroust/Bergsmann (1995), p. 137; Heinrich (1997), p. 17.

Other important advantages are *improvement in flow control*, which leads to greater process reliability, and increased transparency, which greatly improves availability of information. The majority of arguments drew a positive reply from over 60% of the respondents. It can be seen that *cost savings*, by comparison with the other criteria, did *not* stand out as being important. This confirms that the qualitative arguments in the workflow management area outweigh statements of quantity, and demonstrates the difficulty of arguing on the basis of a cost/benefit analysis.

The importance attached to *improvement of resource management* likewise appears to be relatively *small*. This result is interesting, since WfMS fulfil coordination functions (e.g. tasks for monitoring, time and capacity scheduling, or feedback processing) and thus perform the typical functions for control centers.[18]

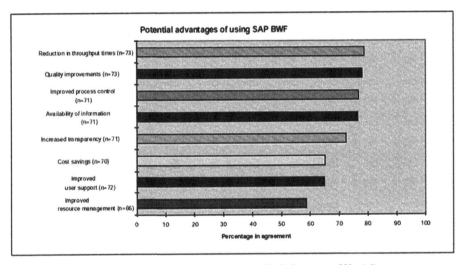

Fig. 7: Potential advantages of using SAP Business Workflow

The evaluation of potential problem areas indicates that technical drawbacks (*higher implementation costs* and *lack of experience in the technology*) are regarded by the respondents as being the most important, with over 70% in agreement (cf. Fig. 8). These are followed by disadvantages that arise in relation to the organization, e.g. *lack of organizational redesign, no clear implementation strategy, lack of user concept* or *minimal consultant expertise* with regard to the use of workflow management.

It will be noticed that all criteria relating to the employee area appear as a whole at the end of the list. This is surprising because employee-specific criteria (e.g. acceptance) are regarded as significant success factors in the implementation of a workflow project.[19] The first factor in the socio-cultural area is called the *"big brother effect"*, which is repeatedly mentioned in connection with the implementation of WfMS and must be regarded as a consequence of increased transparency. This series of potential disadvantages of using SAP BWF is put into perspective by the fact that all arguments received a relatively high score of over 55%.

---

[18] Cf. Scheer et al. (1994), p. 291.
[19] Cf. e.g. Vogler (1996), p. 357; Maurer (1996), p. 23; Altenhofen (1997), p. 24 ff.

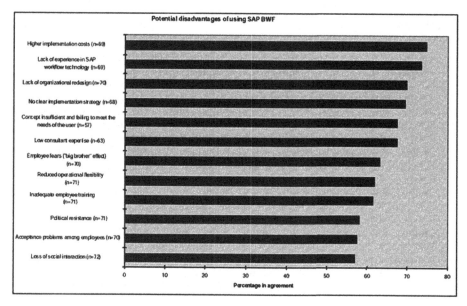

Fig. 8: Potential disadvantages of using SAP Business Workflow

5   Prospects

This paper shows that workflow management is not only a subject for scientific debate, but is also increasingly becoming a topic of discussion for practical purposes. It is possible to show that workflow management, particularly in the R/3 environment, is not merely a "nice to have" feature but a matter that is taken seriously. Initial findings indicate that this workflow concept has the potential to support business processes in the R/3 system. Nevertheless, these initial positive findings must not hide the fact that the cost of implementing SAP BWF has so far been too high for the typical user, and that other projects receive greater priority. However, the use of SAP BWF is expected to increase in the near future.

The findings presented here are selected results of an empirical study: "The importance and application of SAP Business Workflow in Switzerland". The detailed analyses were published in a report which appeared in April 1998. This is available from the Institute of Information Systems, University of Bern. SAP BWF was chosen because it is considered as the most important integrated WfMS.[20] It is a fact that the findings of this empirical study are in some way SAP specific. Nevertheless, as other publications[21] show, some results like the potential advantages and disadvantages of WfMS or the trend to integrate workflow components into existing software are transferable to other products.

---

[20] Cf. e.g. Casonato (1996a); Casonato (1996b).
[21] Cf. e.g. Becker/Vogler (1997); Mohan (1998).

References

1. Altenhofen, C.: Workflowmanagement aus Sicht der Arbeitswissenschaft. In: Becker, J., Rosemann, M. (eds.): Organisatorische und technische Aspekte beim Einsatz von Workflowmanagementsystemen. Proceedings zum Workshop vom 10. April 1997, Arbeitsbericht Nr. 54, Münster (1997) 24-33
2. Becker, M., Vogler, P.: Workflow-Management in betriebswirtschaftlicher Standardsoftware - Konzepte, Architekturen, Lösungen. Arbeitsbericht IM HSG/CC PSI/9, Version 1.0, Institut für Wirtschaftsinformatik, Universität St. Gallen (1997)
3. Berthold, A., Mende, U., Schuster, H.: SAP Business Workflow: Konzept, Anwendung, Entwicklung. Addison Wesley Longman, München et. al. (1999)
4. Casonato, R.: SAP Business Workflow: Do You Need It?. In: Gartner Group (ed.): Research Note, Products P-SAP-261, o. O. (1996)
5. Casonato, R.: Workflow Vendors in Europe: Survey Results. In: Gartner Group (ed.): Research Note, Markets M-WKS-1589, o. O. (1996)
6. Chroust, G., Bergsmann J.: Umfrage: Workflow, Eine Momentaufnahme über Verbreitung, Einsatz und Meinungen über Workflow in den deutschsprachigen Ländern, Umfragezeitraum: 2. Halbjahr 1994. Oldenbourg, Wien München (1995)
7. Derungs, M., Vogler, P., Österle, H.: Kriterienkatalog Workflow-Systeme. Arbeitsbericht IM HSG/CC PSI/1, Version 1.0, Institut für Wirtschaftsinformatik, Universität St. Gallen (1995)
8. Endl, R., Duedal, L., Fritz, B., Joos, B.: Anforderungen an Workflowmanagementsysteme aus anwendungsorientierter Sicht. Arbeitsbericht Nr. 92, Institut für Wirtschaftsinformatik, Universität Bern (1997)
9. Erdl, G., Schönecker, H. G.: Vorgangssteuerungssysteme im Überblick - Herkunft, Voraussetzungen, Einsatzschwerpunkte, Ausblick. In: Office Management 41/3 (1993) 13-21
10. Galler, J., Scheer, A.-W., Peter, S.: Workflow-Projekte: Erfahrungen aus Fallstudien und Vorgehensmodell. In: Veröffentlichungen des Instituts für Wirtschaftsinformatik, Heft 117, Universität Saarbrücken (1995)
11. Georgakopoulos, D., Hornick, M., Sheth, A.: An Overview of Workflow-Management: From Process Modeling to Workflow Automation Infrastructure. In: Distributed and Parallel Databases 3/2 (1995) 119-153
12. Gerber, J.-P., Knolmayer, G.: Informationsbeschaffung zu Softwareprodukten aus Newsgruppen und Mailing-Listen am Beispiel von SAP R/3. In: Wirtschaftsinformatik 38/6 (1996) 633-638
13. Heinrich, W.: Trendanalyse, Integrierte Standardsoftware steigert Prozeßdenken in Unternehmen, Im Workflow-Warenkorb liegen auch faule Eier. In: Computer Zeitung 28/31 (1997) 17
14. Kamath, M., Ramamritham K.: Bridging the gap between Transaction Management and Workflow Management. http://www-ccs.cs.umass.edu/db/publications/nsf-wf.html [as of: 1998-12-20]
15. Knolmayer, G., von Arb, R., Zimmerli, C.: Erfahrungen mit der Einführung von SAP R/3 in Schweizer Unternehmungen. Studie der Abteilung Information Engineering des Instituts für Wirtschaftsinformatik der Universität Bern, 3rd edn. Bern (1997)
16. Maurer, G.: Von der Prozeßorientierung zum Workflow-Management, Teil 2: Prozeßmanagement, Workflow Management, Workflow-Management-Systeme. Arbeitspapiere WI, Nr. 10, Universität Mainz (1996)
17. Meyer, M.: Prozessmonitoring in SAP Business Workflow. Arbeitsbericht Nr. 101, Institut für Wirtschaftsinformatik, Universität Bern (1997)
18. Meyer, M., Pfahrer, M.: Erfahrungen beim Einsatz von SAP Business Workflow und IBM Flowmark. Arbeitsbericht Nr. 93, Institut für Wirtschaftsinformatik, Universität Bern (1997)

19. Mohan, C.: Recent Trends in Workflow Management Products, Standards and Research. In: Dogaç, A., Kalinichenko, L., Özsu, M. T., Sheth, A. (eds.): Workflow Management Systems and Interoperability. Proceedings of the NATO Advanced Study Institute on Workflow Management Systems (WFMS), Istanbul 1997. Springer, Berlin et al. (1998) 396-409
20. Nippa, M., Picot, A. (eds.): Prozeßmanagement und Reengineering: Die Praxis im deutschsprachigen Raum. Campus, Frankfurt a. M. New York (1995)
21. Osterloh, M., Frost, J.: Prozessmanagement als Kernkompetenz, Wie Sie Business Reengineering strategisch nutzen können. Gabler, Wiesbaden (1996)
22. Österle, H.: Business Engineering, Prozess- und Systementwicklung. 2nd edn. Springer, Heidelberg (1996)
23. Petrovic, M., Altenhofen, C.: IBM, Microsoft und SAP werde am häufigsten unterstützt, Fraunhofer untersucht den Markt für Workflow und Dokumentenmanagement. In: Computerwoche Focus, Markt - Technik - Anwendungen, Blickpunkt: Workflow o.J./1 (1998) 8-10
24. SAP AG (ed.): System R/3, SAP Business Workflow, Funktionen im Detail. Walldorf (1996)
25. SAP AG (ed.): Business Process Technology. Compact Disk, Walldorf (1998)
26. Scheer, A.-W., et al.: Modellbasiertes Geschäftsprozeßmanagement. In: Management & Computer 2/4 (1994) 287-292
27. Strebi, S.: Kritische Erfolgsfaktoren bei der Einführung von SAP R/3. Arbeitsbericht Nr. 91, Institut für Wirtschaftsinformatik, Universität Bern (1996)
28. Strong, D. M., Miller, S. M.: Exceptions and Exception Handling in Computerized Information Processes. In: ACM Transactions on Information Systems 13/2 (1995) 206-233
29. Vogler, P.: Chancen und Risiken von Workflow-Management. In: Österle, H., Vogler, P. (eds.): Praxis des Workflow-Managements, Grundlagen, Vorgehen, Beispiele. Vieweg, Braunschweig Wiesbaden (1996) 343-362
30. Vogler, P., Jablonski, S.: Editorial, Workflow-Management. In: Informatik 5/2 (1998) 2
31. von Arb, R.: Vorgehensweisen und Erfahrungen bei der Einführung von Enterprise-Management-Systemen dargestellt am Beispiel von SAP R/3, Dissertation, Universität Bern (1997)
32. Weiss, D., Krcmar, H.: Workflow-Management: Herkunft und Klassifikation. In: Wirtschaftsinformatik 38/5 (1996) 503-513
33. Wenzel, I.: Mit Dokumenten fängt alles an. In: Computerwoche 24/31 (1997) 33-34

Configurable Business Objects for Building Evolving Enterprise Models and Applications

Mike P. Papazoglou and Willem-Jan van den Heuvel

Tilburg University, INFOLAB
PO Box 90153, NL-5000 LE Tilburg
The Netherlands
mikep@kub.nl, wjheuvel@kub.nl

Abstract. To remain competitive organizations must be able to move fast and adapt quickly to change. To achieve this they are required to reconfigure their key business processes as changing market conditions dictate.
This chapter discusses a methodology to link enterprise models to wrapped legacy system modules or off-the-shelf (ERP) components. Moreover, it reveals how such mappings can be retrofitted to address business change requirements.

1 Introduction

Today's increasingly competitive, expanding global marketplace requires that companies cope more effectively with rapidly changing market conditions than ever before. Emerging technologies, such as business objects and components, are generally being perceived as core technologies to successfully deal with these challenges. However, there are a number of important issues which must be addressed before business object technology becomes a reality. These include:

Business-Object Oriented Enterprise Models: Modern organizations seek to streamline their processes and improve customer service through greater connectivity between *both* business processes and key operational systems. Enterprises can only become a full player in the global market place by re-conceptualizing the company as a collection of business operations and processes, by reshaping corporate structures around modern business processes and by making their internal processes align with and support the (integrated) value-chain. This requires that *new business models* are created on the basis of (common) business objects which provide a powerful mechanism for realizing and implementing business models.

Adaptable Business Processes: In addition to improved business modeling it is important to make sure that critical applications can deal with *business change*. Modern value-chain supporting business applications require that system incompatibilities be overcome and that business processes and information systems not only harmonize but also jointly support the ability to react quickly to new opportunities.

W. van der Aalst et al.(Eds.): Business Process Management, LNCS 1806, pp. 328-344, 2000.

Leveraging Legacy Assets: Both of the above items focus attention not only on the need to gracefully accommodate process changes but also on how to synthesize a business process out of fragments, some of which may leverage legacy assets. Legacy systems that often represent millions-of-dollar of business value, and, as a result, may not be ignored when moving to new flexible business architectures.

This chapter addresses these three issues in the following way. Firstly, we will introduce business-object oriented enterprise modeling (section 2) and discuss the essential features of the *BALES* (binding Business-Applications to LEgacy Systems) methodology (section 3) that focuses on parameterizing business objects with legacy data and functionality. Thereafter, we will explain how this methodology can be successfully employed to cope with changed business requirements by retrofitting business object parameters. This chapter concludes with a discussion and a summary.

2   Architecture-centric Business-Object Oriented Enterprise Modeling

Enterprise models reflect the activities, structure, processes, information, actors, processes, goals an constraints of a business. Business objects do not only provide a natural way to model the enterprise, but also at same time guarantee a close link to the business (legacy) applications. Moreover, business object technology provides semantic as well as network interoperability, two key enablers for the virtual enterprise. In this section, we will describe the main ingredients of business-object oriented enterprise modeling based upon an integrated enterprise architecture.

2.1   The Integrated Enterprise Framework

Complex enterprise models need to be founded on an enterprise framework to provide a solid structure that simplifies its interpretation and facilitates future reuse as well as modification.

Figure-1 illustrates an integrated value chain enterprise framework for modeling business applications and for developing and delivering enterprise solutions. This enterprise framework consists of business objects, processes, and workflows defined within, or across, a specific 'vertical' industry. The integrated enterprise framework in Figure-1 provides a base for the effective encapsulation of business practices, policies, and tactics in modular high-level components. Moreover, it facilitates value chain integration, by which multiple organizations (see enterprise A and B in the figure) can collaboratively plan, implement and manage the flow of goods, services and information, and thereby increase their competitive position in the global market.

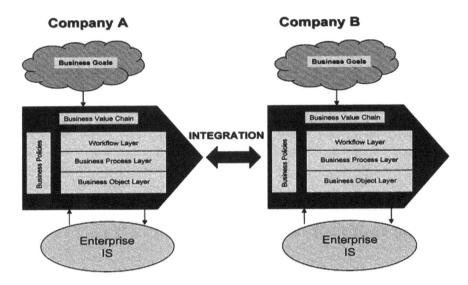

Fig. 1. The Integrated Enterprise Framework.

2.2 Business Objects

Business objects provide a natural way for describing application-independent concepts such as product, order, fiscal calendar, customer, payment and the like. They play a central role in capturing the semantics of actual business entities and processes, in a way that is understandable by the business [1], [11].

Business (entity) objects that reside in this layer essentially contain business data which can only be manipulated by business methods (services). Complex business object variants can be implemented by attaching business policies to them (see below).

Business objects can be divided in various categories. Common Business Objects (CBOs) are business objects that can be shared across multiple domains, e.g., a currency business object. Obviously, they need to be speciliazed to deal with domain-dependent semantics. The second category comprises domain frameworks: specialized business objects which deal with common semantics within a vertical domain. The OMG is currently putting much standardization efforts in both categories of objects (see: http:\\www.omg.org\). ERP package like IBM's SanFrancisco [4] and SAP (Industry Solutions) [18] are currently investing in the development of industry specific as well as common business objects and domain frameworks.

2.3 Business Processes

A business process is the definition of a set of interrelated activities that collectively accomplish a specific business objective, possibly, according to a a set of pre-specified policies. The purpose of this layer is to provide *generic business processes*. These provide a set of basic building blocks for an application in a specific business domain, e.g., procurement management, general ledger, etc. These building blocks can be specialized and extended to capture domain or application specific processes which are realized at the workflow layer.

The business processes are initiated by internal or external events (e.g., a customer request), and result in outgoing events (e.g., the notification that a product is ordered) [2]. Business processes rely on a set of business objects to perform the requested operations.

2.4 Workflows

The workflow layer assigns business processes to actors, and, moves the process forward from one role (that performs an activity) to the next. The workflow layer can be supported by workflow applications.

Workflow objects rely on an extensive foundation of reusable components, viz. the core business processes, that form the basis for building new applications. Workflow-enabled business processes can track transactions across, department, company and enterprise boundaries. This type of distributed workflow layer provides the sequence of business activities, arrangement for the delivery of work to the appropriate inter-organizational resources, tracking of the status of business activities, coordination of the flow of information of (inter and intra-) organizational activities and the possibility to decide among alternative execution paths [5].

Workflow activities may invoke components from existing applications, for instance legacy objects, and combine them with newly developed applications. Several of the workflow activities have a transactional nature which requires long running interactions. The requirements of transactional workflows have been described in [12].

Business processes that need to operate across or between organizations – in order to implement value chains that can be used to deliver cross-enterprise E-commerce applications – may be implemented using a set of workflow definitions that have been created to support segments of the overall process. This approach addresses the problem of how to avoid creating islands of automation in the operation of an end to end business process.

For example, an order activity in a production planning workflow may start an appropriate order entry process at a closely aligned parts supplier. This type of cooperation can only be achieved if the workflow systems of the cooperating companies are loosely coupled. This results in the elimination of supply chain discontinuities that produce delays and waste. Distributed workflows are normally built on a distributed object network infrastructure [3]. This enables a business to change its organizational structure and processes independently of another.

2.5 Business Goals and Policies

It is important that business objects and business processes in the enterprise framework are oriented towards the fulfillment of the business goals. The business mission describes the core competence of an organization, for example, the product-market combination in which the business will be active, the market share the organization tries to gain, and so on and so forth. The business mission is translated in strategic plans and is operationalized in terms of quantifiable Critical Success Factors (CSFs) which determine those facets in which the organization must excel over its competitors [21]. Within the context of *BALES*, the enterprise implements it's goals at all levels of the enterprise architecture by attaching *business policies* to the objects.

Business policies define various implementations of the same business (process) object, e.g., various different policies for credit or order management. These policy objects can be easily adapted to anticipate on changes in the organization's strategy and related CSFs.

In line with the SanFrancisco approach, *BALES* policy objects are based on various object-oriented patterns. The structure of policy objects is based on the *strategy pattern* [19]. The strategy pattern describes an encapsulated, interchangeable family of algorithms. These algorithms can be changed without affecting the composition, as the volatile logic is encapsulated in the strategy object. Policy objects adopt this pattern, providing an alternative to subclassing, and are particularly useful when there exist many variants of a business rule, e.g., the `DetPlanning` policy object in figure 2 that contains a plan-driven business procedure to determine material requirements of a maintenance unit based on the Bill-of-Material (see the next section for an elaborated description). In case of multiple alternative business policies, the selection logic is isolated in a separate selection class that determines which business policy object to use in a particular context, e.g., the `determinePlanning` business policy selection object that encapsulates logic to trigger a deterministic planning policy object (`DetPlanning`) or a consumer based planning policy (`ConsBasedPlanning`) in figure 2. This solution is based on the 'chain-of-responsibility' pattern [19].

The main advantage of business policy objects is that the volatile business logic is stored in an isolated place, and can be easily changed, while minimizing the impact on other parts of the business application. A potential drawback of this patterns is that the clients of the business policy objects must be aware that there exist multiple variants [19].

3 Business Applications

When developing applications based on business objects and processes it is important to address two interrelated factors: (a) the linking of business objects with legacy information systems, and (b) the requirements for change so that business information systems can evolve over time. Thus we view change management dealing with these two essential and interrelated aspects. Any new environment must leverage investments in legacy systems, it must also allow its business processes to adapt to changes enforced by new corporate goals or policies.

3.1   Leveraging Legacy Assets

In an enterprise framework there is a pressing demand to integrate 'new generation' business processes with legacy perspectives, processes and applications. Legacy systems are systems that are critical for the day-to-day functioning of an organization, they normally comprise monolithic applications that consist of millions of lines of code in older programming languages (e.g., COBOL), are technically obsolete with a poor performance and hard to adapt and maintain [6]. However, they are valuable assets of an organization that can be leveraged and integrated into next generation business systems. The break-up of monolithic business units and processes from a business perspective requires a restructuring of the applications that support them and, at a minimum, finding a way to integrate them. Additionally, the nature of many of these new processes means that they must be integrated at the transaction level, not just via replication and batch transfers of data. There are various strategies to deal with legacy systems [6], like discarding, replacement of the legacy system, enhancement of the existing system and selective integration. This last technique makes it easier to integrate parts of a legacy system into new systems.

Object wrappers are a successful technology to support integration of business objects with legacy systems. It allows mixing legacy systems with newly developed applications by providing access to the legacy systems. The wrapper specifies services that can be invoked on legacy systems by completely hiding implementation details. The advantage of this approach is that it promotes conceptual simplicity and language transparency. A detailed study of how legacy relational databases can be transformed to semantically equivalent representations accessible via object-oriented interfaces can be found in [7].

3.2   Adaptability of Business Processes

To remain competitive organizations must be able to move fast and adapt quickly to change. Moreover, they must be able to reconfigure their key business processes as changing market conditions dictate. Enterprises must respond to new requirements quickly without interrupting the course of business. Such changes must be mapped to the business object level and related to already existing enterprise models. New business requirements might require new processes and workflows to be implemented, but the existing business rules and data in legacy systems may only be partially reusable. Using a purely bottom-up approach is not desirable, although many commercial systems support it, as the danger is that we simply perpetuate legacy ways of working.

In the enterprise framework described in Figure-1 we take the classical organizational view that business changes are initiated by changes to business goals. This is in accordance with approaches towards linking the organizational goals to business activities that have been identified in the research literature [8]. It is only natural to expect that these changes would become 'visible' at the workflow level. However, it is virtually impossible for workflows to predict in advance all potential exceptions and paths through a business process. Most workflow products require all exceptions to be predicted and built into the process definition. Rather than insisting that all exceptions are predicted in advance, workflow systems must allow users to change the underlying process model dynamically to support a particular case of work. To achieve this degree of business process adaptability, each case of work must be related to a distinct and corresponding process fragment. A critical challenge to building robust business applications is to be able to identify the reusable and modifiable portions (functionality and data) of an existing business process or object and combine these with 'newer generation' business processes/objects in a piecemeal and consistent manner. These ideas point towards a methodology that facilitates *pro-active change management* of business objects that can easily be retrofitted to accommodate selective functionality from legacy information systems. We refer to objects exhibiting such characteristics as *adaptable business objects*.

4   Linking Enterprise Models to Business Applications

The *BALES* methodology, that is under development, has as its main objective to parameterize business objects with legacy objects. Legacy objects serve as conceptual repositories of extracted (wrapped) legacy data and functionality. These objects are, just like business objects, described by means of their interfaces (services) rather then their implementation. A newer generation business object interface can be constructed by selecting a chunk of an existing legacy object interface. This partition comprises a set of appropriate attribute and method signatures. All remaining interface declarations are masked off from the business object interface specification. This means that business object interfaces are parameterizable to allow these objects to evolve by accommodating upgrades or adjustments in their structure and behavior.

The core of the *BALES*-methodology comprises three phases (see Figure-2): *enterprise modeling* (or forward engineering), *reverse engineering* and *meta-model linking*.

4.1   Case Study: Maintenance and Overhaul of Aircrafts

To illustrate the *BALES* mapping methodology a simplified example is drawn from the domain of maintenance and overhaul of aircrafts (see Figure-2). The upper part of this figure illustrates the results of the enterprise modeling phase of the business domain in terms of workflows, business processes and business objects. The enterprise model is represented in an extended version of UML, called *BALES* UML, that offers basic constructs such as business-objects, and business policies, as UML does not provide the object-oriented reflections of these prototypical business concepts.

The *BALES* UML dialect has been specially designed to enable the generation of *BALES* Component Definition Language (CDL) compliant business object interface descriptions. *BALES* UML extends and refines extends the semantics of UML by adding stereo-types such as <<BusinessWorkflow>>, <<BusinessPolicy>> to respectively denote business workflows and business policies.

As can be seen from Figure 2 the enterprise model is enacted by a Request_Part workflow which comprises three business processes: Request, Prognosis and Issue. The Request_Part workflow is initiated by a maintenance engineer who requests parts (for maintaining aircrafts) from a warehouse. The Request process registers the maintenance engineer's request in an order list. This list can be used to check availability and plan dispatch of a specific aircraft part from the warehouse. The Request process uses the business (entity) objects Part and Warehouse for this purpose. Subsequently, the workflow initiates an Issue process (see Figure-2). The Issue process registers administrative results regarding the dispatching of requested part and updates the part inventory record by means of the Part_Stock business object. The Prognosis process uses information from the Part and Warehouse business objects to run a prognosis on the basis of the availability and consumption history of the requested part.

The lower part of the picture Figure-2, represents the result of the reverse engineering activity in the form of two processes (wrapped applications and related databases) Material_Requirements_Planning and Purchase_Requisition. These processes make use of five legacy objects to perform their operations. Figure-2 also indicates that the enterprise workflow draws not only on 'modern' business objects and processes, but it also leans on already existing (legacy) data and functionality to accomplish its objectives. For example, business processes such as Request and Issue, on the enterprise model level, are linked to the legacy processes Material_ Requirements_Planning and Purchase_Requisition by means of solid dashed lines. This signifies the fact that the processes on the business level *reuse* the functionality of the processes at the legacy model level. In this simplified example we assume that problems such as conflicting naming conventions and semantic mismatches between the enterprise and legacy models have been resolved. A possible solution to this problem can be found in [13].

To formally describe the interfaces of business and legacy objects we use a variant of the Component Definition Language (CDL) that has been developed by the OMG [14].

4.2 *BALES* Component Definition Language (CDL)

CDL is a declarative language to specify the services of collections of business objects, their relations, dynamics, business constraints and attributes. Business objects are not written in CDL, but in programming models for which language mappings are available, e.g., Enterprise Java Beans. CDL is a superset of the Interface Definition Language (IDL), the ODMG Object Definition Language (ODL) and the ODMG Object Query Language (OQL). This specifica-

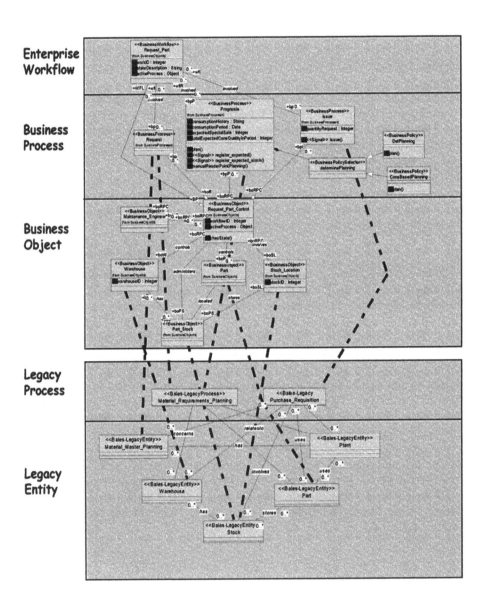

Fig. 2. Developing an enterprise model by means of reusing legacy processes and objects.

tion language extends IDL by adding several 'high-level' constructs to capture more business semantics. IDL indeed merely defines *object methods* to implement language-independent distributed objects, which can be plugged in to a broker (ORB) that provides additional services such as security, concurrency and transaction services. The goal of CDL transcends this rather low-level, inter-object communication purpose of IDL, and is oriented towards delivering distributed (business) objects based on the Business Object Facility (BOF), specifying Common Business Objects and delivering marketable business objects by software vendors. The BOF is a run-time software infrastructure to support business object components, offering services such as transaction management, and messaging.

Obviously, components are the central notion in CDL. According [14], CDL components define collections of business objects, dependents, applicances and subsystems. As explained before, business objects are a special category of objects with clear business semantics, such as customer, bill, and request-for-quotation. Dependents are volatile objects, without identity, that can only persist within the context of a business object, and are commonly used to define attribute types. This category of objects typically does not have a specific business meaning, but adds business semantics by defining the type of business object attributes and parameters. There are five types of dependents: primitives (CORBA data types, such as integer and string), elementary objects (frozen data type objects, such as currency (pounds) and weight (kg)), composite objects, immutable objects (data types that can not be changed) and, lastly, collections (e.g., arrays and bags). Appliances can be attached, or applied, to container objects (e.g., a business object). Individual appliances only have some meaning when applied to a container type, e.g., the policy object 'discount-policy' (the appliance) has only meaning if applied to the business object 'Customer' (the container). All these components can be organized into a coherent collection with a uniform interface, called a subsystem.

BALES CDL adds the following constructs to the core CDL: legacy objects and processes, and, business goal, policy and workflow objects. We have already dealt with business goals, policies and workflows in section 2.5.

A legacy (entity) object consists of wrapped legacy data and functionality (transactions). In case of a relational data model, the legacy objects generally consist of wrapped relations and transactions to update/insert or delete rows of that relation, e.g., a relation 'Employee' in a relational model, can be wrapped an accessed by means of set- and get-methods that surround this table. In [7], we discuss a methodology that articulates an approach to transform legacy relational databases to semantically equivalent representations accessible via object-oriented interfaces and data languages. Legacy processes are objectified programs, subroutines or even procedures depending on their level of granularity, which represent the 'legacy' way of working. Legacy process objects are implemented as control objects that organize legacy object transactions into logical units of work. The state of a legacy process is stored in the legacy (entity) objects.

Finally, *BALES* CDL supports SAP Business Application Programming Interfaces (BAPIs), which can be used to describe SAP Business Object services.

4.3   A CDL Excerpt

In the following we give a CDL-code excerpt to illustrate how the operation *plan* of the business process object `Prognosis` is implemented by a semantically equivalent operation materialized by the legacy business process `Material_Requirements_Planning`, see Figure-2. We first give a CDL definition of the legacy business process, see Figure-3.

```
// Definition of the legacy business process Material Requirements Planning
 LegacyProcess Material_Requirements_Planning {

    // the relations of the process object, with other components
    relationship has References Part;
    relationship for References Plant;
    relationship concerns References Warehouse;

    // the dynamic behavior
    signal register_expected;
    signal start_long_term_planning;
    signal start_stat_analysis;

    // Methods to implement Material Requirements Planning
    // forecast stock on basis of deterministic planning
    void forecastDetModel(in Integer partID, in Integer stockID,
      in Integer warehouseID, in Date consumptionPeriod,
      in Integer consumptionHistory);

    // forecast stock on basis of consumption based planning
    void planProduct (in Integer artID, in Integer stockID,
                in Integer warehouseID);

    // state transition rule of Material Requirements Planning
    apply StateTransitionRule ProgProcessing {
       trigger = {register_exp_stock};
       source  = processing;
       target  = handled;
    }; # end str
 }; // end process Material_Requirements_Planning
```

Fig. 3. CDL definition of the MRP legacy process object.

The CDL excerpt in Figure-3 defines the legacy process `Material_Requirements_Planning` which is associated with the legacy objects `Warehouse`, `part` and `plant` see Figure-2. This legacy process can be used to forecast all the part requirements in the warehouse. For this purpose it uses the legacy operation *forecastDetModel*.

The CDL specification in Figure-4 defines the business object operation `forecast` in terms of the legacy operation `Material_Requirements_Planning`, given in the previous. The legacy operation is embedded in the business process object as a parameter of the `forecast` operation.

4.4   Meta-Model Linking

The enterprise modeling phase defines a conceptual enterprise model into CDL and links this CDL definition to the predefined *Meta-CDL Enterprise Model*.

```
BusinessProcess Prognosis {
  [PRIVATE] attribute Bag consumptionHistory;
  [PRIVATE] attribute Date consumptionPeriod;
  [PRIVATE] attribute Integer expectedSpecialSale;
  [PRIVATE] attribute Integer totalExpectedConsQuantityinPeriod;
  signal register_expected ();
  signal register_expected_stock ();
  relationship boRPC IsPartOf BusinessObjects::Request_Part_Control  inverse bpP;

  // abstract method implemented by policies
  void plan ();
  void manualReorderPointPlanning (in Integer artID, in Integer stockID, in Integer warehouseID);
  }; # end process Prognosis

BusinessPolicySelector determinePlanning {
      relationship BPPProg IsOwnedBy BusinessProcesses::Prognosis inverse BEdetPl ;
  }; // End: determinePlanning

BusinessPolicy DetPlanning : determinePlanning {
  // Plan driven planning policy
  // Mapping of forecasting method to legacy process component MRP
  void plan (Warehouse.Material_Requirements_Planning.forecastDetModel(in Integer partID, in Integer stockID,
      in Integer warehouseID, in Date consumptionPeriod, in Integer consumptionHistory));
  }; // End: DetPlanning
BusinessPolicy ConsBasedPlanning : determinePlanning {
  // Stochastic planning policy
  // Manual reorder point procedure
  void plan (in Integer artID, in Integer stockID, in Integer warehouseID);
  }; // End: ConsBasedPlanning
```

Fig. 4. CDL definition of a business object.

The Meta-CDL Enterprise Model defines and relates all enterprise modeling CDL concepts. During the reverse-engineering phase, that is conceptually equal to the forward engineering phase, legacy object and process interfaces are again represented in terms of CDL and are used to instantiate the *Meta-CDL Legacy Model*. The Meta-CDL Legacy Model is integrated with the Meta-CDL Enterprise Model into a single canonical model and relates all reverse engineering concepts. The CDL descriptions of both the enterprise and reverse-engineered models are then compared to each other in order to ascertain which parts of the legacy object interfaces can be re-used within new applications. To achieve this, we represent and store both business and legacy (Meta-)CDL specifications in a repository system. For this purpose we utilize the ConceptBase system [15] because it has an advanced query language for abstract models (like the CDL meta model) and it uniformly represents objects at any abstraction level (data objects, model components, modeling notations, etc.). The representation language that underlies ConceptBase is based on the logical formalism Telos [16], that has a frame syntax to represent classes and objects. During the meta-model linking phase, queries are used to infer potential legacy components that may be linked to business components. For instance, we can identify business object attributes and/or operations that can be constructed out of legacy object attributes and/or operations. Telos queries are used to retrieve exact or partial matches of signatures of requested components that are stored in a repository. To ensure type safety on method arguments and method results we require the use of *argument contravariance* (expansion) and *result covariance* (restriction).

In the same way as described in the above, the *BALES* methodology can deliver parameterized business objects in terms of ERP component interfaces, e.g., expressed in SAP BAPIs, as long as they can be mapped to the *BALES* metamodel. A detailed description of the *BALES* methodology can be found in [9].

5   Proactive Business Change Management

Business object technology offers *interface evolution* as a resilient solution to business change, as business object interfaces can be changed without affecting the underlying implementation. This enables minimal coupling between business components: an essential condition for serious reuse. The business components are not explicitly bound to each other, rather messages are trapped at run-time by a semantic data object that enforces the binding at the level of parameter passing semantics [10].

5.1   Mapping Business Changes to the Business Object Level

As we have indicated in section 3.2, business changes need to be mapped down to the business object level. In fact, the *BALES* methodology assumes that business change is *goal driven*. This intentionality of the organization is implicitly implemented by linking business policies to the business processes, and their constituents.

According to Ackoff [20], there are various ways to (re)act to change. The first category of business change constitutes reactive change, and refers to an unplanned response to a changed 'reality'. On the other side of the specter we discern planned, or active change management. Active change management assumes that organizational changes can be *designed* by the management, and implemented by the business. It only seems logical that this category of business change does not challenge business application development as much as unanticipated business changes.

BALES advocates a flexible information system architecture to quickly anticipate on reactive change. This strategy is called *pro-active* change management. Therefore, *BALES* defines adaptive, parameterizable business objects that are easy reconfigurable to meet changed market conditions, and can easily be re-parameterized to reallocate the business object to legacy system mapping.

Thus, *BALES* prescribes the following two-step approach to incorporate business change:

1. Adapt existing enterprise model to reflect the new business reality.

Based on their impact and the ability to deal with change within the context of existing organizational procedures, *BALES* considers various mechanisms to pro-actively anticipate on business change:

  - Changes to enterprise goals and value chain.
    In case of strategic business change, the business redefines its value chain, in terms of business goals, policies, products and services. This category entails the most drastic change, and typically leads to changes at all levels of the enterprise architecture, from the business workflows which define

how services are implemented for a (internal or external) customer, to the business objects, on which the business processes flow. Moreover, business goals typically need to be redefined and re-mapped to business processes.

– Changes to enterprise Planning and Control (P&C).

The Planning and Control processes in an organization allocate recourses to operational business processes by a sophisticated material and capacity requirement planning process. Recourse processes support the primary, operational business activities, and improve their effectivity and efficiency, e.g., planning, quality control and human recourse management. Operational business processes constitute the primary value adding business activities, such as inbound logistics, assembly, packaging and sales. Changes in the P&C cycle typically result in changed workflow object definitions. The planning and control workflows are typically organized to implement one of the six reference, co-ordindation mechanisms of Mintzberg [17].

– Changes to Business Processes.

Businesses are required to continuously re-engineer their (key) business processes to adequately respond to a changed environments. A more radical approach is to totally rethink and re-engineer the business as from scratch to considerable improve the business's effectiveness and efficiency. Both types of business process changes obviously result in a redefined business process and object layer in the enterprise architecture.

– Changes to Business Policies.

The changes, we have discussed up till now, can not be handled by existing organizational routines. The organization's structure needs to be transformed to deal with them. In some cases however, a realignment of strategy rather than *transformational* change is sufficient. *BALES* provides business policies to deal with *incremental* change by finetuning the legacy way of working (pro-active change) or slightly adapting (reactive change) the current business rules. In 2.5, we have discussed the policy mechanisms to cope with both types of incremental change.

2. Determine new mapping between enterprise model and legacy systems.

After the business model has changed, the business object implementator needs to determine a new mapping between the business objects from the enterprise model and the legacy system(s).

During this step, the implementator needs to determine the renewed mapping between the enterprise model and the reverse engineered legacy system model, without any side effects to the non-changed objects.

5.2 An Example of Process Changes

Due to a changed political climate the budgets of the Dutch defense organization have been tightened considerably over the past years. Therefore, defense operations need to be implemented more efficiently. These developments substantially influenced the way of working with the warehouse operations which we described in section 4.1.

The enterprise model of the maintenance and overhaul organization (see Figure-2), was based on the legacy business routines, reverse engineered on the basis of employee's requirements and procedure handbooks, and represents the way of working of several years back. Due to pressure of the DoD to minimize costs, the accounting department adviced the defense staff, amongst other things, to modernize the forecasting method and utilize a more cost-aware planning and control cycle for the (required) stocks in the warehouse.

The redesigned `planning` process does not incorporate a simple extrapolation of past inventory levels and demand but rather employs a sophisticated algorithm that optimizes the required inventory stock not only on the basis of required parts but also the inventory costs.

Figure 5 illustrates how we can replace part of an existing business process definition with newer business functionality using CDL specifications. As can be seen in this figure, the proposed *incremental* business changes imply a re-parameterization of the `DetPlanning` policy object that encapsulates the volatile planning business procedure.

```
BusinessPolicy DetPlanning : determinePlanning {
    // Mapping of forecasting method to legacy process component MRP
    plan (in LegacyProcess Warehouse.Material_Requirements_Planning.
        forecastDetModel(in Integer partID, in Integer stockID, in
        Integer warehouseID, in String consumptionHistory), in Currency partCost);
}; // End: DetPlanning
```

Fig. 5. CDL definition of the changed business policy `DetPlanning`.

The new `plan` method reuses the legacy deterministic material requirements planning algorithm `forecastDetModel`, that employs a *gross requirements planning*, and adds a `partCost` parameter in order to determine inventory costs. By doing this, the optimal inventory level of parts is not only calculated on the basis of part quantities (gross requirements) but also on available storage location, plant and order stocks (the so called net requirements, which are computed on the basis of the bill-of-material (BOM)).

Though this example is rather simplistic, it indicates how *BALES* can proactively deal with business change by simply *re-parameterizing* the business (policy) object `detPlanning` which is encapsulated in `Prognosis`, without introducing any side effects to existing objects.

6   Summary

Enterprises need flexible, modular business processes that can easily be configured to meet the demands of business and technology changes. In this chapter we argued that the combination of new business models with controlled change management are the driving forces that will eventually transform relatively independent organizations into cooperating enterprises.

We have described the *BALES* (binding Business Applications to LEgacy Systems) methodology that we are currently developing. The methodology's main objective is to inter-link parameterizable business objects to legacy objects and implement pro-active change management. Business objects are configured so that part of their implementation is supplied by legacy objects or by evolvable business objects. This means that the interfaces of 'modern' business objects are parameterizable (or self-describing) to allow these objects to evolve by accommodating upgrades or adjustments in their structure and behavior.

References

1. F. Manola et al. "Supporting Cooperation in Enterprise Scale Distributed Object Systems", in M.P. Papazoglou and G. Schlageter, editors, *Cooperative Information Systems: Trends and Directions*. Academic Press, London, 1998.
2. T. Curran, G. Keller, and A. Ladd. *SAP R/3 Business Blueprint: Understanding the Business Process Reference Model*. Prentice-Hall, New-Jersey, 1998.
3. S. Paul et. al. "Essential Requirements for a Workflow Standard", OOPSLA'98 Business Object Workshop III, http://www.jeffsutherland.org/oopsla97/, Atlanta, October 1997.
4. S. Abinavam et al. *San Francisco Concepts & Facilities*. International Technical Support Organization, IBM, February 1998. SG24-2157-00.
5. M.P. Papazoglou, A. Delis, A. Bouguettaya, and M. Haghjoo. "Class Library Support for Workflow Environments and Applications", *IEEE Transactions on Computer Systems*, 46(6), June 1997.
6. M. L. Brodie and M. Stonebraker. *Migrating Legacy Systems: Gateways, Interfaces and the Incremental Approach*. Morgan Kaufman Publishing Company, 1995.
7. M.P. Papazoglou and W.J. van den Heuvel. "Leveraging Legacy Assets", to appear in M. Papazoglou, S. Spaccapietra, Z. Tari, editors, *Advances in Object-Oriented Modeling*, MIT-Press, 1999.
8. P. Loucopoulos et. al. *Using the EKD-Approach - The Modelling Component*. Techn. report, WP/T2.1/UMIST/1, UMIST, April 1997.
9. W.J. van den Heuvel, M.P. Papazoglou, and M.A. Jeusfeld. "Configuring Business Objects from Legacy Systems", *Procs. CAISE'99 Conf., Heidelberg, Germany*, Springer-Verlag, June 1999.
10. P. Eeles and O. Sims. *Building Business Objects*. John Wiley & Sons, New York, 1998.
11. M.L. Brodie. "The Emperor's Clothes are Object-Oriented and Distributed" in M.P. Papazoglou and G. Schlageter, editors, *Cooperative Information Systems: Trends and Directions*, Academic Press, 1998.
12. M.T. Schmidt. "Building Workflow Business Objects, Object-Oriented Programming Systems Languages Applications", Proceedings of the OOPSLA'98 Business Object Workshop, Springer, 1998.
13. M.P. Papazoglou and S. Milliner. Content-based Organization of the Information Space in Multi-database Networks", in B. Pernici and C. Thanos, editors, *Procs. CAISE'98 Conf., Pisa, Italy*, Springer-Verlag, 1998.
14. Data Access Technologies. "Business Object Architecture (BOA) Proposal", BOM/97-11-09, OMG Business Object Domain Task Force, 1997.

15. M.A. Jeusfeld, M. Jarke, H.W. Nissen, and M. Staudt. "ConceptBase: Managing Conceptual Models about Information Systems", in P. Bermus, K. Mertins, and G. Schmidt, editors, *Handbook on Architectures of Information Systems*. Springer-Verlag, 1998.
16. J. Mylopoulos, A. Borgida, M. Jarke, and M. Koubarakis. "Telos: Representing Knowledge about Information Systems", *ACM Transactions on Information Systems*, 8(4), 1990.
17. Henry Mintzberg. "The Structuring of Organisations", *Prentice-Hall*, Englewood-Cliffs, 1979.
18. SAP. *http://www.sap.com/products/industry/*,
19. E. Gamma et al. *Design Patterns: Elements of Reusable Object-Oriented Software.* Addison-Wesley Publishing Company, 1999
20. R.L. Ackoff. 'Management misinformation systems', *Management Science*, 14(4):147-156.
21. G. Johnson and K. Scholes. *Exploring Corporate Strategy*, Prentice Hall, 1999

Workflow Management between
Formal Theory and Pragmatic Approaches

Stefan Jablonski

Friedrich-Alexander-Universitaet Erlangen-Nuernberg
Computer Science Department VI (Database Systems)
Martensstrasse 3, 91058 Erlangen, Germany
Stefan.Jablonski@informatik.uni-erlangen.de

Abstract. A general and globally accepted formal theory for workflow management is still not in sight. Since workflow management is said to be very application-driven, the question arises, whether a formal theory is necessary and possible at all. This article identifies the major domains of workflow management and discusses the necessity of formal theory and pragmatic approaches, respectively.

1 Current Situation

Since the advent of workflow management technology at the beginning of the nineties a lot of contributions to this area were made. Although this looks promising the overall goal to develop a generally applicable theory and a conceptual basis for workflow management still has not been met. Very many contributions narrow down to a very particular issue of workflow management; they find a tricky and often very valuable solution for a niche problem. Nevertheless, a step forward towards a generally applicable, conceptual model for workflow management is still not made. Three peculiarities characterize contributions in the workflow management area:

- Contributions are pragmatic.
  Many researchers state that workflow management is a discipline that is totally driven by the application. Since in many applications, theory is not directly applicable, they conclude that a formal theory for workflow management is also not relevant. This results in "how-I-did-it" approaches and solutions which contribute nothing but the single solutions to specific problems with only minor general value.
- Contributions claim to be general but are not.
  There is another group of researchers that are convinced that a formal theory is necessary for workflow management. Thus, many contributions present approaches towards this goal. Among other things, they introduce meta-models that ought to define a global concept for workflow management. Nevertheless, most of these approaches cannot hold what they promise. For instance, [4] investigates some of these approaches and undoubtedly proofs that they fail with respect to general applicability. Also the investigation in [4] is dated back to 1996, the situation has not

W. van der Aalst et al. (Eds.): Business Process Management, LNCS 1806, pp 345-358, 2000

changed significantly. The results of this research are still applicable and valid. The investigations reported in [5] support this observation.

- Contributions are too much influenced by adjacent research areas.
  Workflow management is a discipline on its own. However, many researchers stem from other, mostly adjacent research areas. Database management, in particular transaction management, and Petri Nets are two very dominant examples. Thus, often theories developed within one of these adjacent research areas are transferred into workflow management without critical assessment and necessary adjustment. The question whether these borrowed theories are applicable at all in the context of workflow management is asked too rarely.

In order not to be misunderstood. All three types of contributions are valuable. Although, they do not define by themselves a generally applicable theory for workflow management. They merely contribute valuable, but also limited experiences, methods and concepts with respect to this goal. Nevertheless, without taking into considerations the results of all these approaches a theory for workflow management cannot be formulated.

The need for a theory must be recognized and is not debatable. The more interesting and challenging question asks for the kind(s) of theory that is (are) needed and for the places within workflow management where this theory (theories) is (are) applied. We believe that workflow management can best be characterized by three key domains:

- The development of workflow management applications, i.e. the development of workflows. The emphasis is on the organization of the development process.
- The specification of workflow management applications, i.e. the specification of workflows. The formal model to describe workflows is under consideration.
- The execution of workflow management applications, i.e. the execution of workflows. The system infrastructure required to enact applications is investigated.

Hereby, a workflow management application comprises a set of workflows which altogether implement a specific application system.

The contribution of this article is to investigate the three key domains of workflow management with respect to the question whether either formal theory and/or pragmatics is necessary in order to support the corresponding task adequately. In this paper, pragmatics is interpreted as the application of common knowledge and specifically of experiences gathered in the domain. Therefore, the three key domains of workflow management are investigated in Section 2. This discussion identifies the main features of workflow management. Section 3 then explores the three key domains and finds out where formal theory and where pragmatics can best be applied. Along this line, recommendations for more pragmatic approaches and solutions will be given. Formal theories are named and if available introduced briefly.

Although revealing essential issues of workflow management this chapter does not claim to give definitive answers to the right balance between formal theory and pragmatic approaches nor does it provide a complete theory for workflow management.

2 Workflow Management Systems and Applications

In the former section the three key domains of workflow management are identified. We will see that the discussion of the development process of workflow management applications boils down to the discussion of the relationship between application processes and workflow (Section 2.1). The specification of workflows needs a workflow language. Section 2.2. introduces a general and abstract workflow language. The execution of workflow management applications demands a so-called workflow engine, i.e. an execution infrastructure for workflows. This infrastructure can best be investigated by analyzing its architecture.

The presentations of the three key domains reveals either the major issues of each key domain and identifies the major challenges of a key domain. The discussion in Section 3 then refers to these issues and challenges and discusses the preference of either a formal theory or a pragmatic approach.

2.1 Lifecycle of a Workflow Management Application

Big software systems cannot conceivably be specified by one person. Besides, the development of big software systems will progress steadily into more detail such that a so-called development lifecycle derives. Fig. 1 shows a typical development lifecycle for workflow management applications [11].

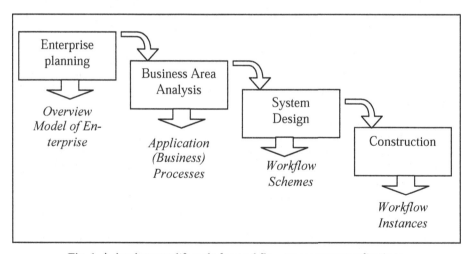

Fig. 1. A development lifecycle for workflow management applications.

In the phase enterprise planning an overview model of an enterprise is built. It is refined in the phase business area analysis. In application systems that are suitable for the deployment of workflow management technology the result of the phase business area analysis will always be a set of application processes, often called business processes [16]. The application processes are transformed into workflow schemes in the subsequent phase system design. Finally, in the construction phase workflow instances are derived from workflow schemes and are executed.

As it is examined in [2] extensively, workflows are derived from application processes. This is very valuable since much information that is relevant for a workflow model (workflow scheme) can be deducted from a corresponding application process directly [7]. Nevertheless, application processes are the result of the analyses of an business area. Their purpose is to describe the main features of an business area in an illustrative way. Therefore, an application process bears the main structure and meaning of the business area. However, since application processes are more descriptive they are not executable normally [2]. In order to execute them they have to be transformed into an executable form. A workflows is one possible form; and it is executable on a workflow management system. Thus, application processes can be regarded as drafts for the design of workflow schemes.

Although it is an important observation and is mostly true, the main difference between an application process and a workflow is not that the former one is illustrative and the latter one can be executed. The main distinction stems from the different purposes they are serving. Application processes are created during business area analysis; they have to describe the contents of an application area. Workflows are created during system design; they are an implementation vehicle - mostly tailored to the enactment of application processes.

We regard the relationship between application processes and workflows as one of the most interesting features within the development lifecycle of workflow management applications. Two key issues have to be mentioned.

- Derive design information for a workflow from the corresponding application processes as much as possible. Often application processes already bear contents and structure that can be borrowed by the workflow designer. Although, it is well proven that this does not always imply a direct mapping from an application process to a workflow [2], the information compiled into an application process is an asset with the specification of workflows. And it has to be stated again, workflows and application processes are not identical. Very often they even show a totally different structure.

- Maintain the relationship between application processes and workflows. To preserve this relationship especially pays off when changes are encountered. For instance, when an application process must be changed, the workflows that also have to be adjusted can be found effectively and efficiently if the relationship between application processes and workflows is kept.

Another issue along the development of workflow management application is the aspect of reusability. When big application systems comprising hundreds of workflows have to be developed, it is very advantageous to leverage on the results of other application system development processes. This means that workflows that already have been developed (in other projects) should be reused. To organize the reuse of whole or parts of workflows (e.g. an organizational policy, a large data structure, a program wrapper) is another challenge.

2.2 An Abstract Workflow Language

The goal of this section is to introduce a general and rather abstract language for the definition of workflows. The major features of such a language should be identified in a general way. Therefore, not a concrete language will be introduced but instead a number of concepts which characterize this language. The concepts then should be applicable to many workflow languages. A brief mapping to a real workflow language will demonstrate the applicability of the concepts developed.

The purpose of a workflow language is to describe workflows. Workflows are derivations of application processes as we have learned in Section 2.1; they can be executed by a workflow management system. In order to find out what language constructs are needed to build a basis for the description of workflows, we want to look into real life and want to see how application processes are enacted there. Hereby, we iterate a few times and refine the concepts identified step by step.

The two main concepts of a workflow language can nicely be derived from the term "workflow": "work" and "flow". Work has to be performed, besides, there is some flow (of work). At first, a place where work is performed must be identified. It is called *work unit*. Thus, work flows between work units, i.e. work is exchanged between work units. Examples of work units in real life are offices, where office work is performed, or shop floors, where manufacturing work is performed. When more the processing task within a work unit is of interest, a work unit is also called *work step*.

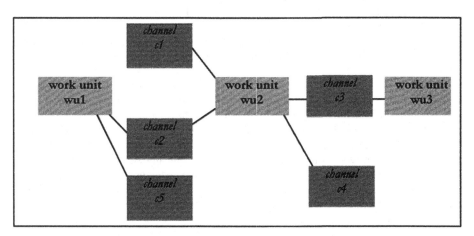

Fig. 2. The two basic concepts of a workflow language: work units and channels

Work units are independent from each other, i.e. each work unit can be set up independent from other work units. However, since work is flowing between them there are connectors between them, called *channels*. We will see later that there are different types of channels. Fig. 1 shows the two major concepts work units and channels. It becomes obvious that channels can connect multiple work units not just two. Furthermore, channels can sometimes bear a direction. This issue will be discussed later in this sub-section.

A next iteration of discussion will refine work units and channels. Refining a work unit reveals the question about its components. Looking at the real world examples from above again, three pieces come into the mind: *people* who perform work at a work unit, *tools* that are needed to carry out work and *operations* that are executed at a work unit. Hereby, operations form logical units of execution; tools are deployed within operations in order to provide the required functionality.

When refining the definition of channels, the concept of work has to be analyzed first. Again, we want to learn from the real world examples. In an office environment, an incoming document folder indicates work for the office clerk. In an manufacturing environment, delivered pieces that have to be assembled also indicate work. In an abstract view, documents and pieces are nothing but data and material. Thus, data and material flow along channels, i.e. *data channels* and *material channels* are introduced. Things that arrive at a work unit are work indicators. Combined with the people who have to carry out work, the tools they will use and operations that must be performed, these work indicators become work.

But there are even more types of channels which will be motivated by the following example. An assembly part is delivered which was painted in the work step before. To become dry, this part must lie for at least two days untouched. Thus, further information must flow along the channels to indicate this temporal restriction. Just the part would indicate that something has to be done with it - without being able to specify this necessary delay. We interpret the situation as if a control token is flowing between the work units, i.e. a *control channel* is defined, c.f. [5]. Control tokens bear temporal and causal information. Together with other items that flow along other channels it forms work for the receiving work unit.

The well-known concept of events also "flows" along the control channel since events are nothing but control tokens that indicate - mostly - that some piece of work can be worked upon.

Specifically in the context of events, the possible sources and sinks of channels have to be discussed. In Fig. 2, sources of channels can be work steps (e.g. work unit wu1 is source for channel c2) or channels does not have sources at all (e.g. channel c1). In the latter case, it is assumed that there is an input to the channel from outside. An equivalent observation applies to sinks. Channels can end in work units (e.g. channel c3 ends in work unit wu3) or can end without any successor (channel c4). The latter case means that the event is sent to some receiver outside the workflow management system. The same applies to all other flow types identified so far. Data and material can come from some place outside the workflow into the sphere of the workflows. The other way round, data and material might be sent to a place outside the workflow. Fig. 3 summarizes the concepts work unit and channels.

The introduction of concepts happens on an abstract level. Nevertheless, it is easy to transform the developed concepts into the workflow management area. The workflow languages of many workflow management systems can be classified according to the components identified in Fig. 2 and Fig. 3. As an example, the workflow language of the **Mobile** workflow management system [8] is studied. This language is selected since the author is very familiar with it and since it nicely demonstrates how the above concepts can be transformed into the area of workflow management.

In **Mobile** the language components are called perspectives. Intra work unit perspectives can be distinguished from inter work unit perspectives. The latter relate to channels and control dependencies between work units; the former organize work at a work unit.

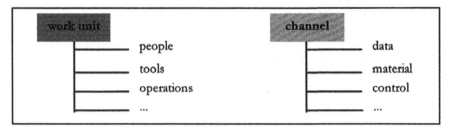

Fig. 3. The components of work units and channels

The group of intra work unit perspectives mainly comprises the organizational and the operational perspective. The organizational perspective defines the people who are eligible and obliged to perform work at a work unit. The operational perspective provides tools and furthermore operations that can be performed at a work unit. The group of inter work unit perspectives is formed by the behavioral perspective that defines control flow dependencies between work units and the informational perspective that defines data flow dependencies between work units. Due to the extensibility of the **Mobile** workflow language the material and event channel would be added as two further inter work unit perspectives with corresponding names. In **Mobile** there is another perspective, namely the functional perspective which is fundamental. This perspectives corresponds to work units, in **Mobile** called workflows. These work units (workflows) define the skeleton of all workflows. All other perspectives are integrated into this skeleton. Besides, the functional perspective allows to hierarchically structure a complex workflow definition by supporting functional decomposition. Thus, sub-workflows can be defined which can be regarded as a refinement of a (super-)workflow.

So far, the main components of a workflow language are introduced together with some kind of abstract syntax, Now, we are going to discuss the execution semantics of the workflow language. In principle, the following rule holds: a work unit can start to perform if all incoming channels are set (if there is a flow on a channel at all which sometimes might be optional). This means for instance, that data has arrived, that material is provided and that control flow (e.g. in form of an incoming control event) permits the work unit to start. For the purpose of this article further details are not necessary. Refer to [8] for more information about execution semantics.

In the following, non-functional requirements of a workflow management system are compiled. The first one is extensibility. Workflow management aims at the broad support of application areas. Thus, it is quite usual that new application-specific constructs must be added to the workflow language in order to adequately model the application scenario. For instance, when an organizational assignment needs to refer to temporary project assignments and this kind of assignment is so far not part of the workflow language, then an corresponding organizational assignment statement has to be included. Thus, extensibility must be a key feature of a workflow language.

Another requirement towards a workflow language can be derived from the close-ness of workflow management to applications. Since the current situation in the mar-ket dictates the vendors to serve each customer individually, a huge number of alter-native application processes for one specific task might evolve quickly. The workflow language must provide means to cope with this issue. Inheritance is one suitable solu-tion [3], however, it is still not experienced whether this means is applicable in huge applications. In general, the management of this high number of alternatives requires expressiveness of the workflow management language.

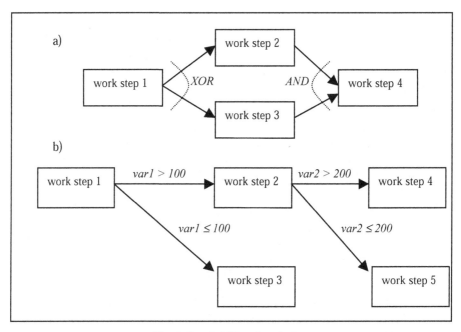

Fig. 4. Reachability of work steps

One of the major challenges in the context of a workflow language is the correct-ness of workflow specification. Hereby, the syntactical correctness of a workflow specification is not that issue, it is easy to check. A good language compiler will be able to do this. The more challenging features are reachability and executability of workflow steps. The former means that one workflow step can be executed at all, i.e. that the execution path can reach this workflow step eventually. An example sheds some light into this definition. In Fig. 4 two examples of simple workflows are given. Only one type of channel is shown, namely the control channel (arrows). The expres-sions adjacent to the arrows indicate conditions that have to be fulfilled if the corre-sponding control path should be followed. The dotted arcs (with attachments "XOR" or "AND") denote an exclusive fork condition and a conjunctive join condition. It becomes obvious that the definition of the workflow in Fig. 4a is incorrect. The fourth work step could never be executed since the AND condition in front of this work step will never be fulfilled. This incorrectness can already be detected when the workflow scheme is analyzed. Whether work step 4 in Fig. 4b can be reached is not decidable. This depends of the relationship between the value ranges of variables var1 and var2 and their interrelation. For instance, if var2 is greater the two times var1 then work step 5 will never be reached.

It is sufficient to have mentioned the non-functional requirements extensibility, expressiveness, and correctness. They cover the main issues and will be analyzed with respect to the applicability of formal methods in Section 3.

2.3 Architecture of a Workflow Management System

While the former section deals with workflow modeling, this section deals with workflow execution. In the context of workflow execution a workflow management system must be investigated. Especially, its architecture must be analyzed in order to find out whether the execution of workflows is adequate with respect to functional and non-functional requirements [15]. To identify these requirements is the issue of this section.

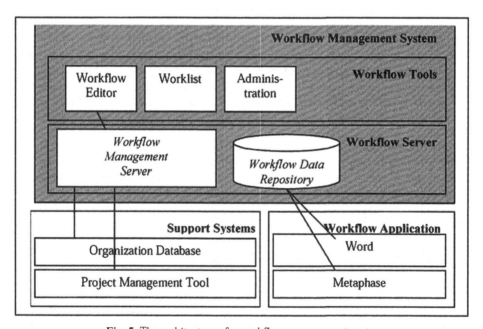

Fig. 5. The architecture of a workflow management system

In Fig. 5 a principle architecture of a workflow management system is shown. The interface of a workflow management system to users is built by a suite of workflow tools; a few are presented in the picture. The modeler of workflows is supported by a workflow editor, end users which execute workflows are supported by worklist tools. Administrators use the administration tool to install and configure a workflow management system. The heart of a workflow management system is constituted by the workflow management server and the workflow data repository [13]. The former bears the logic of workflow modeling and execution; the latter bears all type and instance data relevant for workflow modeling and execution. Workflow applications are business applications that are called in workflows in order to support the execution of a particular workflow step. Support systems are another group of software systems that back the work of the workflow management server.

The functional requirements towards the architecture of a workflow management system are easy to formulate. The perspectives identified in Section 2.2 must be enacted. This specifically implies the implementation of the workflow execution semantics which is also discussed in Section 2.2.

The non-functional requirements can good be motivated by Meyer's criteria and principles of good software design [12]. He states that modularity is one of the key design methods for software systems. Also for workflow management systems such a design method has to be applied to achieve a modular structure of the system. The following criteria help evaluate designs with respect to modularity: decomposability, composability, understandability, continuity, and protection. Furthermore, Meyer identifies the principles linguistic modular units, few interfaces of modules, small interface which provide weak coupling of modules, explicit interfaces, and information hiding which must be observed to ensure proper modularity.

Modularity is the key feature of a workflow management system. Further features which are elaborated now can be enacted best, if the modularity of the workflow management system can be taken as granted. To shorten the discussion of further non-functional requirements we concentrate on two issues: effectiveness and efficiency.

- Effectiveness means to have available functions that solve the application problems adequately. Since applications often change or grow, this involves to adjust or to add new functions from time to time. The feature extensibility is derived from this issue.
- Efficiency means to be able to execute workflows accurately and in time even in the presence of high system load. The feature scalability is derived from this issue.

Section 3 will investigate what formal methods can be used in order to design a workflow management system in such a way that the identified functional and non-functional requirements can be met.

3 Formal Theory and/or Applied Methods

This section is to investigate the identified key domains of workflow management with respect to the applicability of either formal theory or pragmatic approaches. In Section 3.1 a general assessment of this issue is given. Section 3.2 then analyses how the key domains can be supported

3.1 General Assessment

Section 2 shows that the three key domains of workflow management are not independent from each other. The development of workflow management applications directly points to a workflow language in order to model workflows. These workflows then have to be executed. This leads to the conclusion that whatever formal theory and pragmatics will be found, it must be comprehensive and must span all three domains.

Another observation supports the assessment that besides a reasonable amount of formal theory there is a huge area where pragmatic methods are required. One good example to illustrate this issue is the quality of a workflow. There are definitely some standards that are based on formal theory and assess objectively whether a workflow is specified well. For example, if all work steps identified in an application process are somehow mapped to a workflow is an indication for a good transformation. However, it is not clear whether this mapping is good or bad. This is a matter of pragmatic assessment and is not decidable with formal theory. This observation boils down to the fact that workflow specification often has to deal with non-computational issues than with issues that are decidable from a formal logic point of view.

Another issue must be mentioned: optimization. In quite a few publications optimization is named as a key issue for workflow management. In principle, we subscribe to this attitude. Nevertheless, we are convinced that most of the optimization strategies are not generally applicable since most of them are merely driven by quantitative considerations (like time and cost) what is just one possible aspect of good workflow design. One example is to take the number of work steps as criterion to assess a workflow specification. To end up in workflows with few steps is regarded as well designed. However, it might be interesting to have work steps of finer granularity in order to gain modularity. Workflow execution costs might then be slightly higher due to enhanced interpretation costs, though modular extension, adjustment or replacement of work steps is much easier to achieve.

3.2 Discussion of Specific Issues

According to the identification of three key domains of workflow management in Section 1 the following discussion is divided into three part. The discussion starts with the analysis of the development process for workflow management applications. Two issues were identified as most relevant:

1. Workflows should be derived from application processes.
2. The logical relation between application processes and workflows must be maintained.

There are some approaches that formalize the derivation of workflows from application processes by defining a mapping function between these two process formats [9, 10]. This mapping has to be assessed with respect to several criteria. There is a principle difference between application processes and workflows. Both are based on different sets of language constructs. The former more needs descriptive terminology while the latter requires well defined system-oriented vocabulary. Thus, the two languages can be mapped only partially. Even if there is agreement on some language constructs it is not clear whether their interpretation within the two different contexts is concurrent. For example, the specification of sequential processing of steps in an application process can be interpreted either as end-begin synchronization of the two corresponding work steps of a workflow, as begin-begin synchronization or as end-end synchronization.

We think that a formal transformation between application processes and workflows is not adequate since this task is heavily driven by pragmatic assessments and interpretation. However, to maintain the logical connect between application processes and derived workflows is of major interest especially with respect to (software) maintenance. Here, sophisticated concepts are necessary which besides other things are able to record decisions, personal assessments, considerations, etc. that lead to the design of workflows.

The next key domain of workflow management is workflow modeling with the workflow language as major component. The correctness of a workflow specification, its extensibility and expressiveness are identified as major issues (cf. Section 2.2). There is a number of contributions that argue about the correctness of workflow specifications [1]. The criteria reachability and executability are investigated. However, these investigations are always confined to the control flow aspect of a workflow. Other dependencies (channels, cf. Section 2.2) between workflows like data and material flow are not taken into account at all. We think that without the extension of these investigations to all dependencies between work steps these contribution are only of partial value. For instance, what is the benefit to know that a step is reachable with respect to control flow, however, the same step will never be executed since it is not reachable with respect to data flow?

We also see that the extension to arbitrary dependencies is hard to achieve and it is almost impossible to declare a formal theory for this issue since too many non-decidable issues would have to be considered. For instance, the example of Fig. 4b nicely demonstrates that due to the reference of values of variables it cannot be decided whether all work steps of this workflow will ever be executed. Nevertheless, there is a lot of research going on currently that investigates this issue. In contrast to these approaches, we suggest pragmatic methods to check the correctness of workflow specifications. Tool support is appreciated hereby. For example, a tool checks the channels between work units and checks whether there are cycles. Since most cycles cannot automatically be tested whether they loop indefinitely the tool should merely detect them and ask the modeller to check the end condition of the loops. Then, a good and mostly appropriate analyses of the workflow can be guaranteed.

Last but not least the third key domain of workflow management, the architecture of a workflow management system must be investigated with respect to the need of formal theory or pragmatic methods. Whether the functional requirements towards a workflow management system are fulfilled cannot be decided. This would mean to check whether the workflow language is implemented correctly. Modularity as one of the major features of the architecture of a workflow management system also cannot be checked formally. Whether this feature is considered appropriately must be assessed informally, i.e. more pragmatic criteria assess the appropriateness of the design.

Scalability is an issue where formal methods could be applied. There is work done that examines the distribution of workflow execution in order to find an execution strategy that guarantees efficiency. In [14] it is investigated how workflow schema and instance data must be allocated in a distributed system environment to achieve performing workflow execution.

4 Conclusion

This paper identifies the key domains of workflow management, the development life cycle of workflow management applications, the workflow language and the architecture of workflow management systems. These key domains are then investigated with respect to the question whether formal theory or pragmatic approaches are better suited to meet their specific requirements. The overall conclusion is that both formal theory and pragmatic approaches will be required in the realm of workflow management. There are some features of workflow management that can be described by formalisms; other features are more of a pragmatic type such that formalisms are not applicable.

It is not a goal of this paper to aim at completeness. We rather reveal some important issues that have to be considered when the impacts of theory and pragmatics are discussed. Neither do we claim to provide solutions; we rather want to indicate specific solution approaches and more want to trigger and inspire future discussions. These are absolutely necessary since the critical investigation of foundations for workflow management is still not done.

Acknowledgement
Many thanks to my colleague Michael Schlundt whose critical and productive comments clarified the issues discussed in this paper decisively.

References

1.   van der Aalst, W.M.P.: The Application of Petri Nets to Workflow Management. The Journal of Circuits, Systems and Computers, Vol. 8 (1998), No. 1, 21 - 66
2.   Boehm, M.: Systematic Construction of Workflow Types for Workflow Management Applications. PhD Thesis, Technical University of Dresden, 1999 (in German)
3.   Bussler, C.: Towards Workflow Type Inheritance. Proc. First International Workshop on Object Oriented Workflow Management Systems, OOPSLA, 1998
4.   Bussler, C.: Analysis of the Organizational Modeling Capability of Workflow Management Systems. Workshop of the GI Working Group "Workflow Managment", Linz, 1996
5.   Hahn, C.; Neeb, J.: Experiences in Selecting a Workflow Management System for the Car Industry. Technical Report, Friedrich-Alexander-Universitaet Erlangen-Nuernberg, Chair for Database Systems, 1999
6.   Jablonski, S.: MOBILE: A Modular Workflow Model and Architecture. Proc. 4th International Working Conference on Dynamic Modelling and Information Systems, Nordwijkerhout, NL, 1994
7.   Jablonski, S.: On the Complementary of Workflow Management and Business Process Modeling. SIGOIS Bulletin, Vol. 16 (1995), No. 1
8.   Jablonski, S.; Bussler, C.: Workflow Management - Modeling, Concepts, Architecture and Implementation, International Thomson Computer Press, 1996
9.   Karagiannis, D.; Junginger, S.; Strobl, R.: Introduction to Business Process Management Systems Concepts. In: Scholz-Reiter, B.; Stickel, E. (eds.): Business Process Modeling, Springer-Verlag, 1996
10. Krallmann, H.; Derszteler, G.: Workflow Management Cycle - An Integrated Approach to the Modelling, Execution, and Monitoring of Workflow-Based Processes. In: Scholz-Reiter, B.; Stickel, E. (eds.): Business Process Modeling, Springer-Verlag, 1996
11. Martin, J.: *Information Engineering*. Englewood Cliffs, NJ, Prentice-Hall 1990

12. Meyer, B.: *Object-oriented Software Construction.* Prentice-Hall International, Englewood Cliffs, NJ, 1988
13. Neeb, J.: Schlundt, M.; Wedekind, H.: Repositories for Workflow Management Systems in a Middleware Environment. Proceedings 33. Hawaii International Conference on System Science (HICCS'00), Maui, Hawaii, 2000
14. Schuster, H.; Heinl, P.: *A* Workflow Data Distribution Strategy for Scalable Workflow Management Systems. In: Proc. ACM Symposium on Applied Computing (SAC'97), San Jose, 1997
15. Schuster, H.; Jablonski, S.; Heinl, P.; Bußler, C.: *A General Framework for the Execution of Heterogeneous Programs in Workflow Management Systems.* In: Proc. of the First IFCS Conf. on Cooperative Information Systems, Brussels, June 1996, pp. 104-113
16. Stein, K.: Integration of Application Process Modeling and Workflow Management. PhD Thesis, University of Erlangen-Nuernberg, 1999

Documentary Petri Nets:
A Modeling Representation for Electronic Trade Procedures

Ronald M. Lee

Erasmus University Research Institute for Decision and Information Systems (EURIDIS)
Erasmus University Rotterdam
PO 1738
3000 DR Rotterdam, the Netherlands
tel. 31-10-4082601
rlee@fac.fbk.eur.nl

Abstract. This paper introduces the concept of an electronic trade scenario (executable transaction model) as a potential solution to "open" electronic commerce - trade among parties that have no prior trading relationship. The basic idea is that these trade scenarios would be stored in a "global repository", and downloaded by trading parties as needed for a particular trade. A representation, called Documentary Petri Nets (DPN) is used to represent such trade scenarios. The *InterProcs* system is described as a prototyping environment to support the design and execution of such trading systems using this representation. Given that the parties are often trading at "arm's length", a key focus is the development of trustworthy trade scenarios that have sufficient controls and evidentiary documentation.

1 Introduction

Business-to-business electronic commerce has so far been realized mainly through the use of Electronic Document Interchange (EDI) implemented in closed, mainly bi-lateral linkages that are relationship specific. As the demand for electronic trading relationships among businesses becomes greater, there is a need to make these electronic linkages more generic and re-usable. Furthermore, the scope of the modeling needs to encompass not only simple two-party links, but the entire trade or supply chain transaction model, which may include as many as a dozen different parties.

The most complex challenges are in the area of international trade. This is also the area where incredible economic benefits might be found. A conservative estimate of potential savings in transaction costs in the area of international trade is around half a *trillion* US dollars per year. This does not include the potential entry of many new small to medium-sized businesses into international trading.

Current developments in wide area networking (e.g. Extranets) and related component technologies make the notion of global repositories for generic, re-usable transaction models increasingly more feasible. Needed, however, is effective design representations and methodologies for representing complex trade and supply chain

W. van der Aalst et al. (Eds.): Business Process Management, LNCS 1806, pp 359-375, 2000
© Springer-Verlag Berlin Heidelberg 2000

transaction. We thus examine the requirements for such representations. We then present our own solution to this challenge: Documentary Petri Nets (DPN's), which satisfies these representation requirements in a way that supports both bottom-up and top-down design approaches, and also the procedural separation of the business roles. Implementation characteristics of the DPN representation are also examined.

A modeling and prototyping environment, called *InterProcs*, is presented that includes a graphical design interface based on Documentary Petri Nets, which automatically generates functioning prototype transaction models that operate locally or in distributed fashion over the Internet. A simplified documentary credit procedure provides an example of such a Documentary Petri Net model.

But this is only the beginning of the potential we foresee. Once a formal representation for trade procedures is adopted, new functionalities may be developed based on that representation. Following are three directions in our continuing research:

- automated auditing of trade procedures ("auditdaemons"), which use pattern-matching techniques to identify fraud, collusion, and other control weaknesses in the trade procedure [2, 3, 4,11].

- scenario grammars (aka procedure constraint grammars), which allow the sharing and re-usability of chunks of procedural knowledge at arbitrary levels of abstraction. For instance, a car loan, a mortgage, and a documentary credit procedure are all special cases of a more generic secured loan. The use of scenario grammars allows computer aided generation of customized procedures by parties with little or no expertise [12, 14, 15].

- navigation of distributed requirements and constraints - especially for international trade, bureaucratic constraints on the trade procedure may be imposed by governmental agencies (e.g.customs) of the countries included in the trade. Further, these requirements may change without notice. The solution we propose, called the messenger model, allows automatic navigation of these distributed agencies to collect these constraints and to incorporate them into the trade procedure at the time the contract is made [13].

2 Open Electronic Commerce

The focus of this project is on *open* electronic commerce: doing business among parties having no prior trading relationship. What we hope to achieve is computerized support for commerce that is *trustworthy* in the sense that trading partners who do not know each other, and may even come from different countries and cultures, may conduct business with the assurance that their interests will be protected in the event that "things go wrong", whether by accident, negligence, or intentional fraud.

In order to conduct electronic commerce, parties have to know about each others' "way of doing business" before they can start exchanging data electronically. Extra knowledge about the preferred way of doing business of one trading partner has to be conveyed to the other; in other words, the parties have to agree upon the trade scenario they are going to follow [7,8, 21]. A trade scenario is the mutually agreed uponset of procedures, documents and rules that govern the activities of all parties involved in a set of related business transactions. Thus, a trade scenario controls all interactions between the roles involved. A trade scenario stipulates which actions should be undertaken by which parties, the order in which these actions should be performed as well as the deadlines and other timing constraints on the performance of these actions. Actions of parties include the sending and/or receiving of goods, documents or funds.

The need and usefulness of trade scenarios is easy to demonstrate. Consider only a simple post-payment contract for goods. The buyer assumes that an invoice will be sent after delivery to trigger the payment obligation. The seller, on the other hand, abides by the practice that payment becomes due from the time of delivery, and does not send an invoice. Thus, the goods arrive, and the buyer does not pay, waiting for an invoice. Meanwhile the seller becomes irked, and initiates collection proceedings. This is an example of the so-called "battle of the forms". Each party utilizes standardized documents such as a purchase order, delivery agreement, etc. which contain (typically on the backside, in small print) the terms and conditions that are their style of doing business. Unfortunately, the small print is often ignored by the receiving party.

For trade in a well-established industry area, standardized practice becomes generally accepted, and there usually is not a problem. In some cases, guidelines by international bodies such as the International Chamber of Commerce or the UNCID have been established (for instance the Uniform Customs and Practices for Documentary Credits, issued by the ICC, [6]). However, in more open trading situations, that cross national, cultural or sectorial boundaries, such conflicts are much more likely to arise. Many existing EDI applications of course embed the types of document exchange sequencing of a trade scenario. However, these sequences are normally "hard coded" into the application programs, as specified in the terms of the trading partner agreement, a legal, textual document. A key aspect of the architecture presented here is that trade scenarios are "soft coded", in a declarative, rule-based form. This has the virtue that they may be down-loaded from e.g. a central library to meet the needs of a particular contractual situation.

3 Documentary Petri Nets

In Figure 1, the contracting process is divided into three main phases: shopping, negotiation and performance. (While we recognize that this over-simplifies somewhat, it is sufficient for present purposes.) Interpreting this in an electronic commerce context, the shopping phase involves navigating among the product offerings of various vendors (e.g. electronic advertisements on the Web). As a result of this phase, the customer identifies a prospective vendor and specifies the product characteristics to be purchased. During the next phase, negotiation, the parties will arbitrate two things:

    a. *doing* tasks - such as payment terms,delivery terms

    b. *control* tasks - including documentary requirements.

The output of this negotiation will be the specific trade scenario that the parties will follow for the execution of the contract. The negotiation process itself also follows a scenario. For many types of trading, this negotiation scenario remains more or less the same.The documentary controls for such anegotiation scenario will be such standardized (EDI) documents such as purchase order, PO acknowledgement, etc. However, in certain contract domains, additional controls are required. One example is secured loans, such as home mortgages or documentary credits. In these cases, substantial additional control documentation is needed such as credit worthiness of borrower, inspection of the asset, market value of the asset, and so on.

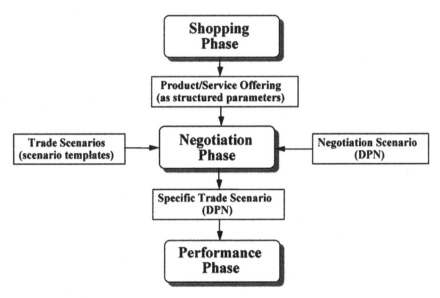

Figure 1. Contracting Phases

In this section we describe the representation called Documentary Petri Nets (DPN's), used to specify the procedural aspects of a trade scenario. A basic issue for this project is how these trade procedures should be represented (a.) from the modeler's perspective, and (b.) from a computation (inferential) perspective. In the course of our prior research, we have examined a wide number of such representations, including state-transition diagrams, marked graphs, event nets, event grammars, the event calculus, process algebras, temporal and dynamic logics. Eventually, we found Petri nets ([1, 18, 19] to be the most appropriate representation for capturing the temporal/dynamic aspects of electronic trade procedures, offering both a graphical representation (for modelers) and a formal basis for the verification of various properties (computational). In addition, Petri nets have become popular in a wide variety of problem domains, including numerous workflow systems, where sequence, contingency and concurrency of activities need to be modeled. This wide acceptance facilitates the training and understandability for electronic trade scenarios. However, Petri nets by themselves offer only a temporal framework for the procedural representation. For that reason, we have found it necessary to add various extensions to the Petri net representation, making it more appropriate for the modeling of trade procedures. We call this extended representation Documentary Petri Nets (DPN's).

Basic Petri nets focus on the representation of discrete dynamic systems, including aspects of concurrency and choice. A Petri net is a bi-partite, directed graph with two types of nodes: *places* (represented as circles) and *transitions* (typically represented as bars or boxes). Arcs connect places with transitions or vice versa (it is not allowed to connect two places or two transitions). The dynamic behavior of the modeled system is represented by tokens flowing through the net (represented as blackening of a place). A transition is enabled if all its input places (i.e., arcs exist from those places to the transition) are marked. If this is the case, the transition removes the token from each input place and instantaneously produces one in each output place (i.e., an arc exists from the transition to the place). This is called the *firing* of a transition.

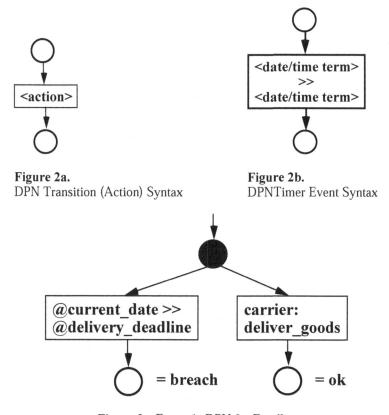

Figure 2a.
DPN Transition (Action) Syntax

Figure 2b.
DPNTimer Event Syntax

Figure 2c. Example DPN for Deadline

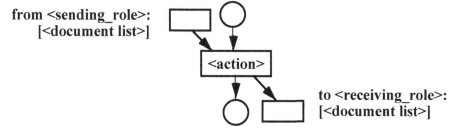

Figure 2d. DPN Document Place Syntax

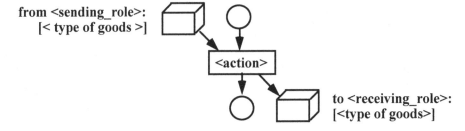

from <sending_role>:
    [< type of goods >]

<action>

to <receiving_role>:
    [<type of goods>]

Figure 2e. DPN Physical Goods Syntax

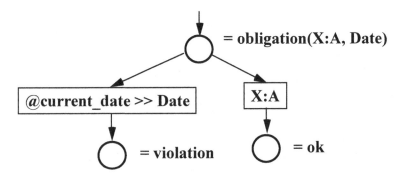

= obligation(X:A, Date)

@current_date >> Date

X:A

= violation

= ok

Figure 2f. DPN Example Deontic Status Labelson Control Places

With Documentary Petri Nets, an important extension to basic Petri nets we make is the interpretation of transitions as the actions of contracting parties, which are indicated by an associated label of the form[1] shown in Figure 2a. Also, whereas basic Petri nets represent *relative* time (as a partial ordering of events), we needed to add certain *absolute* time notations for deadlines, etc. In DPN's, these are included as a special kind of transition, called a *timer event*, having an associated label of the form (">>" is time ordering), as shown in Figure 2b. Most commonly, these involve a comparison of the built-in parameter, **@current_date**, with a another date such as a delivery deadline. For example, see Figure 2c. In this case, the token will be taken by the first transition to occur. Thus, if the event that the current date exceeds the delivery date occurs before the delivery of the goods, the token will more to the state of breach.

---

[1] Here we are presenting the notation for role DPN's, where all the actions in the procedure refer to the same agent. Another form of DPN is possible, called a joint DPN, that models the coordinated actions of some or all of the parties together in a single graph. In that case, the form of the action labels for transition nodes becomes:

<role(s)> : <action>

and the form of the labels for documents places (incoming or outgoing) becomes:

    <sender role> to <receiver role> :[<document list>]

and similarly for physical goods:

    <sender role> to <receiver role> : [<kind of good>]

Another important extension to basic Petri nets that we have added in DPNs, is a representation of *documents*[2]. Syntactically, these are another kind of place node, called a *document place*, drawn as a rectangle. In the role procedures, each document place has an associated label of the form as shown in Figure 2d. Normally, the document list will be only a single document (type), but this allows also for the sending of bundles of documents as a single documentary communication[3]. A frequent type of documentary exchange relates to the transfer of funds. Often, this is a document sent to a bank, such as a payment instruction. In business-to-business transactions, the exchange of actual cash is fairly rare. However, to model such cash payments we also use the same notation of a document place. (Thus, we would consider paper currency as a special kind of performative document.) A variation of document places that is occasionally used is a *goods place*, indicating the exchange of physical goods. The notation for this is a cube, and it has a similar labeling as for document places[4], as shown in Figure 2e.

In addition to the above described labels, any of the control places, document places or goods places may have an additional kind of label, known as a state predicate. These use the same predicate notation as in Prolog, and are used to indicate additional properties and relations that become true when the place is marked. These are commonly used to indicate changes in deontic status, for instance, **obligation(X:A,Date)** which means that party **X** has an obligation to perform action **A** before the deadline, **Date**[5]. This is illustrated in Figure 2f.

One important aspect of modeling trade scenarios is the ability to model the procedures of each role as a separate Documentary Petri Net. This modeling style results in a clear, visual separation of the various the roles, that also enables their geographical separation. Indeed, it is this characteristic of the DPN modeling technique that allows the automated trade scenarios to be executed in a distributed fashion, by legally autonomous parties. *The only coordination between the various role scenarios is by means of the (electronic) documents they exchange.* This directly parallels the way paper-based trade procedures operate today.

---

[2] Typically, these documents will be in a structured format such as UN/EDIFACT or XML/EDI [12]. However, they could equally well bein a logic-based format such as Kimbrough's FLBC [9]. The only requirementis that selected data needed by the procedure be retrievable from the document.

[3] Computationally, the data in these documents is persistent; that is, once a document has been received by a role, it is recorded in the role's local database, and remains there even though the document place may cease to be marked. Functionally, this is similar to the way electronic documents are handled in actual practice. An alternative approach would be to use colored Petri nets [1], where data would be carried through the Petri net by means of structured tokens. We found this latter approach to be unnecessarily complicated for our modeling needs.

[4] Automated trade scenarios, operating over digital networks, obviously do not handle or transport physical goods directly. The use of this notation is usually to describe the larger system, where physical as well as electronic actions are modeled.

[5] This example also illustrates the use of logical variables (as in Prolog) within a DPN. The scope of these variables is the DPN procedure where it appears. By contrast, parameters, which begin with "@" (e.g.@delivery_deadline) may be global in the entire model, or refer to data elements in documents within the role.

4 Modeling Example

As an example problem domain we will analyze the formation and execution of an international contract for the sale of commercial goods [5]. Commonly, international sales contracts are executed by a documentary credits procedure, subject to the rules set forth in the Uniform Customs and Practice for Documentary Credits [6].

Documentary credit procedures were introduced by the banking community in order to solve a common problem in business: the lack of trust among trading partners. When partners do not know whether they can trust each other, the risk for both buyer and seller is very high. For example, the buyer might pay for the goods without being sure of receiving them or the seller may ship the goods without being sure of getting paid. These problems arise particularly when the trade is international, as a common legal and banking system exists when trade is conducted within the same country. The solution that the banks offer to international business is that they take over the risk for the buyer and seller. The buyer and seller may rely on a trusted relationship between their banks.

Documents play an important role in these transactions in that payment for the goods is made not on the delivery of the goods themselves but on the presentation of stipulated documents. Stipulated documents may include a commercial invoice, an insurance certificate, a certificate of origin, and a transport document (e.g., a bill of lading or an airway bill), among others. The seller receives payment by presenting the stipulated documents to a bank (the advising bank) that the buyer has instructed to make payment.

Two attributes make documentary credit procedures a challenging domain for automated trade scenarios. First, these procedures involve numerous agents who often must interact in different native languages. The agents in an international sale using documentary credits may include two or three banks, a forwarder/broker, a liner-agent, a land transport carrier, a customs official, an insurance agent, a stevedore (to load the goods on the ship), a ship's captain, and several others in addition to the buyer and seller. Also, the goods may have to cross several borders in their transit from seller to buyer; thus, multiple versions of documents in various languages may be required. (The multi-lingual interface and text generation capabilities of *InterProcs* are thus useful here as well.)

Second, these procedures are mired in bureaucratic complexity and are subject to a host of confusing rules depending on the countries of the exporting/importing parties. At one time as many as 100 forms (i.e., performative communications) were required to ship goods from one country to another and to arrange payment [7]. The task of processing these myriad forms was so cumbersome that the goods commonly travelled faster than the forms, arriving before the documents did [10]. When the goods being shipped were perishable food stuff, the buyer was placed in the untenable position of watching his goods spoil as he waited for the documents allowing him to claim the shipment. Using information technology to generate, process (i.e., reason about) and transmit these documents can avoid these problems.

In the following example, we present a (somewhat simplified) trade scenario for a documentary credit procedure. The principal roles are:

Consignee: the recipient of the goods (normally the buyer).

Shipper: the party dispatching the goods(normally the seller).

Issuing Bank: the bank issuing the credit (normally in the buyer's country).

Corresponding Bank: a partner bank, which handles paper work at the other side (normally in the seller's country).

Carrier: the transporter of the goods.

Almost all documentary credit procedures conform to the guidelines issued by the International Chamber of Commerce (ICC) Uniform Customs and Practices for Documentary Credits [6]. By including a sentence such as "this letter of credit has been issued under the rules of ICC/ UCP 500" these guidelines become legally enforceable, independent of differences in national legislation of the involved parties' countries. The diagram shown in Figure 3 gives an overview of the document flows among these roles. Following that, Figures 4a-e show snapshots taken from *InterProcs* of the role procedures developed for this trade scenario[6].

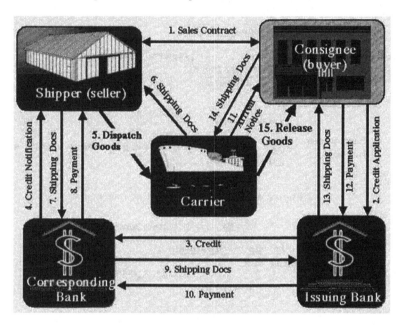

Figure 3. Overview Diagram forDocumentary Credit Procedure

---

[6] This model may also be executed from the Website: http://www.euridis.fbk.eur.nl/Euridis/

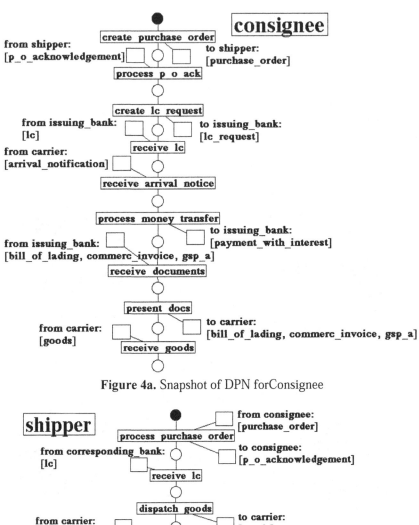

Figure 4a. Snapshot of DPN forConsignee

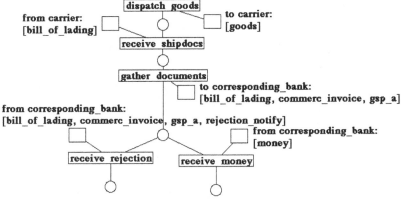

Figure 4b. Snapshot of DPN for Shipper

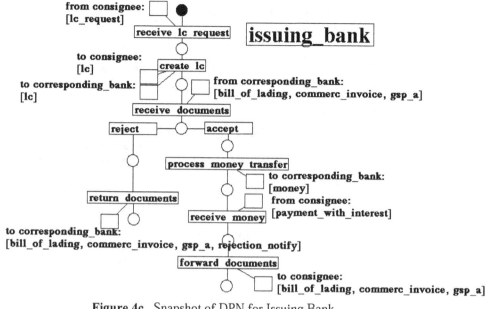

Figure 4c. Snapshot of DPN for Issuing Bank

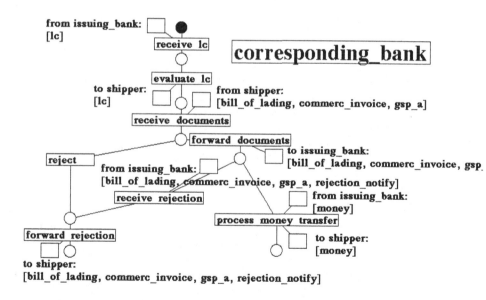

Figure 4d. Snapshot of DPN for Corresponding Bank

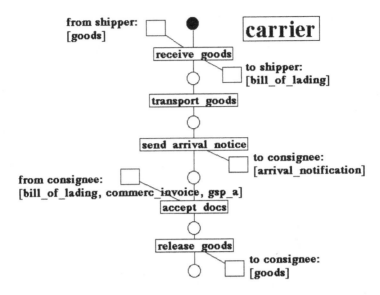

Figure 4e. Snapshot of DPN for Carrier

5 InterProcs

In this section we provide an overview of the *InterProcs* system, which implements the modeling representations we have developed for automated trade scenarios. The motivation behind the development of *InterProcs* is to validate our concepts and representations for electronic trade scenarios, demonstrating their feasibility though realistic prototype transaction models with actual EDI documents. The system divides into two separate systems: *InterProcs Executor*, which executes existing transaction models; and *InterProcs Designer,* a tool for the design and knowledge base development of trade scenarios.

5.1 InterProcs Executor

In this section, we explain the operation of the *InterProcs Executor*. With it, one can view and execute existing trade scenario models in three modes:

Viewer Mode: This mode provides a simulation of the total scenario on a single machine. The trade scenario is accessed as an applet from a Web site. Documents are transmitted among the roles internally within the executing Java program. This mode is useful for design and demonstration purposes. It also provides a convenient means for distant development of models: new versions of a scenario can be put up on a Web site and viewed by clients at remote locations.

Gaming Mode: As the name suggests, the purpose of this mode is for interactive gaming, normally as a single location using a local network, with multiple machines and multiple players. The roles of the trade scenario are downloaded from a Web site, and executed using *InterProcs Executor* as an applet.

Network Mode: The purpose of this mode is for prototype testing of the trade scenario in geographically separate locations. As in the gaming mode, the roles of the trade scenario from a Web site, but here they are executed using *InterProcs Executor* as a stand-alone application (which allows access to local files and databases). Documents are transmitted among the roles via normal Internet email.

5.2 InterProcs Designer

In this section, we explain the operation of the *InterProcsDesigner*. With it, one can design new automated trade scenarios utilizing:

- graphical drafting using Documentary Petri Nets, by role
- re-usable template sub-procedures
- design of electronic documents
- design of detail computations on documents

A principal feature of *InterProcs* is its graphical user interface for designing trade procedures. Furthermore, since the system embeds a Prolog engine, auxiliary rule-bases can be added to a trade scenario model, allowing further automated 'intelligence' such as heuristic navigation of regulatory constraints. *InterProcs* can not only be used to draw trade procedures, it also offers the possibility to simulate them, including graphical animation of the transaction flow. When designing trade scenarios, the scenario actions of each role are represented as a separate Documentary Petri Net, shown in a separate window on the screen. The communication between the roles is exclusively through exchanges of (electronic) documents. (This is a practical as well as legal requirement of trade scenarios.)

Trade scenarios may be constructed either top-down or bottom-up. Using a top-down approach, an integrated version of the overall trade scenario is developed, which is then (automatically) divided into separate sub-scenarios for each of the roles. Using a bottom-up approach, distinct scenarios (procedures) are developed from the perspective of each separate role. By simulating these together as acomplete scenario, one is able to identify and diagnose any incompatibilities among the roles. The result, whether designed top-down or bottom-up, is an automated trade scenario that executes in a distributed fashion, with autonomous parties (at different geographical locations, with different machines) for each role. The characteristic that the resulting automated trade scenarios are distributed in this way is legally essential: since most of the documents handled by a trade procedure have a legal significance, it is vital that each organization have completely independent control of the documents they send out, since they will be legally responsible for theconsequences.

Using the various operating modes of the *InterProcsExecutor*, this distributed execution of the trade scenario may be analyzed and evaluated. In the viewer mode, the distributed execution is simulated on a single machine. Using the gaming mode, for instance in a group collaboration setting, managers can play the different roles, and become evaluate the scenario from the different role perspectives. In the network mode, different organizations may participate in the testing of the scenario from their local sites.

The system at present operates as a design and prototyping tool for trade scenarios. However, it has been developed in such a way (in Java) so as to be able to save the resulting trade scenarios as object-oriented components. These components may be combined with other business system components (e.g. for database access, security, application interfaces) to provide a production-level implementation. With this vision, trade scenarios may be stored in a publicly accessible, global repository, available via the Internet. Thus, the promise is for plug-and-play installation of complex trade transaction models, enabling small as well as larger companies easier entry into new (also international) markets.

6 Automated Generation of Trade Scenarios

A limitation of the manual design approach presented thus far (and as well, a limitation of other open EDI approaches) is that the scenarios produced are *fixed*; that is, they cannot be adapted or adjusted to meet additional needs of a given situation. In this part of the project, we address this problem with an expert system approach, by which scenario components are broken down into reusable component parts, which can be flexibly reassembled to meet the needs of a wide variety of situations. The computational formalism we introduce is called a *procedure constraint grammar* (PCG). As its name suggests, an objective of the PCG representation is to describe procedures by their temporal ordering constraints, rather than the absolute sequence of steps. This allows for more flexible re-combination of procedural components (doing and control tasks).

Using a procedure constraint grammar, the user interacts with the system, specifying constraints and objectives of the contracting situation. Based on these specifications, the system composes a trade procedure, which is presented in graphical form, and which can then be compiled and simulated. Here, the term 'grammar' is used in the linguistic sense of generative grammars, i.e. a set of rules for generating syntactically correct or well-formed sentences in a language. The objective of PCG rules is to generate procedures that are not only well-formed syntactically, but also from a control standpoint. In this aspect, a procedure constraint grammar operates like an expert system shell that may be used to develop knowledge bases about contracting and associated legal and documentary requirements. Unlike language grammars, however, which are typically represented as an integrated hierarchy of rules, PCG's are organized as constraints on a target procedure. It is the job of the PCGconstraint solver to identify a (minimal) solution procedure (according to some preference ordering of the user - e.g. minimal duration vs minimal risk).

Key features of procedure constraint grammars are therefore their *flexibility* to model situation-specific variations of generic trade procedures, and the *re-usability* of procedural knowledge previously developed by domain experts. Our objective is in a sense to obtain the best of both worlds, to allow contracting parties to specify unique requirements of their contract situation, while yet maintaining a legal integrity and controls in the trade procedure. The resulting electronic trade procedure should be *trustworthy* in that each of the parties is assured that preventative or detective controls are in place in case of the other party's non-performance, or other accidental events occur. Other approaches to this objective have been considered, but proved not to be sufficient. These include a sub-procedure approach, where actions of the trade procedure can refer to other substitutable procedures. This proved too inflexible in that the situational variations often need to include a combination from different sources of procedural knowledge: those related to the task; those relating to controls; and those relating to the specific communications media employed. We also considered an object-oriented approach, but found it to have similar difficulties. Object oriented methods handle procedural knowledge mainly by overriding routines in the parent procedure. For our purposes, this is much like the sub-procedure approach. Additionally, the requirement of multiple knowledge sources leads to multiple inheritance, with the associated difficulties of contention.

In our current approach, knowledge specified as independent 'constraints', which can be at arbitrary levels of abstraction. Where different levels of abstraction need to be combined, this is handled by the constraint solver by expanding them to a common lowest level of detail. Where contentions occur, these are dealt with by preference orderings, which are specified in the knowledge base. Further discussion of procedure constraint grammars is found in [12, 14, 15]. The notation used in these papers is a linear one, similar to that used in many AI planning systems. Currently under development is a graphical variant of the current DPN graph notation, that we call *scenario templates*. Using these scenario templates are designed graphically in much the same way as the current DPN's are. Scenario templates can invoke other scenario templates as sub-procedures (with parameters and logical variables as arguments). We allow multiple variations of a scenario template definition, with different selection conditions. (This is like the multiple rules in a grammar). Together, these scenario templates comprise a *scenario grammar* of equivalent functionality to the PCG's described above.

7 Summary, Conclusions

The concept of an electronic trade scenario was introduced as a potential solution to "open" electronic commerce - trade among parties that have no prior trading relationship. The vision is that these trade scenarios would be stored in a publicly accessible electronic library (perhaps a "global repository" maintained by an independent international organization), and downloaded by trading parties as needed for a particular trade. The Documentary Petri Nets (DPN) representation was presented as a candidate representation for such trade scenarios. The *InterProcs* system was presented as a prototyping environment to support the design and execution of such trading systems using this DPN representation. Features included a graphical design interface for trade scenarios, Internet-based scenario execution, audit daemons for detecting control weakness, as well as scenario grammars and supply chain designer for the automated generation of trade scenarios. Future directions include the output of trade scenarios as object-oriented components for assimilation within emerging business component architectures, to support plug-and-play installation of trade scenarios into production transaction systems.

References

[1]   Aalst, W.M.P. van der, "Timed Coloured Petri Nets and their Application to Logistics", *PhD thesis Eindhoven University of Technology*, 1992

[2]   Bons, R. *Designing Trustworthy Trade Procedures for Open Electronic Commerce*, PhD Dissertation, Euridis and Faculty of Business, Erasmus University, 1997

[3]   Bons, R.W.H., Lee, R.M., and Wagenaar, R.W. "Computer-Aided Auditing of Inter-organizational Trade Procedures", *Intelligent Systems in Accounting, Finance and Management*, Special Issue on Electronic Commerce, ed. Jae Kyu Lee, 1998.

[4]   Chen, Kuo Tay. *Schematic Evaluation of Accounting Control Systems*, PhD Dissertation, University of Texas atAustin, 1992.

[5]   Dewitz, Sandra. *Contracting on a Performative Network: Using Information Technology as a Legal Intermediary*, PhD Dissertation, University of Texas at Austin, 1992.

[6]   ICC, *The Uniform Customs and Practices for Documentary Credit Procedures*, International Chamber of Commerce publication number 500, Paris, France, January, 1994.

[7]   ISO, *The Open-edi Conceptual Model*, ISO/IEC JTC1/SWG-EDI, Document N222, 1991.

[8]   ISO, *The Open-edi Reference Model*, IS14662, ISO/IEC JTC1/SC30, 1996.

[9]   Kimbrough, S. "Sketch of a Basic Theory for a Formal Language for Business Communication", *International Journal of ElectronicCommerce*, Vol 3, No 1, 1999.

[10]   Kindred, H.M. "Modern Methods of Processing Overseas Trade."*Journal of World Trade*, December 1988, pp.5-17.

[11]   Lee, R.M., "Auditing as Pattern Recognition", Working Paper, Department of Management Sciences and Information Systems, University of Texas at Austin, August 1991.

[12]   Lee, R.M.: "Dynamic Modeling of Documentary Procedures: A CASE for EDI", *Proceedings of Third International Working Conferenceon Dynamic Modeling of Information Systems*, Noordwijkerhout, NL, June 1992.

[13]   Lee, R.M. "A Messenger Model for Navigating Among Bureaucratic Requirements", *Proceedings of the Hawaii International Conference on System Sciences*, January, 1997, Vol IV, pp.468-477.

[14]   Lee, R.M. "Automatic Generation of Electronic Procedures: Procedure Constraint Grammars" Proceedings of the Eleventh International Electronic Commerce Conference, Bled, Slovenia, 8-10 June, 1998, pp. II:49-85.

[15]   Lee, R.M. "Candid - A Formal Language for Electronic Contracting", Euridis Research Monograph (RM 1998.08.02), August,1998.

[16]   Lee, R.M., Bons, R.W.H., Soft-Coded Trade Procedures for Open-EDI, *International Journal of Electronic Commerce*, pp.27-50, Volume 1, Number 1, 1996.

[17]   Lee, R.M. "Distributed Electronic Trade Scenarios: Representation, Design, Prototyping" *International Journal on ElectronicCommerce*, Vol 3, No 1, 1999.

[18]   Peterson, J. L., *Petri Net Theory and the Modeling of Systems*, Prentice-Hall, 1981.

[19]   Petri, C.A., *Kommunikation mit Automaten*, PhD thesis, University of Bonn, Germany, 1962.

[20]   UN/IPTWG. United Nations / International Trade Procedures Working Group (see www.unece.org/trafix/)

[21]   Wrigley, C.D., "EDI Transaction Protocols in International Trade", *Proceedings Conference on Interorganizational Systems in the Global Environment*, Bled, Slovenia, September, 1992.

ARIS Architecture and Reference Models for Business Process Management

August-Wilhelm Scheer, Markus Nüttgens

Institut für Wirtschaftsinformatik, Universität des Saarlandes,
Im Stadtwald Geb. 14.1, D-66123 Saarbrücken
{scheer, nuettgens}@iwi.uni-sb.de

Abstract. In this article a general business process architecture is presented, which is based on the Architecture of Integrated Information Systems (ARIS) and which is composed of the four levels of process engineering, process planning and control, workflow control and application systems. The ARIS-House of Business Engineering encompasses the whole life-cycle range: from business process design to information technology deployment, leading to a completely new process-oriented software concept. At the same time, the architecture bridges the gap between business process modeling and workflow-driven applications, from Business Process Reengineering to Continuous Process Improvement.

1. New Approaches of Developing Information Systems

There are two fundamental ways of (re-)engineering information systems. The "formal driven" approach is based on the goal of developing and implementing a technical correct running system. The "content driven" approach is based on the goal of developing and implementing an organizational correct running system. By using reference models, content and technology can be combined in a new way.

The content driven approach starts with the design of the strategic business opportunities and the organizational requirements. The resulting models are the basis for an iterative business improvement and technological implementation. The content driven approach can be structured as a layer model and described in an architectural framework for business process management. Reference models as "blue prints" for business engineering can be used to model and optimize business processes.

The term "business process" is defined universally. A business process is described as a procedure relevant for adding value to an organization. It is viewed in its entirety, from beginning to end. Figure 1 illustrates the business process of order entry processing. The initial requirements of the customer lead to order acceptance by the manufacturer's Sales department. Sales then relays information to Purchasing, in order for them to supply bought-in parts. Finally, Production plans and executes the work-order.

W. van der Aalst et al. (Eds.): Business Process Management, LNCS 1806, pp 376-389, 2000
© Springer-Verlag Berlin Heidelberg 2000

Figure1 illustrates this procedure by a series of events triggering functions. The initial event of the process is the customer requirement. The final event is the completion of the product in Manufacturing. Events not only trigger functions, they are themselves the results of functions. Processes can be split into sub-processes. Conversely, sub-processes can be joined together. By introducing logical operators, the control structure with its event-driven process chain (EPC) can be expanded to accommodate variously complex procedures [1], [2], [3].

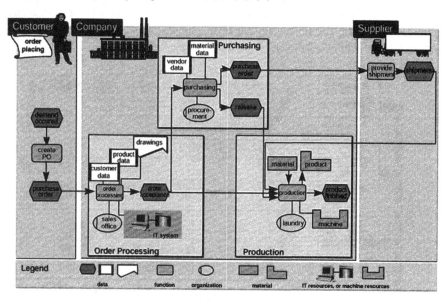

Fig. 1. Modeling of a business process, using event-driven process chains (EPC) [4]

Besides describing the procedural structure of events and functions, there must also be a focus on describing the organizational units assigned to the functions. Many reengineering projects are actually directed at re-allocating functions to organizational units.

Aligning the enterprise along its processes offers the possibility to hit several business targets. But a process-oriented business management not only requires a concept for the systematic design and organization of the business processes themselves (by means of so-called Information System Architectures).

Process-oriented business management also calls for tools and concepts to design the information systems supporting these processes. The aim is to design and control the organizational structures in a very flexible way so they can rapidly adapt to changing conditions (of the market, competitors etc.) [5].

2. ARIS-House of Business Engineering Architecture

Despite an abundance of various reengineering concepts in recent years, business processes have emerged as the focal point of business reengineering [6], [7], [8], [9], [10], [11].

The Architecture of Information Systems (ARIS) can be used as a keystone for Business Process Reengineering and Business Process Management [1], [4], [12]. ARIS-House of business engineering (HOBE) enhances the ARIS process architecture by addressing comprehensive business process management, not only from an organizational, but also from an IT perspective (see Figure 2) [12], [13].

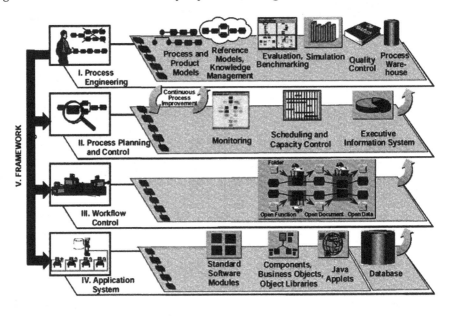

Fig. 2. The 'ARIS-House of Business Engineering' Architecture of Business Processes [4]

Because business process owners need to focus on the „one shot" engineering and description aspects of their business processes, ARIS HOBE provides a framework for managing business processes -- from organizational engineering to real-world IT implementation, including continuous adaptive improvement. HOBE also lets business process owners continuously plan and control current business procedures and devote their attention to continuous process improvement (CPI) [14], [15].

At level 1 (**process engineering**), business processes are modeled in accordance with a manufacturing work schedule. The ARIS concept provides a framework which covers every business process aspect. Various methods for optimizing, evaluating and ensuring the quality of the processes are also available.

Level II (**process planning and control**) is where business process owners' current business processes are planned and controlled, with methods for scheduling and capacity, and (activity based) cost analysis also available. Process monitoring lets process managers keep an eye on the states of the various processes.

At level IV (**workflow control**), objects to be processed, such as customer orders with appropriate documents or insurance claims, are delivered from one workplace to the next. Electronically stored documents are delivered by workflow systems.

At level IV (**application system**), documents delivered to the workplaces are specifically processed, i.e., functions of the business process are executed using computer-aided application systems -- ranging from simple word processing systems to complex standard software solution modules--, business objects and java applets.

The four Levels are interdependently connected. Information at Level II regarding the profitability of current processes, is the point of departure for continuous adjustment and improvement of the business processes at Level I. Workflow Control is linked to Level I, because Workflow Control at Level III requires the description of business processes. At the same time, Workflow Control reports actual data regarding the processes to be executed (amounts, times, organizational allocation) back to Level II. Applications at Level IV are executed from the workflow system at Level III and configured according to the business process models at Level I.

2.1 Engineering Business Processes

Business process engineering aims to achieve the greatest efficiency possible in terms of business-organizational solutions. Organizational departments, reengineering project teams or even business process owners can be responsible for process engineering. While work schedule development for manufacturing processes might be institutionally allocated to a certain department for years as job preparation, other kinds of business processes are not quite as regimented. We would recommend having the same entities responsible for engineering as are responsible for the business processes themselves.

Generally, enterprise business processes, such as a typical purchasing process, are engineered at the type level. Subtypes for certain subforms (orders for spare parts, normal parts or just-in-time parts, for example) can also be created. However, ordering processes are usually not modeled just because specific parts need to be ordered.

On the other hand, work schedules for specific parts in manufacturing processes are indeed documented. This is due to the fact that process descriptions are not only used to support fundamental organizational rules, but also for direct process execution. The more process documentation is utilized for executing business processes, such as for workflow control, the more descriptions for process instances become necessary.

When engineering optimal business processes, reference models can be included, along with available knowledge on best practices. It is also possible to compare alternative procedures (benchmarking) or carry out simulation studies or quality evaluations.

Reference models, which can be developed in real-world situations (best practices) or theoretically, document process know-how that can be utilized for modeling. We can distinguish between procedural models or the implementation of standard software, and business models such as for order processing or product introductions. Models can be specialized for vertical markets (resulting in vertical market reference models). ARIS concept reference models, developed by consultancies with expertise gained in customer projects, are available for practically every vertical market. Thus, documented process expertise results in the development of commercial products.

Reference models can be quite comprehensive, consisting of hundreds or thousands of model objects. This is why various levels of aggregation are used. Reference models provide enterprises with an initial process engineering solution, letting them determine the degree of detail of the model and the business content. Adapted to company-specific requirements, reference models evolve into company-specific models. Actual case studies have shown that the use of reference models in organizational projects can reduce time factors and costs by more than 30%.

Reference models provided by software vendors as software documentation (the most comprehensive model being SAP's R/3 reference model) benefit the customer by utilizing business process know-how, providing the opportunity to compare business software solutions or pinpointing positive or negative implementation issues.

Process know-how is increasingly being regarded as an important component of overriding corporate knowledge management. Corporate knowledge includes know-how regarding the products, technologies, organizational procedures and rules as well as the individual know-how of each individual employee. Documenting, storing, utilizing and enhancing this basic know-how is a key task of knowledge management [16].

While it is essential to evaluate activity based costing and benchmarking results for a single business process, multiple alternatives are generated, studied and analyzed in simulation studies in order to engineer the best possible business process. No methodical enhancements of the business process model are necessary for defining and analyzing the various engineering alternatives in what-if-situations. After analysis, the existing process model serves as the foundation for the simulation. In dynamic simulations, on the other hand, the dynamic behavior of process alternatives is studied. Individual processes are generated in accordance with the process model, their processing is tracked. Thus, processes are defined at the instance level and their interrelationships are analyzed. This pinpoints any potential delays before any processing begins. As far as the process alternatives to be analyzed are concerned, it is possible to define various process structures, processes with different function times and operating behavior, respectively, of the respective organizational units. Alternatives are generated individually, in accordance with empirical studies, or randomly and automatically.

The structure of a simulation model can be derived directly from the general structure process (see Figure 3).

ISO 9000 definitions include criteria for defining the quality of business processes. Companies can have their adherence to these standards certified. The main idea of these certifications is that the quality of the processes is an indication of the quality of the processes themselves.

All around the world, standards such as ISO 9000 and 9xxx, as well as the more rigid QS-9000 in the automotive industry, are now well established. In addition to certifying adherence to basic standards like ISO 9001, they stress management aspects and pave the way for total quality management (TQM). Efforts towards enhancing quality do not grind to a halt, however, once adherence to ISO 9000 standards has been certified. In order to optimize enterprise processes in accordance with certain goals, TQM requires people to think and act in a process oriented manner and to constantly review and improve existing procedures.

The result of systematically capturing, storing and maintaining business process know-how in a repository is called a process warehouse. Process warehouses are fed from a wide range of project sources in which business processes are analyzed. These projects can include reengineering tasks, ISO 9000 certification, implementation of standard software, activity based costing, etc. When various methods and tools are used in these projects, the content of the models in the process warehouse needs to be consolidated and then merged with other models. In consistent and transparent organizational guides, this process know-how can then be made available to additional projects. Finally, Internet and intranet technology enables distribution in global enterprises.

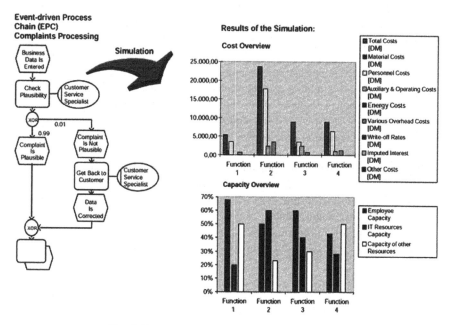

Fig. 3. Example of a simulation with EPCs [4]

2.2 Planning and Controlling Business Processes

Engineering a business process concludes in a kind of template for individual business processes (process instances). In order to be able to plan and control current business processes, the appropriate information must be made available to the persons responsible for the process.

Process monitoring provides the employees involved in and responsible for the business processes with up-to-date status information regarding the current business processes. In addition to the processing status, current process times and process costs can be shown ad hoc. This provides the persons responsible for the business process with transparent information for answering customers' questions and manipulating the remainder of the process if necessary.

Project and production scheduling systems also provide information on "to-be" and "as-is" deviations from the schedule and costs of the business processes that are to be executed. This, as well as other information, is utilized to continuously improve business processes.

Every method used in describing Level I, such as process analysis, model comparison, ISO 9000 certification or simulation, can be employed for CPI. BPR and CPI should be regarded in the same vein. When a certain situation arises, causing a company to reflect on its structures, this in turn can lead to a BPR project. However, even after resolving the problem, processes still change. New organizational concepts can arise. New Best Practice cases become available as reference models. New technologies are invented. New knowledge is obtained from processes, which have just been implemented, leading to an adjustment of the process. Hence, Process Design is a continuous process. Frequently, conflicts of interest lead to apparent disparities between BPR and CPI: applications vendors are sometimes blamed for the lengthy procedure occasionally necessary to implement their software. They are concerned that their product could be held responsible for any additional delay if they are connected with a BPR project. Therefore, they oppose BPR strategies and recommend rapid installation of their software and subsequent CPI. Due to their interest in selling consulting services, consulting companies, on the other hand, recommend the opposite approach: first, develop a new engineering (organizational) concept and then support it with the new software. This prevents unnecessary and awkward procedures from being carried over into the new software concept. The contradictions of these two approaches are resolved in the 'ARIS-House of Business Engineering' because BPR and CPI are so closely intertwined.

The integration of a process costing component within ARIS is important for implementing a permanent Improvement Process (see Figure 4).

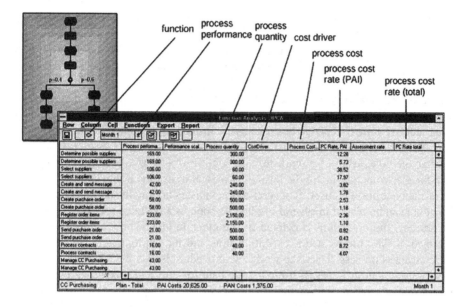

Fig. 4. Supporting process costing with EPCs [13]

The intense debates in business administration circles in recent years regarding process costing generally dissipate if one adheres to this basic view of business processes [17], [18]. Process costing has always been around, however, only in areas in which process descriptions are available, such as in calculating manufacturing processes. That is why we use terms like concurrent calculation, where as-is costs of a manufacturing order, and thus of a manufacturing process, are determined in parallel with an ongoing process.

Process data can also be summarized in an executive information system (EIS) or data warehouse, supporting process management.

2.3 Workflow Control

Business process engineering and business process planning levels, respectively, are geared to business oriented managers. Workflow control converts business processes into IT tools.

Generally, it is not possible to administer an entire business process with one application software system. Very often, a variety of systems for sales, purchasing, manufacturing or accounting is necessary. Even integrated standard application packages have gaps which have to be filled by custom systems or standard applications from other vendors. None of these systems is individually capable of determining the status of the entire process (for example, every processing state of a particular order). It therefore makes sense to allocate the responsibility for comprehensive process control to an explicit system level rather than distributing it across several systems. This level is called „workflow".

Workflow systems pass the objects (documents) to be processed from one work place to the next. Ideally, they do this electronically, from the computer system of one workplace to the next operation step's system. This requires a detailed description of the procedure, customized for the individual process type, and of the respective employee [19].

Figure 5 illustrates how a specific process in the execution level is derived from the procedure defined in Level I. Instead of the general attributes of the organizational unit, we now find actual business users. Instead of the general term, we find an order that is linked to an actual customer.

After the conclusion of a workstep, the workflow system retrieves the document from the electronic out-bin of the business user and transports it into the electronic in-bin of the next business user. If several business users are involved in processing, the procedure can be placed in several in-bins. As soon as a business user has begun with the process, the procedure is deleted in the other in-bins. The workflow system is informed of the process status, execution time and the appropriate business user of every business process. Thus, the workflow procedure is also the foundation for Process Management in Level II. It reports the data for cost and scheduling evaluations and provides process information for process monitoring. An agreement by the Workflow Management Coalition, a group of Workflow vendors, has standardized interfaces. Now, various workflow systems can be linked with one another [20].

The process representation of workflow systems can also be used to guide business users. This increases their knowledge of the interrelationship of organizational business processes.

The specific procedure in Figure 5 (right box) follows from the general business process procedure. You create a specific procedure by giving information on particular business users and by selecting a certain path outlined in the general business process description. Thus, business users can always see how their activity is embedded in the process, who will precede and who will succeed them within the process. For example, they can also see that only the left branch of a business process is relevant for them; the control flow of the right branch might be deleted. Since a particular process has not been created for the business user of the succeeding activity, only the department name, "Warehouse", is listed. Depending on the capacity situation at that time, the business user of the next workstep is not determined until the conclusion of the task. During Process Workflow, processes with precisely defined procedural structures can be differentiated from processes with only roughly defined procedural steps.

In many operational or repetitive procedures (such as order or loan processing), functions, their procedural branches and organizational units are determined from the start. Thus, the process is well-structured and can be described with the EPC method. On the other hand, other processes can only be described partially since functions become apparent during the process. This is also the case when the sequence of the process steps is determined ad hoc or the organizational units to be processed become apparent on an ad hoc basis. In these cases, we define the process as being poorly structured. It can only be modeled in an imperfect way. For example, functions can only be presented in a "TO DO" list; the sequence will be determined by the project team during the process. It is at this time that the person to whom the task has been assigned, is also determined.

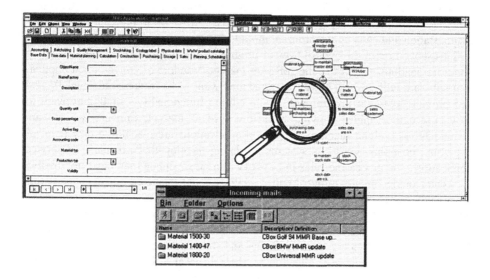

Fig. 5. The workflow component guides users according to processes [13]

Workflow systems seem to be more suitable for controlling well-structured processes. Likewise, less structured processes are supported by groupware systems, which only offer tools such as electronic mail, video conferencing, shared conferencing etc., but which do not require logical knowledge of the processes. In real-life situations, we will always find a mix of these two structure forms. Thus, workflow systems are capable of "exception handling", that is, procedure control can be changed ad hoc during processing. This functionality can be linked with groupware tools, complementing workflow and groupware. In the future, these two systems will even grow together.

2.4 Application Systems

Current vendors of integrated software systems are splitting their systems into smaller modules. Many of them are now just loosely coupled. This makes it possible to release upgrades for each individual module and not across-the-board for the entire system. On the whole, there is a strong tendency today towards splitting application software into individual components (componentware). These modules are reassembled into complete solutions according to process models. The operational data in these applications are managed by database systems.

In the object-oriented approach, data and functions are encapsulated and communicate via a messaging system, which performs material handling for the workflow system. The objects correspond to the "folder" and provide references to data and functions. It is important to note that Level III is responsible for the entire process of the operation. It calls up objects to be processed, such as electronic forms for filing insurance claims, loan application forms for loan processing operations or customer orders for customer order processing. It then passes them on to the appropriate processing station and calls up the program modules.

This separation of the control flow of programs and function execution is bringing about tremendous changes in the software market. Vendors of conventional application software will have to decide whether they want to be brokers' at Level IV and just provide "componentware" with some editing functionality - or if they want to move up to the rapidly growing workflow systems market. Conversely, software manufacturers without much experience in applications are reaching a new point of departure, now that workflow systems are being developed. Particularly in service applications, the processing rules in Level IV can be so simple that they only involve data entry or document editing. Many functions could therefore be executed at this level, such as calling up a spreadsheet or a word processing program. This makes workflow systems that control the coherence of a procedure all the more important.

What this means for users is that a new architecture for application software is on its way. Service providers, such as banks and insurance companies, do not have a large selection of standard applications at their disposal to support their operational procedures. Now they can document (model) their business procedures in Level I and can control their procedures by implementing a workflow system in Level III. In Level IV, they can still use their existing software to support the processing rules. Nevertheless, today it is necessary to split software in Level IV and make it accessible to workflow control. By separating procedure control from function execution statements, information systems are split into data management, procedure control and function execution.

Figure 6 shows a prototype of such an integrated process-oriented information system. The left window represents the user interface of the modeling tool and the features that can be used to design and analyze information models on Level I and II. The models stored in the repository can be used to configure and activate workflow processes. The window in the middle shows an activated workflow process on Level III. The application software on Level IV is pushed by the workflow management system and represented in the right window.

3. Customizing and Configuration with Reference Models

When supporting business processes in their entirety, it is not sufficient to simply split the whole process into the four parts intellectually or as a physical system, as described above. We must also separate their links with one another. We have already noted that the individual business events in the Process Workflow Level are generated by copying the business process design in Level I. The generating of this business design is thus a link between the business process modeling tool and the workflow system. In the Workflow Management Coalition, experts are working on creating accepted standards for this link [20]. The same goes for delivering workflow results to Level II, for example, by delivering details regarding as-is schedules or as-is amounts to Level II for evaluation purposes.

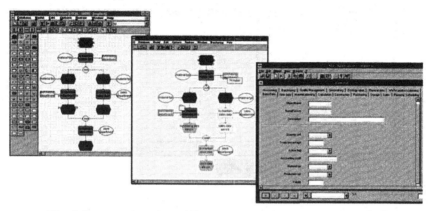

Fig. 6. Process-oriented, workflow-supporting application software [13]

These two links make it possible to immediately update a business process procedure, even in execution and evaluation levels. This occurs without having to manipulate any computer programs. Thus, organizational Design Level I plays a tremendous role within the whole architecture.

From an organizational point of view, the link between Level I and Level IV is equally important. Thus, the modeling level not only generates procedure control, but also processing rules and data transformation. After starting with a group of processing rules that are only very roughly defined, for example, it is possible to filter and adapt only those that are really important for the business procedures.

Application Systems of the future have to be consistent in carrying through this concept of model-driven customizing:

Changing the attributes of the data model in Level I alters the data tables in Level IV (see Figure 7). Modifying process models, in turn, varies the sequence of function procedures. Changing function models either switches off or activates functions. Finally, employing the organizational model allocates functions to certain organizational units and determines the screen sequence. Application Systems are derived directly from industry-specific market reference models described according to the ARIS Method. Using the Modeling tools, they can then be developed into company-specific "to-be" models.

ARIS Model:
attribute allocation diagram:
master data ITEM

screen:
master data ITEM

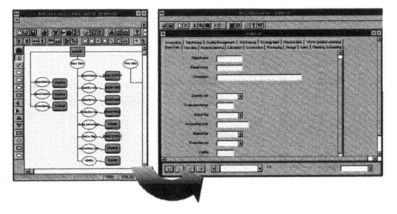

Fig. 7. Model-based customizing with ARIS-House of Business Engineering [13]

In order to transfer the model into application software, a build-time-system, class library and configuration model is relevant. The build-time-system converts the company-specific ARIS model, based on object-oriented programming, into an operational application system (run-time system). The build-time system utilizes a class library consisting of predefined business administration and data processing classes. The processing rules for this conversion are comprised in the configuration model. Here is an example: Processing rules guarantee the DP-conversion of the ARIS models into database objects. They further govern the description of database objects and links between external and internal identifiers (e.g. for tables and columns). Besides modifying procedure rules, model-based customizing enables the adjustment or expansion of data models, dialogue masks and process organization. Thus, the application is derived directly from the process model of the enterprise and then configured from business-objects.

References

1. Scheer, A.-W: Architecture of Integrated Information Systems: Principles of Enterprise-Modeling. Berlin et al.. (1992)
2. Keller, G.; Nüttgens, M.; Scheer, A.-W.: Semantische Prozeßmodellierung auf der Grundlage "Ereignisgesteuerter Prozeßketten (EPK)". In: Veröffentlichungen des Instituts für Wirtschaftsinformatik (ed. Scheer, A.-W.), Nr. 89, Saarbrücken (1992) (http://www.iwi.uni-sb.de/iwi-hefte/heft089.zip)
3. Scheer, A.-W.: Business Process Engineering - Reference Models for Industrial Enterprises, 2nd ed., Berlin et al. (1994)
4. Scheer, A.-W.: ARIS – Business Process Frameworks, 2nd ed.. Berlin et al. (1998)

5. Scheer, A.-W.; Nüttgens, M.; Zimmermann, V.: Rahmenkonzept für ein integriertes Geschäftsprozeßmanagement, in: Wirtschaftsinformatik, 37/1995/5. (1995) 426-434.
6. Davenport, T. H.: Process Innovation - Reengineering Work through Information Technology. Boston. (1993)
7. Gaitanides, M.: Prozeßorganisation: Entwicklung, Ansätze und Programme prozeßorientierter Organisationsgestaltung. München (1983)
8. Harrington, H. J.: Business process improvement: the breakthrough strategy for total quality, productivity and competitiveness. New York et. al. (1991)
9. Donovan, J.J.: Business Re-engineering with Information Technology. Englewood Cliffs (1994)
10. Hammer, M., Champy, J.: Business Reengineering: Die Radikalkur für das Unternehmen. 5. ed., Frankfurt/Main-New York (1995)
11. Harrington, H. J.: Business Process Improvement. New York et al. (1991)
12. Scheer, A.-W.: ARIS – Business Process Modeling, 2nd ed. Berlin et al. (1998)
13. Scheer, A.-W. Industrialisierung der Dienstleistung. In: Veröffentlichungen des Instituts für Wirtschaftsinformatik (ed. Scheer, A.-W.), Nr. 122, Saarbrücken (1996)
14. Scheer, A.-W.: Workflow-Systeme: Jetzt auch im Büro. In: Harvard Business Manager 19(1997)1, pp. 115-122.
15. Thome, R., Hufgard, A.: Continuous System Engineering, Entdeckung der Standardsoftware als Organisator. Würzburg (1996)
16. Rolles, R. Schmidt, Y.; Scheer, A.-W.: Workflow im Umfeld von Schulung und Ideenmanagement. In: Scheer, A.-W.; Nüttgens, M. (ed.): Electronic Business Engineering, Physica Verlag, Heidelberg (1999), pp. 725 – 743
17. Cooper, R. and Kaplan, R. F.: Measure costs right: Make the right decisions. In Harvard Business Review. 66/1988/5, (1988)p. 96-103.
18. Johnson, H. P. and Kaplan, R. F.: Relevance lost: The rise and fall of management accounting. Boston (1987)
19. Galler, J. and Scheer, A.-W.: Workflow-Projekte: Vom Geschäftsprozeßmodell zur unternehmensspezifischen Workflow-Anwendung. Information Management 1/95, (1995) pp. 20-27
20. Hollingsworth, D.: The Workflow Reference Model. In: Document TC00-1003, Draft 1.1 (ed. Workflow Management Coalition) (1995)

Author Index

Lecture Notes in Computer Science

For information about Vols. 1–1720
please contact your bookseller or Springer-Verlag